Recent Research in Psychology

Wm J. Baker Leendert P. Mos
Hans V. Rappard Henderikus J. Stam
Editors

Recent Trends in Theoretical Psychology

Proceedings of the
Second Biannual Conference of the
International Society for Theoretical Psychology,
April 20–25, 1987, Banff, Alberta, Canada

With 14 Illustrations

Springer-Verlag
New York Berlin Heidelberg
London Paris Tokyo

Wm J. Baker
Leendert P. Mos
Center for Advanced Study in
Theoretical Psychology
University of Alberta
Edmonton, Canada T6G 2E9

Hans V. Rappard
Department of Psychology
The Free University
1007 MC Amsterdam
The Netherlands

Henderikus J. Stam
Department of Psychology
University of Calgary
Calgary, Alberta
Canada T2N 1N4

Library of Congress Cataloging-in-Publication Data
International Society for Theoretical Psychology. Conference (2nd : 1987 : Banff, Alta.)
Recent trends in theoretical psychology / proceedings of the Second Biannual Conference of the International Society for Theoretical Psychology / editors, William J. Baker ... [et al.].
p. cm. -- (Recent research in psychology)
Conference held in Banff, Alta., Canada, Apr. 20-25, 1987.
Bibliography: p.
1. Psychology--Philosophy--Congresses. 2. Psychology--Methodology--Congresses. I. Baker, William J. II. Title.
BF38.I545 1988
150'.1--dc19 88-12164

Camera-ready text prepared by the editors.
Printed and bound by Edwards Brothers, Inc., Ann Arbor, Michigan.
Printed in the United States of America.

9 8 7 6 5 4 3 2 1

ISBN 0-387-96757-5 Springer-Verlag New York Berlin Heidelberg
ISBN 3-540-96757-5 Springer-Verlag Berlin Heidelberg New York

PREFACE

This volume constitutes the proceedings of the second biannual conference of the International Society for Theoretical Psychology (see Epilogue) held in Banff, Alberta, Canada, April 20-25, 1987. Thirty-nine papers were presented during the four days of the conference including an invited address by Kenneth Gergen. Unfortunately, even after severely restricting the length of the written papers, the required limitation on printed space permitted only 34 of these to be included in these proceedings. While most of the papers required editorial adjustment, the authors had final word on style and content.

The classification of conference papers tends to be somewhat arbitrary, but we decided to structure the chapters under four headings: philosophy, metatheory, methodology, and theory. By *philosophy* we refer primarily to issues in the philosophy of science as these pertain to the discipline of psychology. *Metatheory* refers to theory, drawing on the philosophy of science and having implications for methodology, about psychological theories. *Methodology* refers to both theory of inquiry and specific methods of investigation as these derive from philosophical and metatheoretical considerations. By *theory* we refer to both analyses of the foundations of extant theory, including historical and sociological analyses, and the advancement of substantive theory.

Eight papers have been included under *philosophy*. Rejecting any notion that theories progress towards greater fidelity with nature, *Gergen* envisions scientific progress in terms of alternating periods of meaning stabilization and transformation. The former leads to maximum social coordination and value expression and the latter, as social institutions become progressively restrictive, to social change. Theories, on his view, are devices which increase the range of our intelligibility and serve to mold society anew time and again. *Terwee* in his critical review of Gergen's rhetorical conception of social psychology maintains that the latter's rejection of foundationalism is all but impossible. A revised interpretative conception of psychology is sketched which leaves room not only for empirical-analytical, phenomenological, hermeneutical, and rhetorical methodologies, but adheres to truth founded in our practices and certainties of everyday life. *Tolman* recognizes a crisis of disunity in psychology. In order to achieve theoretical unification, he makes a case for a materialist foundation of the discipline and a realist view of its evolutionary and historical contexts. *Vroon* examines the incompatible 'root metaphors' which have permeated psychology's explanations and despairs of theoretical unity as, from a historical perspective, the discipline has a penchant for enriching either the mind or the world. *Shames* argues for the role of metaphor in scientific epistemology and, together with *Royce*, whose focus is on 'weak' theory, for an exploration of the 'context of discovery' in our appraisal of psychological theories. *Salner* reviews the role of epistemic beliefs in the world views held by psychologists. Also working within the context of discovery, she notes the structural similarities between individuals and scientific communities in the process of coming to understand social reality. *Kirsch* and *Hyland* complete this section with a discussion of complementarity and causal isomorphism with respect to mind-body philosophies. The authors draw out the implications of their monism for both theoretical and empirical questions of psychophysiological phenomena. While these diverse contributions adhere to a range of ontological and epistemological stances, they nearly all appear within a post-positivistic philosophy of psychology which eschews the strictures of logicism.

Under the heading of *metatheory* we have included eight papers. *Danziger* points, by way of a historical case study, to the ontological and theoretical presuppositions informing methods of inquiry. Whereas on the received view of science any method may be legitimately employed to test a theory, if theory and method are indeed interdependent it is incumbent upon the investigator to demonstrate that the presuppositions of method do not conflict with those of the theory being tested. But then, methods do not merely serve to test theories, but to demonstrate them in action. That methods are indeed theory-laden and serve to structure the domain of inquiry is exemplified by *Ratner* who, from a critical examination of biological explanations of psychological phenomena, argues for the relative autonomy of psychological theory. *Hezewijk* draws attention to the same point, that methods and theories are informed by ontological presuppositions, with reference to the representationist and presentationist styles of theorizing by von Helmholtz and Mach, respectively. In his distinction between predicational and mediational theorizing, *Rychlak* elaborates not only on the asymmetry in the explanations offered by psychologists of their own behavior and the behavior of others, but also his teleological conception of psychology which demands a view of the 'predicating organism ready to take a position in life experience'. *Madsen*, in a meta-analysis of Skinner's psychology, notes how his materialist monism and radical empiricism lead to mediational theorizing which, however, can well withstand the criterion of piecemeal testability. *Maiers*, in his ironical critique of the claim that psychology follows a natural science model, argues against those who would demarcate the sciences from the humanities. He, instead, rejects antiscientism by avoiding the bifurcation in favour of a historical-empirical study of 'real practices': a critical psychology in the Marxist tradition. In concluding this section, Mos and Smythe independently address various issues in the foundations of contemporary cognitive psychology. Thus *Mos*, with reference to phenomenology, argues that the current focus on the concept of representation in cognitive theory fails as an account of the semantic relation of 'aboutness' and, hence, as an explanation of intentionality which is the mark of the mental. *Smythe* distinguishes between propositional and skillful knowing in terms of propositional attitude theory and forcefully formulates the challenge that this distinction poses for any psychological theory of cognition. What is notable in these eight contributions is that they invoke not only issues in the philosophy of psychology but that their metatheoretical analyses have implications for both methodology and theory construction.

Under the heading of *methodology* we have included eight papers. In a critique of the concepts of reliability and validity, *Giorgi* presents a phenomenological understanding of these concepts as achievements of intentionality. Both logical empiricism and phenomenology share the common goal of determining the proper evidence for knowledge claims. But phenomenology, in distinguishing between acts and objects, takes validity as an essential description of an intuited essence and reliability as such an essential description in use. *Horley* examines the assumptions, criteria, and implications for his proposed units of analysis in the description and explanation of human action. Similarly, *Kuiken* and *Wild* are concerned with the analysis of units but specifically from within and with regard to the development of a phenomenological methodology. Drawing on both the horizon analysis of meaning and paraphrase in discourse analysis, they propose a psychological analysis of language which is fully concordant with human subjectivity. *Rappard*, from a historical perspective, proposes a systematization rather than a unification of psychology and illustrates how the 'founding definitions' of such a systematization affect empirical research in social psychology. *Mishara*, with reference to the theory of irreversible dynamics in physics, presents a model for conceptualizing processes of behavioral change. *Van Geert*, too, is concerned with describing a model of change but with a model of developmental transitions. He reviews the various properties of transition concepts in developmental theories with a view towards comparing and evaluating them. *Rogers*, in a social-historical analysis of the concept of construct validity, argues that its resilience derives from unwarranted metatheoretical assumptions which continue to plague contemporary personality assessment. In the final paper of this section, *Thorngate* presents a social-psychological analysis examining the implications of his proposed principles of 'attentional economics' in an evaluation of information produced and consumed in the marketplace of psychological research. Again, the contributors in this section cling to a range of philosophical presuppositions, but what they have in common is a sensitivity to how methods of inquiry are informed by metatheory and have implications for theory appraisal.

Nine papers have been included under the final heading of *theory*. The first paper presents an overview of the contributions of Ludwig von Bertalanffy. *Weckowicz* describes the late theoretician's influence, especially by way of his systems theory, on psychology and philosophy as well as biology and cybernetics. The remaining papers by Jorna, Lewicka, Kose and Heindel, Stam, Parrott, Yeudall, Hague, and Cartwright and Peckar address foundational issues pertaining to current theories or domains of inquiry in the discipline. *Jorna's* paper examines the implicit assumptions of two contemporary cognitive theories, Anderson's and Tulving's, and finds their formulations wanting at both the descriptive and explanatory level. *Lewicka* compares theories of rational judgment in terms of her distinctions between subjective and objective anchoring, and sufficient and necessary conditions of cognitive acts. In the process, she mediates between constructivist and realist views of human cognition. The latter distinction is also addressed by *Kose* and *Heindel* in their critical examination of contemporary interpretations of Piagetian theory which have variously misconstrued his genetic epistemology. Taking Piaget's central problem as the 'formation of cognitive structures', the authors focus on the 'activity of the subject' and its implications for psychological theory. *Stam* argues that the absence of theoretical foundations in the domains of health psychology and behavioral medicine is motivated to ensure that these psychological specialties do not clash with those of the health care professions. In a historical review, *Parrott* takes seriously the phenomenological experience of emotion and argues for a conceptual reintegration of affect and cognition in order to account for those cognitively complex emotions which have no unique physiological basis. *Yeudall* proposes a comprehensive three-dimensional model of brain functioning in relation to psychopathology. In doing so, he exemplifies the interdependence of theory, clinical practice and research. *Hague* argues for the intuitive basis of moral objectivity as rooted in Dabrowski's conception of authentic subjectivity. In concluding this section, *Cartwright* and *Peckar* argue, from a review of theories in the physical and biological sciences, for a layered-structure conceptualization of contemporary personality theories. These nine contributions to theoretical psychology address not merely issues of substantive theory but also those of methodology, metatheory and, even, philosophy. Finally, *Baker* in his *Epilogue* presents a brief overview of the conference.

In the preparation of this volume we gratefully acknowledge Evelyn Murison who entered the text and Casey Boodt who provided editorial assistance and prepared the tables, figures, and author index. The University of Alberta financed the facilities and resources at the Center for Advanced Study in Theoretical Psychology which made it all possible.

The Editors
February, 1988

34

TABLE OF CONTENTS

CONTRIBUTORS

Wm J. Baker, Center for Advanced Study in Theoretical Psychology, University of Alberta, Edmonton, AB, Canada T6G 2E9

Desmond S. Cartwright, Department of Psychology, University of Colorado, Boulder, CO, U.S.A. 80309-0345

Kurt Danziger, Department of Psychology, York University, North York, ON, Canada M3J 1P3

Paul van Geert, Department of Psychology, University of Groningen, 9712 GK Groningen, The Netherlands

Kenneth J. Gergen, Department of Psychology, Swarthmore College, Swarthmore, PA, U.S.A. 19081

Amedeo Giorgi, Graduate School and Research Center, Saybrook Institute, San Francisco, CA, U.S.A. 94123

William J. Hague, Department of Educational Psychology, University of Alberta, Edmonton, AB, Canada T6G 2G5

Patricia Heindel, College of Saint Elizabeth, Convent Station, NJ, U.S.A. 07961

René van Hezewijk, Department of Psychonomics, University of Utrecht, 3508 TC Utrecht, The Netherlands

Jim Horley, Department of Psychology, University of Guelph, Guelph, ON, Canada N1G 2W1

Michael E. Hyland, Department of Psychology, Plymouth Polytechnic, Plymouth, Devon, England PL4 8AA

René J. Jorna, Institute for Management and Organization, University of Groningen, 9700 AV Groningen, The Netherlands

Irving Kirsch, Department of Psychology, University of Connecticut, Storrs, CT, U.S.A. 06268

Gary Kose, Department of Psychology, Long Island University, Brooklyn, NY, U.S.A. 11201-5372

Donald Kuiken, Center for Advanced Study in Theoretical Psychology, University of Alberta, Edmonton, AB, Canada T6G 2E9

Maria Lewicka, Faculty of Psychology, University of Warsaw, 00-183 Warsaw, Poland

K. B. Madsen, Laboratory of General Psychology, Royal Danish School of Educational Studies, Copenhagen NV, DK 2400 Denmark

Wolfgang Maiers, Psychological Institute, The Free University of Berlin, 1000 West Berlin 33, Federal Republic of Germany

Brian L. Mishara, Department of Psychology, University of Quebec, Montreal, QB, Canada H3C 3P8

Leendert P. Mos, Center for Advanced Study in Theoretical Psychology, University of Alberta, Edmonton, AB, Canada T6G 2E9

W. Gerrod Parrott, Department of Psychology, Georgetown University, Washington, DC, U.S.A. 20057

Helene Peckar, Department of Psychology, Norwich University, Northfield, VT, U.S.A. 05663

Hans V. Rappard, Department of Psychology, The Free University, 1007 MC Amsterdam, The Netherlands

Carl Ratner, Department of Psychology, Humboldt State University, Arcata, CA, U.S.A. 95521

T. B. Rogers, Department of Psychology, University of Calgary, Calgary, AB, Canada T2N 1N4

Joseph R. Royce, Center for Advanced Study in Theoretical Psychology, University of Alberta, Edmonton, AB, Canada T6G 2E9

Joseph F. Rychlak, Department of Psychology, Loyola University, Chicago, IL, U.S.A. 60626

Marcia Salner, Graduate School and Research Center, Saybrook Institute, San Francisco, CA, U.S.A. 94123

Morris L. Shames, Department of Psychology, Concordia University, Montreal, QB, Canada H3G 1MB

William E. Smythe, Center for Advanced Study in Theoretical Psychology, University of Alberta, Edmonton, AB, Canada T6G 2E9

Henderikus J. Stam, Department of Psychology, University of Calgary, Calgary, AB, Canada T2N 1N4

Sybe J. S. Terwee, Department of Theoretical Psychology, University of Leiden, 2312 KM Leiden, The Netherlands

Warren Thorngate, Department of Psychology, Carleton University, Ottawa, ON, Canada K1S 5B6

Charles W. Tolman, Department of Psychology, University of Victoria, Victoria, BC, Canada V8W 2Y2

Pieter A. Vroon, Department of Psychonomics, University of Utrecht, 3584 CS Utrecht, The Netherlands

Thaddeus E. Weckowicz, Center for Advanced Study in Theoretical Psychology, University of Alberta, Edmonton, AB, Canada T6G 2E9

T. C. Wild, Department of Psychology, University of Alberta, Edmonton, AB, Canada T6G 2E9

Lorne T. Yeudall, Department of Neuropsychology, Alberta Hospital, Edmonton, AB, Canada T5J 2J7

THE CONCEPT OF PROGRESS IN PSYCHOLOGICAL THEORY

Kenneth J. Gergen

Swarthmore College
Swarthmore, PA, U.S.A.

SUMMARY: The deterioration of empiricist metatheory raises the critical question of whether psychological theorizing is a progressive activity. By considering psychological theories as performative rather than descriptive, a new conception of progress is invited. Theories enable scientists, as social collectives, to carry out a range of activities. During a stabilization phase theories solidify certain ranges of actions within the community. During a transformational stage, they undermine the taken for granted, and open vistas to new forms of activity - both within science and society.

Introduction

The traditional benchmark for evaluating theory within the sciences has been that of objective correspondence. In one form or another, it is argued that theories are to be prized to the extent that they furnish accurate reflections of nature. For logical positivist philosophers this desideratum was vigorously pursued in the form of various accounts linking propositions (terms or logical atoms) at the theoretical level, via correspondence rules, to punctate facts or events in the observational realm. Theories are valorized to the extent that real world predictions confirm their utility. To the extent that theories are verified through successful prediction, one might justifiably view them as approximating a hypothetical truth. For Popper and the 'critical rationalists' this emphasis on verification was replaced with a logic of progress through disconfirmation. The mere accumulation of verifications need not contribute to the truth value of a theory, argued Popper. Rather it was the ability of a theory to withstand attempts at disconfirmation that justifies its value. Progress in science is thus the result of a continuous winnowing process, in which rigorous observational work serves to reject false propositions, leaving us in the end with pure and nourishing grains of truth. Even instrumentalist philosophers of science, while not wishing to speak of truth but of pragmatic gain, credit those theories serving to predict events in nature. It is this collectivity of views that has served as the life support system for the widely shared belief in progress in psychological science. As held since the virtual inception of the discipline, empirical corroboration should be the major criterion of theoretical acceptability. Yet, let us reconsider.

The romance with empirical correspondence was most compelling during the halcyon years of the science - roughly from the 1920s-60s - when one could cleanly separate theories from facts, facts from values, and values from logic. Subjected to close and continuing scrutiny, foundationalist assumptions about the objective nature of scientific theories have begun to crumble - timorously with Popper, and then with increasingly devastating eruptions with the critiques of Quine, Toulmin, Hanson, Kuhn, Taylor, Feyerabend and others. Let us consider but a few results of this litigenous literature:

1. There is as yet no viable account of how theoretical propositions can be derived from observation - how language about the world could ever spring from the soil of sensory input. Popper allocates this problem to the inarticulable domain of the 'context of discovery'. However, until the problem is solved we are left with the possibility that the initial postulates with which science commences are tangential to the actual nature of things. Verification would only increase our confidence in such diversions; falsification would only reduce their range to the trivial.

2. The preceding problem is compounded by arguments demonstrating the impossibility of separating out observational language from theoretical presuppositions. That is, in order to count something as a fact or a datum one requires a forestructure of theoretical understanding - terms or concepts that are already sensible. These orienting terms are embedded within more elaborated theories, whether implicit or explicit. Thus, what counts as observation is determined by preexisting theoretical commitments, and these commitments do not themselves spring from the soil of observation. As we see, then, there is nothing that would save an initially false theory from being self-perpetuating. As theories furnish the forestructure by which facts are identified, there is nothing that could be empirically located (so long as one remained within paradigm) that could challenge the theory.

3. This latter argument is further extended by the contention that theories operate much as miniature ontologies. They specify the ingredients of the world (or some part of it) and how it operates. Thus, once formulated, the theory will determine what counts as evidence, confirmation and disconfirmation. Competing theories, implying alternative ontologies, are thus incommensurable; no empirical comparisons are possible unless theories share the same ontology. To illustrate, a voluntarist can never unseat a mechanist by virtue of empirical data, because a mechanist would simply not recognize voluntary processes as a constitutent part of the universe. In the same way, neither voluntarist nor mechanist could empirically challenge a spiritualist who claimed that God's spirit insinuated itself into human action.

4. There is no viable account of how it is that theories actually predict phenomena in nature. Words acquire their meaning within particularized contexts; when extricated from these contexts they cease to have the same meaning - or sometimes, any meaning at all. The proposition that the average temperature is lower in December than June seems ineluctably true, and to do a good job of predicting from year to year - unless you happen to be living in Argentina. Strip the proposition from its common context of usage and it ceases to inform. At the more general level it may be proposed that theories themselves cannot make predictions. Theories themselves are stated in a manner that is context free; their context of applicability remains unspoken, and in principle unspecifiable. For example, what if we correct our earlier prediction by adding a clause reversing our temperature forecasts for Argentina and other nations in the southern hemisphere. Yet, how can I apply this forecast unless I know how to instantiate the terms of this added clause? And these instantiations are not furnished by the proposition itself. What I mean by Argentina, for example, depends on whether we are looking at a world atlas, reading a history book, requesting that it not cry for me, planning a visit, and so on. But what if we now begin the task of specifying what terms like Argentina and southern hemisphere mean. We shall rule out the atlas, the song, the travelogue and so on as places where temperature predictions apply. Yet, what are we now to make of the terms 'atlas', 'history', 'song', or 'travelogue'? These terms as well have different meanings in differing contexts of usage. As can be seen, verbal specification of the predictive implications of a theory leads one into an infinite regress: each attempt at specification of meaning depends itself on further specification. In conclusion, it is not theories that predict, but people; theories in themselves are mute in this regard.

Many additional criticisms have been leveled against the various forms of empiricist foundationalism. We have arguments for the inseparability of factual statements from valuational commitments, the historical perishability of social knowledge, the interpretive or hermeneutic (e.g., non-observational) basis for accounts of human action, the inapplicability of covering laws and mechanistic formulations to the understanding of human action, and so on.

I do not intend this paper as an exigesis on the deterioration of empiricist foundationalism. Most interested parties are now in agreement that the search for foundations of objective knowledge is a failed program. Rather, my central point is that there are no compelling reasons for retaining the position that theories within the sciences (including psychology) should primarily be evaluated against standards of correspondence, predictive utility, empirical fact, resistance to falsification or other such criteria. And, for those concerned with psychological theory, it becomes a question of greatest importance to gain clarity on precisely what positive function (if any) theories could possess within the discipline. Are there any alternative means for evaluating theory; what are we now to view as criteria of progress? I daresay few would wish at this point to fall back on such secondary virtues of theory construction as coherence or parsimony. To the extent that such virtues are demanded by the objectivist programmatics, they succumb in the same manner as correspondence criteria; to the extent that they are not demanded, they appear at this juncture to be merely matters of aesthetic taste.

At times my work has been characterized as nihilistic. This label is primarily used by those who feel that life would be thrust into a chaotic void should we give up claims to objective knowledge. Yet, I suspect that the vast majority of the world's population are little concerned with what conclusions we in the Western academy reach on such matters. They live quite adequately without knowing whether or not there is such a thing as 'objective knowledge', and their world will hardly be more or less chaotic by virtue of our decision on such matters. Yet, regardless of the strength and implications of previous critique, my purpose in the present offering is a positive one. Essentially I wish to take up the challenge which the critique of empiricist foundationalism deposits as its legacy. I wish to embark on a preliminary account of how we might understand theoretical work within psychology as a progressive endeavor. That is, I wish to offer a post-empiricist account of how theoretical positions might be evaluated within the discipline.

Description as Performative

To develop this account successfully a precis is required concerning the more general character of language use. It is useful in this instance to return to a distinction made by J. L. Austin in 1955, a distinction that continues to inform much work in linguistics and semantics. Austin distinguished between *constative* propositions, those used for the description of the world, and what he termed *performative* propositions - linguistic formations that did not describe or report on states of affairs, that could not be verified as true or false, but were themselves actions in the world. For example, the sentence 'The bat is on the mat' would be considered constative; one can verify the utterance through observation. In contrast, the utterances, 'On your mark, get set, go...', 'hello', 'goodbye', or 'here's to you', are performative. They are a doing in and of themselves - starting a race, greeting, parting, toasting, and so on. Let us examine the performative aspect of language more fully, for in an important sense, our previous discussion has raised vexing questions concerning the constative function of language. Our summary critique of empirical foundationalism simultaneously threatens the view that language can be a map or mirror of the world. Recall that no way would be located of explaining how scientific theories could be derived from observation nor, once established, how such theories could predict events in the world. By elaborating on the performative function of language - and ultimately scientific theory - we shall be able to return to the problems of language as picture with a new vision - and thus a new perspective on evaluating psychological theory.

As Austin went on to propose, performatives are to be evaluated, not according to correspondence with fact, but according to their *felicity* within what he called a *procedure.* A procedure was essentially some form of social convention; a felicitous utterance is one that fits appropriately into the conventional states of interpersonal affairs; infelicitous utterances do not. To mumble 'On your mark, get set, go...' suddenly and spontaneously while dining with a companion would be regarded with deep suspicion. The utterance would be infelicitous. Its felicity would be restored should we relocate the utterance in the context of a children's race. In effect, a proper understanding of the performative character of language requires that we move our attention outward from the linguistic acts themselves to the broader patterns of interaction in which they occur. To put it more directly, we may say that the performative value of an utterance is derived from its position within a more extended pattern of relationship.

It is also implied by Austin's analysis that these more extended procedures or conventions are not merely verbal. In Wittgenstein's (1953) terms, we may view utterances as constituents of more extended *life forms* - which may include both actions (other than verbal) and objects or environments. The point is made very easily with matters of gesture and facial expression. Both gestures and expressions contribute to the context that renders speech meaningful - giving it status as a particular kind of performative. There are only a limited number of non-verbal expressions for example, that may precede the announcement, 'I love you' and simultaneously place that utterance within the achieved relational pattern we may felicitously call romance. A grimace, a sinister laugh, or a dazed look will simply not qualify the remark in this way. It also follows that various actions, such as running, lifting, or striking at a moving object, may all be constituents of interpersonal procedures or life forms. Their performative value is determined by felicitously placed words as much as the performative function of words depends on such actions. Consider the game of tennis, for example. Here various utterances are indeed constituent parts of the game as social achievement. Such phrases as 'your serve', 'thirty-love', 'The games are five to three' and so on are essential parts of the event. Their performative value typically depends on an extended set of physical actions both preceding and following the utterances; the actions in turn require such utterance for them to proceed appropriately. It is also important to notice in this case, that we are not only including extended sets of actions within the relational patterns, but objects as well, balls, rackets, nets, and so on. Objects, actions and words must all be coordinated for the social achievement of the game (or life form) to occur.

We must now move to the central conclusion of this precis. We began with Austin's distinction between constatives and performatives, and we bracketed the problem of how words, including theoretical propositions in the sciences, could be said to furnish pictures of an independent reality. Now that we have expanded the analysis of the performative function of words we can return to the problem of empirical correspondence in a more effective way.

In particular, let me first propose that when we engage in actions that we call 'describe' 'explain' or 'theorize' we are essentially engaging in a performative ritual or life form. When we say that such and such an utterance is 'accurate' or 'inaccurate', 'true' or 'false' we are not judging it according to some abstract or idealized standard of verisimilitude; it is not its pictorial accuracy that is at stake. Rather, we are indicating its degree of felicity or infelicity in particularized circumstances. The proposition that the world is round and not flat is neither true nor false in terms of pictorial value, i.e., correspondence with the objective world. However, by current standards, it is more felicitous to play the game of round world truth when flying from Cologne to Kansas; and more felicitous to 'play it flat' when touring the state of Kansas itself. Let me next propose that the felicity of utterances we call descriptive is derived from other performative rituals. That is, the capacity to function as a performative in the game of description depends on the way in which the utterance is embedded within more primitive practices. Let me illustrate these two proposals.

Consider my youthful attempt to serve as a summer assistant to a wall plasterer. When my boss Marvin, an irrascible but exacting individual, climbed to the top of a ladder, his arms working the plaster toward perfection on the ceiling above his head, it was exceedingly important that I furnish him at a moment's notice mixtures of water and plastering compound that were exactly to his specifications. At times the mixture had to be moist - so it could be subtly worked and reworked; at others it had to be dry, so that it could be laid on thick and fast. Thus, he would bellow, 'skosh' (for a wet mixture) and 'dry one' (for a drier compound), depending on his progress. These words were of course quite alien when I began my servitude, but within a few days I became quite proficient in producing the desired mixtures. In effect, 'skosh' and 'dry one' became part of a relational dance in which we were engaged - words we needed to achieve a perfect finish.

Yet, let us see what has been achieved as a byproduct of this primitive dance of words, actions and objects. After two weeks of immersion in this procedure, Marvin and I could have been exposed to a series of mixtures, and with very little error, I suspect, we could have agreed on which were 'skosh' and which 'dry ones'. If I said 'dry one coming up' this would also inform Marvin of what he might predict on that occasion. This prediction could have been confirmed or disconfirmed. In effect, by virtue of their function within the relational form, such terms as 'skosh' and 'dry one' developed the capacity to function within another game - the game of description and verification. The words themselves do not describe the world; but because of their successful functioning within the rudimentary, performative ritual, they could then serve as 'descriptors' within the rules of the derivative game. This is to say that Austin's first term in his distinction, the constative or descriptive, is more properly to be considered a special case of his second or performative mode. Because of their success in coordinating relationships various utterances come to occupy a useful place in those rituals by which we determine truth and error, make predictions, and so on. To say that words describe, picture, or map (the world of plastering in this case) must be seen as a byproduct of their embeddedness within the joint achievement of a relationship. The words do not in fact furnish a picture any more than finger motions and whistles do. We would not wish to compare which of two melodies more exactingly captured the nature of the world, nor on this account, should we ask competing scientific theories to be compared in this way.

Scientific Theory and Social Pragmatics

There is a sense in which the presentation thus far has played out two partitas on the same melody; both threaten the semantic link once traditionally believed to hold between theories about the world and the actual nature of what there is. Both in questioning empiricist foundationalism, and then in tracing the genesis of description to the pragmatics of human relationships, we are challenging the traditional assumptions that theories can spring from the soil of observation, may be compared with respect to their adequacy in describing an independent world, and serve as generalized predictive guides for future action. In the initial critique of empiricist foundationalism we were confronted with the question of why, then, theories at all? Of what utility are theories within the sciences, and how might we valorize one over the other? Our second analysis, focusing on the performative basis of description, enables us now to take some preliminary steps toward solving the problem of progress in theory.

As we see, verbal language - and here we may now include theoretical description and explanation, are constitutive elements of broader patterns of human interchange. Language plays a pragmatic function within interactional achievements. From this perspective, we may now begin to delineate the ways in which theoretical language features within scientific practices. Two of these practices deserve special attention.

At the outset, the sciences have traditionally been engaged in the achievement of prediction. This is most obviously the case in the many of the natural sciences, in which, for good or ill, technologies have been developed that enable us to generate atomic energy, fly round the world, and reduce deadly diseases on a reliable basis. The predictive capacity of the psychological sciences is far less awesome, but we have developed technologies that enable prediction, at better than chance, of various problematic behaviors, performance in a variety of settings, the formation of affective ties, and so on. In all these various cases, the process of generating predictive technology is essentially reliant on a community of scientists - developing various measures, employing them in different populations and contexts, applying or developing various statistical devices and so on. As we have seen, theories within these sciences do not themselves make these predictions; the predictions cannot in any way be derived logically from the theoretical premises. However, theories would appear to play a positive function in the collaborative process by which collectivities of scientists generate predictions. That is, theoretical language is constitutive of the pragmatic interchange of which predictions are the ultimate achievement. Like 'your serve', 'thirty love' and 'my add' in tennis, they serve as the common argot enabling scientists to coordinate their activities one with another. If I join a group of scientists concerned with the prediction of what they call 'academic performance' I must not only employ this term, but a series of additional terms, including for example, 'IQ tests', 'anxiety indictors', 'achievement motivation', and the like. Such terms must also be embedded not only within a set of relationships with my colleagues but with sets of objects - papers, pencils, scoring keys, students and the like. The theoretical terms do not make predictions, then, but operate as vehicles through which scientific practitioners coordinate themselves to achieve such ends.

A second scientific outcome demands attention. In my view, the human sciences such as psychology have furnished relatively little in the way of predictive technology to the culture at large. To be sure, we have produced various forms of testing and measurement that might be counted as technological byproducts of the psychological sciences, along with various procedures for treatment of problematic persons in the society. For a variety of reasons, however, including the historical dependency of most patterns of action (Gergen, 1982), I am not sanguine that prediction will ever be a major outcome of the human science. Rather, it is my opinion that the major contribution of the psychological sciences to the society more generally has scarcely achieved notice. This is the contribution of theoretical descriptions and explanation to the repository of cultural discourse. This latter point deserves brief expansion.

As previously proposed, discourse is constitutive of relational practices that include persons, places, objects, and so on. Should the discourse be removed, such practices would be vitally altered; should the discourse undergo change, so might the practices in which such discourse is embedded. In a broad sense it may be said that existing social patterns are highly dependent on the forms of a discourse available to people for conducting their affairs. At the same time, one of the chief products of the psychological sciences is discourse about people - accounts of what they are doing, and why they are doing it. Regardless of the range and rigor of our observational techniques, the size of our samples, and the complexity of our statistical analyses, such research efforts are transformed in the end into ordered discourse. And much of this discourse enters into public life - theories of child development in psychology enter into widely disseminated manuals of child care; theories of mental health into numerous therapeutic settings, the courts, screening procedures of large organizations, and the like; theories of cognition into educational institutions; theories of attitudes and decision making into the enclaves of political and market strategists; theories of motivation into the ranks of organizational management; and so on. Psychological intelligibilities also insinuate themselves into the deepest interiors of daily life - into our relationships with our children, intimates, and friends. In effect, psychologists furnish the culture with a significant range of discursive devices, ontologies of the interior, and rationales with which we justify or carry out myriad forms of relational activity. The discipline furnishes the vital constituents of our most significant patterns of interchange.

Evaluating Theory in the Stage of Normal Science

We have now positioned ourselves to view theoretical discourse within the sciences principally as a vehicle for achieving social outcomes. Armed with this perspective, let us turn more directly to the chief problem at hand, namely furnishing an account of scientific progress, and most particularly, advancement within the realm of theory. To accomplish this task it is useful to return to Kuhn's (1962) distinction between normal and revolutionary science. Under conditions of normal science, scientists more or less agree on a given ontology, methods for charting relations among events, and explanations for these relations. These coordinated agreements go into the makeup of what Kuhn calls *paradigmatic* science. Scientific revolutions are essentially alterations in basic paradigms - from the Ptolmaic to the Galelian view of astronomy, from Newtonian to relativity theory in physics, and so on. Parenthetically, I do have grave reservations concerning Kuhn's account of how scientific revolutions occur. Critical to Kuhn's account of scientific revolutions is the emergence of what he terms 'anomalies', critical empirical facts that cannot be explained by the existing theories. Yet, putting aside the capacities of scientists to extend theories in light of seeming disconfirmations, (a la the Quine-Duhem method of elaborating ancillary suppositions), it is difficult to see how such anomalies could emerge. As we have seen, facts are themselves theoretically saturated; for a fact to exist requires a preliminary set of suppositions concerning the make-up of the world. In effect, ontological suppositions must precede the construction of the scientific fact rather than follow derivatively. Thus, empirical anomalies could not, as Kuhn would have it, precede the development of a new paradigm. The new paradigm must precede the establishment of the anomalie. However, in spite of these reservations it is useful for the present to retain Kuhn's distinction with minor modifications.

In particular, let us distinguish between *normal science* - a phase during which the problems to be solved are more or less agreed upon among communities of scientists, and what may be termed *transformational science.* In this latter case I am abandoning Kuhn's term, 'revolutionary' because the term is reserved for only those cases of radical change. I wish to denote here a form of scientific activity that is more or less continuous - existing coterminously with the normal, and undertaken by those who are often themselves engaged in normal activity. I propose this distinction between normal and transformational scientific activity - because, as we shall see, theories may be evaluated differentially within these two phases. Criteria for progress within normal science differ from those occurring within the transformational stage.

Let us first consider the phase of normal science. As we have seen, one of the chief aims of the sciences, including psychology, is that of generating more or less reliable predictions. Psychologists wish to be in the position of forecasting schizophrenia, identifying the suicidal, predicting the effects of a persuasive message on people's actions, determining whether a learning deficit is congenital, predicting whether certain individuals can withstand space flight, and so on. Now, as we have reasoned, theories themselves do not generate predictions. Theoretical propositions cannot carry instructions as to the manner in which they may be instantiated. During this normal phase of scientific activity, then, the chief use of theory may be viewed as that of coordinating the actions among persons within the profession around the task of enhancing prediction. As we have seen theoretical accounts serve as the major pragmatic vehicle for conjoining the efforts of individuals in achieving this common end.

It is at this juncture that we can generate a more compelling rationale for the functional value of some of the secondary criteria of theoretical evaluation in traditional lore. That is, certain of the secondary rhetorical criteria come to acquire a positive functional value within this context of social coordination. For example, the criterion of *logical coherence* becomes valuable, not because the world is itself logical and thus requires a description that mirrors its properties, but because in the process of coordinating activities among scientists it is important to maintain consistency in what various events, indicators, actions and the like are to be called. By distinguishing between a stimulus and a response, a demand characteristic and a neutral condition, a manifest and latent content, and so on, and using these distinctions consistently within the more expanded patterns of action in which prediction is the outcome, the possibilities for confusion across the community of scientists is decreased. Similarly, the criterion of *parsimony* comes to be more than an aesthetic consideration. The more elaborated the theoretical account of various phenomena in question the more complex the process of social coordination. In effect, traditional criteria of internal coherence and parsimony have a restored value for the discipline; they are not inherent goods within a theory. Their value is primarily limited to a specific phase of scientific activity, and within this phase their value is derived from their pragmatic function in the coordination of the scholarly community.

Let us turn to the second major outcome of psychological theory, that of furnishing intelligibilities to the society more generally. In this case a new range of evaluative criteria are invited. As we have seen, theoretical terms cannot be selected by virtue of their accuracy; the terms selected for uniting the scientific community cannot be chosen because they are the most accurate in describing of what is taking place. After all, except for its clumsy and undifferentiating qualities, the scientist could use sign language or periodic grunts and groans to carry out the task of coordination. Thus, considerable latitude is open for the psychologist regarding whether he or she uses, for example, mechanistic or organismic formulations, behavioral theories or rule-role formulations, cognitive or humanisitic means of accounting, and so on. And, because these formulations hereafter come to be disseminated to the society - putatively accounting for the way things are, and deriving unwarranted rhetorical power from the accompanying sets of predictions - they must be carefully scrutinized. What kinds of social practices are desirable, what sorts of patterns are eschewed by the favored theory? In effect, valuational critique is required.

Here one cannot be definitive regarding the kinds of criteria that may be brought to bear. This is so because there is available within the culture a rich range of valuational perspectives - moral, political, ideological, religious, and so on. All furnish discourse frames from which theoretical accounts in psychology may be assessed. Marxists justifiably use political grounds in selecting organismic as opposed to mechanistic theories; feminists may see severe ideological limitations in the choice of theories that express a self-contained individualism; humanists hold that deterministic theories have deplorable effects on the common consciousness and thus prefer accounts in which agency plays a pivotal role. At this juncture I would not wish to delimit the range of societal critique that may be brought to bear on psychological formulations. Critical theorists, feminists and humanists have been among the few participants in this kind of dialogue thus far and there is a vital need to expand the spectrum of moral and ideological sensitivity.

Theory in the Transformational Stage of Science

Thus far it has been proposed that during the stage of normal science theories may properly be compared with respect (1) to their ability to coordinate the scientific community around the task of prediction, and (2) their capacity to reflect the valuational commitments of the scientist. Theories that enhance the coordination of the scientific community and reflect more fully the moral commitments of a given community may be viewed as superior within this phase. Yet, should scientific activity be fixed in a given path of prediction or committed to a single vision of the good, we might view the sciences as both stagnant and myopic. Recall that theories are constitutive of broader patterns of relationship - both within the science and the society more generally. Thus, to remain fixed to a delimited range of theories is to constrain the potential of culture both scientific and otherwise. To remain in the 'normal phase' is to foreclose on new options of prediction, to delimit our possibilities for solving problems, and reduce the opportunity for realizing human potentials. Required are new criteria for theoretical evaluation in the transformational stage of science.

To elaborate, in terms of the problems of prediction, a truncated range of theories will mean that the patterns of relationship among scientists will remain relatively fixed allowing only refinements within a limited range of prediction. For example, to the extent that theories of perception remained 'bottom-up', as they did for many years, exclusive attention was paid to the effects of variables in the stimulus world. The more recent development of 'top-down formulations', opened the way to consideration of a wider range of internal antecedents, to what we term 'perception'. With the shift in perspective from 'bottom up' 'to top down' new kinds of prediction are invited. The network of predictive relationships is expanded. With regard to the effects of psychological discourse on social practice, theories of well being primarily concerned with internal dynamics (e.g., psychoanalytic theory) have led to holding individuals responsible for their actions. Aberrant behavior is the result of problematic psychological processes, and treatment must be directed to the defective individual. Yet, as theories of social systems enter in to the vocabulary of the scientist (and thus the culture more generally), we now have the option of viewing an individual's problems as the result of defective groups - families, educational systems, economic institutions and the like.

We now have sanction for broad social change, which sanction was not available with theories of individual based functioning.

It is in this vein that I have written previously of *generative theory* (Gergen, 1982). A generative theory is designed to undermine commitments to the prevailing systems of theoretical construction, and thereby generate new options for action. It is the generative criterion that can, in my view, most effectively bring about a transformational shift. Generative theorizing may frequently begin with critiques of existing accounts. Then, as the conceptual implications of the critique are progressively elaborated, the contours of a new ontology or world construction may slowly emerge. In this sense, critique is to be highly valued within the sciences, for it begins to lay important groundwork for succeeding theories of generative capacity. A good example of generative theorizing - commencing with critique and continuing through a dislocating ontology - is provided by feminist writings of recent years. Many feminist scientists became justifiably concerned over the pervasive tendency for research to demonstrate the inferiority of women in comparison to men. Various studies showed women to be less mature in their levels of moral thought, less achievement oriented, more conforming, more field dependent, more depressive, and so on, than their male counterparts. Is it possible, it was asked, that such findings were biased, and in particular might they be the result of the androcentric prejudice of male scientists? Such doubts then lead to criticisms of the ways in which ideology insinuated itself into the research process and the products which it engendered. As these criticisms were more fully elaborated, feminists began to develop theoretical means of reconstructing sex differences. Masculine theories, as masculine science, lays stress on independence, control, and power - all of which are viewed by feminists as societally problematic. As a contrast, it was possible to redefine women's perspective as more relational - sensitive to the subtle patterns of interdependence that unite or connect human beings. Armed with such theories of sex difference, feminists have set out to demonstrate predictive patterns - patterns in which women are shown to have a separate conception of morality from men, to be more socially sensitive, more oriented toward equality in social groups, and so on. A new view of human functioning is simultaneously emerging, one that holds social relationships to be the fundamental units of society - with individuals as derivatives. Contrast this to the traditional view in psychology of individuals as the central units of action and relationships as artificial byproducts. In effect, here is a case in which critique at the socio-political-moral level lead to an undermining of confidence in traditional research outcomes, the development of new theory, the search for new predictions, and I believe most importantly, a newly emerging discourse on the nature of human functioning. It is this latter discourse that now serves to inform the actions of many women and to invite alterations in social practice.

Summary and Conclusion

To summarize, we may envision the scientific process as composed of two opposing tendencies. The first opts toward the stabilization of meaning systems, focused prediction and the affirmation of particular values. The second aims toward transformation, where established patterns and values are uprooted and the range of available alternatives - both within science and society - is broadened. Under conditions of stabilization the criteria of theoretical evaluation are different from what they are under conditions of transformation. To achieve stabilization, theories are required that lead to the maximum of social coordination and value expression. When the attempt is to transform, the theorist must press against the borders of absurdity, shaking up the sedimented presumptions, arguing critically and audaciously. In the end, successful moves toward stabilization should lend themselves to transformation. Once theories at this stage have become embedded within secure traditions, their value becomes progressively lessened and their favored social institutions progressively restricting. At the same time, successful moves toward transformation will, in the end, give way to stabilization. As the audacious becomes commonplace, the metaphoric becomes literal, and value possibilities become realized in new forms of institution, transformational theory becomes normalized. Ideally the psychological sciences should thus move through periods of stabilization, decay, challenge, growth, and subsequent stabilization. Our theories do not thus move inexorably toward greater fidelity with nature; we come no nearer to truth (whatever that may be) through this procedure, but we do offer to the culture an increasing range of predictive devices and most important, an increasing range of intelligibilities. With a range of forecasts available, and the generation of intelligibilities that enable us to mold society anew, one might be confident in speaking of psychology - even in this age of post modern despair - as a discipline with unlimited progressive potential.

References

Austin, J. A. (1955). *How to do things with words.* Cambridge, MA: Harvard University Press.

Gergen, K. J. (1982). *Toward transformation in social knowledge.* New York: Springer.

Kuhn, T. S. (1962). *The structure of scientific revolutions.* Chicago: The University of Chicago Press.

Wittgenstein, L. (1953). *Philosophical investigations.* Oxford: Blackwell.

NEED RHETORICAL ANALYSIS LEAD TO RELATIVISM?

AN EXAMINATION OF THE VIEWS OF K. J. GERGEN

Sybe J. S. Terwee

Leiden University
Leiden, The Netherlands

SUMMARY: This article examines Kenneth Gergen's rhetorical conception of social psychology. Gergen's criticism of certain positivist assumptions of mainstream academic psychology is seen as valuable and basically valid. While his arguments do not imply the ***impossibility*** of empirical-analytical psychology, the persistent beliefs concerning the value-neutrality, testability, and applicability of empirical hypotheses do seem to be in need of revision. However, some of Gergen's arguments are reinterpreted. His rejection of foundationalism is shown to be virtually impossible in the light of Ludwig Wittgenstein's analysis of certainty and doubt. Hence, Gergen's claim that interpretations are open to infinite revision is consequently relativized. A revised interpretative conception of psychology is sketched in the conclusion.

Here one must realize that complete absence of doubt at some point, even where we would say that 'legitimate' doubt can exist, need not falsify a language-game. Wittgenstein (1969, p. 375)

Empirical-analytical Versus Interpretative Psychology

Discussions about psychology's fragmentation and the possibilities for unification and progress often center around the concept of *interpretation.* To suppose that psychological knowledge has interpretative aspects is seen by many as a potential danger for the objective status of the discipline as it is traditionally understood, namely as an empirical-analytical science modelled after the natural sciences. Customarily, the ensuing discussion centers around the question of whether psychology has to be strictly regarded as an empirical-analytical ('natural') science which avoids interpretation, or whether it can or should be conceived as an interpretative-hermeneutical enterprise (cf. Schlenker, 1974).

Interest in this discussion has never waned altogether, although the terms in which these matters are discussed have changed considerably. In this paper, I propose we look at the problem in a somewhat different way. I propose to look upon the interpretative and the empirical-analytical methods as two equally valid, but different, approaches to an understanding of the world. Both of them are perfectly legitimate within the scientific context of studies in the humanities. There are pragmatic, and not primarily epistemological, reasons on which we can decide to use the one or the other. Without attempting to list all the good arguments by proponents of interpretative methods in psychology (e.g., Gergen, 1982; Taylor, 1971; Peters, 1958), it suffices to say that there are also good reasons to prefer empirical-analytical method. The question is: do empirical-analytic methods enable researchers to avoid interpretation altogether? The answer is an unambiguous but multi-faceted 'no'. Every observation is theory-laden and in that sense is an interpretation of the world in the light of a theoretical framework (Popper, 1959). The positivist myth of neutral data has long been abandoned in philosophy. Science is a rule governed enterprise and even methodological rules imply selective and sometimes highly biased points of view. Such selective viewpoints are necessary and need not be regarded as a sign that psychology can no longer be a science or present testable hypotheses. The point is that there are many contacts between viewpoints or values and psychology, so that psychology cannot be regarded as an isolated tower of neutrality (Duintjer, 1974). Values are present in every experiment or investigation as shown, for example, by Morawski and Goldstein (1985) in the case of nuclear war research. Unfortunately, such viewpoints or values usually become clear only when we have the benefit of hindsight. For example, Samelson (1980, 1981) has shown that historical work can be very useful in the critical reflection upon psychology. Experimental research and scientific observations - we come to know about them as a result of all kinds of valuations, (cf. Peters & Ceci, 1982) - do not form a foolproof safeguard against subjectivity, rather, they are themselves based upon interpretation.

All this does not imply that the empirical-analytical method is basically wrong. The only thing is, that it does not provide us with the kind of ideal neutrality that is sometimes taken for granted. Working with experimental, quantitative methods still obliges one to make value-based decisions and interpret human reality. When this fact is not acknowledged, then interpretations and decisions are made implicitly and without proper reflection on their importance.

My intention in this paper is to show that Gergen's work is a reflection on the nature and suppositions of empirical-analytical psychology with its dilemma of interpretations.

Psychology as Rhetoric

Gergen's reflections spring from experimental social psychology, which he labels as positivist-empiricist in character. He observes that this kind of science hopes to attain objective and enduring truth or certainty, and is built on the belief in progress through the accumulation of facts.

According to Gergen (1980), there are three assumptions inherent in empiristic social psychology which are untenable. First, there is the assumption of empirical evaluation. Empiricistic psychology supposes that a theory may be evaluated against 'the facts', against observations or empirical evidence. Traditionally, theorists hold that this must result in falsification or confirmation of the theory. Gergen argues that testing in this empiricist sense is impossible in psychology. Due to the interpretative nature of psychological facts, any theory may be related to any set of facts. What Gergen shows is that the same experimental results may be explained by different theoretical models and these results may also be used as support for virtually any theory. The relationship between theoretical concepts and empirical exemplars is fundamentally ambiguous (Gergen, 1980, 1982). It is important to note that all of the examples of the ambiguous nature of facts that Gergen provides stem from social psychology. Second, the empiricist assumes the accumulation of knowledge. However, following the first assumption, namely, that the theories are insulated from empirical evidence, the elimination of incorrect theories is impossible in any straightforward way. This means that the chances for progress are very small indeed if one clings to the traditional criterion of verisimilitude. Third, the empiricist assumes that the application of social psychological theories to achieve social good involves prediction and control. But as should be clear from the above, the predictive capabilities of psychological theories are small because predictions are highly ambiguous. Hence, the value of basic theory must be sought in a direction different from prediction and control (Gergen, 1980),

However, the foregoing cannot be read as a criticism of empirical psychology. It is a critique of certain assumptions of empiricistic psychology. It is *within that framework* that empirical evaluation is impossible or, rather, turns out to be something different from what it is believed to be.

The problems inherent in these three assumptions of empiricistic social psychology are illustrated by the so-called interpretative dilemma. Gergen poses this dilemma by describing a situation from everyday life. Ross and Laura approach each other at a social gathering, and Ross reaches out and momentarily touches Laura's hair. Precisely what is observed if we see this happen? What action has occurred? How do we normally solve the essential problem of behavioral identification? (Gergen 1980, 1982, in press). Different interpretations of the action can be given. Indeed it is not easy to say which meaning this action actually has for the participants, or for observers. Was the touching of Laura's hair a signal of affection? Or an act of derision? It all depends on the context and, if we turn for additional information to the retrospective and emergent contexts, we can easily imagine how more and more interpretations become plausible.

Gergen (1980) draws three conclusions from this example.

1. The identification of any given action is subject to infinite revision.

2. The anchor point for any given identification is not fundamentally empirical, but relies on a network of interdependent and continuously modifiable interpretations.

3. Any given action may be subject to multiple identifications, no one of which is inherently superior (pp. 241-243).

If one applies these conclusions to the interpretative basis of social psychology, it becomes clear that the traditional empiricist assumptions are undermined. Gergen concludes that the traditional aims of the discipline must be modified, and sketches the possibilities of a social psychology as an interpretative enterprise. In short, instead of describing and explaining a pre-existing reality, a theory should be concerned with descriptions of rule systems and conceptual transformations of social life. Common forms of interpretation and their relation to social action might be systematically elucidated. One might also challenge the guiding assumptions of a culture, foster reconsideration of that which is taken for granted, and furnish fresh alternatives for social action. The challenging of common-sense interpretation is what Gergen means by generative theory. Philosophically speaking, we might call this emphasis on the change of common interpretations a rhetorical or deconstructionist position.

In a reader dedicated to social constructionist inquiry (Gergen & Davis, 1985), Gergen observes that psychology might look for kinship to the traditional interpretative disciplines. Psychology might gain a lot by developing an affinity with disciplines chiefly concerned with rendering accounts of human meaning systems, for example, literary theory.

Gergen (1985) draws an important distinction between two innovations that his alternative conception offers. The first concerns the object of research. This is no longer seen as naturally 'given', but as constituted by social rules and norms. This means that psychology becomes a derivative of social process: "the explanatory locus of human action shifts from the interior region of the mind to the processes and structure of human interchange" (p. 12). The second innovation is on the level of metatheory. Earlier, Gergen cast doubt on the process of objective warranting. His conclusions apply also to the accounts of social construction. "Such accounts can enable one to escape the confines of the taken for granted. However, the success of such accounts depends primarily on the analyst's capacity to invite, compel, stimulate, or delight the audience, and not on criteria of veracity" (Gergen, 1985, p. 14). Gergen addresses the possible criticism that such rhetoric may lead to relativism by observing that empiricism does not seem to fare any better in this respect, for the so-called objective foundations for knowledge still have to be justified. But, he does acknowledge that "...constructionism offers no foundational rules of warrant, and in this sense is relativistic. However, this does not mean that 'anything goes'. Because of the inherent dependency of knowledge systems on communities of shared intelligibility, scientific activity will always be governed in large measure by normative rules" (Gergen, 1985, p. 14).

In a paper called *If persons are texts* (Gergen, in press), Gergen addresses the question of how his rhetorical position relates to the hermeneutic approach in psychology. Hermeneutics, generally connected with the work of the German philosopher H. G. Gadamer, maintains that there is at least one legitimate alternative to the scientific, methodical, approach to reality. The interpretative approach used in the cultural and historical disciplines is not methodical in empirical analytical terms, but it nevertheless leads to knowledge. This interpretative kind of knowledge is not arbitrary and it is open to validation. However, its character is historical, which means that it is part of 'effective history' (Wirkungsgeschichte) in the sense that later generations may judge differently from their vantage-points. Not only does knowledge change, but *the standards* change with which knowledge is evaluated. Gadamer seems to be ambiguous as to the question of progress in the hermeneutical disciplines, sometimes he suggests that a new understanding implies a better understanding, in other contexts he calls it a 'different understanding'.

As a rhetorician, Gergen is more inclined to challenging existing forms of understanding and to analyze the way persuasion works. As we have seen above, he casts doubt on the notion of a 'correct' interpretation or 'the best' interpretation. Similarly, he cannot accept the common understanding by the 'hermeneuticists' of Gadamer's position. Gergen prefers the ideas of "literary theorists in general" and "deconstructionists in particular" (Gergen, in press, p. 21; quotations and page numbers from a typed manuscript). In literary theory, the *reader* has displaced the *text* as the center of concern. However, the ensuing deconstruction of the text and its author presents us with another impasse. It seems that human understanding is impossible. To quote Gergen again: "In the process of reading, both the text and its author are obliterated. The individual again falls back into isolation, unable to know, and unable to communicate" (p. 22). In reaction to these problems, Gergen sketches an alternative for the metaphor of person as text. This alternative rests on the assumptions that (a) the dualism between interior and exterior must be abandoned. Human actions are what they are; we can only confront each others' actions directly, and (b)the words of others' are of significant consequence for our actions; we are not self-contained monads.

This last move is puzzling. It seems that Gergen falls back on what seems to be, essentially, Gadamer's position. Gadamer can certainly not be accused of being a dualist of exterior (actions) and interior (intentions). Intentions are absolutely irrelevant and futile to Gadamer and, within his work, never play a role in interpretation. Further, he acknowledges the necessity of interpreting in those cases where a natural, direct understanding, is impossible; for example, the reading of an ancient text, or the understanding of a culture different from our own. Even then, we can confront others' actions directly, or approach the text directly in the hermeneutic circle. Indeed, in the process of following the hermeneutic circle, the words of the object are of significant consequence for our actions. Our own preconceptions are brought into play. The horizon of the interpreter's understanding is affected by reading of the text. When we reach a fusion of the horizons of understanding - even in the process of reading a text - it is hardly possible to view the reader or interlocutor as a 'self-contained monad', to use Gergen's terms. It seems that Gergen unwittingly moves back into the realm of Gadamerian hermeneutics. Certain formulations he uses at the end of the article form evidence for this surmise.

For example, he writes, that "the meanings of words, gestures and actions are realized within the unfolding patterns of relationship" (p. 24). We may look, not inward, "but outward into the continuously expanding horizon of the relationship" (pp. 24 and 25). Gergen mentions the expression of depression as an example. "As our participants showed us, there are only a limited set of discursive moves that may be made" (p. 27). Following this new metaphor of the game, the dance, or the relationship, we may explore the embedding of relational scenarios. "Rather than exploring the unknown world of the interior, one moves to the level of client-therapist relationship" (pp. 28-29). "Questions of validity are replaced by queries into the forms of relatedness into which our verbal expressions (among others) fall, and into their implications and alternatives (p. 30).

These quotations show that there is at least one recurring theme in Gergen's work: the opposition between validity, truth, objectivity and stable insight on the one hand, and changing meanings, developing insights, open-ended interpretations, and relative truth on the other. Let us now have a closer look at some philosophical presuppositions of this theme and the rhetorical position in general.

An Evaluation of the Rhetorical Position

Earlier, I called Gergen's conception of the foundations and nature of psychology a rhetorical conception of social psychology. It is not surprising that various forms of criticism have been raised against these ideas, because they run counter to established psychological theorizing. Gergen so strongly denies the possibility of objective knowledge, that his ideas have become a threat for the very enterprise of social psychology. While I would maintain that this is not a necessary conclusion from his rhetorical position, there are aspects in Gergen's writings which invite this reading. Let me try to elucidate the discussion by raising three questions in connection with the evaluation of the rhetorical conception of social psychology.

1. Gergen views the interpretation of human action as essentially ungrounded and open to infinite revision. But is this view not premised on a misconceived dilemma: either there are rational foundations, or there are no foundations at all? My contention is, that most of the interpretations we give are not rationally justified, but still they are not arbitrary or subjective, because they are grounded in the practice of our form of life (culture or scientific paradigm).

2. The contextual validation of interpretations of human action is regarded by Gergen as essentially impossible. The problem of evaluating theories and interpretations in the context of empirical-analytical research are convincingly posed. However, is the endless revision of interpretations, as Gergen describes it, also possible in contexts of everyday life, and even if it is possible, does it constitute an actual problem for a discipline that does not work on empiricistic assumptions? It seems that traditional interpretative disciplines have found ways to deal adequately with the evaluation of interpretative theories.

3. Gergen has formulated an alternative aim for social psychology. In this rhetorical conception, psychology must provide alternatives for common forms of understanding, and form a generative theory. However, may these alternative aims not be seen as an enrichment of empirical-analytical and hermeneutical-interpretative psychologies, rather than as an antidote? Empirical-analytic research could be part of the rhetorical task.

The Basis of Knowledge

The idea that knowledge has certain and rational foundations has been gradually undermined in this century. Generally, philosophers do not believe that a complete justification of knowledge claims is possible. Let me review some important lines of development.

Popper (1959/1934) was first in demonstrating that the logical positivists' claim that scientific knowledge rests on certain foundations was unwarranted. Instead, Popper posited a conventional basis for our knowledge claims. Scientific knowledge rests on basic propositions. These are accepted by decision, and if all scientists agree on them there is no need to test them further. However, testing is always possible in principle, and offers a guarantee against dogmatism. The character of scientific knowledge is that it cannot be justified by reference to indubitable facts. Rather, it may be corroborated by tests; testability is the criterion for science.

About thirty years later, Thomas Kuhn (1962) radicalized the falsificationist ideas about the foundations and the development of scientific theories. According to Kuhn, the nature of science has traditionally been misunderstood. This basis of science is not propositional, rather, it consists of exemplars of good research. In last resort, a scientist is not able to justify his theories with the help of knowledge claims or methodological rules: he must refer to paradigms of what counts, in his science, as sound research (cf. Wittgenstein, 1969, p. 139). On this account, knowledge is further undermined, or better, relativized: knowledge and rationality are valid concepts when measured against the standards of a certain paradigm or disciplinary matrix.

Kuhn's ideas were clearly inspired by Wittgenstein. In *Philosophical Investigations* (1953) and *On Certainty* (1969) Wittgenstein addresses the philosophical problem of the foundations of knowledge. He stresses the imbeddedness of all our knowledge in language games and, eventually, forms of life. His analysis of rule following behavior demonstrates that rules alone are not sufficient to guide human action. In the end, justification is impossible; and we act, without rational grounds, but with certainty. Wittengenstein also shows that any application of a rule involves a decision, for example, when a pupil fails to continue a number series, we are unable to give him rational grounds; instead we become involved in a fruitless discussion about the concept of 'sameness', and in the end we are forced to admit that something is right "because we all do it". (Wittgenstein, 1953, p. 186: "It would almost be more correct to say, not that an intuition was needed at every stage, but that a new decision was needed at every stage.")

Wittgenstein (1969) is even more clear in this respect: "Giving grounds, however, justifying the evidence, comes to an end; - but the end is not certain propositions striking us immediately as true, that is, it is not a kind of *seeing* on our part; it is our *acting,* which lies at the bottom of the language-game" (Wittgenstein, 1969, 204). The concept of certainty is a second and related way in which Wittgenstein indicates the nature of the basis of our knowledge. Knowledge and certainty form mutually exclusive categories for him. If we know something, we are able to present evidence and grounds for it, and so we are not certain. But if we are certain (for example, that these are real human people, who are sitting in front of me), we are not able to give grounds for our belief, nor are we generally able to doubt. "If you tried to doubt everything you would not get as far as doubting anything. The game of doubting itself presupposes certainty" (Wittgenstein, 1969, 115; cf. 120, 370, 391).

What implications might these philosophical analyses have for the rhetorical position? I believe that Wittgenstein convincingly shows the non-rational, but, nevertheless, indubitable foundations of human knowledge. Normally we accept these foundations and only in exceptional cases are we willing and able to doubt. When Gergen points to the lack of rational foundations for our everyday interpretations, he is entirely correct. But this does not open the door to unlimited doubt and continuous revision of all our interpretations. Though some revisions are possible in principle, they would only actually occur in exceptional cases. Not some rational ground, but only the traditional practices and a system of certainties present in every human culture provide safeguards against subjectivity and arbitrariness in interpretation.

The Revision of Interpretations

In Gergen's view, the context of an action does not help us in determining the meaning of an action. The example of Ross and Laura shows that enlarging the context only tends to complicate the interpretation; more information about the context tends to create more possibilities of interpretation.

However, the example must not blind us to the innumerable situations in everyday life where we directly perceive the meaning of actions. And if it is not a question of unproblematic perception, we usually find out in conversation what is at stake. Problems of interpretation do not have to be denied, but they must be properly situated, in a Wittgensteinian manner, as exceptions against the backdrop of reasonably well-ordered language-games of everyday life.

There is one special situation which artificially creates problems in interpretation: the psychological experiment. Usually the normal context is removed, and subjects are asked to react to certain contrived manipulations. Here, indeed, it is very difficult to say what the resulting responses mean. It is significant that Gergen only takes one example from everyday life as evidence for his thesis that interpretations are open to infinite revision. And one wonders whether the problem of Laura and Ross actually occurs that often in daily life. The rest of Gergen's evidence is taken from the field of social psychology, and it tells us more about the difficulties inherent in empiricist research than it does about the interpretations of actions in natural contexts (cf. Brandt, 1982).

Generative Theory: Psychology as Rhetorics

In the analysis of mainstream social psychology, it becomes clear that investigations which fail to challenge common-sense knowledge in our culture, are not so easily challenged by alternative explanations of the results. This leads to conservatism: "the review process ensures that the scientific literature will not deviate markedly from 'what every reasonable person' already knows" (Gergen 1980, p. 254). This is certainly a good reason for propagating audacious theorizing. But does rhetorical analysis exclude all kinds of explanatory and interpretative understanding of existing norms, rules and forms of action? Confronted with empiricist defenders of neutrality, it seems necessary to stress the variable and continuously changing nature of human reality. But these changes take place against a massive background of continuity - also in the cultural domain. It seems that one cannot even tell whether certain norms are right or wrong, desirable or undesirable, without studying and interpreting human language-games. The stress on the flexible character of interpretation and the aim of audacious theorizing may be seen as useful antidotes against empirical-analytical dogmatism, but these need not become values in themselves. If they do, they must be deconstructed in turn (Carveth, 1984).

Does Rhetorical Analysis Lead to Relativism

The tendency in Gergen's work to stress the infinite diversity of human behavior and to deny the possibility of discovering regularities by means of more traditional research is criticized by Jahoda (1986). Jahoda argues that the conception of persons as free and autonomous is also a typical Western ideal. Of course, this is a legitimate value to defend, also when it is a basis for theorizing. In part, Gergen's emphasis on freedom may be ascribed to the fact that he is in constant discussion with his empiricist opponents. For after all, it is empiricist metatheory which has as its aim timeless truths and general laws, but has produced only limited knowledge of a reduced reality heavily impregnated by temporary norms.

However, the radical move to the opposite position, namely, that psychology must not aim at the truth, must not seek validation for its knowledge claims, and must restrict itself to persuasion, seems somewhat too simple. When Gergen says: "the success of such accounts (of social construction) depends primarily on the analyst's capacity to invite, compel, stimulate, or delight the audience, and not on criteria of veracity" (Gergen,1985, p. 14), I think he creates a contrast which is not based on a real opposition. The audience within psychology is only compelled or stimulated by work which meets certain criteria of veracity. Of course, this veracity has nothing to do with old-fashioned ideas about transhistorical truths, or absolute justifications of knowledge. Relativism is inevitable in the sense that historical evolution might change the standards with which scientific knowledge is evaluated. Also, psychological knowledge may be seen from different vantage-points: there is more than one theoretical-value-orientation. It is not always possible to reach an inter-subjective judgment about certain matters. These are restrictions which must be kept in mind when one defends a claim to knowledge. Nevertheless, accepting limits to our knowledge does not prevent us from believing that we are searching for the truth. This is a simple distinction between different levels of discourse: within science, we aim for the best interpretations possible with respect to truth, veracity, and relevance. But taking the vantage point of the philosopher, and reflecting upon science, we realize that the knowledge acquired does not transcend historical and cultural limitations. Rhetorical analysis aims to show the fluctuating character of reality. In this process, fixed meanings are deconstructed. Yet, even when rhetoricians deconstruct their own positions, they claim to be truthful about reality, and to reveal important aspects of reality. In this sense, empirical-analytical psychology, hermeneutics and rhetorics share an important goal, that is, they all aim for the truth. In his critiques of the assumptions of empiricist psychology, Gergen has demonstrated that the empirical-analytical method presents us with psychological knowledge that is dependent upon the cultural and historical context. The same holds true for his rhetorical conception. The conclusion may sound paradoxical: in his radical rejection of the aims of empiricist psychology, Gergen remains entangled in one central presupposition of the empirical-analytical world-view. He assumes that apart from the realm of natural science, no real knowledge may be found, and that any pursuit of truth in the humanities is futile. However, this presupposition rests on a shaky basis indeed.

Alternatives for the Acceptance of Relativism

How valid is the hypothesis that interpretative research leads to inherently subjective results? The literature, both within and without the field of psychology, presents us with a variety of arguments that undermine this conception of interpretation. Runyan (1982) has pointed out that even where a variety of plausible interpretations may be given, a critical assessment of the evidence presented is crucial. We may encounter such a plethora of interpretations in clinical studies (Terwee, 1985; Fosshage & Loew, 1978), in psychobiography (Runyan, 1982), in history and traditional philology (Oudemans & Lardinois, 1987), and in cognitive psychology (Erdelyi, 1985). The authors mentioned all share the belief that the pursuit of knowledge and truth is essential in such studies. Some provide rules and methods for sound interpretative work (French & Fromm, 1964) while others stress the fact that interpretations ought to be tested against evidence (Erdelyi, 1985; Runyan, 1982). Some warn against the quantitative methodological imperative in psychology (Danziger, 1985), others reject empirical-analytical thinking as a world-view (Hekman, 1984; Terwee, 1987; De Boer, 1983). It seems that interpretative disciplines may offer us real knowledge, though a different kind of knowledge than many psychologists would expect.

References

Boer, Th. de (1983). De vraag naar de psychologie: Kritik der unreinen Vernunft. In J. J. D. Drenth, et al. (Eds.), ***Psychologie in Nederland. Enkele ontwikkelingen in 1982*** (pp. 1-24). Lisse: Swets & Zeitlinger.

Brandt, L. W. (1982). ***Psychologists caught. A psycho-logic of psychology.*** Toronto: University of Toronto Press.

Carveth, D. L. (1984). The analyst's metaphors: A deconstructionist perspective. ***Psychoanalysis and Contemporary Thought, 7,*** 491-560.

Danziger, K. (1985). The methodological imperative in psychology. ***Philosophy of the Social Sciences, 15,*** 1-13.

Duintjer, D. D. (1974). Moderne wetenschap en waarderijheid. In Th. de Boer & A. Köbben (Ed.), ***Waarden en wetenschap*** (pp. 20-45). Baarn: Ambo.

Erdelyi, M. H. (1985). ***Psychoanalysis: Freud's cognitive psychology.*** New York: W. H. Freeman.

Fosshage, J. L., & Loew, C. A. (Eds.).(1978). ***Dream interpretation - a comparative study.*** New York: Spectrum Publications.

French, T. M., & Fromm, E. (1964). ***Dream interpretation. A new approach.*** New York: Basic Books.

Gadamer, H. G. (1960). ***Wahrheit und Methode.*** Tübingen: J. C. B. Mohr.

Gergen, K. J. (1980). Towards intellectual audacity in social psychology. In R. Gilmour & S. Duck (Eds.), ***The development of social psychology*** (pp. 239-270). London: Academic Press.

Gergen, K. J. (1982). ***Toward transformation in social knowledge.*** New York: Springer.

Gergen, K. J. (1985). Social constructionist inquiry: Context and implications. In K. J. Gergen & K. E. Davis (Eds.), ***The social construction of the person*** (pp. 3-18). New York: Springer.

Gergen, K. J., & Davis, K. E. (1985). ***The social construction of the person.*** New York: Springer.

Gergen, K. J. (1986). Interpreting texts of nature and culture: A reply to Jahoda. ***European Journal of Social Psychology, 16,*** 31-37.

Gergen, K. J. (in press). If persons are texts. In S. B. Masser, K. E. Gergen & K. E. Davis (Eds.), ***Hermeneutics and psychological theory*** (p. 14). New Brunswick, NJ: Rutgers University Press.

Hekman, S. (1984). Action as a text: Gadamer's hermeneutics and the social scientific analysis of action. ***Journal for the Theory of Social Behaviour, 14,*** 333-354.

Jahoda, G. (1986). Nature, culture and social psychology. ***European Journal of Social Psychology, 16,*** 17-30.

Kuhn, T. S. (1962). ***The structure of scientific revolution.*** Chicago, IL: University of Chicago Press.

Morawski, J. G., & Goldstein, S. E. (1985). Psychology and nuclear war. A chapter in our legacy of social responsibility. ***American Psychologist, 40,*** 276-284.

Oudemans, Th. C. W., & Lardinois, A. P. M. H. (1987). ***Tragic ambiguity. Anthropology, philosophy and Sophocles' Antigone.*** Leiden, The Netherlands/New York: E. J. Brill.

Peters, R. S. (1958). ***The concept of motivation.*** London: Routledge & Kegan Paul.

Peters, D. P., & Ceci, S. J. (1982). Peer-review practices of psychological journals: the fate of published articles, submitted again. ***The Behavioral and Brain Sciences, 5,*** 187-155.

Popper, K. R. (1959). *The logic of scientific discovery.* London: Hutchinson.
Runyan, W. M. (1982). *Life histories and psycho-biography.* New York: Oxford University Press.
Samelson, F. (1980). J. B. Watson's little Albert, Cyril Burt's twins, and the need for a critical science. *American Psychologist, 35*, 619-626.
Samelson, F. (1981). Struggle for scientific authority: The reception of Watson's behaviorism, 1913-1920. *Journal of the History of the Behavioural Sciences, 17*, 399-425.
Schlenker, B. R. (1974). Social psychology and science. *Journal of Personality and Social Psychology, 29*, 1-15.
Taylor, C. (1971). Interpretation and the sciences of man. *Review of Metaphysics, 25*, 3-51.
Terwee, S. (1985). The evaluation of interpretations Freud's case of little Hans. (unpublished).
Terwee, S. J. S. (1987). Grünbaum's foundations of psychoanalysis. *Psychoanalysis and Contemporary Thought, 10*, 347-372.
Wittgenstein, L. (1953). *Philosophical investigations.* Oxford: Basil Blackwell.
Wittgenstein, L. (1969). *On certainty.* Oxford: Basil Blackwell.

THEORETICAL UNIFICATION IN PSYCHOLOGY:

A MATERIALIST PERSPECTIVE

Charles W. Tolman

University of Victoria
Victoria, British Columbia, Canada

SUMMARY: The case for a materialist foundation for psychology is described in which theoretical unification emerges as an on-going historical process, not as a state. Theoretical indeterminacy is overcome through appeal to evolutionary and historical contexts which allow evaluation of theories in terms of essentiality and relevance.

The problems of theoretical indeterminacy, disunity and fragmentation in psychology will not be solved by the revival of any form of positivism (e.g., Staats, 1986). It is well known that the Humean epistemology that defined positivism made it impossible to find a satisfactory solution to the problem of objectivity, and that, as a result, the ultimate goal of a unified science remained chimerical. Many psychologists saw that down the positivist epistemological road lay the dreaded end of solipsism (e.g., Wertheimer, 1972, p. 126). The only reasonable alternative between the Scylla of solipsism and the Charybdis of dogmatism seemed to be some form of metaphysical pluralism. Some of us settled, in short,- however uncomfortably - for the indeterminacy and fragmentation that mark what others now see as a crisis in our discipline.

Despite all the critiques of positivism, we seem to be no further ahead. The reason is that most critiques have not penetrated to the skeptical-subjectivist epistemology that is the root cause of its problems. As a result, the tendency has been to reject the scientistic *appearances* of positivism, while preserving its *essential* defect, which, from the point of view of objectivity, and therefore also of theoretical determinacy and unification, is the inability to specify an independently existing, nonarbitrary ground to serve as a basis for resolution of theoretical differences.

Philosophical materialism[1] claims to avoid this defect. If, as materialism claims, such a ground exists and is knowable, then the foundation of a unified conception of science is possible. I can only hope to

[1]The materialism represented here is dialectical materialism (e.g., Tolman, 1987). Psychologists are most likely to be acquainted with dialectical materialism in the works of Vygotsky (e.g., 1978) and Luria (e.g., 1979).

sketch out this possibility here.

Materialism asserts that there is no limit, in principle, to our knowledge of the external (or internal), objective, mind-independent world. This does not mean, however, that knowledge cannot be partial or mistaken. It is almost always the former and too often the latter. This is accounted for by two characteristics of knowledge. First, knowledge is developmental: it is a process of 'getting to know'. In this development we almost never come to know a thing completely because, as we come to know more about it, we also come to recognnize that there is more to be known. It is reasonable to suppose that things are epistemologically inexhaustible. The result is that our knowledge of anything at any given time must be partial from one perspective or another.

Second, a distinction must be made between perceptual and conceptual knowledge. The blind men examining the elephant had correct, but inadequate, perceptual knowledge, and jumped to premature, and thus largely mistaken, conclusions about what it was they were touching. From the materialist point of view, the probability of true conceptual knowledge increases as the fund of perceptual knowledge increases. Continued, cooperative exploration of the elephant would eventually have led the blind men to its correct conceptualization.

It follows from this that truth is relative, not to some kind of arbitrary 'framework' as in skeptical/relativist theories of truth, but to the objective content of knowledge, i.e., the extent to which knowledge reflects not sense data, but the object itself.

The acceptability, indeed necessity, of theoretical pluralism is thus relative to the extent of objective knowledge about something. At an early stage when ignorance dominates, pluralism is necessary and facilitates getting-to-know. As the objective content of knowledge increases through practice, pluralism ought to decrease. Once the elephant has been adequately explored, there will tend to be agreement that it is an elephant, and anyone who continues to insist that it is an umbrella will be regarded as intransigent and disruptive. Thus pluralism represents a *developmental stage* of knowledge and not a permanent condition.

Materialists also insist that knowledge is social. No single individual does, or can, bear the burden of discovering everything by and for himself. That is why we have schools, books, computers, research organizations, and conferences. This means that individuals transcend whatever biological limits might exist for the various cognitive functions. Whoever has acquired the skill of reading and some simple rules of access 'possesses' the whole fund of historically accumulated knowledge contained in the library.

Opponents of a unitary conception of science often charge its advocates with dogmatism. The implication is that only skepticism/pluralism can save us from this end. The correct response is to show that skepticism, like pluralism, is not a position, but the absence of one, and that its proper historical role is to overcome itself. As exemplified in the work of Descartes, skepticism is a means, not an end. The metaphysical skeptics and pluralists simplistically assume there to be only two extreme possibilities: complete knowledge or none at all. But this is itself a form of dogmatism that materialism successfully avoids. Metaphysical pluralism is vulnerable to dogmatism precisely because it denies any independent rational criterion for the resolution of theoretical differences. The materialist is not suggesting that resolution be brought about by weight of traditional or other arbitrary authority, but rather on the basis of appeal to the thing itself, which is the surest way of avoiding dogmatism.

But what makes materialists believe they can appeal to the 'thing itself'? The answer is most easily given by another question: Why *shouldn't* they believe it? Why, when seeing a chair, should one claim to be seeing anything other than the chair itself? Those who deny access to things in themselves (as did Hume & Kant) generally do so because they hold to an indirect realist or representationalist theory of perception. But such a theory has been shown to be both incoherent (e.g., Wilcox & Katz, 1984) and unnecessary (e.g., Gibson, 1966). I shall not attempt here to make the case for a direct realist theory of perception; it is sufficient for present purposes to indicate that materialism ultimately relies upon such a theory.

Summarized to this point, my argument is that a materialist epistemology is plausible, and that only materialism - certainly not positivism in any form - can provide the necessary foundation for a truly unified psychology. It must be emphasized, however, that the development of a unified and cumulative psychology is not a simple function of time and effort. Nor is it a simple function of materialist assumptions. This is abundantly clear from the fact that, despite much positivist rhetoric, most experimental psychologists in this century have operated according to roughly materialist norms. Yet, the 'historical truth' is that "opposing theories have survival value, and that an appeal to the facts as a way of choosing between theories is a very complex process, not nearly as decisive in practice as we might expect it to be" (Hilgard & Bower, 1966, p. 9).

Materialism, time, and effort are necessary, but something more is needed to make a sufficient condition. According to Hilgard and Bower (1966): "Accumulation of knowledge means neither mere fact-gathering nor isolated hypothesis-testing, but thoughtful systematic approaches to meaningful questions leading to *conclusive thinking* ... Some good high-level thinking is needed, keeping in mind *criteria of relevancy,* so that significant controversies are resolved on the basis of firmer knowledge ... We need, along with contemporary *model-building*, some general *psychologizing,* that is, repeated reflection upon the larger questions of psychology, to determine whether or not our approaches are indeed leading to their answer" (p. 583).

The kind of program which Hilgard and Bower appear to be recommending has been underway at the Free University of Berlin (and elsewhere in West Germany, Denmark, and the Netherlands) under the rubric of 'Kritische Psychologie' for almost 20 years. I shall describe the main points of the materialist critical-psychological formulation of the problem and its solution as it was summarized by Klaus Holzkamp in 1977 (1978).

Start with a typical psychological theory, say, a 'consistency' theory in social psychology. From the theory we deduce hypotheses which are then translated into independent and dependent variables. Experimental design and statistical assessment are used to ensure both necessity and sufficiency of the independent variable conditions with regard to the expected result. If the result occurs and is judged reliable, the hypothesis and theory are treated as having been confirmed.

In this procedure there are two sources of theoretical indeterminacy, one minor and one major. The minor one is what might be called 'weak confirmation'. Our experimental and statistical methods have come to be so highly refined that under existing rules of procedure almost any selected relationship has very favourable chances of being confirmed. Holzkamp has called this 'Bestätigungsfreundlichkeit' (confirmation-friendliness). Holzkamp shows how this is supported by our standard criteria for Null hypothesis testing. With the right sample size and 'alpha level', very little explained variance can count as a confirmation of the experimental hypothesis.

Holzkamp is not saying that this is wrong in itself. Nor is he saying that these methods should be relaxed or abandoned. That would surely only make matters worse. Rather, he is pointing out how our methods allow the confirmation of hypotheses, which, though correct, may be entirely *irrelevant* and *inessential.*

The major source of theoretical indeterminacy is a lack of broader perspective. While we may go on confirming our 'consistency' theory *ad infinitum,* we will never learn from our efforts whether 'consistency' is actually relevant or essential to human sociality. Another theorist, interpreting sociality in other, even opposing, terms, and adopting similar experimental procedures, may likewise be able to find infinite confirmation. The resolution of the differences between the theories is therefore not to be sought in further empirical confirmation or further refinement of experimental methods, but in a broader perspective on sociality that can allow us to judge the relevance or essentiality of particular theories.

What, then, is meant by *relevant* and *essential?* According to Holzkamp (1978):

> Relevance is...a *real* mark of status within the dimensional structure, such that theories become scientifically more relevant, i.e., capable of containing more real knowledge, to the extent that they conceptually embrace more relevant dimensions: dimensions are...more ***essential*** than others to the extent that they are more ***fundamental***, i.e., depend less on others than others on them, and consequently a variety of different superficial phenomena, the variability of which derives from less essential dimensions, are lawfully related to one another by virtue of relation to them (p. 157).

How is essentiality determined? From an evolutionary point of view, essential is what contributes to survival. It is essential that an organism respond appropriately to the demands placed upon it by its environmental context. Essentiality of a process can thus be determined by a study of the evolutionary or other developmental context that has shaped it.

Holzkamp calls this approach to essentiality 'functional historical' and it is clearly akin to the ecological approach of J. J. Gibson (1966). An important difference between the two is Holzkamp's insistence upon the centrality of the distinction between phylogenetic and societal-historical contexts. Human beings relate to the world both as evolved organisms and as societal-historically conditioned beings. The distinction is important for psychology because its subject matter is a more immediate reflection of the latter than of the former.

What this means at the *organismic level* is illustrated by Gibson's (1966) discussion of "The Environment as a Source of Stimulation" (Chap. 1). "In considering the problems of perception in man and animals the first question to ask should be, what is there to be perceived?" Gibson identifies the organism-relevant dimensions of the physical environment such as rigidity, gravity, and electromagnetic radiation, and shows how each contributes to the evolution of perceptual capacities. What emerge as essential to perception are those characteristics which contribute to the survival of individual organisms, that is, that make possible the identification of food, predators, features of the terrain for purposes of getting about, etc.

At the *societal level* a uniquely human quality emerges and transforms the *organism-world* relationship into a *person-world* relationship. Humans have come to live in a world which they have themselves produced through collective, planned intervention in Nature. Children may be considerably developed before they ever come into contact with Nature (if they *ever* do). Meanwhile, children have to deal with language, spoons, prepared foods, diapers, toys, strollers, etc., all parts of an environment that has been manufactured for them by their fellow human beings.

At least two significant contrasts with the organism-world relationship should be noted. First, whereas animal social formations depend for their survival upon the survival of individuals, human individuals depend for their survival upon the survival of their group or society. Humans no longer live in Nature; they are evolutionarily suited only for survival in society. Second, while adaptation in the original biological sense may still play a role in human existence, it has been displaced in importance by a process of acquiring the skills necessary for the survival of society. This process has been called *appropriation* ("Aneignung," Holzkamp, 1973, p. 53).

It is important to note the historical nature of the societal environment that shapes personality and the special psychological processes. A child born into a traditional feudal society faces very different problems of adaptation and appropriation than a child born into an advanced industrial capitalist society.

What is being proposed here is that, just as we cannot gain an *unequivocal* understanding of an animal's perceptual capacities without having first identified the relevant dimensions of the environment in which they have developed, we cannot hope to understand human psychological processes *unequivocally* without having first identified the relevant societal dimensions in which they have developed.

It is useful here to be reminded how radically traditional psychology has evaded questions of developmental context. In a fairly well known passage, Lewin (1969, cited in Holzkamp, 1978, p. 168) advised that if we want to understand the behavior of an unruly child who has been threatened by his mother with the police, it is not its actual relations with the police that matter, but rather only what the child believes about the police. In short, explanation of the behaviour comes from what is in the child's mind, not from the context that shaped its mind.

This kind of thinking has been very common in psychology. Zajonc (1968), cited in Holzkamp (1978), wrote that:

> The physical and objective properties of social stimulation and incentives have always been assumed to be less significant for the analysis of social behavior than their subjective counterparts. There is less correspondence between the objective properties of social stimuli and the way in which they are perceived than there is in the case of other forms of stimulation, for example hue. Why this is true is not understood even now, but the lack of systematic dependence of social perception on objective properties of stimuli has prompted social psychologists to focus on the cognitive representations of social stimuli and incentives themselves (p. 170).

But if it is the objective societal world in which we are born, raised, and must work effectively in order to guarantee continued survival of the species, such a lack of correspondence ought to be of immense and urgent concern. Nothing will be learned about it if we continue to withdraw to the level of 'cognitive representations'. What's more, we won't be able to develop unequivocal theories about 'cognitive representations' and behaviour. The current theoretical confusion in social psychology provides ample proof of that.

Holzkamp recognizes at least three distinct ways in which theories can be irrelevant or inessential. First, they may be confused about conceptual distinctions and classification boundaries. This is evident in the distinction between learned and innate. Based on work by Lorenz and other ethologists, Holzkamp-Osterkamp (1975, pp. 112ff.) showed that the two are not exclusive, that learning *is* an innate strategy, and that the real distinction is one of adaptive strategies varying in potential flexibility with respect to external contingencies. At the societal level, Holzkamp (1973, pp. 173ff.) identified similar theoretical difficulties stemming from a false exclusion of subjective and objective factors in human perception.

Second, theories may be falsely extended from one level (e.g., organismic) to another (e.g., societal). A recent example is the early version of sociobiology. Genetics may be an entirely relevant and essential dimension for a theory of insect social behaviour. In a theory of human social behaviour, however, it can obscure what is *really* essential and relevant: the influence of the historical societal context of human development.

Third, theories can falsely universalize that which is true in particular instances. Ute Holzkamp-Osterkamp (1975) demonstrated that much of our understanding of classical and operant conditioning is in fact a misunderstanding of broader, evolutionarily determined flexible adaptive strategies. The theory of reinforcement, for example, evaporates in the broader view as an extreme instance of a particular strategy. None of this can be seen if attention is confined, as it usually is, to the abstracted variables specified by operant theory. And from this restricted view it will remain forever impossible to understand how the grain of truth in operant theory can be integrated with the grains of truth in opposing theories. Only the broader evolutionary perspective makes that possible.

The advantage of any materialist theory is that differences of opinions and interpretations pertain to matters of fact. The resolution occurs through a direct appeal to those facts. It is on this basis that a materialist expects that competing theories will eventually merge into a single, unified theory and that there will be an accumulation of genuine knowledge. The levels of fact and hypothesis have never been particularly problematic. Serious problems have existed at the level of theory because we have not known to which objective facts we should appeal. We have now learned where to look, and that is at the phylogenetic and historical developmental contexts of the process under study. Until very recently psychologists have simply not done this in any systematic way.

It should be noted, finally, that unification cannot be understood as an absolute state, even potentially. Rather, it is a process. What can be expected is that *relative* unification will occur as theoretical differences regarding specific processes are resolved. This, however, will lead to the recognition of new problems and thus create a new relative 'disunity' marked by renewed theoretical pluralism.

What distinguishes this process from that which now exists is that psychologists will, in recognition of it, act with the aim of resolving differences and producing an increasing fund of real knowledge, instead of capitulating to metaphysical pluralism and producing a rag-bag of seemingly incommensurable bits of knowledge-pieces. This promise, it seems to me, makes materialism worth taking seriously.

References

Gibson, J. J. (1966). *The senses considered as perceptual systems.* Boston: Houghton Mifflin.

Hilgard, E. R, & Bower, G. H. (1966). *Theories of learning.* (3rd ed.). New York: Appleton-Century-Crofts.

Holzkamp, K. (1973). *Sinnliche Erkenntnis: Historischer Ursprung und gesellschaftliche Funktion der Wahrnehmung.* Frankfurt: Athenäum Verlag.

Holzkamp, K. (1978). Die überwindung der wissenschaftlichen Beliebigkeit psychologischer Theorien durch die Kritische Psychologie. In K. Holzkamp (Ed.), *Gesellschaflichkeit des Individuums.* Köln: Pahl-Rugenstein. (Originally in *Zeitschrift für Sozialpsychologie, 1977, 8,* 1-22, 78-97.

Holzkamp-Osterkamp, Ute. (1975). *Grundlagen der psychologischen Motivationsforschung.* Frankfurt: Campus Verlag.

Lewin, K. (1969). *Grundzüge der topologischen Psychologie.* Bern/Stuttgard/Wien: Huber.

Luria, A. R. (1979). *The making of mind.* Cambridge, MA: Harvard University Press.

Staats, A. W. (1986b). Unified positivism. *International Newsletter of Uninomic Psychology, 2,* 10-12.

Tolman, C. W. (1987). Dialectical materialism as psychological metatheory. In H. Stam, T. Rogers, & K. Gergen (Eds.) *The analysis of psychological theory* (pp. 221-229). New York: Hemisphere.

Vygotsky, L. S. (1978). *Mind in society.* Cambridge, MA: Harvard University Press.

Wertheimer, M. (1972). *Fundamental issues in psychology.* New York: Holt, Rinehart and Winston.

Wilcox, S., & Katz, S. (1984). Can indirect realism be demonstrated in the psychological laboratory? *Philosophy of the Social Sciences, 14,* 149-157.

Zajonc, R. B. (1968). Cognitive theories in social psychology. In G. Lindzey & E. Aronson (Eds.), *Handbook of social psychology* (Vol. 1, 2nd ed., pp. 320-411). Reading, MA: Addison-Wesley.

PSYCHOLOGY BETWEEN ECOLOGICAL LAWS AND THE SCIENTIFIC REVOLUTION

Pieter A. Vroon

University of Utrecht
Utrecht, The Netherlands

SUMMARY: In view of the limited accessibility of mental life to introspection, psychology has frequently resorted to technological metaphors. These metaphors are related to the scientific revolution and the root metaphor 'the world is a machine'. It implies that stimuli in the environment are to be described in physical terms and that 'enriching' processes take place in the mind. Recently, this approach has been challenged by, for example, ideas about ecological relevance, naive explanations in psychology, and the Gibsonian movement. It is argued that several fields of psychology show a development reminiscent of the Aristotelian tradition and the ancient metaphor 'the world is a humanlike organism'. Apart from that, there is a revival of other general metaphors such as contextualism and realism. This simultaneous use of scarcely compatible ontological positions describes a part of psychology's disunity. Psychology appears not to optimize the accumulation of knowledge since it either advocates a complex, enriching mind or a complex, enriched environment.

Introduction

An important historical problem in psychology is the belief that introspection is of limited value. We feel *that* mental processes take place, but we do not know intuitively *how* these processes go on. This issue of the mind's relative inaccessibility has frequently been approached by comparing mental life with technological products such as clocks, steam engines, telephone exchanges, radios, radar systems and computers. These metaphors have functioned as sources of heuristic inspiration in research and theory construction (Vroon & Draaisma, 1986, for an overview). Both the choice of the metaphors and the dynamics of metaphor-based research and theorizing are complicated matters. Thus, research founded on particular technological products may be abandoned after the discovery that certain findings no longer fit in with that metaphor *or* the realization that the metaphor does not allow the study of classes of mental processes that have been discerned at an intuitive level.

The use of technological metaphors dates back to the seventeenth century. At that time, the focus of the physical sciences shifted away from a universe that was *built* to the way in which it *moved.* In the physical sciences, this transition is denoted as the scientific revolution (Kuhn, 1957; Westfall, 1977). Analogously, the perspective of psychological thinking changed from mental *states* to mental *processes.* Mental states are as a rule known in experience but this is not true of mental processes. Early on in psychology, physical and chemical concepts were applied directly to mental processes (mental mechanics and mental chemistry). Later, mechanical models of the mind were constructed.

Psychology is now partly at a loss however because contemporary theories based on the computer metaphor have become so intricate. This has led to a renewed interest in the origins of the scientific revolution; namely, the Aristotelian tradition. A salient feature of current developments in psychology is an opposition against mechanistic models of the mind. I will try to show that parts of contemporary psychology are, indeed, involved in a widespread revision of basic mechanistic assumptions.

A Contrast

A Dutch psychological journal published an article on astrology by De Rooij (1985). An introductory remark is worth noting. "A connection is possible between astrology and psychology. A number of modern theories of personality resonate with astrological ideas. In a practical sense, too, there are various opportunities for applying astrology to our advantage". This paper should not be considered exceptional; over the past ten years, numerous similar remarks have been made, and there are also many empirical studies.

A month later, the same journal published an article by Michon (1985). Psychologists, he claims, are tormented people, constantly worrying about the practical relevance and the range of their knowledge. He writes: "I am convinced that there is an obvious, accessible road towards a science that will have a high degree of practical relevance. All one has to do is select an external environment, such as the school, traffic or visual space, and then describe its structure. This description should preferably be made in terms that bear a superficial resemblance with the conceptual framework of physics or technology."

Clearly there is a world of difference between Michon's views and those of De Rooij. Unfortunately, there are still many psychologists who tend to ignore or deny signs of dissent in their discipline. But no one can deny that psychology has diversified into many theoretical specializations which publish their own journals, organize their own congresses, and, apparently, benefit little from developments and advancements in other theoretical specializations. Often, the exchange of information between the specializations is impeded by a fragmented and rigid intellectual view of their particular domains.

Another example can be found in Fodor (1983), who advocates the modularity of the mind. People are a *unity of meaning* in whom everything is interrelated, but there are classes of psychological processes, such as perception, functioning according to specific laws, and they are barely influenced by other psychological processes. The encapsulated nature of perception had, however, already been described by Gestalt psychologists at the beginning of this century. Also, as early as 1977, Eccles maintained that modules can be distinguished in the cerebral cortex (Popper & Eccles, 1977, and Koestler, 1967 had already considered this issue over twenty years ago).

Consequently, we cannot deny that something is wrong in psychology. Spangenberg and Nijhuis (1985) refuse to believe that there is a *crisis*, since the number of publications along these lines is limited. This is correct. On the other hand we should realize that it is not quantity that counts; a handful of critical publications can profoundly affect research in the field. Before launching on this discussion, the contrast between the general views I mentioned has to be considered more closely.

Two Subdivisions

Four types of scientific discourse can be distinguished. I refer to Pepper's (1942) book on world views or ontological root metaphors that describe general ways of thinking - namely *organicism, mechanicism, realism* and *contextualism.* (An epistemological dichotomy is proclaimed by van Hezewijk, 1985 and in this volume.)

The premise of realism is the experience of similarity between forms and phenomena. In this tradition phenomena are described and classified. A central question is whether things exist or not. In psychology and the physical sciences, realists are primarily concerned with the *structure* of the universe and the mind. This (Platonic) view has rivalled the more influential Aristotelian tradition of organicism. Organicism presumes that every phenomenon is embedded in a whole that resembles a living being. This implies that everything interacts with everything in a human-like environment. Mechanicism originated in the seventeenth century and considers the world as a machine. Every phenomenon has a primary cause and this one cause (in a chain of causes) must be identified for giving an explanation. Contextualism, finally, views the world as an assembly of events. Since everything is part of an event, all phenomena have many causes operating at the same time. In terms of these world views, there have been two 'ancient' types of psychology: a tradition that aimed to outline man's mental states (realism) and a way of thinking that endorsed the influential and longlasting Aristotelian tradition (organicism).

Pepper shows that the four root metaphors clash since they differ widely in their basic assumptions about the world as well as their methods and definitions of truth. Consequently, 'facts' that have been established in one tradition may mean nothing to another.

Aristotelian Thinking

According to Aristotle, reality is revealed by naive observation. The elements are earth, water, fire and air. They manifest themselves to us by way of specific sensations: dry, moist, cold, warm, and so on. These qualities are not only attributes of the perceiver, but also of the perceived objects (Wallace, 1976). Object and perception cannot be separated; perception refers directly to the world. Visual perception is not based upon internal processes; perception is *direct.* Aristotle describes the way in which an objects is perceived in the following way: "just as sealing wax receives the impression of the seal, but not the iron or the gold that makes up the seal...the object touches the inner chamber of the eye."

Traces of the Aristotelian tradition can still be found in the history of contemporary psychology. Gestalt psychology presumed that reality has a certain structure that is revealed through perception. Perception is immediate, and linked to natural laws and forces which are reflected in the physiological organization of the brain. Köhler promoted this viewpoint and spoke in its defense as recently as the 1959 American Psychological Association convention. He was, however, received coldly, and we shall see why.

European phenomenology is a second (philosophical) doctrine that even belongs more strongly to this tradition. Consciousness is linked to objects and the nature of man can be derived from his existence in the world. Unbiased descriptions of phenomena clear the way for an understanding of man.

At the end of the sixteenth century, the Aristotelian tradition gradually gave way to the metaphor of the world as a machine. Three centuries later, psychology started to develop as a separate, experimental discipline. By that time, technology had progressed sufficiently to supply metaphors for mental *processes.* The use of technological metaphors is characteristic for this development. It is understandable that approaches such as phenomenology did not dominate psychology: the mechanistic approach of the physical sciences had also to be used to study mental processes.

Psychology has been influenced in two ways by the scientific revolution and the physical sciences. Not only the world, but also the mind was 'mechanized'. An important aspect of the scientific revolution was the distinction between primary and secondary qualities. Primary qualities were often defined so as to allow mathematical computations and measurement with instruments. This principle was adopted in psychology, so that very *frugal* definitions of stimuli were used. It was clear that perception could not be described in this way so that many 'enriching processes' had to be postulated in the mind. This meant that reality became increasingly 'empty' and our heads increasingly 'full'. Neisser (1967), one of the founders of cognitive psychology, emphasized that "we have no direct, immediate access to the world... Whatever we know about reality has been mediated, not only by the organs of sense but by complex systems which interpret and reinterpret sensory information". Wilcox and Edwards (1982) are right in saying that this approach is based upon the fact that psychology traditionally apes the natural sciences. To cite Titchener: "We may compare sensation, the element of the idea, to the elements treated in chemical science. An idea is a compound; it consists of a number of elemental processes". Also current psychology considers physical descriptions of sensory information as the input of the perceptual system, and not the environment as experienced by the subject. In this framework, Fechner and the psychophysicist distinguished between sensation and perception. Sensations are related to physical definitions of the stimulus. Another example is Watson: "As stimuli we name such things as waves of light of different wave lengths; sound waves differing in amplitude, length, phase and combination; gaseous particles, solutions which contain particles of matter." As a consequence, the development of stage models describing the processing of physically defined information and stimuli, became unavoidable.

Recently, however, the enormous amount of data and stage models have led to feelings of dissatisfaction, which has been particularly voiced by Fodor (1983) and Gibson (1979). These developments can be clarified by Pepper's work.

Modules of the Mind

To Fodor, several psychological processes behave as encapsulated modules. The mind can be divided into functions that only partially penetrate each other. Fodor opposes the view that perception and cognition are interwoven. Perception, he argues, is an encapsulated process that may initially be related to other mental processes, but subsequently it leads its own life. Such a perceptual module may be complicated, but it can be considered as a 'special purpose computer'.

Fodor also objects to the 'bottom-up' research strategy, since the processes under study are more likely to represent the physical prejudices of the psychologist than reality. He is equally severe in his censure of the 'top-down' strategy which is inconsistent with his premise that higher mental processes are not involved in lower ones. Moreover, higher cognitive processes function in a Quinean manner: modifications of one part of the system affect all other parts. These 'free floating' processes cannot be contained in stage models. Consequently, psychology is in a predicament: both predominant research strategies are considered inadequate. This has also been grist to the mill of the ecologists, led by the Gibsonians.

Many cognitive psychologists, too, express doubt about the fruitfulness of stage models. Their criticism of the bottom-up strategy is as the same as Fodor's. They argue that there may be an organic link between mental processes and requirements ensuing from the environment. The use of ecologically valid descriptions would create good possibilities for psychology. If we just look around us meticulously, we can do without the processing stages. Moreover, structural theories of perception argued that information is not contained in the perceiver but in the stimuli. The connection with Fodor's views is that classes of categories in reality correspond with mental processes.

This seems to recall Gestalt psychology's concept of isomorphism and even phenomenology. Has psychology come full circle? We started by imitating the physical sciences, where elimination of secondary qualities had proved successful. The definition of the human environment became impoverished so that psychology had to postulate numerous processes and stages in the mind. This implied a rejection of the Aristotelian tradition, and also Gestalt psychology and phenomenology. However, now it seems that we are not only remobilizing these approaches, but also reinstalling Aristotle himself.

The Gibsonians

Reality, according to Aristotle, has characteristics that are derived from naive observation. The elements are, earth, water, fire, and air. Perception is immediate, reason plays a negligible role and no mental processes are involved.

Also according to Gibson (1979), speculations about internal mental processes are superfluous, since the information reaching the senses is much richer and much more organized than traditionally is assumed. We never see light, not even sunlight, but objects and surfaces. Reality is filled with organized stimuli that manifest themselves without the intervention of reason. The concept of 'empty space', is not relevant to psychology. The elements are earth, water, fire and air. Substances are to distinguished by their *phenomenal* characteristics. Perception does not involve information processing. Some quotations illustrate his Aristotelian position: "The environment of animals and man is what they perceive... . The distinction between primary and secondary qualities is quite unnecessary... We do not live in space, space is filled with substances". Consequently the environment is being enriched, and our minds are 'empty' once again. The core of Gibson's ideas is that psychology should escape from the shadow of physics. The environment we live in is human-like and not those of the physicist. Gibson proposes *direct realism* in an epistemological sense, just like phenomenology does and as the Aristotelian tradition did earlier. There is no mental-physical dualism, the concept of sensation is abandoned, we do not infer the world by information processing, but are directly confronted with it in a meaningful way. In terms of Gestalt psychology there is isomorphism between environment, experience and action (Wilcox & Edwards, 1982). A similar position is defended by Prigogine (1980). "We are in a period of scientific revolution...a period not unlike the *birth of the scientific approach in ancient Greece.*" (italics mine), and he says that everything should be considered as connected with everything else.

In short, two thousand years of scientific stagnation came to an end by launching an offensive against Aristotle, and psychology seems to be back where it started. The mind has returned to reality, the universe is anthropomorphous once again, and well known phenomena such as *misperceptions* cannot be explained and are taken for granted. Psychology seems to be in danger of landing in stagnation again. Even phenomenological psychology which was unproductive in explaining, controlling and predicting behavior and mental life, is being propagated again in the English speaking world. (Turvey, Shaw, Reed, & Mace, 1981).

Mixing Metaphors

Two current root metaphors about the nature of reality have been briefly described: the world as an organism and the world as a machine. However, there are two more possibilities. The world may also be considered as an assembly of forms, patterns or formal systems (realism). This metaphor functioned in introspective studies up to the 20th century and is currently manifest in the structural information theory which uses a mathematical-linguistic description of reality to explain perception and even higher cognitive processes.

The fourth root metaphor mentioned by Pepper is that of the world as an assembly of events (contextualism). Psychology is concerned primarily with human beings. They are involved in events that usually occur in the environment and we should be concerned with these events. It is not the objects and relations between objects that are invariant; each event has its own laws. Much contemporary research can be viewed in the light of this root metaphor (Hoffman & Nead, 1983). We study memories for commercials, the weather forecast and autobiographies. When Neisser turned his back on cognitive psychology in 1976, he not only proclaimed that mechanisms such as iconic memory have hardly any significance in daily life and perhaps do not even exist, but he also emphasized that ecological, personalist studies of memory were much more valuable than traditional memory research (Neisser, 1982). Definitely, a trend from 'hard' to 'soft' research can be discerned (Duindam, 1984). Psychology is focusing less on physical features of stimuli and more on meaning and intentionality. Instead of artificial, short-term situations in the laboratory, real-life events are becoming more important. Not only ecological psychology places human functioning in a much broader context than before, recent information processing theorists have developed an analogous approach. They reject the idea of discrete stages and allow, for example, the influence of long-term memory on sensory information processing. In psycholinguistics, the focus has shifted from syntax to meaning, from words to stories, and from individual linguistics to sociolinguistics. The trend is not only to study 'higher' functions, but also to place them in a broader setting. In short: the context of psychological research has broadened. There is even a renewed interest in the philosophy of the Romantic period (Jung, graphology, astrology), and in research in social psychology and personality, naive interpretations have receive much attention recently.

Of course it makes sense to concentrate on phenomena of daily life, if only because psychology has often been incapable of applying its research findings. We should seriously consider whether experimental, laboratory research in fact can be generalized to reality. The danger of this development, however, is that the 'real world' is *studied* along an Aristotelian line of thought and that *naive* observation becomes the starting point again. This combination must be avoided or else we may be penalized by another period of scientific stagnation.

The Future of Psychology

It is hard to foresee where all this will lead to. Our historical consciousness is amazingly small and certain theoretical viewpoints are sometimes rejected scornfully, only to set the tone in a different jargon a few years later. Basically there are two types of disunity in psychology. *Synchronic disunity* means that there is a mixture of incompatible root metaphors so that different products of knowledge cannot be combined and integrated. This simultaneous use of world hypotheses is unique: in the physical sciences only *one* world view at a time was dominant. Perhaps only in physics is there currently a rise of several intellectual circuits analogous to what happens in psychology. Physicists are interested in the structure of the universe (realism), others in the study of motion (mechanicism), the complex relationships between natural events (mystic organicism); and finally the 'bootstrap physics' (contextualism) proclaiming that physics is about complex relationships and events that cannot be reduced to particles or fields. The same may be occurring in the field of medicine (Vroon, 1986).

Diachronic disunity in psychology involves the loss of empirical material that does not correspond to currently fashionable thought (see Vroon, 1987, for examples). The current opposition to mechanistic models may have arisen because human beings have an intuitive, metaphysical self-image that jars with knowledge accumulated through mechanistic analogies. In this sense, a renewed link with nature, which was typical for the Aristotelian tradition, is attractive. Linschoten (1964) distinguished two natures in human beings. The first nature is the one studied in psychological research, the second corresponds with common sense. The role of the psychologist implies that the first nature should not diverge *too much* from the second. The psychologist is influenced by *both* natures of people, for he or she is not only a scientist but also an ordinary person.

Pepper's work on root metaphors has a two-fold significance for studying these phenomena and our ambiguous relationship with technology. In the first place, many parts of the field can be categorized with the help of his four 'world views'. Many debates can be cleared up by analyzing these basic ideas. In the second place, Pepper argues that the root metaphors are, for the most part, incompatible: something that is studied within the framework of one metaphor does not fit in the other. This explains parts of both types of disunity mentioned.

I have tried to show that these four theoretical circuits also exist in modern psychology, and that the rule 'don't mix metaphors' is not followed. Gibsonians are affiliated with organismic thinking, traditional cognitive psychologists follow the metaphor of human beings as machines, structural information theorists support the realist's metaphor, and several views briefly discussed correspond with contextualism. Whoever wishes to endorse a unified science should consider the question whether Pepper's root metaphors can somehow be made to correspond with one another so that knowledge can be bundled in a historical and contemporary perspective. However, no significant progress has yet been made in this respect and there is still a poor exchange or diffusion of insights and data among those committed to different metaphors.

A final question one might ask is: Why do we make curious choices? Why must *either* human beings *or* the world they live in be complicated? Why not accumulate our knowledge by linking complexity of the environment to complexity of the mind? In that case we can benefit more from each of the traditions in psychology and we may overcome the enormous 'scientific amnesia' of our science.

References

Duindam, V. (1984). *Het vlees is woord geworden.* Unpublished Master's thesis, University of Utrecht.

Fodor, J. A. (1983). *The modularity of mind.* Cambridge: MIT Press.

Gibson, J. J. (1979).*The ecological approach to visual perception.* Boston: Houghton Mifflin.

Helson, H. (1964). *Adaption-level theory: An experimental and systematic approach to behavior.* New York: Harper.

van Hezewijk, R. (1985). *Vooronderstellingen en interpetatiestijlen in de psychologie.* Utrecht: Elinkwijk, doctoral dissertation, University of Utrecht.

Hoffman, R., & Nead, J. M. (1983). General contextualism, ecological science and cognitive research. *The Journal of Mind and Behavior, 4(4),* 507-560.

Koestler, A. (1967). *The ghost in the machine.* London: Hutchinson.

Kuhn, T. S. (1957). *The Copernican revolution.* Cambridge: Harvard University Press.

Linschoten, J. (1964). *Idolen van de psycholoog.* Utrecht: Bijleveld.

Michon, J. A. (1985). Bottom up en top down. *De Psycholoog, 20(6),* 275-280.

Neisser, U. (1967). *Cognitive psychology.* New York: Appleton.

Neisser, U. (1982). *Memory observed.* San Francisco: Freeman.

Pepper, S. C. (1942). *World hypotheses.* Berkeley: University of California Press.

Popper, K. R., & Eccles, J. C. (1977). *The self and his brain.* Springer International.

Prigogine, I. (1980). *From being to becoming: Time and complexity in the physical sciences.*

De Rooij, J. (1985). Tijd voor astrologie. *De PsychoIoog, 20(5),* 229-236.

Spangenberg, J. F. A., & Nijhuis, F. J. N. (1985). Crisisperceptie in de psychologie. *Nederlands Tijdschrift voor de Psychologie, 40,* 348-359.

Turvey, M. T., Shaw, R. E., Reed, E. S., & Mace, W. M. (1981). Ecological laws of perceiving and acting: In reply to Fodor and Pylyshyn. *Cognition, 9,* 237-304.

Vroon, P. A., & Draaisma, D. (1986a). *De mens als metafoor.* Baarn: Ambo.

Vroon, P. A. (1986b). Denkstijlen in de geneeskunde. *Nederlands Tijdschrift voor Integrale Geneeskunde, 1,* 18-26.

Vroon, P. A. (1987). Man-machine analogs and theoretical mainstreams in psychology. In Wm J. Baker, M. E. Hyland, H. van Rappard, & A. W. Staats (Eds.), *Current issues in theoretical psychology* (pp. 393-414). Amsterdam: North-Holland.

Wallace, E. (1976). *Aristotle's psychology.* New York: Arno Press.

Westfall, R. S. (1977). *The construction of modern science.* Cambridge: Cambridge University Press.

Wilcox, S., Edwards, D. A. (1982). Some Gibsonian perspectives on the ways that psychologists use physics. *Acta Psychologica, 52,* 147-163.

SCIENTIFIC EPISTEMOLOGY: A PSYCHOLITERARY APPROACH

Morris L. Shames

Concordia University
Montreal, Quebec, Canada

SUMMARY: The asseveration that metaphor is woven into the fabric of the creative enterprise - scientific epistemology included - is so well established that it virtually defies impugnment. There is, for instance, a corpus of literature attesting to its ratiocinative significance (Bruner, 1962; Sacks, 1979) and the significant role it plays in scientific, among other epistemologies (MacCormac, 1976, 1983). In fact, it has been suggested that the provenance of consciousness itself is rooted in metaphor (Jaynes, 1976, 1986) and that it is essentially a "mental principle" (Gordon, 1961). Nonetheless, none of these analyses has been sufficiently systematic in their expatiation on metaphor as underwriting such a cognitive process. This paper proffers such an analysis based upon a conflation of Frye's (1957) systematic treatment of symbols and metaphor and Jung's analytical Psychology (de Laszlo, 1958). Although these seem to be disparate domains there is a natural confluence of theories here which serves to adumbrate the intuitionistic side of scientific epistemology, that is to say, the creativity underlying scientific discovery.

The propaedeutic literature has almost entirely focused on *scientific method* as characterizing the cognitive substrate of the practising scientist to the neglect of virtually all other cognitive processes. This model has drawn heavily from the Edisonian dictum that scientific genius is primarily a matter of "perspiration", that is to say, hard work which can be broken down into delineable stages of thought and activity and, therefore, universally taught and, in consequence, universally practised. More proveniently, this methodocentrism can be traced to Mill's (1843/1919) attempts to rigorize induction by means of a handful of methods or "canons", as they are ofttimes called. In short, this has been the century of *collective* epistemology where "yeoman science" (Shames, 1984, 1985b) has held sway over its intuitionistic side, that is to say, where performance, not competence, has been in the ascendant owing to the view of science "as a paradigm-governed social activity whose essence is to periodically undergo *revolutionary* transformations in its own *normative self-definition*" (Doppelt, 1983, p. 109).

This methodcentric thrust, grounded as it is on the historico-critical side of the Piagetian epistemological equation (Piaget, 1950), has faced - but has not yet yielded to - a virtual revolution in cognitive science which has witnessed the resurgence of competence and the embracement of interdisciplinarism in cognitive science (Gardner, 1985). In keeping with this general tack a fundatorily different approach to scientific epistemology has been proposed whereby the focus is shifted to the "inspirational" side of science, that is to say, to the science of discovery rather than the traditional justificationist and falsificationist experimental paradigms (Shames, 1984, 1985a, 1985b, 1987). This approach turns on the understanding that despite the paucity of attention accorded insight and intuition they have played a disproportionately important role in the historical record of science. They, among other factors, represent the proveniently cognitive, creative moment which finds expression in analogy and metaphor.

The disproportion of attention accorded the creative side of science is the consequence of its perceived aleatory nature, that is, its nonlogical scripting which by that very fact defies "scientific" scrutiny. For instance, as Imre Lakatos has pointed out:

> For Kuhn scientific change - from one 'paradigm' to another - is a mystical conversion which is not and cannot be governed by rules of reason and which falls totally within the realm of the ***(social) psychology of discovery.*** Scientific change is a kind of religious change. (Worrall & Currie, 1978, p. 9)

The roles of intuition and insight in scientific epistemology have long since been recognized (e.g., Bunge, 1962; Medawar, 1969; Meynell, 1976); their treatment in systematic, if not apodeictic terms, however, is quite another matter.

In this respect various tropes have been appropriated owing, I assume, to the implicit relationship between language and thought and, as such, they are apposite reflections of those cognitive processes mediating insight and intuition. Chief among these has been metaphor and its precursor, analogy. For instance, during the period when logical positivism was in the ascendant, the physicist, N. R. Campbell (1920) was proffering an impassioned plea for analogies arguing that they:

> are not "aids" to the establishment of theories; they are an utterly essential part of theories, without which theories would be completely valueless and unworthy of the name.. It is often suggested that the analogy leads to the formulation of the theory, but once the theory is formulated the analogy has served its purpose and may be removed and forgotten. Such a suggestion is absolutely false and perniciously misleading. (p. 129)

Notwithstanding this definitive asseveration it should be recognized that analogies, irrespective of their presumed paramorphic or homeomorphic character (Weitzenfeld, 1984), are precursive to metaphor which more aptly reflects the processes of insight and intuition. After all, analogy, by its very insistence upon functional similarity, if not structural similarity, imposes some limitation upon the spontaneity which characterizes insight. Metaphor, on the other hand, is not thus limited and, in consequence, has been more closely associated with scientific insight.

Jerome Bruner (1962), in adumbrating the conditions of creativity, has proposed three forms of effectiveness - predictive effectiveness, formal effectiveness and metaphorical effectiveness to account for those acts which produce 'effective surprise,' the hallmark of the creative enterprise. For him the metaphor is a ubiquitous heuristic which does not yield the *product* commonly referred to as science; however, the scientific *process* "seems rather shot through with metaphor at critical moments in the history of science" (Bruner, 1962, p. 11). The logician, Quine (1979), has also made the case for metaphor arguing for its epistemological universality in that "it flourishes in playful prose and high poetic art, but it is vital also at the growing edges of science and philosophy" (p. 159). So committed to metaphorical thinking is Quine (1959) that he postulates:

> Along the philosophical fringes of science we may find reasons to question basic conceptual structures and to grope for ways to refashion them. Old idioms are bound to fail us here and only metaphor can begin to limn the new order." (p. 159)

Working from the 'tension theory' of metaphor, MacCormac (1976) has delineated two aspects of metaphor, the suggestive and the expressive, which give rise to two different uses of metaphor - metaphors of conveyance and 'root-metaphors.' By dint of this analysis he argues for the similarity between the scientific and religious enterprises based not upon the similarity of content of metaphors in both of these disciplines, nor the intentions behind these metaphors, but in terms of "the linguistic methods by which both enterprises achieve legitimate meaning" (p. xi). His argument, however oblique, thus speaks to the issue of cognitive processes since, in the case of science and religion, "both employ metaphors to suggest new hypotheses, both seem to confirm their hypotheses in human experience, and both often create myths by forgetting the hypothetical character of their metaphors" (MacCormac, 1976, p. xviii). In short, in respect of the scientific enterprise, "the use of scientific metaphors represents the scientist's cognitive effort to produce imaginative hypotheses through the juxtaposition of concepts not normally associated" (MacCormac, 1983, p. 66).

Metaphor, it is clear, is widely regarded as crucial in scientific epistemology but, overall, its treatment has been less than systematic. For instance, it has recently been averred that "there is, *in fact,* (italics mine) evidence to suggest that scientific enquiry rests directly on the conceptual innovations arising from the use of metaphor in scientific settings"

(Rothbart, 1986, p. 163). After citing a few examples as 'evidence', the author concludes that "a theory-expanding metaphor represents one element of a paradigmatic picture of reality. In this respect scientific knowledge is continually constructed and reconstructed by these fertile representations of the world" (p. 165). Analyses of this order, however, are usually imperiled by their very form of argumentation, the *circulus ad demonstrandum* which seemingly weaves metaphor through the fabric of science and then argues for 'creative science' as founded upon tropical thinking. Aside from some generic definition which turns on the notion of innovation, there has been little in the way of a systematic and profound definition of metaphor, and virtually nothing in respect of the evolution of tropology as a cognitive process reflected in cultural content and which engineers the creative dimension in scientific thought. The following exposition seeks to fill these most crucial lacunae in the literature.

It has recently been argued that there is "an epistemic drive present in man (which) provides the basis for the development of symbolizing activity" (Royce, Coward, Egan, Kessel & Mos, 1978, p. 340) and, it would seem, this drive is as fundamental as are the primary drives. This is, after all, in keeping with Jung's psychiatric superstructure where the symbol is the focal point of his entire research project (de Laszlo, 1958). It is a living symbol which expresses an essential, unconscious factor and which permeates *all* creative activity. Even consciousness - its very provenance, in fact - is rooted in such symbols in that "it arises from the power of language to make metaphors and analogies" (Jaynes, 1986, p. 137).

An assay of the cultural contents of Western civilization reveals the evolution of this all-important metonymous cognitive capacity, that is, the linguistically-grounded ability to mutate human experience into a variety of symbolic forms. Northrop Frye's (1957) Olympian, sweeping analysis of Western literature has yielded, perhaps, the most systematic, extant theory of symbols and metaphor. It is, perhaps, not mere fortuity that this theory - which deals explicitly with the sweep of Western literature - is hierarchically organized in that, extended, it reflects a fundamental cognitive process, a fundament of human nature, as it were, and as Simon (1973) has pointed out, "nature loves hierarchies" (p. 5). Succinctly stated, Frye's theory of metaphor, which derives from his theory of symbols, is the centre-piece of this model where metaphor is taken as the *medium* for the creative process whose compass comprises not only literature and religion - the breeding-ground of exegesis - but science as well. Its heuristic character, furthermore, derives from its confluence with *analytical psychology,* specifically, an understanding of the collective unconscious as a repository of archetypes.

Frye's theory regards symbols as isolated units which enter into a hierarchy of phases. At the perigeal point of this hierarchy there are the fundamental *literal* and *descriptive* phases of symbolism where the symbol is understood as inextricably *sign* and *motif* both, the sign functioning as "a verbal representative of a natural object or concept" (Frye, 1957, p. 367) while a motif is understood to be "a verbal unit in a work of literary art" (p. 366). On a higher level of organization, the *formal* phase of symbolism, the symbol is apprehended in terms of the *imagery* it evokes where the image is regarded "as a formal unit of art with natural content"(p. 366). At yet a higher level of cognitive organization there is the *mythical* phase of symbolism where the symbol is *archetypal*, "usually an image which recurs often enough in literature to be recognizable as an element of one's literary experience as a whole" (p. 365). At the apogeal point of this hierarchy, the *anagogic* phase of symbolism, the symbol assumes a virtually apocalyptic, *monadic* nature where the symbol is at the very heart of one's total literary experience yielding - given the entire taxonomy of these symbols - the *dianoia*, or meaning of literature which Frye's *logos* of literature intended, that is to say, "the shaping word which is both reason and, as Goethe's Faust speculated, *praxis* or creative act" (p. 120).

Thus far, the analysis has turned only on symbols as isolated units. The creative imagination, however, is more clearly bespoken by the relationships between and among symbols, the unit of relationship representing one form or other of metaphor. Thus, Frye's theory of metaphor grows directly out of his theory of symbols. This theory is grounded in the *literal* level of meaning where metaphor assumes no form other than straightforward *juxtaposition*. The exegetical possibilities are widened considerably on the *descriptive* level where there is "the double perspective of the verbal structure and the phenomena to which it is related" (Frye, 1957, p. 123), that is to say, where there is the postulation of the property of *likeness* or *similarity*. This assay of Western literature reveals yet a higher level, the *formal* level of metaphor, "where symbols are images or natural phenomena conceived as matter or content" (p. 124) and where metaphor is thus conceived as an *analogy* of natural proportion which, according to the author, requires four terms of which two share a common factor. There is, seemingly, a syllogistic dimension underpinning this level of metaphor. The level of organization becomes considerably more complex as one approaches the concrete universal, or *archetypal* metaphor. In this instance the symbol is *associative*, that is, archetypal in the sense that such a metaphor "unites two individual images, each of which is a specific representative of a class or genus" (p. 124). The *anagogic* dimension of meaning enjoys apical status in this hierarchy involving, as it most certainly does, the radical form of metaphor. The cognitive colouration here is one of hypothetical *identity* where "identity is the opposite of similarity or likeness, and total identity is not uniformity, still less monotony, but a unity of various things" (p. 125). It seems clear from this that this form of metaphor is far and away the least contrived and, as such, its wellspring must be sought elsewhere, other than Western literature.

Jung's analytical psychology, in particular, the collective unconscious and its ancestral, inherited symbolism speaks most appositely to an understanding of anagogic metaphor. Once this psychological substrate is recognized, it is at once appreciated that anagogic metaphor is not a *mere* literary device but, rather, it implies a profound psychological process whose epistemological reach has rather universal proportions. Jung himself has argued that:

> Inasmuch as every scientific theory contains a hypothesis, and therefore, an anticipatory designation of a fact still essentially unknown, it is a symbol. Furthermore, every psychological phenomenon is a symbol when we are willing to assume that it purports or signifies something different and still greater, something therefore which is withheld from present knowledge. (de Laszlo, 1959, p. 275)

The archetypes are such symbols of the unconscious and these "are not disseminated only by tradition, language and migration, but these can rearise spontaneously, at any time, at any place, and without any outside influence" (Jung, 1959/1969, p. 13). They are, in short, the anagogic material out of which dianoia is forged - in the realms of science and literature both!

This model appears to be hierarchical in nature by dint of immanence, not arbitrariness. For example, synectics theory argues for both *descriptive,* or decorative, and *generative,* or inductive metaphors where the latter is the resultant of an essentially subliminal process (Gordon, 1961). In this analysis, metaphor is essentially a mental principle which is "inherent in language and grounded in the nervous system" (p. 113). Therein lies the key to its hierarchical character since:

> our capacity to use language has been dulled and the consequence is a limitation of ability to grasp new relationships. Contemporary theory about language holds that language is essentially metaphorical in its nature and development. This theory is grounded in the school of neurophysiology which maintains that symbolization is an inherent function of the nervous system, that the nervous system does not return direct impressions of the external world but indirect symbolical representations. This position further maintains that the rudimentary symbolization process of the nervous system ***is elaborated on higher and higher levels, culminating in the brain*** (italics mine). (Gordon, 1961, pp. 111-112)

To add even further to this evidentiary mass, there are interesting data of recent vintage from the world of "artifical intelligence" which form a striking correspondence to this psycholiterarily grounded model of cognitive functioning. It should be noted at the outset that what Searle

(1980) has called "Strong AI" has come under considerable and cogent attack in the last decade. Among the consistent critics, in this respect, have been Hubert and Stuart Dreyfus (1986) who argue - in their text, *Mind over Machine* - that human beings simply possess an intelligence that machines cannot match. Their argument is based on an analysis of human skills, that is to say, 'cognitive' skills, and thus forms a striking parallel with the psycholiterary model which I have proffered. For instance, they delineate five levels of human skill, - 'novice,' 'advanced beginner,' 'competent performer,' 'proficient performer' and 'expert' - all of which comprise a hierarchy which reflects an important aspect of intelligence. At the lowest level, there is simply the manipulation of rules and symbols since the novice simply knows basic facts about a subject and context-independent rules for using those facts. The 'advanced beginner' goes further since he can formulate rules for action, based on examples, and thus he can take context into account. Further up the hierarchy, the 'competent performer' is highly personally involved in the subject and, in consequence, the behaviour in question is strongly goal-oriented. The person is able to react reflexively, without conscious thought about the rules involved and is able to reason analytically about situations. Near the apex of the hierarchy, the 'proficient performer' is distinguished by recalling whole situations and, in consequence, applies them to the present without reductionistic decomposition. The highest level of skill involves what they call 'know-how', where the expert is fully involved in the situation, has little awareness of the skill involved, and, in consequence, he makes little conscious use of analytic reasoning. This apical skill involves operating in a larger world, as it were, where one visualizes and manipulates whole objects and situations. There is a compelling resemblance here to *anagogia,* the radical form of metaphor, as there is similarity throughout the entirety of both models. In fact, the Dreyfuses appear to be proffering worthwhile descriptors of the cognitive processes underlying the various levels of metaphorical epistemology although this has clearly not been their express intention.

In light of this analysis it comes as no surprise whatever when the Dreyfuses conclude that stored-program computers, in using rules to process facts, *cannot* perform at high levels of skill. Even pattern computers - a wholly unknown quantity at this time - are not likely to come to the rescue here since the anagogical character of 'know-how' is not readily - if ever - simulable. After all, metaphor, - conceived in radical anagogical terms - by virtue of its very nature, that is, its largely unconscious, holistic, 'know-how' approach, is, therefore, something which is not simply learned from others but, like Heidegger's (1949) philosophy derived from *dasein*, is something individuals and even generations must start over again for themselves. Thus, metaphor, like any good symbol has the hermeneutical character which oftimes leads to perplexity, which is to say that it is understood to be of immeasurable epistemological significance yet sufficiently unapprehendable, in principle, so that the epistemology cannot be simulated nor can it be transmitted in the usual, straightforward, pedagogical manner.

It comes, therefore, as no surprise when people rhapsodize over metaphor and its epistemological universality. It has been variously considered as a 'mental principle' which is either unconscious, pre-conscious or, even conscious, in nature. Jaynes (1976), for instance, has promulgated the following argument:

> The most fascinating property of language is its capacity to make metaphors. But what an understatement! For metaphor is not a mere extra trick of language, as it is so often slighted in the old schoolbooks on composition; it is the very constitutive ground of language. (p. 48)

Armed with this asseveration, Jaynes concludes that:

> subjective conscious mind is an analog of what is called the real world. It is built up with a vocabulary or lexical field whose terms are all metaphors or analogs of behavior in the physical world. Its reality is of the same order as mathematics. (p. 55)

Metaphor, by this analysis, is the provenance of consciousness which *is*, after all, based on language.

It seems clear, therefore, that the absolute democratization of science and scientific praxis by virtue of a formulary method - as, perhaps, Mill had intended - is a noble aim but, likely, futile in its realization. This approach does indeed impinge meaningfully on 'yeoman science', that is, the collectively-practised, paradigmatic science of Kuhn (1962/1970) but it speaks not at all to the issue of 'creative science,' the science of insight and discovery and this is, after all, related to the discovery-justification distinction first postulated by Reichenbach (1938) and still hotly debated today (Lugg, 1985; Nickles, 1985). In light of this argument one should no more expect uniformly creative science from the extant cohort of practising scientists any more than one would expect the likes of 'Ulysses' and 'Remembrance of Things Past' from all those who put pen to paper. Discovery in science, after all, is an aptitude no less and no different in kind than the genius one finds in literature. They are both - it must be remembered - grounded in metaphor and, as Aristotle has pointed out, he is the best interpreter of dreams who can best grasp similarities, that is, he who is a master of metaphor, which is "the one thing that cannot be learnt from others" (Bywater, 1909, p. 101)

This is not mere speculation since a critical reading of the historical record reveals that metaphor is woven through the entire fabric of science. Notwithstanding the problems attendant upon peeling away layers of the unconscious and, for that matter, probing the conscious mind with its oftimes unconscious motivation, such as experimenter effects (Rosenthal, 1976) and the like, there is a wealth of testimony to the metonymous mind of science where symbolism, imagery, and metaphor are regnant. Newton, it has been argued, employed his famous metaphor of sound in order to expatiate upon and explain optical phenomena (North, 1980). In subsuming optics into a system of general dynamics for matter in motion, Maxwell (1890) himself reflected that:

> the figure of speech or thought by which we transfer the language and ideas of a familiar science to one with which we are less acquainted may be called Scientific Metaphor. There are certain electrical phenomena again which are connected together by relations of the same form as those which connect dynamical phenomena. To apply to (electrical phenomena) the phrases of dynamics with proper distinctions and provisional reservations is an example of a metaphor of a bolder kind. (p. 227)

Bohr's model of the atom, too, with its central proton surrounded by orbiting electrons drew heavily from the solar system itself as its metaphorical provenance (Jaynes, 1976). Even more interesting, Bohr himself claimed "that the idea of complementarity in physics came to him first in metaphoric form: that one could not know somebody simultaneously in the light of love and the light of justice" (Bruner, 1962, p. 10).

Gruber (1981) has used Darwin as his 'living metaphor' of scientific creativity. His argument rests principally upon Darwin's use of key metaphors in the evolution of his thought, chief among these being the branching tree of nature, artificial selection, war, wedges, the tangled bank and contrivances. As convincing as these examples may be, perhaps the most arresting, archetypal metaphor for this metaphorical model of perception and cognition are the reminiscences of Kekulé in respect of his structural theory of the atom and his discovery of the benzene ring. The former grew out of a reverie while riding home on a near-deserted omnibus and the latter was born out of a dream where images grew into serpents and "one of the serpents seized its own tail and the form whirled mockingly before my eyes. I came awake like a flash of lightning" (Libby, 1922, p. 264), he wrote.

These few, but representative examples, make clear that the task of scientific discovery - not unlike the tasks of literary genius and theological insight - has been left to those with a clear metaphorical predilection - an aptitude which, as Aristotle has suggested, is not readily learned.

References

Bruner, J. (1962). The conditions of creativity. In H. Gruber, G. Terrell, & M. Wertheimer (Eds.), *Contemporary approaches to creative thinking* (pp. 1-30). New York: Atherton Press.

Bunge, M. (1962). *Intuition and science.* Englewood Cliffs, NJ: Prentice-Hall.

Bywater, I. (1909). *Aristotle on the art of poetry.* London: Oxford University Press.

Campbell, N. R. (1920). *Physics, the elements.* Cambridge: Cambridge University Press.

de Laszlo, V. S. (1958). *Psyche and symbol: A selection from the writings of C. G. Jung.* Garden City, NY: Doubleday and Company.

de Laszlo, V. S. (1959). *The basic writings of C. G. Jung.* New York: Modern Library.

Doppelt, G. (1983). Relativism and recent pragmatic conceptions of scientific rationality. In N. Rescher (Ed.), *Scientific explanation and understanding: Essays on reasoning and rationality in science* (pp. 107-142). Lanham, MD: University Press of America.

Dreyfus, H., & Dreyfus, S. (1986). *Mind over machine.* New York: Free Press.

Frye, N. (1957). *Anatomy of criticism: Four essays.* Princeton, NJ: Princeton University Press.

Gardner, H. (1985). *The mind's new science: A history of the cognitive revolution.* New York: Basic Books.

Gordon, W. J. J. (1961). *Synectics: The development of creative capacity.* New York: Harper & Row Publishers.

Gruber, H. E. (1981).*Darwin on man: A psychological study of scientific creativity.* Chicago, IL: University of Chicago Press.

Heidegger, M. (1949). *Existence and being.* (W. Brock, Trans.) London: Vision Press.

Jaynes, J. (1976). *The origin of consciousness in the breakdown of the bicameral mind.* Boston, MA: Houghton Mifflin Company.

Jaynes, J. (1986). Consciousness and the voices of the mind. *Canadian Psychology, 27(2),* 128-139.

Jung, C. G. (1969). *Four archetypes: Mother/rebirth/spirit /trickster.* Princeton, NJ: Princeton University Press. (Originally published, 1959).

Kuhn, T. S. (1970). *The structure of scientific revolutions.* Chicago, IL: University of Chicago Press. (Originally published, 1962).

Libby, W. (1922). The scientific imagination. *Scientific Monthly, XV,* 263-270.

Lugg, A. (1985). The process of discovery. *Philosophy of Science, 52(2),* 207-220.

MacCormac, E. R. (1976). *Metaphor and myth in science and religion.* Durham, NC: Duke University Press.

MacCormac, E. R. (1983). Scientific metaphors as necessary conceptual limitations of science. In N. Rescher (Ed.), *The limits of lawfulness: Studies on the scope and nature of scientific knowledge* (pp. 61-68). Lanham, MD: University Press of America.

Maxwell, J. C. (1890). In D. Niven (Ed.), *The scientific papers of James Clerk Maxwell.* (Vol. 1). New York: Dover.

Medawar, P. B. (1969). *Induction and intuition in scientific thought.* Philadelphia: American Philosophical Society.

Meynell, H. A. (1976). *An introduction to the philosophy of Bernard Lonergan.* London: The Macmillan Press Limited.

Mill, J. S. (1919). *A system of logic: Ratiocinative and inductive.* London: Longmans, Green & Company. (Originally published, 1843).

Nickles, T. (1985). Beyond divorce: Current status of the discovery debate. ***Philosophy of Science, 52(2)***, 177-206 .

North, J. (1980). Science and analogy. In M. Grmek, R. Cohen, & G. Cimino (Eds.), ***On scientific discovery*** (pp. 115-140). Boston: D. Reidel.

Piaget, J. (1950). ***Introduction a l'epistemologie génétique.*** Paris: Presses Universitaires de France.

Quine, W. V. (1979). A postscript on metaphor. In S. Sacks (Ed.), ***On metaphor*** (pp. 159-160). Chicago: University of Chicago Press.

Reichenbach, H. (1938). ***Experience and prediction.*** Chicago: University of Chicago Press.

Rosenthal, R. (1976). ***Experimenter effects in behavioral research: Enlarged Edition.*** New York: Irvington Publishers, Inc.

Rothbart, D. (1986). Scientific unification through metaphor. In D. M. DeLuca (Ed.), ***Essays on creativity and science*** (pp. 163-166). Honolulu: Hawaii Council of Teachers of English.

Royce, J. R., Coward, H., Egan, E., Kessel, F., & Mos, L. (1978). Psychological epistemology: A critical review of the empirical literature and the theoretical issues. ***Genetic Psychology Monographs, 97***, 265-353.

Sacks, S. (Ed.). (1979). ***On metaphor.*** Chicago: University of Chicago Press.

Searle, J. R. (1980). Mind, brains and programs. ***Behavioral and Brain Sciences, 3***, 417-457.

Shames, M. L. (1984, August). ***A systems model of analogical thought and transcendance.*** Paper presented at the First International Conference on Systems Research, Informatics and Cybernetics, Baden-Baden.

Shames, M. L. (1985a, February). ***On demarcation and the primacy of scientific epistemology.*** Invited address given to the McGill chapter of Sigma Xi, the Scientific Research Society, Montreal.

Shames, M. L. (1985b, August). ***Literary theory, analytical psychology and the scientific imagination.*** Paper delivered at the XVII International Congress of History of Science, University of California, Berkeley.

Shames, M. L. (1987). Methodocentricity, theoretical sterility, and the socio-behavioural sciences. In W. J. Baker, M. E. Hyland, H. van Rappard, & A. W. Staats (Eds.), ***Current issues in theoretical psychology*** (pp. 261-282). New York: Elsevier Science Publishers B.V.

Simon, H. A. (1973). The organization of complex systems. In H. H. Pattee (Ed.), ***Hierarchy theory: The challenge of complex systems*** (pp. 1-27). New York: George Braziller.

Weitzenfeld, F. S. (1984). Valid reasoning by analogy. ***Philosophy of Science, 51(1)***, 137-149.

Worrall, J., & Currie, G. (Eds.). (1978). ***The methodology of scientific research programs: Philosophical papers, Volume 1, Imre Lakatos.*** Cambridge: Cambridge University Press.

THE IMPLICATIONS OF DIFFERENTIAL THEORY APPRAISAL AND THE CONTEXT OF DISCOVERY FOR ADVANCING THEORY IN PSYCHOLOGY

J. R. Royce

University of Alberta
Edmonton, Alberta, Canada

SUMMARY: The bulk of theory appraised by philosophers of science has been based on strong theory - theory capable of offering valid explanations. This means that weaker forms of theory, such as descriptive and programmatic theory, have been neglected. However, recently the philosophers have begun to analyze the context of discovery (Nickles, 1980). They have found, for example, that there are three phases in scientific discovery: the generation of ideas, the pursuit of these ideas, and preliminary evaluation. It is also necessary to develop a method of differential theory appraisal so that the relative strength of the theory can be ascertained. This involves identifying the many dimensions common to all forms of theory, and determining the weight to be assigned to each variable as the predictor for the successful development of programmatic, descriptive, or explanatory theory. It is anticipated that these developments will be more relevant to less advanced disciplines such as psychology, but that it will require several decades before they have an observable impact on development as theory in psychology.

In previous papers on theoretical psychology Royce (1978, 1985) presented a program of metatheoretic analysis based on a philosophy of constructive dialectics. A major metatheoretic problem is psychology's theoretical pluralism - the existence of a large number of theories in each of psychology's major domains.

In a recent analysis of this problem Royce ended up with the paradoxical conclusion that the best way to deal with theoretical pluralism is to produce more theory - but with the qualification that the new theory be more theoretically powerful than its predecessors.

But this kind of judgment is heavily dependent upon a valid method of theory appraisal. However, theory appraisal has been stymied by the fact of theory incommensurability - the well documented fact that not all of the theories under consideration are of the same genre. The point is that competing theories from highly disparate genres (e.g., behavioristic and psycho-analytic) are based on disparate or non-comparable criteria as to what constitutes valid theory. It would appear that the problem can only be resolved if a method can be developed which is equally adequate for the full range of theories, thereby rendering them commensurate and amenable to critical analysis and comparison.

Over the past few decades the philosophers of science have provided extensive analyses of the nature of theory. However, these analyses have lumped all theory into the single category of theory. Thus, they have failed to recognize that what they are actually confronted with is a multitude of theories, ranging widely from weak to strong. A major consequence of this failure has resulted in inadequate methods of theory appraisal.

To be more specific, theory appraisal has been elaborated within the context of the philosophy of justification - that is, the attempt to specify the basis for accepting a theory as valid or rejecting it as not valid. This means that the philosophers of science have focused their attention on strong theory - theory which is capable of offering valid explanations. The argument is that only this kind of advanced theory has the potential of being valid, and that less advanced theory has no such potential.

But what about weaker classes of theory? Have they nothing to contribute to the advancement of science? The philosophers appear to have taken this stance.

But scientists say otherwise, or else they would not have produced weaker forms of theory. Furthermore, the history of science clearly shows that most of its advanced theory evolved from weaker theory. Lakatos, who has leaned heavily on historical analysis, is one of the few philosophers of science to give it adequate recognition. He does this via his concept of research programs - referring to scientific research which either moves forward by developing increasingly powerful theory or regresses by failure to do so.

In his analysis of the theory continuum (ranging from weak to strong), Royce identified (1978) three classes of theory. These three categories range from programmatic at the weak end of the continuum to explanatory at the strong end, with descriptive in the middle.

The point is that advancement in all scientific fields varies, and that theory varies accordingly. For example, even in the physical sciences theory reflects varying degrees of progress. Thus, although explanatory theory covers most physics domains, it does not include geophysics. For example, although earthquakes can be accurately described they cannot be predicted. This means there is no adequate explanation regarding their cause. Thus, in this domain the available theory is descriptive rather than explanatory.

This also applies to evolutionary theory and biology in general. And, as we move to the behavioral and social sciences, the theories become even weaker. Broadly speaking, we can characterize physical theory as explanatory, biological theory as descriptive, and social science theory as programmatic. And, unfortunately most of psychology's theory is either descriptive or programmatic. I know of no theory in psychology which can claim explanatory status. Hullian learning theory constitutes the most significant attempt in this direction, but it failed. That is, it failed as explanatory theory, and can, therefore, more accurately be described as semi-explanatory, or as descriptive with intimations of explanatory power.

What does this mean? Does this lack of advanced or explanatory theory in psychology mean we should close up shop? Does it mean we have failed as science? Some scholars think so. I don't.

What it means is obvious. It means that psychology just isn't an advanced science. Thus, it is inappropriate to subject it to the standards of advanced science.

But this is exactly what happens when psychological theory is analyzed in the context of justification. For philosophical analysis in the context of justification is based on advanced theory in the physical sciences.

A major concern of this paper is to develop a method of theory appraisal so that the relative strength of a theory can be ascertained. The relative strength of a theory is actually a complex which is composed of many dimensions or characteristics of a theory; items such as the following: empirical testability, degree of empirical-formal fit, comprehensiveness or scope, parsimony, depth of penetration into the problem or domain under investigation, degree of formalization, degree of cohesiveness, and explicitness of conceptualization. Although this inventory of theory dimensions is merely suggestive it is sufficient to bring out the complexity of the concept of theoretical power or strength of a theory. This complexity implies that degree of theoretical development is some unknown, optimally weighted combination of the dimensions.

However, there is an additional complication. A careful review of the dimensions inventoried reveals that they describe relatively advanced theory. Thus, if we now add dimensions which are more characteristic of descriptive and programmatic theory, such as the number of empirical laws contained in the theory, and the further research the theory provokes, the complexity becomes even greater. In short, different dimensions will be more relevant to one or other of the three kinds of theory.

This leads to the main thesis of this paper - a differential method of theory appraisal - that is, different criteria for each kind of theory. The number of kinds of theory is an open question. And we may eventually be able to conduct empirical analyses for the three categories identified by Royce. However in this context only two categories are relevant - relatively developed or strong theory and under-developed or weak theory. What is the overall criterion for each of these classes of theory? They are theoretical power or explanatory value for developed theory and heuristic value for undeveloped theory. However, we must also deal with the problem of incommensurability of theory. This is at least alluded to by developing a common set of dimensions. That is, an exhaustive set of dimensions must be developed - dimensions which are meant to be characteristic of all theory, both weak and strong. However, the dimensions will be differentially weighted. Those that are totally irrelevant to a given class of theory will be weighted zero, and those that are of greatest importance will be weighted one. The remaining dimensions will receive values in between, the higher the value the greater the relevance.

The determination of these differential weights can be investigated both rationally and empirically. The rational approach involves the kind of conceptual analysis the philosophers typically provide. And the empirical approach involves standard procedures developed in psychometric theory and studies of personnel selection. These methods involve correlating a large number of predictor variables with a criterion variable. This involves computing a multiple correlation coefficient and determining beta coefficients or weights for each of the predictors. Making observations for some of the theory dimensions may be difficult, but in principle they appear to be amenable to empirical investigation. For the easy cases the observations will be accompanied by a number, such as the rank order of the theory out of the total number of viable theories in a given domain or the total number of investigations a theory has spanned since it was formulated. For the difficult aspects of the theory, such as the degree of formalization and the degree of conceptualization, the observation will also be accompanied by a number, but the number will reflect a judgment, such as in rating scales. Thus, although observations can be recorded they'll be complex and subjective rather than the simple nose counting or meter reading we'd prefer. Despite the subjectivity this introduces, reliable empirical studies of this kind of data are possible. Subjectivity is the price that must be paid when empirically investigating complex questions.

The point is that successes in weak theory provide a promising direction for further research - a direction sorely needed on problems about which we are essentially ignorant.

Eysenck's analysis focused on the role of predictions in weak theory. But there are also other points to be made, such as what is involved in the generation of ideas, and what is involved in their further pursuit once generated. Consideration of such issues has been dubbed the context of discovery by the philosophers of science. And, although they originally consigned these issues to empirical investigation by such fields as psychology, anthropology, and sociology, there are signs that a rejuvenation of context of discovery is in progress (see Nickles, 1980).

The major focus of philosophy of science has moved from justification to logicality, and from there to a very broad concept of rationality which includes discovery as part of the problem. It has further been realized that the logical nature of discovery is not a matter of deductive logic or rules, but a matter of scientific judgment or reasoning. It has more to do with suggestions or heuristic possibilities than rigid deductions.

Furthermore, studies in the history of science have sensitized philosophers of science to the realization that to ignore the discovery aspect of science, as they have for the past fifty years, is to *ignore* most of the scientific enterprise - that is, not only the most interesting aspects of science, but that having to do with scientific progress. It seems to be agreed that there are two senses of the discovery/justification distinction - the temporal and the logical. The temporal distinction refers to the fact that discovery occurs early in the doing of science and justification occurs late in the process. The logical distinction refers to reasoning about discovery and confirmation. A rational reconstruction which focuses on the generation of ideas in the case of discovery, and a rational reconstruction which focuses on ideas in their finished state in the case of justification.

Furthermore, it is highly likely that there are three rather than two phases in science - a pursuit phase in between the generational and the evaluative phases. Pursuit is concerned with evaluating which of several alternatives is most worthy of further effort - that is, preliminary evaluations of what is most likely to pay off after further investigation.

This means that we can anticipate that the philosophers will eventually provide us with the same kind of deep and penetrating analyses of the discovery aspect as we have already received for the justification aspect. What we cannot anticipate are clarifications of the following: (1) a formal logic or algorithm of conceptual alternatives, (2) to predict the content of discoveries, (3) to be able to predict which, if any, of alternative approaches will succeed, and (4) to be able to justify content - that is, general rules by means of which to rank the likelihood of alternative approaches to yield discoveries. On the other hand, we can anticipate clarification of the following: (1) a cognitively useful classification of conceptual alternatives, (2) acceptable patterns of inference employed in hypothesis generation, (3) identification of cognitive and non-cognitive factors affecting the context of discovery, and (4) identification of factors bearing on plausibility, trustworthiness, and justification in the context of discovery (Burian, 1980). In short, philosophic insights for producing the kind of theory we have in psychology is finally on the way. Judging by what has happened regarding the analysis of justification, however, it will be two or three decades before they come up with insights that might be of help in furthering the advancement of theory construction in psychology.

References

Burian, R. M. (1980). Why philosophers should not despair of understanding scientific discovery. In T. Nickles (Ed.), *Scientific discovery, logic, and rationality.* Dordrecht, Holland: D. Reidel Publishing.

Eysenck, H. J. (1985). The place of theory in a world of facts. In K. B. Madsen & L. P. Mos (Eds.), *Annals of theoretical psychology (Vol. 3, pp. 17-72).* New York: Plenum.

Nickles, Thomas (Ed.). (1980). *Scientific discovery, logic, and rationality.* Dordrecht, Holland: D. Reidel Publishing.

Royce, J. R. (1978). How we can best advance the construction of theory in psychology. *Canadian Psychological Review, 19,* 259-276.

Royce, J. R. (1985). The problem of theoretical pluralism in psychology. In K. B. Madsen & L. P. Mos (Eds.), *Annals of theoretical psycholgy* (Vol. 3, pp. 297-316). New York: Plenum.

EPISTEMIC BELIEFS AND THEIR DEVELOPMENTAL RELATIONSHIP TO POST-POSITIVIST PSYCHOLOGY

Marcia Salner

Saybrook Institute
San Francisco, CA, U.S.A.

SUMMARY: This paper describes post-positivist epistemological assumptions and their development since the 1950s. As a vehicle for organizing the discussion, two recent articles in ***American Psychologist*** (Manicas & Secord, 1983, and Gergen, 1985) are reviewed and compared. Both articles have a similar purpose - to describe post-positivist psychology - but they differ in terms of how social reality is conceptualized. This difference points to an open issue in theoretical psychology and to the role of epistemic beliefs in the world views that psychologists accept or reject. In order to emphasize the need for more attention to the psychological development of epistemic beliefs (and of psychological theorizing itself), the historical evolution of post-positivist assumptions in psychology is viewed through the lens of Perry's (1970) theory of intellectual development. The structural similarities between individual intellectual development and the evolution of formal epistemology suggest that both individual and collective advances in psychological and philosophical reasoning take place against the same social background and result from socially given dilemmas and problems that individuals must confront.

Several years ago, I acknowledged to a well known philosopher of science that the discipline of philosophy has been very usefully applied to the problem of creating psychological knowledge. I asked him whether he thought that the reverse relationship might apply, that is, could the discipline of psychology be usefully applied to the study of philosophy. The philosopher appeared uncomfortable with my question and began to talk about a certain philosopher, dead now for several centuries, who had exhibited florid symptoms of paranoid schizophrenia. The philosopher of science grudgingly admitted that it seemed important to analyze the relationship between this ancient philosopher's mental illness and his work, and that this might constitute an important contribution of psychology to philosophy. However, this was not what I had in mind in asking my question about the application of psychological theory to the study of philosophy. First, I do not consider the discipline of psychology to be limited to the study of abnormal behavior. Rather, I had in mind the general issue of cognition, specifically the role played by epistemic beliefs

- those beliefs that we invoke to answer such questions as "What is knowledge?" "How do we know?" "How do we *know* that we know?" What is the psychological function of epistemic beliefs in human experience? What relationship do they have to personality? To life history? To social experience? These questions seem to imply a relationship between philosophy as a formal pursuit and individual intellectual development that is rarely pursued by either psychologists or philosophers.

I have been struck by the dearth of scholarship which uses psychological knowledge to study how psychological knowledge itself is produced. Psychological theories have been used to study the characteristics of scientists, (Eiduson, 1962; Roe, 1952; Maslow, 1966; Mahoney, 1979). Some notable exceptions that delve into the more problematic relationship between knowledge and individual psychology include Richard Coan's (1979) study of "the personal and theoretical pathways" of a sample of psychologists, and the extensive work around the concept of psycho-epistemology by Joseph Royce and his many colleagues at the Center for Advanced Study in Theoretical Psychology at the University of Alberta (e.g., Royce, 1972, 1974, 1975; Royce, Coward, Egan, Kessel, & Mos, 1978; Powell & Royce, 1978; Diamond & Royce, 1980). Piaget (1970) is perhaps the best example of a philosopher who turned his attention to psychological theory in an effort to ground philosophy in the evolution of human mental processes. However, the amount of attention that has been devoted to the study of psychological knowledge *from a psychological perspective* has been a relatively small percentage of the vast literature in both the disciplines of philosophy and psychology.

I see a need for renewed interest in the psychology of knowledge because of an anomaly within psychology and the human sciences generally, particularly as these disciplines are practiced within the United States. This anomaly stems from the fact that the majority of research work being carried out by psychologists today is based on theories of inquiry drawn from physical science models to which a positivist aura still clings. (I will return in a moment to the specifics of what I mean by 'a positivist aura.') Second, the work of philosophers of science has, during the past thirty years, seriously undermined positivist assumptions as a secure basis for the development of knowledge. Hence, the discipline of psychology is plagued by inconsistency: the very foundations of the theories of inquiry on which psychologists depend for generating psychological knowledge have been discredited. We are operating in a post-positivist climate whether we like it or not and the future of psychology as a discipline may revolve around how, and how quickly we can adjust our theoretical and epistemological perspectives.

To amplify on this point I will contrast some of the positivist assumptions to which contemporary psychology still clings with some of the post-positivist assumptions that have been advanced as an alternative.

Two recent articles in *American Psychologist* can facilitate this discussion which must, in the interests of space, be abbreviated to an alarming degree. These two articles both have the same intent: to describe a post-positivist psychology. However, each takes a somewhat different slant reflecting contemporary schisms within the human sciences around whether or when, observational science or hermeneutic interpretation yields the appropriate logic to guide us.

The first article, by Peter Manicas and Paul Secord (1983), compares traditional empirical science with both the Kuhnian critique that emerged in the 1960's, and with a more recent critique - scientific realism, or as they term it, a "new philosophy of science." First, they describe traditional science and identify five of its major assumptions:

1. It has a foundationist epistemology, in which the test of the truth of propositions is 'correspondence' between theory and data. Hypotheses are to be tested against the 'facts'.

2. Theories are deduced from these 'factual' data.

3. Research is more or less a-theoretical, with many researchers avoiding theory, as far as possible, and seeking to test only those hypotheses related to variables that can be closely tied to observation.

4. A Humean conception of causality and of lawfulness is taken for granted.

5. Explanation and prediction are exactly symmetrical (p. 400).

In short, traditional empirical science assumes, in Cartesian fashion, that the theories of the human observer are separable from the data of an observable world which is real, exists as it appears, and is a reliable determinant of the truthfulness of theories.

Manicas and Secord remind us that, by 1950, there were many philosophical challenges to this foundationist epistemology of science, but it was not until Kuhn published his *Structure of Scientific Revolutions* (1962/1970) that debate about scientific epistemology became widespread within the academic community. Manicas and Secord (1983) note that:

> Kuhn attacked empiricist epistemology...He argued...that observation was "theory laden" and that science must be understood as a social activity in which disciplines develop their own rules of practice...Scientists were human observers and science a social activity, which subjected it to normative or paradigmatic influences operating apart from the internal criteria of science (pp. 400-401).

The paradigmatic critique of traditional science was an important spur in the evolution of thinking about science; however, it brought with it problems of its own. Manicas and Secord (1983) comment, "The problem was clear enough: If there is no theory-neutral data base (foundationism) and if disciplines constitute their own scientific practice, what are the criteria of truth?" (p 401).

It is attempts to resolve the particular problem of adequate truth criteria that has led some philosophers of science to a third alternative. Manicas and Secord ascribe the following essential features to this new alternative to traditional empiricism. Relying heavily on the work of Harré (1970, 1972) Harré and Madden (1975), and Bhaskar (1975, 1978, 1979, 1982), they call it the "realist view":

1. It argues that knowledge is a social and historical product. Epistemologically, there can be nothing *known* to which our ideas (sentences, theories) can correspond. But it is precisely the task of science to invent theories that aim to represent the world. Thus, the practices of science generate their own *rational* criteria in terms of which the theory is accepted or rejected. Since our theories are constitutive of the known world but *not* of the *world* we may always be wrong, but *not* anything goes.

2. The realist theory views the natural world as nonreductive or emergent. A simple crude example may be helpful. The compound NaCl is a complex of elements, Na and Cl. Each have causal properties and Na Cl has causal properties that are not true of either sodium or chlorine. But at still another level, sodium and chlorine are themselves complexes of electrons, neutrons, quarks and so on.

3. Scientific laws are *not* about events or classes of events, regularly or stochastically conjoined, but are about the causal properties of structures that exist and operate in the world. Thus, not only is the world stratified (i.e., nonreductive or emergent) but it is a complex of structures and structural processes. On the realist view, 'things' of the world never operate under conditions of complete closure. This explains why we have the experience of patterns, of tendencies, and of probabilities.

4. The realist theory of science rejects in toto the idea that explanation and prediction are symmetrical. We may often be in a position to explain some event once it has occurred, when it would have been impossible - even in principle - to predict it. The past is, in a sense, 'determined.' That is, what happened

> can be causally *explained*. But the future is *not* determined precisely because the complexly related structures and systems of the world are constantly being reconfigured (Manicas & Secord, 1983, pp. 401-403).

In short, Manicas and Secord are describing an epistemology of contexts that posits a dialectical relationship between the knower and the known, and in which the source of truth lies neither in the world nor in the human knower, but in the (human) 'experience of patterns'.

Manicas and Secord are describing a view of science that is holistic, phenomenological, and dependent on socially constructed rules (such as linguistic rules). When we examine the set of assumptions which they set forth, we can see in them evidence of the impact of general systems theory, with its emphasis on holism, levels of analysis, and structure. Similarly, an emphasis on phenomena, *as they appear*, reflects the impact of the phenomenological philosopher, Edmund Husserl, on modern scientific thinking. The philosophy of the new realism is also heavily dependent on the psychology of cognition in its emphasis on gestalts and the 'experience' of patterns. And, finally, there is a recognition of the element of creative unpredictability in human life, which incorporates into the traditional realm of science a rational understanding that has come from the humanities disciplines.

However, the realist emphasis has its limitations when applied to the human realm, where we are not so much concerned with natural objects and the dynamic processes that govern these objects as we are with human meaning and its elaboration into complex systems: linguistic, political, legal, familial, religious, and so forth. It is here that we see that the realm of inquiry is not so much *given*, in the realist sense, as it is *constructed* through human action into artifacts (e.g., culture, language, societies, texts, works of art, technologies, etc.). The importance of this distinction between real (natural) objects, given by nature, and constructed (humanly processed) artifacts is discussed in the second article I wish to draw on, authored by Kenneth Gergen (1985). Gergen argues the importance of the social construction as a process that is intrinsic to the human realm that the human science researcher investigates.

Social constructionism, as a philosophical position, departs from the position of scientific realism in one important regard. The historical realist assumes the existence of a real natural world, which lies, albeit 'through a glass, darkly', behind our cognitive experience of contextualized patterns. Social constructionists, on the other hand, doubt the utility of this assumption when it comes to investigation of the human realm. Gergen (1985) notes:

> Social constructionism ... begins with radical doubt in the taken-for-granted world - whether in the sciences or daily life - and in a specialized way acts as a form of social criticism. Constructionism asks one to suspend belief that commonly accepted categories or understandings receive their warrant through observation.
>
> The terms in which the world is understood are social artifacts, products of historically situated interchanges among people. From the constructionist position the process of understanding is not automatically driven by the forces of nature, but is the result of an active, cooperative enterprise of persons in relationship. In this light, inquiry is invited into the historical and cultural bases of various forms of world construction (p. 267).

Where scientific realism and social constructionism differ is in whether they regard the 'real' world as a natural given or as a social construction. Despite this major difference between the realist view, set forth by Manicas and Secord (1983), and the constructionist view, set forth by Gergen (1985), in several essential respects they are similar. Both ground knowledge and truth claims in the shared intelligibility of scientific communities which are historically and culturally situated. Both presume a dialectical interaction between knower and known that is radically different from foundationist, or positivist epistemology. Both emphasize the formal rational constraints which contexts place on 'anything goes' relativism.

Gergen (1983) comments on this relativism:

> Constructionism offers no foundational rules of warrant and in this sense is relativistic. However, this does not mean that "anything goes." Because of the inherent dependency of knowledge systems on communities of shared intelligibility, scientific activity will always be governed in large measure by normative rules. However, constructionism does invite the practitioners to view these rules as historically and culturally situated - thus subject to critique and transformation. There is stability of understanding without the stultification of foundationalism. Further, unlike the moral relativism of the empiricist tradition, constructionism reasserts the relevance of moral criteria for scientific practice (p. 273).

The debate about the relative merits of a realist versus a constructionist view is not one that will be resolved in favor of one camp or the other inasmuch as the essential contradiction in the debate is over the role which humanity plays in the creation of the world! Underneath the superstructure of epistemology lies the bedrock of metaphysics and its bowdlerized relative, ideology. How the differences between epistemological realism and epistemological constructionism should be resolved or harmonized within contemporary psychology is an appropriate issue for further study by theoretical psychologists inasmuch as the province of the discipline cuts across phenomena that are both given (e.g., neurophysiology, maturation, aging) and constructed (e.g., social rules, language, organizations).[1] However, I am more interested for the moment in what the positions espoused by Manicas & Secord (1983) and Gergen (1985) have in common that serves to define a post-positivist direction for the discipline of psychology. Both positions are, strictly speaking, constructionist, although they differ in the degree of emphasis on this point. What both point to is a shift in the focus of attention in philosophy from a positivist concern with 'getting through' to the reality 'out there' to a concern with mental processes themselves, for example, Manicas & Secord's interest in the 'experience of patterns.' A similar shift has been visible within psychology as post-positivist challenges to behaviorism have resulted in the emergence of cognitive science and a focus on the manner in which stimuli from 'out there' are mediated by the human mind itself. However, and this is my point, *we do not find cognitive psychologists applying their knowledge of cognitive processes to the study of how knowledge about cognition is itself produced.* Instead, such study is given over to philosophers whose methodology is dependent exclusively on rational argumentation, that is, on methods themselves derived from cognitive processes. Thus our study of the mind is sealed in by the failure of psychologists to recognize that the very epistemic foundation of post-positivist philosophy depends heavily on the psychological, that is, cognitive, domain. This is why I contend that a psychology of knowledge is as essential today as the more familiar study of the philosophy of knowledge.

By way of illustration, I would like to re-examine this brief review of historical changes in epistemological thinking (that Manicas & Secord, 1983 have provided) from the perspective of psychological theory. I will use William Perry's (1970) theory of intellectual and ethical development, based on his longitudinal study of Harvard undergraduates. Perry was particularly interested in individual psychological development through time in the same way that Manicas and Secord are interested in accounting for historical evolution in the philosophy of science. Both projects are concerned with understanding temporal change - why and how it occurs.

When we examine Perry's (1970) theory of epistemological development side by side with Manicas' and Secord's (1983) account of collective epistemological development, we can see that, structurally, the main lines are similar. This should not be surprising since both the evolution of philosophical ideas and the development of individual student's ideas

[1]For more discussion of the philosophical positions briefly described above, the reader is referred to Leplin, J. (Ed.), (1984). *Scientific realism.* Berkeley & Los Angeles: University of California Press; and Berger, P. L. & Luckman, T. (1966). *The social construction of reality: A treatise in the sociology of knowledge.* New York: Irvington.

take place within the same cultural context and within a similar academic social context. Thus, both philosophers of science and college students share some, though of course not all, the features of the general intellectual landscape that characterizes contemporary America. Furthermore, part of a college student's learning process is to confront on a personal level some of the same intellectual questions that puzzle and preoccupy philosophers. Briefly, Perry (1970) found when he encouraged students to speak about this experience, that, as a group, they revealed the existence of a series of stages which describe intellectual development. Perry found a developmental progression among students in that they tended to move from a position of 'dualism' (in which the source of knowledge is to be found in the external world), through 'multiplicity' (in which knowledge becomes a jumble of competing perspectives, each with its own legitimacy depending on the unique position of the knower), to 'contextual relativism' (in which knowledge is viewed in relation to reasoned personal commitment within the social, cultural and historical contexts in which knowledge evolves.)

A similar developmental trajectory can be seen within the philosophy of science. Traditional science is based on a foundationist epistemology, in that knowledge and its truth claims are evaluated against an external referent. Knowledge and truth are 'out there' - an epistemological view that is shared, albeit naively, by Perry's 'dualists'. Perry found that his dualist subjects can function very competently, as long as they are able to stave off confrontation with ideas or experiences that undermine the credibility of their belief that the way things are personally experienced is the way they are. Similarly, the traditional scientist is not troubled about the foundations of his or her assumptions unless confronted with contrary perspectives that defy assimilation (e.g., light as wave or light as particle; the velocity or a particle versus its position).

The Kuhnian critique of foundationist (or dualist) epistemology unnerved many traditional scientists with its emphasis on the relativity of perspectives. Contact with multiple conflicting paradigms, each with its own particular merits and demerits, apparently has the same disorganizing effects on scientist and Harvard undergraduate alike: it throws both of them back and away from ontic belief in the authority of the external world and toward a concern with the (subjective) role of the human knower. Both must puzzle over the source of knowledge. In each case, the resulting issue is the same: "If there is no theory-neutral data base...what are the criteria of truth?" (Manicas & Secord, 1983, p. 401).

Perry found that his subjects were allowed a temporary solution to this epistemological problem that, fortunately or unfortunately, depending upon your values, is not available to the philosopher or scientist who wishes to remain within the purvue of academic rationality. This solution is marked by recourse to the authority of gut feelings, or the elevation of subjectivity to a position that pre-empts efforts to intellectually understand objective claims to truth. Perry labeled these subjects "multiplists." The multiplist's solution of relying on the messages of the 'gut' for legitimizing truth claims eventually failed some of Perry's subjects for similar reasons that cause it to fail as a strategy for the philosopher of science. It is a chaotic and anarchistic view of intellectual life which does not take one anywhere except into the recesses of philosophic solipsism. In order for his subjects to remain committed to multiplistic beliefs, Perry found that they had to find some life space where the ambiguity and conflict of multiple paradigms were tolerable.

Similarly, the general tolerance within the academic community for the co-existence of multiple and competing paradigms, along with frequently encountered cynicism about the possibility of any eventual resolution at a higher order of generality, suggests to me that our society, at least academically, is normatively committed to a multiplistic set of epistemic beliefs. Or, to put it another way, a Kuhnian view of truth is beginning to prevail over that of positivist science.

However, there is enormous dissatisfaction expressed within every discipline with the 'rampant relativism' that seems to prevail as a result of the challenges that have been mounted against the foundationist assumptions of positivism. It is the search for a reasoned basis on which to ground truth claims emanating from various perspectives that fuels the development of both Perry's multiplist subjects and contemporary philosophers of science to search for the next stage in the development of epistemic beliefs. This effort addresses the epistemological issue raised by the Kuhnian critique: All truth is relative, but *relative to what?* The answer appears in an emphasis on logical, social, temporal, and physical contexts. We see a transition to a relational, that is, structural, definition of truth. In the philosophy of science we see emerging a qualified realism that is focused on the dynamic between the theoretical perspective of the knower and the external world; the latter now viewed, through the lens of the knower's experience of patterns, as a complex organization of interacting systems in a continuously emerging process of reconfiguration. This set of beliefs is labeled by Perry as 'contextual relativism.'

Contextual relativism, as described by Perry (1970), arises in college students out of psychological frustration encountered with multiplistic epistemic beliefs. The subjective emphasis of the multiplist leads to a kind of epistemic alienation, because if every idea is logically as good as any other, how is it possible to choose anything to which one can make a commitment? Contextual relativism represents the subject's increased awareness of the importance of contexts in defining truth and value. Pluralism is accepted as a condition, but the evolution of intellectual standards and reasoned commitment is much more stringent and complex than 'anything goes' relativism. Epistemologically, contextual relativism is dialectical and interactive; it does not look for truth either in the world (as the dualist thinker does), or in the self (as the multiplist thinker does), but in the interaction between self and world that results from committed, existential action.

The descriptions of post-positivist epistemology that are put forth by both Gergen (1985) and Manicas & Secord (1983) are 'contextual relativist' positions according to Perry's (1970) definition. As such, they are incompatible with either 'dualist' or 'multiplist' epistemic beliefs. Debates about which of the epistemic positions is the 'correct' one for psychologists to hold can continue indefinitely, perhaps serving only to illustrate Kuhn's (1970) portrayal of 'the incommensurability of paradigms'. On the other hand, if we take a developmental perspective, there may be some hope of resolving contradictions.

I have presented a *developmental* view of both philosophy of science and of epistemic cognitive processes because the concept of development incorporates the idea of dynamic change. We can see in epistemic change, whether in philosophically naive students or professional philosophers, a response to questions that depends less on mere temporality than it does on the intrusion of certain environmental challenges in the form of human problems to be cognitively solved (e.g., accounting for multiple perspectives, and the necessity to develop standards for evaluating competing knowledge claims).

According to the developmental view - argued, for example, by Piaget (1970) - chronologically prior cognitive schema, or organizing principles, are neither rejected nor lost in this perpetual confrontation with challenges. Rather, they are incorporated into new and more complex structures at a higher level of inclusiveness. Just as Einsteinian theory does not invalidate Newtonian theory, but merely qualifies it, so it is that later developments in formal epistemology and in cognitive processes can subsume earlier developments, and lead to greater flexibility and differentiation in subsequent applications. As a result, we need not necessarily conclude that post-positivist psychology should (or should not) eschew traditional empirical methods based on dualist (foundationist) assumptions, or that 'rampant relativism' and the methodological proliferation that it breeds is (or is not) desirable. Rather, historically prior theories of inquiry need to be carefully qualified with respect to the particular phenomena to which they can most appropriately be applied. New methods for dealing specifically with exceptions to those prior categories of understandable phenomena need to be developed and used.

In conclusion, I would like to stress that the task of understanding 'ideas about knowledge,' or what I have called epistemic beliefs, falls clearly within the domain of the discipline of psychology. In order to further that understanding, we need considerably more research on cognitive processes in human individuals before we can establish how epistemic beliefs are related, first, to cognitive development generally and, second, to formal philosophical reasoning as it evolves over time. A number of cognitive factors have already been identified that are important developmentally: postformal relativistic reasoning (Sinnott, 1984); problem finding versus problem solving (Arlin, 1986); dialectical thinking (Basseches, 1986); reflective judgment (Kitchener & King, 1981; Kitchener, 1986); empathy (Benack, 1984); and, moral judgment (Armon, 1984; Rest, 1986).

In addition, formal epistemology needs to be explored further by psychologists, who cannot take for granted that the epistemic assumptions that they have adopted along with the discipline's accepted methodologies and theories is, like most mothering, 'good enough'. Epistemology is a living process, not a formal intellectual game. Although it is the domain of philosphers, it is psychologically active in human cognition in a far more general way. It is possible that through psychological examination of epistemological development we may be able to create a useful psychology of knowledge that can then serve both the disciplines of psychology and philosophy in developing a post-positivist epistemological framework which does not founder in either subjectivity or relativism.

References

Arlin, P. K. (1986). Problem finding and young adult cognition. In R. A. Mines & K. S. Kitchener (Eds.), *Adult Cognitive Development* (pp. 22-23). New York: Praeger.

Armon, C. (1984). Ideals of the good life and moral judgment: Ethical reasoning across the lifespan. In M. L. Commons, F. A. Richards, C. Armon (Eds.), *Beyond formal operations* (pp. 357-380). New York: Praeger.

Basseches, M. (1986). Dialectical thinking and young adult cognitive development. In R. A. Mines & K. S. Kitchener (Eds.), *Adult cognitive development* (pp 33-56). New York: Praeger.

Benack, S. (1984). Postformal epistemologies and the growth of empathy. In M. L. Commons, F. A. Richards, & C. Armon (Eds.), *Beyond formal operations* (pp. 340-356). New York: Praeger.

Berger, P. L., & Luckman, T. (1966). *The social construction of reality: A treatise in the sociology of knowledge.* New York: Irvington.

Bhaskar, R. (1975). *A realist theory of science.* Leeds, England: Leeds Books.

Bhaskar, R. (1978). On the possibility of social scientific knowledge and the limits of behaviorism. *Journal for the theory of social behavior, 8,* 1-28.

Bhaskar, R. (1979). *The possibility of naturalism.* Brighton, England: Harvester.

Bhaskar, R. (1982). Emergence, explanation and emancipation. In P. F. Secord (Ed.), *Explaining social behavior: Consciousness, behavior, and social structure* (pp. 275-310). Beverly Hills, CA: Sage.

Coan, R. (1979). *Psychologists: Personal and theoretical pathways.* New York: Irvington.

Diamond, S. R., & Royce, J. R. (1980). Cognitive abilities as expressions of three "ways of knowing". *Multivariate Behavioral Research, 15,* 31-56.

Eiduson, B. T. (1962). *Scientists: Their psychological world.* New York: Basic Books.

Gergen, K. (1985). The social constructionist movement in modern psychology. *American Psychologist, 40,* 266-275.
Harré, R. (1970). *The principles of scientific thinking.* Chicago: University of Chicago Press.
Harré, R. (1972). *Philosophies of science.* Oxford, England: Oxford University Press.
Harré, R., & Madden, E. H. (1975). *Causal powers.* Totawa, NJ: Littlefield Adams.
Kitchener, K. S. (1983). Cognition, metacognition and epistemic cognition: A three-level model of cognitive processing. *Human development, 26,* 222-232.
Kitchener, K. S. (1986). The reflective judgment model: Characteristics, evidence, and measurement. In R. A. Mines & K. S. Kitchener (Eds.), *Adult cognitive development* (pp. 76-91). New York: Praeger.
Kitchener, K. S., & King, P. M. (1981). Reflective judgment: Concepts of justification and their relationship to age and education. *Journal of Applied Development Psychology, 2,* 89-116.
Kuhn, T. S. (1970). *The structure of scientific revolutions* (2nd ed.). Chicago: University of Chicago Press (1st ed., 1962).
Leplin, J. (Ed.). (1984). *Scientific realism.* Berkeley/Los Angeles: University of California Press.
Mahoney, M. J. (1979). Psychology of a scientist: An evaluative view. *Social Studies of Science, 9,* 349-375.
Manicas, P. T., & Secord, P. F. (1983). Implications for psychology of the new philosophy of science. *American Psychologist, 38,* 399-413.
Maslow, A. (1966). *The psychology of science: A reconnaissance.* Chicago: Henry Regnery.
Perry, W. (1970). *Forms of intellectual and ethical development in the college years.* New York: Holt, Rinehart & Winston.
Piaget, J. (1970). *Genetic epistemology.* New York: W. W. Norton.
Powell, A., & Royce, J. R. (1978). Paths to being, life style and individuality. *Psychological Reports, 42,* 98-1005.
Rest, J. R. (1986). Moral development in young adults. In R. A. Mines & K. S. Kitchener (Eds.), *Adult cognitive development* (pp. 92-111). New York: Praeger.
Roe, A. (1952). *The making of a scientist.* New York: Dodd, Mead.
Royce, J. R. (1974). Cognition and knowledge: Psychological epistemology. In E. C. Carterette & M. P. Friedman (Eds.), *Handbook of perception, vol. 1: History and philosophical roots of perception* (pp. 149-175). New York: Academic Press.
Royce, J. R. (1975). Epistemic styles, individuality and world view. In A. Debons & W. J. Cameron (Eds.), *Perspectives in information science* (pp. 259-295). Leyden, The Netherlands: International Publishing Co.
Royce, J. R., & Rozeboom, W. W. (1972). *The psychology of knowing.* New York: Gordon and Breach.
Royce, J. R., Coward, H., Egan, E., Kessel, F., & Mos, L. (1978). Psychological epistemology: A critical review of the empirical literature and the theoretical issues. *Genetic Psychology Monographs, 97,* 265-353.
Sinnott, J. D. (1984). Postformal reasoning: The relativistic stage. In M. L. Commons, F. A. Richards, & C. Armon (Eds.), *Beyond formal operations* (pp. 298-325). New York: Praeger.

COMPLEMENTARITY, CAUSAL ISOMORPHISM, AND THE MIND-BODY PROBLEM[1]

Irving Kirsch

University of Connecticut
Storrs, CT, U.S.A.

Michael E. Hyland

Plymouth Polytechnic
Plymouth, England

SUMMARY: The rise of cognitive psychology has heralded a revival of interest in the mind-body problem. As a heuristic, Hyland (1985) suggested that mind terms and body terms be thought of as complementary descriptions of the same event. Complementarism precludes causal relations between mental and physiological events, and instead posits identity relations between these two types of variables. Independently, Kirsch (1985) proposed that for all causal sequences linking one mind state to another, there is a corresponding causal sequence of physiological states. Rather than being mind-body philosophies, complementarity and causal isomorphism are shown to be logical consequences of virtually all monist philosophies, including those that are currently most prominent. Their heuristic value is demonstrated with respect to empirical questions about psychophysiological phenomena.

Introduction

The rise of cognitive psychology has heralded a revival of interest in the mind-body problem. As a heuristic for theory construction, Hyland (1985) suggested that mind terms and body terms be thought of as complementary descriptions of the same event. Complementarism precludes causal relations between mental and physiological events, and instead posits identity relations between these two types of variables. Independently, Kirsch (1985) proposed that for all causal sequences linking one mind state to another, there is a corresponding causal sequence of physiological states.

The purpose of this paper is to extend our work in two ways: first, we demonstrate that the heuristic principles of complementarity and causal isomorphism are logical consequences of most monist mind-body philosophies. Therefore, these principles are not bound to any one particular

---

[1]An expanded version of this paper appears in ***The Journal of Mind and Behavior, 8***, 1987, 417-434. Printed here with permission. Requests for reprints should be sent to Irving Kirsch, Department of Psychology, U-20, Room 107, University of Connecticut, 406 Cross Campus Road, Storrs, CT 06268

metaphysic; second, we demonstrate the heuristic value of complementarity and isomorphism with respect to empirical questions about psychophysiological phenomena.

Complementarity

The concept of complementarity was introduced by Bohr (1934, 1949) specifically to account for certain phenomena in physics. Mackay (1958) developed and extended Bohr's idea of complementarity so as to make it applicable to any discipline. Mackay argued that complementarity is a logical consequence of certain sorts of descriptive language and is therefore not just a working model but a true representation of reality. He suggested that "complementary statements are essential when one chosen language-system is logically precluded from representing some of the distinctions or relationships which are discernible in the subject matter" (p. 121). According to Mackay, descriptions of minds and brains are complementary because each precludes some of the distinctions discernable in the other.

Hyland's (1985) use of the term 'complementarity' derives from Mackay's, but with two differences. First, Hyland does not commit himself as to whether complementarity is a true representation of reality or only a working model. He suggests that whether ultimately true or not, complementarity is a pragmatic viewpoint to accept at this present stage of psychology's development. As such, Hyland treats complementarity as a metatheoretical heuristic rather than a metaphysical statement. Second, Hyland uses 'surplus meaning' as a criterion for distinguishing different types of complementary description in psychology. All hypothetical constructs contain surplus meaning, and the surplus meaning specifies the ontological status of the construct as well as acting as a heuristic for empirical predictions. Hyland argues that there are categories of surplus meaning in psychology. One category provides insight into the relationship between mind states and behavior, and the other provides insight into the relationship between physiology and behavior.

One assumption underlying theoretical complementarity, as well as metaphysical complementarity, is that causal relations cannot occur between different types of complementary descriptions. Hence, Hyland suggests that causal relations can occur only between mind and mind states, or between body and body states. However, mind-body connections are established through identity relations which are complementary descriptions of the same event. Causal and identity relations should be used together in psychosomatic explanation as shown in Figure 1. In this and subsequent figures, horizontal arrows represent causality and vertical lines denote identity relations.

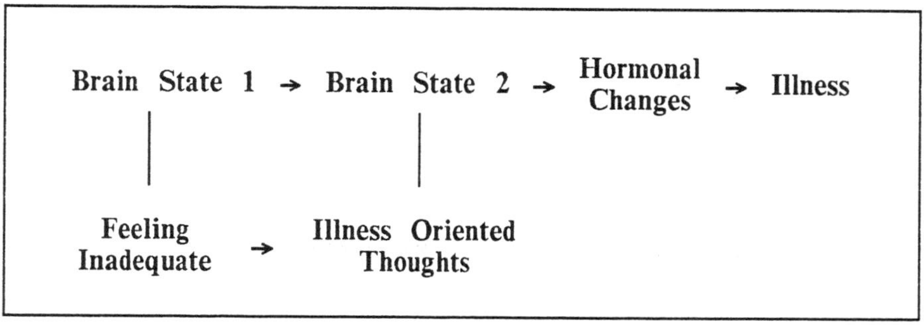

Figure 1. Causal and identity relations in the development of psychosomatic illness.

Causal Isomorphism

The idea of causal isomorphism was proposed by Kirsch (1985) as a means of accounting for some of the effects of placebos on psychological function. Placebos (and active drugs as well) induce expectancies for changes in subjective experience. For example, people expect to become relaxed if they take tranquilizers and energized if they take stimulants. These "response expectancies" are self-confirming. People report feeling relaxed and drowsy after taking a placebo tranquilizer, and they report feeling more tense and alert after taking a placebo stimulant.

In addition to affecting subjective experience, placebos have physiological effects. Placebo tranquilizers produce decreases in blood pressure and pulse rate; placebo stimulants have opposite effects. The question that these data pose is: How can these *physiological* changes be produced by expectancy, which is, after all, a *mental* construct?

Kirsch's (1985) answer to this question begins with two assumptions: First, there is (in principle) a physiological counterpart to any instance of a mental event. Second, the relation between a mental event and its physiological substrate is one of identity rather than cause and effect, an assumption that is equivalent to Hyland's (1985) independently conceived notion of mind-brain complementarity.

The idea of causal isomorphism is a logical consequence of the two assumptions described above. If there are physiological substrates to all mental events, then for any causal sequence of mental events, there must be a corresponding sequence of physical events. In other words, for any true statement indicating that one mental event has caused another mental event, there must be a true statement about two corresponding physiological states. Figure 2 illustrates the consequences of this assumption for understanding placebo-induced changes in pulse rate. Properly speaking, the change in pulse rate is not caused by expectancy. Rather, it is caused

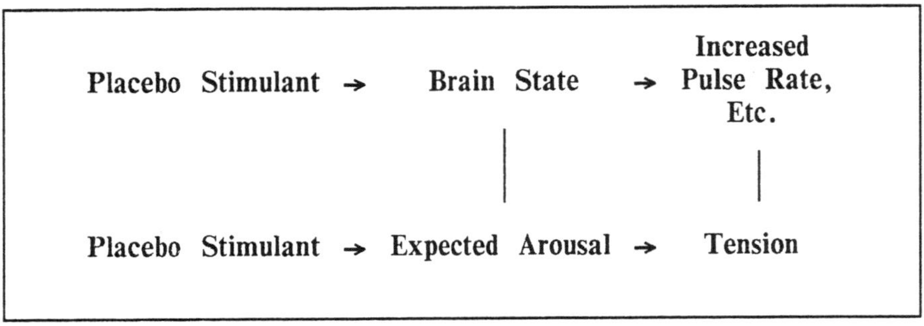

Figure 2. Causal isomorphism as illustrated through the effects of a placebo stimulant.

by the brain state with which the expectancy is identified.

Complementarity, Causal Isomorphism, and Philosophies of Mind

Hyland introduced the assumption of complementarity as a heuristically useful linguistic convention, rather than as an ontological statement. Similarly, Kirsch introduced the related notion of causal isomorphism without implying any particular philosophy of mind. Specifically, complementarity and causal isomorphism are metatheoretical statements. That is, they are statements about relationships between theoretical terms and relationships between theories containing these terms. They are not metaphysical statements about minds and bodies. In this section, we examine the relation between these metatheoretical statements and the most prominent current mind-body philosophies.

We begin with central state identity theory, a modern formulation of materialism (Boyd, 1980; Smart, 1963). The defining claim of materialist philosophies is that the universe is entirely composed of physical phenomena. Mentalistic terms are either meaningless or refer to physical phenomena. According to the identity thesis, 'mental' events *are* physical events, in the same way that water *is* H_2O. Specifically, they are states of the nervous system. Clearly, this mind-body philosophy stipulates both of the assumptions from which causal isomorphism can be logically deduced: the assumption of a physical counterpart to any meaningful mental term and the assumption of complementarity (i.e., that the relation between mental and physiological terms is one of identity rather than causality).

We turn next to metaphysical functionalism. Functionalism is a recent philosophy of mind inspired by the field of artificial intelligence (Block & Fodor, 1968). It begins with the materialist assumption that there is a physical substrate for any mental event, but it rejects the assumption that the physical substrate is *necessarily* a state of the central nervous system, an assumption that would limit mind to organisms containing central nervous systems and thereby preclude the possibility that a computer might think.

Functionalists propose that although any particular mental state is a physical event, its classification as a *type* of mental state does not depend on its physical structure. Instead, the classification of mental states depends on their causal relations to stimuli and responses, and to other mental states. For example, although any particular pain can be identified as a specific physical state, different pains may be different physical states. In human beings, pains are physiological states; pain in a computer would presumably be an inorganic physical state. The classification of both states as instances of pain would be based on shared functional characteristics, such as being consequences of physical damage and leading to avoidance of the situations in which they occur.

In postulating that mental states are physical events, functionalism posits complementary rather than causal relations between mental events and their substrates. Because every instance of a mental event is presumed to have a particular physical substrate, a functional relation between mental states implies a corresponding functional relation between the substrates. Furthermore, these causal relations provide the basis for the classification of mental states. Thus, functionalism not only posits causal isomorphism, it also makes it the criterion by which mental terms are defined.

Although most current mind-body philosophies are variants of materialism, double-aspect monism has always had wide appeal among psychologists. Double-aspect theorists view mind and body as two aspects - or ways of viewing and describing - the same thing. As originally proposed by Spinoza, it pertained to all phenomena, including inorganic objects, thereby resulting in panpsychism. However, psychologists who adopt a double-aspect position (e.g., Wundt, 1897/1969) typically restrict it to a subset of living organisms. Clearly, both versions of double-aspect monism imply a physical aspect corresponding to all mental events, and since mind and body are seen as aspects of the same underlying reality, the relation between them is clearly one of identity. Thus, double-aspect monism implies both complementarity and causal isomorphism.

Finally, we turn to Pribram's (1986) structural realism. Structural realism is similar to functionalism in its emphasis on relations between events. However, rather than beginning with the assumption of a materialist metaphysic, Pribram adopts a neutral monist stance in which "informational structure" is seen as the underlying essence of which mind and brain are "realizations" or "embodiments." In giving ontological primacy to informational structure, Pribram's position seems to be at least distantly related to Plato's theory of forms. In any case, since these informational structures implicitly include causal relations, the idea of causal isomorphism necessarily follows.

We have examined the most prominent current monist philosophies and have shown that they logically imply both complementarity and causal isomorphism. In fact, virtually all monist philosophies imply complementarity and causal isomorphism. The only exceptions are radical materialism, which denies any meaning to mental terms, and radical subjective idealism, which denies any meaning to physical terms. But any monist philosophy that accepts both mental and physiological terms as meaningful *must* imply complementarity (and as a consequence, causal isomorphism as well.) This is true because to allow both types of terms without specifying that they refer to the same thing is, by definition, dualism.

Dualist theories begin by denying that mental states can be *identified* with states of the nervous system. The fundamental question for dualism is to account for the apparent correlation between mental and physical events. Interactionism and epiphenomenalism are clearly incompatible with complementarity and causal isomorphism because they are based on the assumption of causal relations between mind and body. Parallelism, on the other hand, posits an isomorphic relation between sequences of mental and physical events. Although physical events correspond to mental events, the relationship between the two is not one of identity. Nevertheless, because direct causal relations between mental and physical events are precluded, the heuristic consequences of parallelism may not be appreciably different from the assumptions of complementarity.

Heuristic Implications

We have demonstrated that although the assumptions of mind-brain complementarity and causal isomorphism are inconsistent with some philosophies of mind (e.g., interactionist dualism), they do not require a commitment to any particular alternative. Not only are they consistent with virtually all monist philosophies, they are logical consequences of them. In this section, we demonstrate the heuristic value of these assumptions. In particular we intend to show that the most common alternative generates pseudo-answers to improperly formulated questions.

Of all mind-body philosophies, only interactionist dualism allows that mind can have a direct causal effect on the body. There are abundant data of mental events influencing bodily processes, but we also want to know the mechanism by which this occurs. A typical dualist strategy is to look for some physiological variable that may mediate the relation between a mental cause and a physical effect, a strategy that is also used to provide 'explanatory' mechanisms for mind-mind causal sequences. Endorphin release, for example, has been proposed as an explanation of placebo-induced pain reduction. However, this is really a pseudo-explanation, in that it leaves at least as much unexplained as before. Let us suppose that increased endorphin release *is* associated with placebo-generated expectancies for reduced pain. (In fact, the current data are inconclusive.) Instead of answering the original question: "How can expectancy reduce pain?", it merely replaces it with a new and more complex question: "How can expectancy cause an increase in endorphin release?". From an interactionist perspective, this could be answered only by finding some new intervening physiological event, which would in turn require explanation.

In contrast to dualist interactionism, the assumptions of complementarity and causal isomorphism preclude asking the question: "What physiological variable mediates the effects of mental states?" They thereby avoid the infinite regress to which that question leads. In its place, the following questions are posed: (a) What are the causal relations between mental states; (b) What are the physiological states with which those mental states are identified; and (c) What nonconscious physiological processes mediate the effect of one physiological state on another? The first of these questions provides a complete psychological explanation, the third provides a complete physiological explanation, and the second establishes the correspondence between the two. A complete psychophysiological explanation thus requires answers to all three questions.

Technically, the assumptions of complementarity and causal isomorphism suggest that the question: "How does a mental state produce a physiological effect?" is improperly formulated. The proper questions are: (a) What are the psychological consequences of the identified mental state; (b) What is its physiological counterpart; and (c) How does that physiological state generate the observed physiological effect?

Figure 3 illustrates how the question: "How does perceived danger produce an increase in pulse rate?" might be approached given the assumptions of complementarity and causal isomorphism. Let us assume that perceived danger leads to fear, and that there are no *psychological* (i.e., mental) states intervening between the perception of danger and the experience of fear. In other words, we are assuming that the relation between perceived danger and fear is immediate and that at the psychological level, the causal explanation is complete. At this point, we may say that the perception of danger leads to an increase in pulse rate because it causes fear, and because increased pulse rate is part of the physiological substrate of the experience of fear.

Conclusion

Theoretical complementarity and causal isomorphism constitute a set of rules for psychosomatic theory construction. These rules are as follows. (1) Causal relations occur only between mind and mind states or

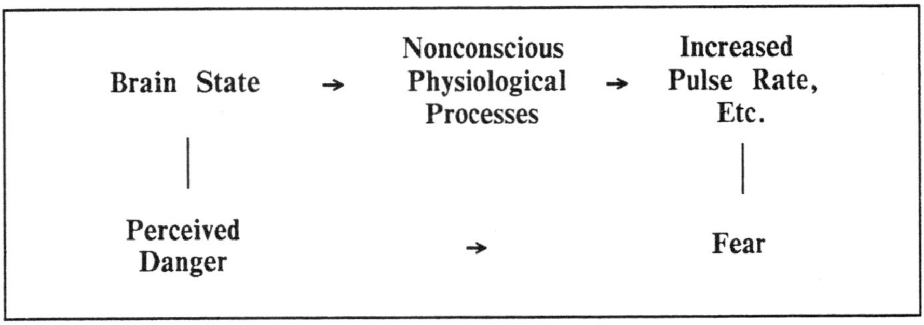

Figure 3. Complementarity and causal isomorphism as heuristic to questions of how mental states 'cause' physiological effects.

between body and body states. Direct causal relations between mind and body states are precluded. (2) Identity relations occur when an event can be described in both mental and physiological terms. (3) For any true statement indicating a causal relation between two mental states, there must in principle be a true statement causally relating two corresponding physiological states. (4) Complete psychophysiological explanations therefore require a combination of statements specifying causal relations and statements specifying identity relations.

These four rules are logical consequences of almost all monist mind-brain philosophies and are therefore independent of any specific metaphysic. The rules are inconsistent with dualist interactionism and epiphenominalism. However, these latter positions have little heuristic value for psychosomatic theory. Interactionism leads to an infinite regress; epiphenominalism suggests that psychosomatic theory might be abandoned altogether. It is therefore proposed that theoretical complementarity and causal isomorphism be adopted as linguistic conventions regulating the joint use of mental and physiological terms.

References

Block, N., & Fodor, J. A. (1972). What psychological states are not. *Philosophical Review, 82,* 159-181).

Bohr, N. (1934). *Atomic theory and the description of nature.* Cambridge, England: Cambridge University Press.

Bohr, N. (1949). Discussions with Einstein on epistemological problems in atomic physics. In P. A. Schilpp (Ed.), *Albert Einstein, philosopher-physicist* (pp. 199-242). Evanston, IL: Northwestern University.

Boyd, R. (1980). Materialism without reductionism: What physicalism does not entail. In N. Block (Ed.), *Readings in philosophy of psychology* (pp. 67-106). Cambridge, MA: Harvard University Press.

Fodor, J. (1968). *Psychological explanation: an introduction to the philosophy of psychology.* New York: Random House.

Hyland, M. E. (1985). Do person variables exist in different ways? *American Psychologist, 40,* 1003-1010.
Kirsch, I. (1985). Response expectancy as a determinant of experience and behavior. *American Psychologist, 40,* 1189-1202.
Mackay, D. M. (1958). Complementarity II. *Proceedings of the Aristotelean Society, 32,* 105-122.
Pribram, K. H. (1986). The cognitive revolution and mind/brain issues. *American Psychologist, 41,* 507-520.
Smart, J. J. C. (1963). Materialism. *Journal of Philosophy, 60,* 651-662.
Wundt, W. (1969). *Outlines of psychology* (C. H. Judd, Trans.). St. Clair Shores, MI: Scholarly Press. (Original work published in 1897)

ON THEORY AND METHOD IN PSYCHOLOGY

Kurt Danziger

York University
North York, Ontario, Canada

SUMMARY: Methods involve the application of specific ordering principles in order to construct empirical domains. These principles are not theory neutral but are based on definite ontological presuppositions. Where the presuppositions of a method conflict with those of a particular theory, that theory cannot be appropriately tested by an application of this method. However, it is an important function of methods, not only to 'test' theories, but also to demonstrate them in action. Where the theories in question refer to the foundations of human social action appropriate methods are those which constitute empirical domains that reflect the structure of such action.

Traditional research practice in psychology proceeded as though theories and methods were, in some fundamental sense, independent of one another. Methods were assumed to be theory neutral, so that, in principle, any method could be used to confirm a theory. The choice of methods was supposed to be determined by considerations that were seen as purely technical in nature, considerations like precision and reliability, for example. What was not addressed was the question of the adequacy of the methods in terms of doing justice to the theories to be tested. Within this ideology of research practice theories did not enjoy the same high status as methods. Theories were seen as the personal products of individual theorists and therefore subject to accidental and irrational influences. Methods, on the other hand, were treated as though they were purely rational constructions. In fact, the rationality of the whole enterprise was guaranteed by the nature of its methodology and not by any quality of its theoretical constructions.

Because theories were regarded as containing a strong arbitrary element, while methods were regarded as subject only to rational considerations, theories had to justify themselves before the tribunal of methodology. But to do its work with justice this tribunal had to apply the same law to all. This law consisted of a set of methodological prescriptions which were considered to be generally applicable because they were held to embody universal principles of scientific reasoning.

However, when we turn from ideology to the actual history of modern psychology we find that major differences of theoretical orientation were generally associated with non-accidental differences in methodology. By way of illustration we need only remind ourselves of the different methodologies of behaviourists, Gestaltists and psycho-analysts, though many other examples could be cited, e.g., the methodological divergence among the major varieties of neobehaviourism (Smith, 1986).

Furthermore, the development, among post-positivist philosophers of science, of more differentiated views about the interrelationship of theory and method (Laudan, 1977; Laudan, 1984; Nickles, 1974; Shapere, 1984) leads to the rejection of any simplistic notions about the theory-neutrality of method. In this paper I plan to explore certain consequences of this reorientation.

Let me begin by characterizing the nature of method. A method consists of an ordered set of practices whose employment will yield a special kind of product which we call data. The ordering of practices proceeds according to identifiable rules, which may be either explicit or implicit. In other words, a method is a specifically structured set of activities for the production of a specifically structured kind of outcome. There is a necessary relationship between the structure of the procedures and the structure of what those procedures produce. Typically, a certain methodological structure will produce data that display a particular structure and will be incapable of producing differently structured data (Danziger, 1985).

By way of illustration, let us turn to Ebbinghaus' ground breaking work on memory, which involved the use of apparently meaningless nonsense syllables. These were structured in a way that has become very familiar. However, if we limit ourselves to saying that Ebbinghaus experimented with nonsense syllables we will have missed the crucial structural feature of his method. He himself was very clear about the fact that his instrument was not the nonsense syllable but the *series* of nonsense syllables. All his data are based, not on a mere collection of syllables, but on a specific arrangement of syllables. The structure of this arrangement is that of a linear sequence of equivalent units with a determinate length that is countable in terms of the number of units. The use of such an instrument necessarily yields numerically structured data, because this is the structure that was built into the method (Danziger, 1987a).

But that is only one side of Ebbinghaus' method. The other side involves a further structuring of the experimental subjects's activity. The process of the subject's familiarization with the stimulus material is deliberately broken up into a number of equivalent segments, called trials, which follow one another in a linear chronological sequence. In other words, the structure of an arithmetic series recurs in the activity of the experimental subject.

To appreciate the significance of this methodological arrangement, which has become utterly taken for granted in modern psychology, we need to compare it with what had gone before. In more traditional investigations experimental subjects might also have to engage the stimulus situation repeatedly, but these repetitions did not constitute a cumulative series. They were not 'trials' but repetitions of the experimental observation for the purpose of increasing reliability and decreasing observational error. This aspect also recurs elsewhere in Ebbinghaus' methodology, but of course the point of repeated attempts at memorizing a particular list lies not in mere repetition but in *cumulative* repetition.

Ebbinghaus' method is therefore based on the confrontation of two arithmetically structured series, the stimulus series of nonsense syllables and the series of trials which represent the activity of memorizing. This makes it possible to establish functional relationships between what are now two sets of variables. The method is tailor made to yield this type of result.

So much for the structural homology of a method and its products, but where does theory come in? It should be clear that Ebbinghaus' method is custom made, not only for producing a certain type of data, but also for verifying a certain type of theory. This theory will have to be of the kind that makes predictions about functional relationships between quantities of effort expended by an individual and quantities of memorized material. That was just the kind of theory Ebbinghaus was interested in, because, as we know from the unpublished first draft of his classic monograph *On Memory,* he started out with the basic conception of memory as a kind of *work*. He needed a method that would enable him to study the mental work of memory in a manner that was analogous to the techniques for measuring physical work.

This historical example illustrates a general point about the relationship of method and theory. The point is that the application of a particular method entails certain presuppositions about the nature of that to which the method is applied. Moreover, these presuppositions can never be refuted by any application of the method because they constitute an axiomatic basis that is built into the very structure of the method. Nor can there be a method of investigation that does not entail ontological presuppositions about the object investigated. This is so because a method is a way of ordering observations, of embedding any single observation in a particular network of relationships to other observations. Applying a method means applying certain principles of ordering, in order to produce a constructed empirical domain. Whether any regularities in this domain have any relevance for another domain (i.e., for another constructed domain or for the natural world) will depend on the appropriateness of the ordering principles built into the method.

In modern psychology we are not concerned with purely speculative theories but only with theories that are linked to specified empirical domains. These empirical domains are created by the application of particular methodologies which embody certain principles of ordering. Theoretical psychology therefore involves two levels which should be clearly distinguished. On the one hand, there is the familiar level of substantive theory which is concerned with explaining, making sense of, and predicting relationships within the relevant empirical domain *once such a domain has been brought into existence.* But there is also another level of theory which is necessary in order to *constitute* the empirical domain in the first place. This level involves the theoretical assumptions which provide the foundations for the methods by which relevant empirical domains are created. This constitutive level of theory is never put at risk by any *specific* empirical content belonging to the domain it has helped to create. The only way in which this level of theory can be judged is by putting a value on its related empirical domain *as a whole.*

While we have to make a sharp analytical distinction between the theoretical presuppositions that are necessary to constitute an empirical domain and the specific theories that can be tested within that domain, this does not mean that constitutive principles ever become irrelevant to the testing of theories. On the contrary, such principles are always presupposed when a theoretical prediction is made. Strictly speaking, any theoretical prediction should always be preceded by the conditional clause, 'given an empirical domain ordered according to principles X, Y, Z,' followed by the specific prediction. In practice this conditional statement is generally left implicit because everyone understands what kind of empirical domain is meant. This does little harm, as long as the relevant constitutive principles remain in operation. But psychology is characterized by a multiplicity of constitutive principles and hence by a multiplicity of empirical domains. When specific predictions are transferred from one domain to another the outcome will be meaningless unless it is accompanied by an appropriate theoretical transformation.

For instance, epidemiological studies of psychopathological syndromes are strictly irrelevant to psycho-analytic theory because in order to constitute the empirical domain of epidemiological data we have to make theoretical assumptions that are entirely different from those that are presupposed by the psycho-analytic situation (Caplan, 1986; Edelson, 1986). We could of course develop a new theory, a theory about epidemiological aspects of psycho-pathology, and this new theory might be in part inspired by certain *conclusions* of psycho-analysis, but this new theory would not be a psycho-analytic theory. It would be as inappropriate to test this new theory in the psycho-analytic situation as to test psycho-analytic theory in the epidemiological domain.

This type of problem illustrates the need to pay more attention to the methodological commitments that have invariably been part of the various theoretical positions adopted within twentieth century psychology. To do this effectively, however, requires a considerable amount of historical and conceptual analysis. The norms of scientific discourse which psychologists have followed obliged them to be explicit about their *specific* theories and *specific* procedures, but they did not oblige them to be equally explicit about their most general methodological assumptions. It is therefore incumbent on those who are interested in general theoretical questions to make up for this limitation of everyday disciplinary discourse and to make explicit what is commonly taken for granted within the different types of research practice (cf. Gigerenzer & Murray, 1987).

One extremely successful type of research practice, for example, is based on a statistical ordering of empirical domains. It must be emphasized that this is not at all equivalent to the use of statistical techniques in psychological research. Such techniques can be employed in one of two ways. They can be used simply as techniques for further analysis of an empirical domain that already exists prior to this procedure, or they can be used to *constitute* an empirical domain which owes its very existence to the application of statistical principles (Danziger, 1987b). It is only in the second case that these principles function as fundamental ordering principles of the type discussed here. For example, if we apply statistical methods to estimate the likely error of a set of observations, they do no more than provide a gloss on an empirical domain that already exists. However, when we construct a psychometric instrument for assessing individual differences the statistical principles play a much more fundamental role, because they are crucial to the constitution of the empirical domain as such. There are theories that are relevant to such statistically constituted domains, and there are theories that are irrelevant or even incompatible with the assumptions on which such domains are based.

One of the few psychologists who explicitly recognized the theoretical significance of the constitutive use of statistics was Kurt Lewin. As we know, he coupled this recognition with a plea for an alternative set of principles to be used in the construction and ordering of psychological data domains (Lewin, 1935). He initiated the use of a type of empirical domain which was constituted by a system of interdependent and co-existing elements whose inter-relationship was neither scalar nor temporal but was that of situational forms. Lewin saw, what most of his American students do not seem to have accepted, namely, that this way of constituting an empirical domain was fundamentally incompatible with statistical principles of ordering that require the abstraction of individual properties to form aggregate classes of inter-individual elements (Lewin, 1981). A distinctively Lewinian theory could not survive such a fundamental reconstruction of its co-ordinate empirical domain.

Freudian theory represents a somewhat similar case in that it too is intimately bound up with the construction of a special empirical domain according to its own characteristic ordering principles. It is astonishing how rarely attempts at 'testing' psycho-analytic theory have confronted the question of a possible incompatibility between some of Freud's theoretical assumptions and those necessary for the constitution of the empirical domain in which the testing is to take place.

More generally, a recognition of the interdependence of theory and method involves a changed conception of their functional relationship. In the received view that relationship was dominated by the function of testing. Methods had the function of testing theories. But if the application of methods is itself theory laden then it is unlikely that they will be able to carry out this testing function fairly. This is not to say that methods can *never* be employed to test theories, but it does mean that they can only be so employed under rather special conditions. Ideally, any application of a specific methodology for the purpose of testing a particular theory should be preceded by a demonstration that the ontological presuppositions of the methodology do not conflict with those of the theory to be tested in any relevant respect. Unfortunately, because of the pervasiveness of the belief in the theory neutrality of method, this issue is virtually never addressed in psychological research practice.

But while our reorientation calls for a restriction of the testing function of methods vis-à-vis theories it should also revive our interest in other functions. Under the influence of logical empiricism psychological research practice came to be dominated by norms that elevated the testing function to the only legitimate relationship between method and theory. This has made us forget that in past scientific practice, including that of psychology, the role which method was called upon to play was generally not one of *testing* theories but of *demonstrating* or applying them. This distinction may be illustrated by referring to the difference between a logical deduction and a working model. I may employ a particular methodology to test specific outcomes that are logically derived from a theory, or I may employ it to construct a working model that demonstrates the theory in action.

The kinds of working models we are familiar with involve the use of formal and physical principles, as in the case of physical simulations and logic machines. However, when one is dealing with psychological theories that have reference to human social conduct, it is not possible to construct non-trivial empirical domains solely by the use of formal and physical principles. To give such domains their intended ontological status we have to identify them as belonging to the category of social action or interaction. For instance, the sequence of marks on paper produced by a subject in a social psychology experiment are to be understood as the social actions of a person in the (perhaps hypothetical) presence of another person. To make these marks mean what we want them to mean we have to see them as part of a social situation. But our understanding of social situations is also constructed according to certain, albeit implicit, rules. Giving a social meaning to our empirical domain therefore entails the presupposition that its elements are ordered in the manner characteristic of a social situation.

One consequence of this is that the construction of a 'working model' that has reference to interpersonal conduct will be more like a process of staging or dramatization than like machine construction. Social psychology experiments show this aspect very clearly, and I would suggest that it is fruitful to look at the practice of psycho-analysis in the same way (cf. Lorenzer, 1970). In both cases there is a pre-existing framework for a scenario which is provided by a theory, and certain specific details must be filled in by the participants. What we end up with is a demonstration of the theory in action, but certainly not a logically rigorous testing of it (cf. Holzkamp, 1986). The pretence that social psychological theories are 'tested' in social psychological experiments or that psycho-analytic theories are 'tested' in therapeutic sessions has been a source of endless confusions and difficulties for both areas. This pretence is of course a product of the belief that the only legitimate relationship between theory and method is constituted by the testing function. However, a recognition of the interdependence of theory and method should lead to a more differentiated view of a variety of fruitful relationships that may exist between them (cf. Gergen, 1982).

Social psychological experiments and psycho-analytic sessions may or may not provide powerful demonstrations of certain theoretical claims. But if they were weak it would not be because they failed as tests but because they failed as demonstrations. The criteria of a good demonstration are not identical with the criteria of a good test. If we undertake to judge these methods as tests we are asking the wrong kind of question.

In the last analysis scientific methods have the function of producing the conditions for a special kind of 'witnessing' (Shapin & Schaffer, 1985). These conditions necessarily contain both social and logical components. As a result of long established and successful practice we may lose sight of the social component because it has come to be taken for granted. In that case we may be tempted to regard scientific witnessing as a purely logical process. In the physical sciences this may not matter much because the social component does not need to be reflected on the theoretical level. But in certain areas of psychology the methods are essentially devices for producing an empirical scenario that is claimed to be an enactment of a theoretical scenario. The worth of such demonstrations cannot be judged on purely logical criteria; the criteria for their evaluation will also have to be based on social categories.

References

Caplan, A. (1986). Comment on Grunbaum. *Behavioural and Brain Sciences, 9,* 228-229.

Danziger, K. (1985). The methodological imperative in psychology. *Philosophy of the Social Sciences, 15,* 1-13.

Danziger, K. (1987a). Herman Ebbinghaus and the psychological experiment. In W. Traxel (Ed.), Ebbinghaus and the psychological experiment, (Ebbinghaus-Studien 2), *Passauer Schriften zur Psychologiegeschichte, 5,* 217-224.

Danziger, K. (1987b). Statistical method and the historical development of research practice in American psychology. In G Gigerenzer, M. Morgan, & L. Kruger (Eds.), *The probabalistic revolution: Ideas in modern science* (Vol. 2, pp. 35-47). Cambridge, MA: MIT Press.

Ebbinghaus, H. (1983). *Urmanuskript "Ueber das Gedaechtnis" 1880* (W. Traxel, Ed.). Passau: Passavia.

Edelson, M. (1986). The evidential value of the psychoanalyst's clinical data. *Behavioral and Brain Sciences, 9,* 232-234.

Gergen, K. J. (1982). *Toward transformation in social knowledge.* New York: Springer.

Gigerenzer, G., & Murray, D. J. (1987). *Cognition as intuitive statistics.* Hilsdale, NJ: Lawrence Erlbaum.

Holzkamp, K. (1986). Wieweit können sozialpsychologische Theorien experimentell geprüft werden? *Zeitschrift für Sozialpsychologie, 17,* 216-238.

Laudan, L. (1977). *Progress and its problems: Towards a theory of scientific growth.* Berkeley: University of California Press.

Laudan, L. (1984). *Science and values.* Berkeley: University of California Press.

Lewin, K. (1935). The conflict between Aristotelian and Galileian modes of thought in contemporary psychology. In K. Lewin *Dynamic theory of personality.* (pp. 1-42). New York: McGraw-Hill.

Lewin, K. (1981). Gesetz und Experiment in der Psychologie. In C. F. Graumann & A. Métraux (Eds.), *Kurt Lewin Werkausgabe* (Vol. 1). Bern: Huber.

Lorenzer, A. (1970). *Sprachzerstörung und Rekonstruktion.* Frankfurt: Suhrkamp.

Nickles, T. (1974). Heuristics and justification in scientific research. In F. Suppe (Ed.), *The structure of scientific theories.* (pp. 571-599). Urbana, IL: University of Illinois Press.

Shapere, D. (1984). *Reason and the search for knowledge.* Dordrecht: Reidel.

Shapin, S., & Schaffer, S. (1985). *Leviathan and the air-pump: Hobbes, Boyle and the experimental life.* Princeton: Princeton University Press.

Smith, L. (1986). *Behaviorism and logical positivism.* Stanford, CA: Stanford University Press.

PSYCHOLOGY'S RELATION TO BIOLOGY:

QUALITATIVELY DISTINCT LEVELS

Carl Ratner

Humboldt State University
Arcata, CA, U.S.A.

SUMMARY: Biology is construed as a broad substratum which is necessary for psychology but which does not strictly determine it. This model of 'relative autonomy' is supported by evidence from human genetics, neurophysiology, sexual behavior, and aggression. Psychology's relative autonomy is contrasted with animal behavior and neonatal activity, and is shown to be the source of our creativity, freedom, intelligence, individuality, and culture.

Although psychology was born from biology over a century ago, it has not yet emancipated itself from its intellectual heritage. A strong biologistic bias persists which regards biology as directly causing, determining, and explaining psychological phenomena, to some extent or another. Some examples of this biologism are *sociobiology*, which posits genetic determinants of aggression, religion, private property, ethics, aesthetics, and marriage customs, *psychobiological explanations of mental illness,* which emphasize genetic and/or neurotransmitter defects, *Chomsky's linguistic* notions of a universal grammar and a language acquisition device; and the *study of individual differences* which posits genetic determinants of individual and gender differences in cognitive skills and personality.

This brief list indicates the pervasiveness of biologism which is further confirmed by a recent survey which found that 70% of psychologists believe that intelligence is inherited to some extent (Snyderman & Rothman, 1987).

Most biologistic formulations recognize other determinants of psychology (such as physical and social experience) in addition to biology. Most biologistic theories are therefore *multifactorial.* While this appears to betoken a broad open-mindedness to diverse factors, the multifactorial position is ultimately unsatisfactory. One reason is that the various factors are not integrated in a consistent formulation, they are merely posited as co-existing with each contributing some amount of 'weight' to psychology. What must be answered is how biology and experience *function* together, not simply how much weight each throws into the pot. The multifactorial position persists in construing biology as a factor with specific determining properties. Such 'interactionism' does not recognize that biology must be qualitatively transformed in order to blend with experience. Experience cannot simply be added onto biological factors in some external, haphazard, and unspecified fashion. Finally, multifactorial theories usually consider biology to be the most important factor, as in claims that intelligence and schizophrenia have heritability factors of 80% (Gottesman & Shields, 1982), in Piaget's recognition that cognitive stages are universal with social experience only affecting the age-speed at which they arrive, in Chomsky's disparaging of particular syntax and semantics in favor of biologically programmed universal structures, and in Freud's relegating of socialization to facilitating or inhibiting natural psycho-sexual stages of development.

I contend that the biological and multifactorial models are wrong, not simply in the weight they attribute to biological influences, but in the entire conception of biology being a causal factor at all. Instead of biology being a causal factor on the same level with social and physical experience, I maintain that biology is rather a necessary substratum for all psychological activities which does not directly determine any of them. Psychology is functionally autonomous, or qualitatively different, from biology and functions according to its own principles. Indeed, this autonomy is the very basis of our creativity, freedom, intelligence, and fulfillment which biological determinism restricts. This notion of different *levels* may be called the 'multilevel' model in contrast to the multifactorial notion of different factors on the same level of functioning. The two models are diagrammed in Figure 1.

Before verifying the multilevel model, let me illustrate it's plausibility with the following rough but useful analogy of the relation between a car engine and driving. While the engine and driving behavior are interdependent in certain ways, they do not stand in a one to one relationship: Obviously, normal driving requires an intact engine, and a faulty motor impairs all driving. The physical parameters of the engine set certain limits on performance; however, a car with a normal engine can be driven in a wide variety of ways, some good, some bad, which have nothing to do with the engine itself. Good driving skills must be learned in their own right, they are not by-products of car engines. Similarly, most driving problems are due to human errors in judgement, *not* to engine misfunctions. Ameliorating these problems requires conscientious attention to driving, not to the engine. Only the comparatively few driving errors which are exclusively due to faulty engines can be entirely corrected by mechanical means. Furthermore, adequate driving skills cannot be improved by supercharging a normal motor; again, only diligent learning and practice of *driving principles* will suffice. In fact, most drivers will most probably drive more recklessly with a supercharged car as they will erroneously assume that greater speed is equivalent to skill. Finally, indi-

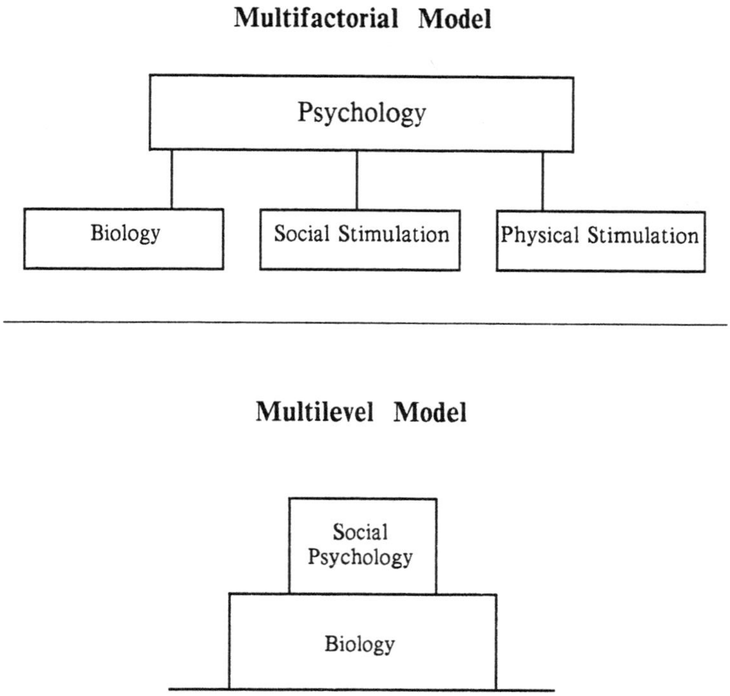

Fig. 1. Multifactorial and Multilevel Models.

vidual differences in cars have little, if any, impact on driving skill or the destination to which one drives.

Human biology has even less direct impact on psychology than car engines do on driving. Both fulfilling and deleterious psychological activities are developed in their own right and are not explainable in biological terms. The vast majority of psychological disturbances occur in healthy bodies and are as inaccessible to physiological treatment as tailgating is to car repair. Similarly, attempting to enhance normal psychology by advancing normal physiology will be as unsuccessful as souping up a car engine is in improving normal driving skills. Finally, individual physical differences have little bearing on adult psychology which is a function of physical and social experiences.

This qualitative distinctiveness of levels has been cogently advocated by Alex Novikoff (1945) who stated:

> Each level of organization possesses unique properties of structure and behavior which, though dependent on the properties of the constituent elements, appear only when these elements are combined in the new sys-

tem. Knowledge of the laws of the lower level is necessary for a full understanding of the higher level; yet the unique properties of phenomena at the higher level can not be predicted, ***a priori***, from the laws of the lower level. The laws describing the ***unique*** properties of each level are qualitatively distinct, and their discovery requires methods of research and analysis appropriate to the particular level (p. 209).

Just as biology has unique properties which have emerged from combinations of physical and chemical matter and cannot be reduced to them, so "man's social relationships represent a new level, higher than that of his biological make-up." Indeed, "Socio-economic or cultural forces come to dominate biological factors in directing man's actions." "The concept of integrative levels, as it stresses the need to study the interrelationships between the biological and sociological, emphasizes the fact that the two constitute two distinct levels. Blurring this distinction leads to anthropomorphism and to mystical, often dangerous, statements about society" (Ibid).

We shall now verify the multileveled relationship between biology and psychology by examining evidence regarding the non-determining role of genetics, hormones, and neurophysiology in psychology. Some of the evidence is well known, but my purpose is to go beyond its empirical truth to demonstrate broader implications for the general question we are addressing. In other words, I want to generalize from particular examples to necessary truths about any and all instances of the phenomena. It is not a matter of whether hormones determine one or another activities but whether their function in human nature enables them to determine *any* psychological activity. Moreover, evidence concerning hormones, genetics, and the cortex do not simply tell us about the effects of these particular systems on psychology, but rather enable us to understand the more general question of *biology's* relation to psychology. As the rationalist philosophers so cogently argued, particulars give us insight into general essences.

Genetics

Many anthropologists have described the autonomy of human *activity* (as opposed to anatomy) from *strict* genetic determination. This is especially evident historically where LaBarre, Kroeber, Leakey, Montagu, and Pannekoek observed that cultural, mental, and technological changes have occurred over many millenia without any significant corresponding genetic transformations. The same genetic structure obviously supports an enormous variety of activities without determining them, and therefore functions as a general substratum which engenders only the most abstract capacities, rather than particular processes. As Montagu (1957, p. 16) explained, "man alone is the creature who possesses a genotype, a genetic endowment, with the maximum capacity for phenotypic adjustment."

Human adaptation and survival depend on intelligently devised actions, not on organismic, genetically produced, changes (Montagu, 1962, p. x). Human evolution occurs through mastering the environment, not by genetically adjusting to it (Dobzhansky, 1960, p. 206). LaBarre (1955) explains the advantage that extra-biological evolution gives humans:

> Machines not only can do man's flying, diving, and superhuman seeing and hearing for him, but also ***they do his evolving for him***...The old-style evolution by body adaptation is obsolete. All previous animals had been subject to the ***autoplastic*** evolution of their self-substance, committing their bodies to experimental adaptations in a blind genetic gamble for survival. The stakes in this game were high: life or death. Man's evolution, on the other hand, is through ***alloplastic*** experiments with objects outside his own body and is concerned only with the products of his hands, brains, and eyes - and not with his body itself...(p. 90).

It is not only the genetic freedom of man's new kind of evolution that is significant; one has to consider the fantastic speed of it as well. It took millions and millions of years from fish to whale to evolve a warm-blooded marine mammal: but man evolved submarines from dream to actuality in a mere few centuries and at no genetic price in physical specialization (Ibid., p. 91).

Animal evolution via physical specialization results in the creation of entirely new species. Human's nonbiological evolution, in contrast, leaves the basic character of the species intact. (Pannekoek, 1953, pp. 88-90). By retaining all the variations within itself, the species undergoes a tremendous broadening of skills. In the animal kingdom, by contrast, skills are apportioned to different species which remain narrowly specialized. The elimination of genetic-physical evolution as a mechanism of behavioral change is thus a tremendous advantage.

Human's superior form of evolution occurs on a social rather than an individual level. "The real evolutionary unit now is not man's mere body; it is '*all mankind's brains together with all the extrabodily materials that come under the manipulation of their hands*'. Man's very physical ego is expanded to encompass everything within reach of his manipulating hands, within sight of his searching eyes, and within the scope of his restless brain" (LaBarre, 1955, p. 91).

The human surpassing of evolution exemplifies the higher level dialectical *aufhebung* of lower processes that Novikoff described above. That is, Darwinian evolution brought about the human species; however, we now react back on and control this process. We consciously decide which genotypes to propogate, both in our own and other species. The laws of evolution which created man continue to operate in the sense that genetic mutations are selected or deselected to propogate or eliminate physical characteristics; however, control over the laws shifts from blind adaptation via natural selection to conscious human selection. Control has shifted from lower processes determining higher ones ('bottom-up') to higher processes determining lower ones ('top-down').

Hormones

Research into hormones further confirms the conclusions from genetics. The behavior of low animals is directly controlled by hormones; however, the influence decreases in the higher animals and is unimportant in man. This is evident in sexuality and aggression.

As Washburn (1960) points out, whereas sex among animals is "subject to physiological - especially glandular - controls, in man these controls are gone, and are replaced by a bewildering variety of social custom." Of course, higher animals manifest somewhat greater independence from hormones than lower animals do; however, in most cases even nonhuman primates' sexual behavior is biologically regulated. This is demonstrated in four areas (Beach, 1947, 1958).

(a) Sexual activity is rigidly tied to estrus and the secretion of estrogen in the female animal, but not in the human female who is unique in being continuously receptive throughout the menstrual cycle, regardless of hormonal changes.

(b) Removal of animals' gonadal hormones through castration or ovariectomy prevents adult sexual activity if done before puberty, or eliminates it if done after puberty (Hoyenga & Hoyenga, 1979, p. 124, 126), however, reduction in hormonal levels has little if any affect on human sexual behavior. Ovariectomy and menopause in a high proportion of women produce no change in sexual desire, just as oral contraceptives, which inhibit ovarian, hypothalamic, and pituitary hormones, have no inhibiting affect on sexual activity (and, if anything, increase it!). Healthy males show a wide range of testosterone values (from about 350 to 1000 nanograms per 100 milliliters of blood) and variations within this range have no significance for sexual behavior (Rosenzweig & Leiman, 1982, p. 403). Castration of males sometimes leads to reduced interest in sex, however many individuals maintain an undiminished sexual drive and coital ability for several decades.

(c) Addition of hormones to depleted animals restores sexual behavior regardless of the age of original removal, however hormonal therapy to enhance sexual desire is not particularly effective in many men and women.

(d) Normal pre-pubescent animals (males and females) whose gonadal hormones have not begun secreting show no sexual activity (except in the case of apes where pre-pubertal males and females do often copulate); however, human children (especially in societies that encourage them) are known to indulge in sexual activities years before gonadal hormones have begun functioning (Rosenzweig & Leiman, 1982, p. 404).

Summing up the evolutionary changes which have resulted in the diminished influence of hormones on sexual activity, Beach (1947) concludes:

> Evidence pertaining to prepuberal sexual activity, to the correlation of sexual behavior with cycles of [hormonal] secretion and to the effects of ovariectomy [as well as castration] followed by replacement therapy suggests that advancing phyletic status is accompanied by progressive relaxation of rigorous hormonal control over sexual receptivity. It appears that in the course of mammalian evolution, and specifically in the development of the primate stem, the physiological basis for sexual behavior has undergone certain modifications which have tended to free...sexual responsiveness from complete dependence upon...hormones (p. 300, 303).

Exactly the same evolutionary trend toward independence from biological determination exists in the case of aggression. Lloyd (1975) cites several works which indicate decreased hormonal control over aggression with evolutionary ascent to the higher species. In mice, reduction in the level of circulating androgen produced by castration is associated with profound reduction in intermale aggressive behavior. Accordingly, reduction in androgens results in a lowering of rats' and mice's social dominance position. Restoring testosterone by injection in castrated animals increases fighting behavior in mice in a dose-related manner. Androgens likewise enhance the social position of chickens and fish.

Effects of androgen on aggression are even less pronounced in primates. Investigations done on castrated rhesus monkeys have failed to find any straightforward relationship between castration and the lessening of aggressive behavior or social dominance (Lloyd, 1975, p. 190). Actually, among primates hormonal levels appear to be a *consequence of* responses to environmental conditions rather than a cause of behavior. Thus, it is *after* attaining a position of social dominance that rhesus monkeys displayed a two to three-fold increase in testosterone levels. Introduction of these same males into groups of strange males where they were subject to sudden defeat resulted in declines in their levels of plasma testosterone (Lloyd, 1975, p. 189, 196).

Among humans, aggression is a function of consciously controlled experience, not hormones. Rosenzweig & Leiman (1982, p. 535) have written "it is not clear that levels of androgens in intact men is related to aggressiveness." Anne Fausto-Sterling (1985, chapter 5) has comprehensively reviewed and evaluated studies dealing with the relation between hormones and aggression. She effectively demolishes the belief that testosterone causes aggression and that reducing testosterone via castration or other chemical means reduces aggression. For example, one study of castrated men found the treatment so ineffective that nine out of 16 subjects subsequently died as a result of aggressive encounters. "The few studies on the effects of 'chemical castration' on violent or aggressive behavior conclude that the procedure is not particularly effective" (Fausto-Sterling, 1985, p. 127).

Cortex

The human cortex manifests the same indeterminacy with regard to behavior that hormones and genes do. In fact, the cortex is the mechanism which enables voluntary action, and learning through experience, to occur. Contrasting cortically mediated activity with subcortically controlled behavior, Beach notes:

> Heredity, as represented by the relatively stereotyped and inflexible functions or capacities of the subcortical neural mechanisms and the gonadal hormones, plays the major role in the courtship and mating of subprimate species. Environment or experience, as it affects the more modifiable cortical functions and the capacity of cortical activity to alter the responsiveness of lower centers, is of primary importance in the sexual behavior of the higher mammals (Beach, 1947, p. 310).

In other words, the cortex, suppresses biology as a directly determining force and transforms it into a general underpinning for consciousness. Paradoxically, the cortex accomplishes this by virtue of its distinctive *physical* characteristics, which means that consciousness is ultimately a form of materialism, but a unique kind of materialism which transcends its given materiality and fosters extra-biological conscious, social and technological mediations.

Roger Sperry (1965, 1969, 1970, 1980, 1986) has formulated this with unsurpassed clarity, and his work should be intensively studied in order to understand the full nature of this mind-brain relationship. Employing the dialectical notion of 'emergence' with great sophistication, Sperry emphasizes how, on the one hand, consciousness is composed and constituted of physiological and physiochemical elements, is inextricably linked to and inseparable from them, and is not a supernatural element apart from and added onto them. Yet, consciousness is a new form or organization of brain functions which possesses new 'macro-properties' and laws which are subjective, mental, and volitional. "The subjective qualities are recognized to be real and causal in their own right, as subjectively experienced, and to be of very different quality from the neural, molecular, and other material components of which they are built" (Sperry, 1980, p. 204).

Sperry (1980) describes how, in 1965, he, John Eccles, and Karl Popper all revised their earlier reductionistic conceptualizations, which explained consciousness as nothing but neurophysiological processes *without any emergent properties of its own,* into a dialectical model in which consciousness is both physical and more than physical, or mental. Sperry rejects mechanistic materialism (that is, reductionism, or mind-brain identity) and also dualism which posits the mind apart from the brain. The mind is part of the brain but a unique *mental* part. This is, in our terms, a 'dialectical monism' which recognizes the mind and brain as inseparable parts of the same continuous hierarchy, yet recognizes the mind as a unique, subjective, function in this hierarchy. The subjective mind does not negate or by-pass micro-processes, it supersedes and supplements them, using them for its own ends by virtue of belonging to the same system as they do. Addressing the humanistic implications of his brain model, Sperry (1965) eloquently states:

> Mind and consciousness are put in the driver's seat, as it were: They give the orders, and they push and haul around the physiology and the physical chemical processes as much as or more than the latter processes direct them...It is a scheme that idealizes ideas and ideals over physical and chemical interactions, nerve impulse traffic, and DNA. It is a brain model in which conscious mental psychic forces are recognized to be the crowning achievement of some five hundred million years or more of evolution...In the brain model described here, man is provided in large measure with the mental forces and the mental ability to determine his own actions. This scheme thus allows a high degree of freedom from outside forces as well as mastery over the inner cellular, molecular, and atomic aspects of brain activity. Depending on the state of one's will power, the model also allows considerable freedom from lower-level natural impulses... (p. 78, 87).

As the cortex develops phylogenetically and ontogenetically, it subsumes more functions under its control and removes them from innate, fixed mechanisms such as genes and hormones (Rose, 1976, p. 195; Birch & Lefford, 1963, 1967).

Human biology, especially the cortex, is a paradoxical force which transcends itself in allowing *non-biological* (or extra-biological) influences on activity. It exposes the organism to the world via conscious, social, and technological mediations, rather than providing natural direct responses to stimuli. The cortex controls the peripheral nervous system and lower parts of the central nervous system *not* by *imposing* biological imperatives on them but by *removing* biological determinants, thereby allowing experience and volition a unique measure of control.

Intelligence is only possible given the *elimination* of constraining biological determinations, which makes the search for such determinants quite misguided. Indeed, the transformation of biology from a determining role to a general substratum weakens it as a factor accounting for individual psychological differences since it doesn't account for any specific psychological functions. Actually, individual differences are more pronounced in man than in animals because our experience is diversified, while animals' experience is relatively homogeneous due to its being constrained along species-wide biological lines. Human capacity is universal whereas performance is highly individualized; animal competence varies with the species and subgroups within the species. However, all members of each group manifest similar performance. Human performance is differentiated from biological capacity while animal performance is tied to (regulated by) biological capacity.

Finally, the elimination of biological determination in man leads to its replacement by culture. Biological determination prevents culture from developing by imposing pre-given constraints on behavior, and this is why animals have no significant culture. Culture, as Geertz observes, is a human necessity because our biology does not tell us how to act. "A fully specified, adaptively sufficient definition of regnant neural processes in terms of intrinsic parameters being impossible, the human brain is thoroughly dependent upon cultural resources for its very operation; and those resources are, consequently, not adjuncts to, but constituents of, mental activity" (Geertz, 1973, p. 76).[1]

The multifactorial model which posits culture as one factor operating on the same level as, and added to, biology is therefore fallacious and cannot explain why animals have not been able to add culture onto their biologies. The correct integration of social-psychology and biology must recognize a qualitative difference in levels and functions which is uniquely pronounced in humans. Biologistic and multifactorial models persist in accommodating biological determinism which only occurs among animals, human infants, and biologically abnormal human adults. Neither of these models has been or will be able to account for the psychology of biologically normal human adults.

References

Beach, F. A. (1947). Evolutionary changes in the physiological control of mating behavior in mammals. *Psychological Review, 54*, 297-311.

Beach, F. A. (1958). Neural and chemical regulation of behavior. In H. F. Harlow & C. Woolsey, (Eds.), *Biological and biochemical bases of behavior* (pp. 263-284). Madison: University of Wisconsin Press.

Bernard, L. L. (1924). *Instinct, a study in social psychology.* New York: Holt.

---

[1]Cognitive and cultural developments are not only potentiated by a reduction in biological determinism, they also act on it: they constitute a selective pressure to weaken biological determinism because they are more adaptive than it is.

Birch, H., & Lefford, A. (1963). Intersory development in children. *Monographs of the Society for Research in Child Development, 28,* 5.

Birch, H., & Lefford, A. (1967). Visual differentiation, intersensory integration, and voluntary motor control. *Monographs of the Society for Research in Child Development, 32,* 2.

Fausto-Sperling, A. (1985). *Myths of gender: Biological theories about women and men.* New York: Basic Books.

Geertz, C. (1973). *The interpretation of cultures.* New York: Basic Books.

Gottesman, I., & Shields, J. (1982). *Schizophrenia: The epigenetic puzzle.* New York: Cambridge University Press.

Hoyenga, K., & Hoyenga, K. (1979). *The question of sex differences.* Boston: Little Brown.

LaBarre, W. (1955). *The human animal.* Chicago, IL: University of Chicago Press.

Lloyd, J. (1975). Social behavior and hormones. In B. Elftheriou & R. Sprott (Eds.), *Hormonal correlates of behavior* (Vol. 1, Chap. 4). New York: Plenum.

Montagu, A. (1957). *Anthropology and human nature.* Boston: Porter Sargent.

Novikoff, A. (1945, March 2). The concept of integrative levels and biology. *Science,* 209-215.

Pannekoek, A. (1944/1953). *Anthropogenesis, a study of the origin of man.* Amsterdam: North-Holland.

Rose, S. (1976). *The conscious brain.* New York: Vintage.

Rosenzweig, M., & Leiman, A. (1982). *Physiological psychology.* Boston, MA: Heath.

Scheler, M. (1961). *Man's place in nature.* New York: Schocken.

Snyderman, M., & Rothman, S. (1987). Survey of expert opinion on intelligence and aptitude testing. *American Psychologist, 42,* 137-144.

Sperry, R. W. (1965). Mind, brain, and humanist values. In J. Platt (Ed.), *New views of the nature of man* (Chap. 4). Chicago: University of Chicago Press.

Sperry, R. W. (1969). A modified concept of consciousness. *Psychological Review, 76,* 532-536.

Sperry, R. W. (1970). An objective approach to subjective experience: further explanation of a hypothesis. *Psychological Review, 77,* 585-590.

Sperry, R. W. (1977). Problems outstanding in the evolution of brain function. In R. Duncan & M. Weston-Smith (Eds.), The encyclopaedia of ignorance (pp. 423-433). New York: Pergamon Press.

Sperry, R. W. (1980). Mind-brain interaction: mentalism, yes; dualism, no. *Neuroscience, 5,* 195-206.

Sperry, R. W. (1986). Macro - versus micro-determinism. *Philosophy of Science, 53,* 265-270.

Washburn, S. L. (1960, Sept.). Tools and human evolution. *Scientific American,* 63-75.

INTERPRETATION STYLES OF PSYCHOLOGISTS AND THEIR CONSEQUENCES FOR PSYCHOLOGY

René van Hezewijk

University of Utrecht
Utrecht, The Netherlands

SUMMARY: One source of (dis)unity in psychology is often ignored, namely differences among psychologists in the way they relate theories and data to the world. Personal differences between ***interpretation styles*** contribute to disunity and discontinuity within psychology. The same data as well as the same concepts and theories may be interpreted in different ways, thereby adding fuel to misunderstanding, apparent 'incommensurability', etc. In this paper two opposite styles of interpretation are introduced. The works of Hermann von Helmholtz and Ernst Mach serve as examples. The paper concludes by noting the consequences of different interpretation styles in contemporary psychology.

Introduction

Insofar as theoretical disunity is a problem in psychology, three possible sources can be identified: ontological, methodological, and sociological. That is, theoretical disunity may be the result of the nature of the subject matter of psychology, of the strategies of research, and of the social organization of the scientific enterprise.

In this paper, I will not be concerned with any of these three sources of possible disunity (see Gholson & Barker, 1985; Staats, 1983; Vroon, 1987), instead a source of disunity is introduced that is seldom mentioned, namely, differences in the interpretation styles of psychologists.

I will begin with a short characterization of what is meant by 'interpretation style.' I will then describe two interpretation styles that represent opposite poles on a 'style' continuum of how data, concepts, and theoretical propositions are interpreted. Finally, I will analyze the differences between interpretation styles of Hermann von Helmholtz and Ernst Mach. In concluding I will give several examples of interpretation styles by referring to recent work in psychology.

Interpretation Styles

By now it is well accepted that there is no *a priori* way to decide whether a fact definitely and exclusively belongs to a theory (Quine, 1953, 1969; Popper, 1972, 1983). It takes a theory to make an event a fact; and it is the logical syntax of a proposition or statement which makes a fact a verifying or falsifying datum (Hezewijk, 1987). What is missing in this characterization is that individual researchers must interpret their concepts and data *as* concepts and data about reality. And in this interpretation, scientists who might otherwise agree, differ.

In other words, conflicts among views of individual scientists, even among those working within the same research programme, might be explained in terms of differences in the interpretation of how their data, concepts, and theories relate to reality. So by 'interpretation style' I am referring to invariances in the way a particular scientist relates data, concepts, and theories to reality, to the world. My understanding of interpretation style is closely related to the work of John T. Blackmore (1972; 1983) who revived a distinction made by William Hamilton (1852) between presentationalism and representationalism.

Presentationalism

Suppose that your sense organs by which you acquire knowledge change substantially, (for example, that the eye becomes sensible to a different range of light). What assertion would you most agree to?

1. "We would experience the world differently." or
2. "We would be living in a different world."

The presentationalist would more readily agree with the second assertion. Presentationalists presuppose, often without awareness, that the way we acquire knowledge of the world determines the way the world is. Reality reflects our information acquisition devices; the world is the way we know it. Thus the world is *present* to us precisely in the way our acquisition devices present that world; in short, knowing-being. Epistemologically the data we have access to *are* reality; what is inaccessible is non-existent and cannot be referred to.

Of course what one takes the world to be like still depends upon what one takes to be the media of information acquisition. Thus, sensationists who maintain that the world is given by the workings of our senses - sensation = being - would reject the existence of an entity which is not sensible. Or, again, phenomenologists maintain that the world is the way it appears in consciousness and what does not appear in consciousness does not exist. Epistemological idealism, direct and naive realism are all presentationalist in nature. Whatever other differences there might be among these positions, as presentationalist interpretation styles they resemble one another in an important respect, namely, the world is how we know, perceive, or experience it. *Esse est percipi.* There is nothing in the world beyond appearances.

Representationalism

Representationalists would tend to agree with the first assertion. Representationalists presuppose that reality is independent of our sensation, perception, or knowledge. Reality is always beyond, or more than we can directly know. Our knowledge of reality is always partial; appearances are mere tokens of reality. Our knowledge will never be a complete or certain copy of the world. Knowledge is merely a clue to reality. According to representationalists there is only one world which is hidden by a veil of appearances and of which we can only glance glimpses; there is no privileged access to the world as it is.

Presentationalism and Representationalism in Psychology

The distinction between presentational and representational styles is an important one for, especially, psychology where interest is focused on the not very observable domain of the mental. Thus, while 'narrow' presentationalists are unlikely to even recognize the existence of human cognitive, affective, and conative characteristics, the less narrow presentationalists, like the phenomenologists, would still identify the world with what has been, as it were, *a priori* decided upon. Representationalists face a different problem, namely how to discover what is characteristic of the human mind behind appearances.

The contrast between both styles, and the relevance of the distinction becomes clear when comparing two nineteenth century scientists: Hermann von Helmholtz (1821-1894) and Ernst Mach (1838-1916). Both had the same interests, both contributed to psychological research and theory, both stood in the German scientific and philosophical tradition, both were physicists by profession, and they can be considered as, more or less, contemporaries.

Hermann von Helmholtz

Helmholtz strongly defended empiricism. He was inclined to accept materialism and to reject vitalism. He did not accept any of the varieties of Kantianism that were popular in nineteenth century Germany. Helmholtz believed the task of science was to formulate the laws of nature. But note the way he interpreted this view on the task of science, and the role of observation and theory.

Helmholtz accepted that beyond appearances there were things-in-themselves. However, as an empiricist he distrusted all 'metaphysical speculation' about the real nature of these things. We do not have access to things-in-themselves and we never will. He did not conclude, however, we are totally shut off from reality. In science, observations are the source of hypotheses and laws concerning observable regularities. In turn, we try to understand the natural world with the aid of these laws. But in doing so, we presuppose that the laws are about real causes, about real forces, in nature. Although it is by means of observation that science can progress, we must assume there also are real but invisible objects, events, powers, and causal relationship among them, to which we have no privileged access except by means of their observable effects.

Helmholtz' psychology resembles his epistemology. Sensations, are caused by real objects and, hence, sensations must be considered as *signs*, each of which encodes some property of the object. Yet we see objects and not sensations. According to Helmholtz, we have learned to unconsciously interpret sensations as tokens of real objects: the images ('Vorstellungen') we form out of sensations *represent* external reality, but they are not copies or pictures of the world.

On Helmholtz' account, sensations are reliable clues about objects and, yet, due to perceptual decoding errors or encoding ambiguities, one can be mistaken. Psychologically, it is the role of learning, and epistemologically, it is the task of science, to discover which clues are 'real' and which clues are not. Thus, it is by finding regularities in sensation and perception that we discover the hidden order (see Helmholtz, 1962, 1865, 1871, 1876; Warren & Warren, 1968; Koenigsberger, 1902, 1903; Meijering, 1981).

An interesting consequence of Helmholtz' theory is, that on the one side there can be reliable clues about aspects of objects at the sensational level, whereas on the other hand there can be mistakes too. They are mostly due to perceptual decoding errors, or to encoded ambiguities. Psychologically speaking it is the task of learning processes, and epistemologically speaking it is the task of science, to discover which clues are 'real' and which ones are not. Thus, according to Helmholtz, by finding regularities in perceptions and sensations, we *discover* the hidden order. (Cf. Helmholtz, 1962, originally three volumes published 1856, 1860, 1867; also Helmholtz 1865, 1871, 1876; Warren & Warren, 1968; Koenigsberger, 1902, 1903, 1903; Meijering, 1981.)

Ernst Mach

Mach, like Helmholtz, was an empiricist, materialist, anti-Kantian, and had the same view on the task of science, namely, to formulate general laws of nature. While Helmholtz took sensations to be a very important source of information about the world beyond sensation, Mach was a presentationalist and to him empiricism meant that there were nothing but sensations. It is our order which we impose upon sensations; sensations neither have an abstract order themselves, nor are the apparent regularities of sensations caused by some underlying, insensible, yet real order. Mach's famous Principle of Economy was a norm for science to be as economical as possible in organizing sensations. It was also considered as an empirical claim: thought is nothing but the economical summarizing of sensations. Like Helmholtz, Mach justified his principle with reference to biology, but unlike Helmholtz who referred to the possible order of nature itself, Mach referred to the instrumental usefulness of the projected order.

Consequently, the way Mach treated sensations was entirely different from the way Helmholtz did. Mach looked for correlations between supposedly physiological stimulations and sensory experiences without postulating any causal connection. Whenever different physiological stimulations gave rise to the same experience, Mach looked for quantitative changes taking place in the sense organs. Sensations provided the elements out of which ideas were made. Physicists focused on sensations as physical events, whereas psychologists focused on the immediate features of sensations. (Mach developed this viewpoint independently of Wilhelm Wundt.) But they only studied two aspects of one reality, the reality of sensations. Consequently, concepts were only shorthand for impulses to activity which gave rise to new sensations (e.g., 'triangle' economically summarizes the counting of angles, the drawing of lines, etc.). Ideas were only images of organized sensations (Mach, 1959/1885; Mach, 1976/1905).

Some Consequences

Mach identified 'sensation' with experience, and experience with a physical source of stimulation and, therefore, he identified sensations with the world. Consequently, a concept was nothing but an economical summary of sensations. Helmholtz interpreted sensations as indexes of external reality and, hence, took a concept to be about an object, or about aspects of an object, or about some relation between objects.

Mach, for instance, could not accept atomic theory while Helmholtz did; and Mach ignored the mind-body problem (believing that he unmasked it as a fictitious problem), while Helmholtz contributed to the unveiling of mental and physical aspects of perception. This is not to say that Helmholtz did not sometimes miss the mark, for example, in the details of his resonance theory of pitch hearing (Goldstein, 1984), or that Mach did not make some important discoveries, for example, the phenomenon known as Mach bands (Blackmore, 1972). Indeed, one would expect a presentationalist to be alert to experiences and contradictions in experiences which are more than only contradictions between one's concepts. Mach also had some good intuitions about the explanation of the Mach band phenomenon (Ratliff, 1965). He actually suggested that it might have to do with the characteristics of inhibitory networks of 'retina points' as he called them (Mach, 1865). That he had the right intuition in this case is not a coincidence either. Being a sensationist of the presentational kind, he looked for explanations in the working of the sense organs themselves, preferably in those parts of the sense organs where physical features can be identified with psychical features. For Mach assumed that "Every psychical event corresponds to a physical event and vice versa" (Mach, 1865).

Mach's sensationism may have led him to another discovery as well: the sense of equilibrium. Of course, this sense was noticed before, but it was Mach who concluded that this sixth sense was located somewhere in the semicircular canals. Again he was aided by his presentationalist inclination to look for correlational constancies between psychical and physical processes (Blackmore, 1972). However, it did prevent him from finding an explanation for hearing which he relegated entirely to the structure of the ear.

So it seems that Mach was successful both in the discovery and explantion of sensory phenomena if the cause was sensational. However, he was less successful when the cause was mental. Perhaps, in the long run, presentationalism may prove to be less fruitful, especially in psychology. The concept of unconscious inference may serve as an example. For Mach, and for any version of presentationalism, concepts and hypotheses which go beyond the information given, are merely shorthand for sets of sensations. Therefore, abstract and hypothetical relations between physical and psychical processes can only be postulated without supposing they might refer to *real* connections, or to real processes between physical and psychological events. It comes as no surprise, then, that Mach could not accept Helmholtz' theory of unconscious inference.

Helmholtz, being a representationalist, considered rational beliefs to have an empirical basis. But he was aware of the restrictions of this view. He explicitly assumed, or at least implicitly presupposed in later publications, that there was necessarily an unjustifiable and transempirical presupposition all organisms take for granted, namely, that whatever our experiences, they have some independent cause. It was this one Kantian category he did accept in, what he called, unconscious inferences. Organisms, in perceiving objects, were supposed to make use of inferential (mental) processes, the features of which still had to be discovered. These inferential processes were not directly visible, of course, but Helmholtz accepted them as real for the real was not exhausted by the sensible. Reality is beyond the immediately given; beyond conscious experiences.

Modern Psychology

Mach's presentationalism was actualized in positivist philosophy of science which very much hindered the exploration of the mind's unconscious inferences. By now no philosopher of science is a Machian positivist anymore. Yet the Machian interpretation style is not yet dead. In psychology many psychologists still have his interpretation style (or one like it) with respect to the relationship of psychological theories and data to the world of the mental. Concepts and theories are still considered as *mere* hypothetical constructs, projecting *our* order in data, without claiming that these hypotheses do refer to real entities. It is a safe strategy of course, if a restrictive and boring one. Unfortunately, is even the critics of modern psychology read psychology with presentationalist eyes, thus combating a straw man.

I only can mention a few examples. One is the way the concept of 'representation' is interpreted in cognitive psychology (Fodor, 1986; Sperber & Wilson, 1986). Presentationalists tend to stress the *copy* or picture or mapping features of representations, while representationalists will put the emphasis on the indicative and signicative functions of representations. According to representationalists, a cognitive scheme is a way to encode relevant aspects of the represented. According to presentationalists such a representation should copy as many features as possible of the represented object; it should be 'true to the given.' The presentationalist wishes to minimize 'loss' of information, so as to avoid abstraction or idealization, and ignores both relevant and irrelevant aspects. According to the representationalist, however, information is something to be inferred and, hence, it can lead to information revealing other, not directly represented features, because representations 'imply' presuppositions (Sperber & Wilson, 1986). According to the presentationalist, all information is 'there', 'in the *experienced* world,' and a representation only *transmits* the information to the viewer. For example, in theories of mental imagery, or of perception, presentationalists will stress the picture-like features of images or percepts, whereas representationalists will stress the indicative characteristics of (parts of) pictures or images (Kosslyn, 1980; Pylyshyn, 1981).

Another example can be found in the conflict between defenders of direct versus of indirect perception, that is, between 'Gibsonians' and 'the Establishment View' (Fodor & Pylyshyn, 1981). A third example is the research program on mental imagery, that is, in differences between the work of Roger Shepard and Michael Kosslyn. Shepard has a more or less representationalist approach and therefore stresses that what is imagined is a rotating object. Kosslyn being a presentationalist stresses that it is the *image* that is mentally rotated. Moreover, Shepard emphasizes more often the investigation of three-dimensional imagery, whereas Kosslyn is often found to focus on two-dimensional imagery (Shepard & Cooper, 1982; Shepard, 1984; Pylyshyn, 1981; Kosslyn, 1980). Yet the differences here are small: the research program on imagery has a strong heuristic which leaves little room for individual differences in interpretations. A somewhat older example is the debate between Chomsky (1959) and Skinner (1957; 1985). The conflict between them can be explained by the differences in their representationalist and presentationalist interpretation styles.

A last example is the social constructivist view of psychology, in the wake of Wittgensteinian presentationalism (e.g., Coulter, 1979; Gergen, 1985). I suggest that social constructivism, the view that ideas about minds, feelings, thoughts etc., are only social constructs, is another manifestation of presentationalism not moving one iota beyond the 'hypothetical constructs of positivism' it is supposed to transcend. Gergen (this volume) criticizes psychology for its picture and mirror theories of representation and the mind. However, many of the important theorists never had it in mind in the literal form that Gergen suggests. Neither Locke and Descartes, nor Helmholtz, Freud, Fodor, Johnson-Laird, Bühler or Külpe ever considered the mind to be mirror-like as a passively reflecting, copies or pictures producing device.

Conclusion

The distinction between presentationalism and representationalism presented in this paper has a limited scope. It is not suggested that interpretive differences will explain all disunity in psychology, or that these will explain all theoretical and empirical progress. Nor does it provide an answer to social historical explanations of the growth of psychology. Interpretation styles are only proposed to play a role in 'filling in the gap' between ideas, and theories, observation statements, concepts etc, on the one hand, and what individual scientists do with, and see in or through them on the other. It may explain why psychologists' interpretations of the same data and concepts differ *within* research programs, *within* schools and systems of psychology, as well as *between* them. It does not explain where data, concepts and theories come from, it only explains what psychologists do with them. The consequences, nevertheless, may be important. For if today's psychology departs from yesterday's psychology, the *a priori* presupposition about the way theories, methods, data relate to reality is surely of relevance.

References

Blackmore, J. T. (1972). *Ernst Mach. His work, life, and influence.* Berkeley: University of California Press.

Blackmore, J. T. (1983). Philosophy as part of internal history of science. *Philosophy of Social Sciences, 13*, 17-45.
Chomsky, N. (1959). A review of 'Verbal behavior' (1957). *Language, 35*, 26-58.
Coulter, J. (1979). *The social construction of mind.* London: Macmillan.
Fodor, J. A. (1986). Information and association. *Notre Dame Journal of Formal Logic, 27.* (pages not numbered).
Fodor, J. A., & Pylyshyn, Z. (1981). How direct is visual perception? *Cognition, 9*, 139-196.
Gergen, K. J. (1985). The social constructionist movement in modern psychology. *American Psychologist, 40*, 266-275.
Gholson, B., & Barker, P. (1985). Kuhn, Lakatos, and Laudan. Applications in the history of physics and psychology. *American Psychologist, 40*, 755-769.
Goldstein, E. B. (1984). *Sensation and perception* (2nd ed.). Belmont: Wadsworth.
Hamilton, W. (1852). Of presentative and representative knowledge. In W. Hamilton (Ed.), *The works of Thomas Reid* (pp. 804-815). Edinburgh: Blackwood, 1846-1863.
Helmholtz, H. von (1865/1871/1876). *Populäre wissenschafliche Vorträge* (Popular Scientific Lectures, 3 Vols.) Braunschweig: Vieweg.
Helmholtz, H. von (1962). Treatise on physiological optics. In J. Southall (Ed.), *Helmholtz' Treatise on physiological optics.* (2 vols.). New York: Dover. (Original work published 1856, 1860, 1867).
Hezewijk, R. van (1987). Modularity, mental models, and tertiary qualities. In Wm J. Baker, M. E. Hyland, H. van Rappard, A. W. Staats (Eds.), *Current issues in theoretical psychology* (pp. 115 - 133). Amsterdam: North Holland.
Koenigsberger, L. (1902/1903/1903). *Hermann von Helmholtz.* (3 vols.). Braunschweig: Vieweg.
Kosslyn, S. M. (1980). *Image and mind.* Cambridge, MA: Harvard University Press.
Mach, E. (1865). On the effect of the spatial distribution of the light stimulus. In F. Ratliff (Ed.), (1965), *Mach bands.* (pp. 253-271). San Francisco: Holden Day.
Mach, E. (1868). On the dependence of retinal points on one another. In F. Ratliff (Ed.), *Mach bands* (pp. 307-320). San Francisco: Holden Day.
Mach, E. (1959). *The analysis of sensations and the relation of the physical to the psychical.* (C. M. Williams, Transl.). New York: Dover. (Original work 1st ed. 1885 as Beiträge zur Analyse der Empfindungen).
Mach, E. (1976). *Knowledge and error.* (B. McGuinness, Transl.). Dordrecht: Reidel. (Original work published 1905 as Erkenntnis und Irrtum).
Meijering, Th. C. (1981). *Naturalistic epistemology. Helmholtz and the rise of a cognitive theory of perception* (2 vols.). (Ph.D. thesis, University of California)
Popper, K. R. (1972). *Objective knowledge. An evolutionary approach.* Oxford: Clarendon Press.
Popper, K. R. (1983). *Realism and the aim of science.* London: Hutchinson.
Pylyshyn, Z. W. (1981). The imagery debate: analog media versus tacit knowledge. In N. Block (Ed.), *Imagery.* Cambridge, MA: MIT Press.
Quine, W. V. (1953). Two dogmas of empiricism. In W. V. Quine (Ed.), *From a logical point of view* (pp. 20-36). Cambridge, MA: Harvard University Press.
Quine, W. V. (1969). *Ontological relativity and other essays.* New York: Columbia University Press.
Ratliff, F. (1965). *Mach bands. Quantitative studies on neural networks in the retina.* San Francisco: Holden Day.
Shepard, R. N. (1984). Ecological constraints on internal representation. Resonant kinematics of perceiving, imagining, thinking, and dreaming. *Psychological Review, 91*, 417-447.

Shepard, R. N., & L. A. Cooper (Eds.). (1982). *Mental images and their transformations.* Cambridge, MA: MIT Press.

Skinner, B. F. (1957). *Verbal behavior.* New York: Appleton Century Crofts.

Skinner, B. F. (1985). Cognitive science and behaviorism. *British Journal of Psychology, 76,* 291-301.

Sperber, D., & Wilson, D. (1986). *Relevance. Communication and cognition.* Oxford: Basil Blackwell.

Staats, A. W. (1983). *Psychology's crisis of disunity.* New York: Praeger.

Vroon, P. A. (1987). Man-machine analogs and theoretical mainstreams in psychology. In Wm J. Baker, M. E. Hyland, H. van Rappard,& A. W. Staats (Eds.), *Current issues in theoretical psychology.* (pp. 393-415). Amsterdam: North Holland.

Warren, R. M., & Warren, R. P. (1968). *Helmholtz on perception. Its physiology and development.* London: Wiley.

PREDICATIONAL VERSUS MEDIATIONAL THEORIZING IN PSYCHOLOGY

Joseph F. Rychlak

Loyola University of Chicago
Chicago, IL, U.S.A.

SUMMARY: Mediational theorizing focuses on mediate or interdependent considerations in a line of action, and can be construed in completely mechanistic terms as when we describe the actions of a lever or a thermostat. Predicational theorizing focuses on the immediate organization of meanings in relation to each other and cannot be understood mechanistically. Mediational theorizing is said to occur in the midst of a left-to-right flow of influence, whereas predicational theorizing is said to occur from a broader to a narrower extension of meaning. Predications can therefore be thought of in either a top-down or a right-to-left alignment as well as the left-to-right direction of meaning extension. It is argued that psychologists are willing to take a predicational view of their own behavior as theoreticians and scientists, but that they describe the human beings they study in terms of a mediational formulation. Historical reasons for this state of affairs are presented. It is also shown how mediational theorizing is flawed, requiring informal 'homuncular' theories to enter into the presentation. The presentation closes with a request that psychologists make themselves the measure of their subject matter, and that therefore more predicational theorizing be attempted in the future.

Introduction

The International Society of Theoretical Psychology is dedicated to the study of how we psychologists frame our understanding of people. There is the added realm of sub-human behavior to consider, of course. But in the final analysis, psychologists have the unique task of understanding people, and, since we are included in this categorization, we must also understand ourselves. This suggests to me that we cannot talk about ourselves as theoreticians, about our assumptions and descriptive styles, without at the same time commenting upon human behavior in general. But invariably, there is a contradiction that arises when we look at psychologists discussing, for example, their paradigmatic assumptions on the one hand, and their formal theoretical description of human learning and behavior on the other.

That is, paradigmatic assumptions or schools of thought are akin to premises, influencing what can be known by those who affirm them and bring them to life in theoretical conceptualizations. As we discuss our preferences in theoretical premises, singling out the philosophical precedents leading to our particular outlook, we have the sense of actively doing something with the concepts employed. There is a psychological appreciation here of being a 'conceptualizer,' of framing things one way rather than another, or of revising what a colleague might contend in light of our personal judgment. And yet, when we now turn to the formal understanding of human learning that psychology has to offer, either by way of traditional learning theories or the more recent formulations of information-processing models, this sense of premising and active conceptualization is always lost in the translation.

The upshot is that we psychologists seem to talk about our theorizing one way and the object of our theories - human behavior - another way. And there is a fundamental contradiction between these two kinds of talk, two kinds of theoretical understanding. I would like to outline for you a distinction between mediational and predicational theorizing in psychology, since I believe it will clarify the contradiction in theoretical explanation that I am concerned about. It is also my hope that once this distinction is better understood, future psychologists will see the necessity to frame predicational forms of explanation.

Mediational Versus Predicational Theorizing

To mediate is to intervene or come between other active processes, bringing about some kind of action indirectly. The mediator is one who settles disputes between parties, each of whom has framed a grounding point of view that conflicts with the other party to the dispute. The conflicting parties are the direct or "immediate" parties to the dispute, acting on a first-hand basis. Immediacy signifies instantaneous organization of experience. Mediacy signifies interdependent organization of experience.

Now, it is possible to think of mediation as involving a human being trying as best he or she can to resolve a disagreement between two disputants, such as the negotiators for labor and management during a strike settlement. Such a mediator might well do what we in conferences such as the present one often do - that is, attempt to ferret out the assumptions underlying the conflicting sides to our disputes over the nature of our discipline. Possibly there is some common ground that the disputants do not recognize, and if it is made clear to them they will begin to resolve their disagreement. But there is also a kind of mediation in events that does not address such assumptive understandings. It is possible to think of a purely mechanical process taking place between events as a mediator of those events. A simple lever serves in such a mediational capacity, whereby a downward pressure applied at one end results in a force of lift at the other end. The mediational influence varies depending upon the placement of the lever on the fulcrum. Another form of mediation occurs when a thermostat in an automobile engine opens or closes depending upon the temperature of the coolant in the radiator, allowing for greater or lesser circulation of the coolant through the engine while it is running.

The meaning of 'mediation' changes dramatically when we move from the negotiator between disputants to the mechanical processes of levers and thermostats. Yet, the fact is that psychology has *not* taken cognizance of the differences between mediating conflicting points of view and mediating mechanical processes. Psychologists continue to pretend that they are accounting for the former by employing theoretical descriptions relying upon the latter. In an effort to separate these two forms of explanation, I would now like to suggest that we call the descriptive analysis that deals with assumptions a *predicational* theoretical model and the one looking at mechanical changes over time a *mediational* theoretical model.

I choose the term 'predication' to represent the assumptive or "point of view" style of explanation because this is what a predication always entails. Predication is concerned with meanings and not with automatic actions. In what sense does one meaningful item enhance or enrich another? Predication is on the side of immediacy, because once a predicate relation is joined, denied or qualified the meaning captured is instantaneous. We are not concerned with the passage of time in speaking of predication. We might define predication as follows: *Predication is the act of affirming, denying, or qualifying certain patterns of meaning in relation to other patterns of meaning.* We predicate when we say that "George is reliable" or "A human being is like a precious flower," and so on.

There is no motion taking place here, no force flowing from one levered end to another, no valves shutting or opening to let liquid through depending upon temperature levels. Nor is there a stimulus cueing a response along, or an input triggering an output by way of a long-term memory storage. The 'direction' of meaning-extension in predication is always from a *broader* range of meaning to a *narrower* range of meaning. Whereas mediation conceptions are always pictured as extending meaningfully from left-to right, or from sooner-to-later, the predication conception is independent of directionality per se. In a syllogism, the major premise predicates the flow of meaning through the minor premise to a conclusion in a top-down fashion. And in our examples of predication - "George is reliable" and "A human being is like a precious flower" - meaning can be symbolized as flowing from right-to-left. If we think of the Euler circles, a predicate is the larger circle within which we place a smaller circle, symbolizing that meaning extends from the broader concept to the narrower without regard for the passage of time. Thus, many people besides George can be described as reliable (i.e., placed in the larger circle of 'reliable people'), and we could doubtless classify animals other than humans as akin to a precious flower. The broader meanings here - reliability, preciousness, flower-likeness - extend to the narrower, targeted items of a person or a class of human organisms.

It is important to stress at this point that predication is not simply a linguistic convention, a matter of language syntax. Predication is concerned with semantics, with meanings, and meanings-within-meanings to be understood as the interlacing relations of a logical corpus. Syntax undoubtedly devolves from the semantic requirements of human reason, a reasoning process founded upon predication. The distinction between a logical premise and a linguistic statement or sentence is thus merely one of convenience. Both involve predication because this is how human beings seem to reason intrinsically.

The Origins of Mediational Theorizing in Natural Science

As I have already suggested, the tradition in psychological theorizing is to presume that all of human reasoning is done mediationally. There is a historical precedent for this theoretical bias. The science of psychology was patterned on Newtonian scientific description, in which scientists take an extraspective stance, looking 'at' their objects of study in an effort to write theories in third-person fashion (Rychlak, 1981, p. 27). This is how we would explain the 'behavior' of a rock, rolling down a hill, or a raindrop falling from the sky. We would look 'at' the rock or raindrop, accounting for its behavior by singling out antecedent forces relating to a principle of gravity or some such. This theoretical stance fixes our attention in a 'left to right,' 'sooner to later,' or 'antecedent to consequent' fashion rather than in the 'broader to narrower' sense of predication. The notion of time's passage is fundamental to a mediational explanation, because something earlier and 'left-lying' is pushing something later or 'to the right' along, in the traditional sense of stimulus-response or, more recently, input-output.

If we were to explain the rock or raindrop based on a predicational theoretical model we would find it impossible to do so. Rocks and raindrops do not predicate. They have no meanings to join, no broader understanding to focus on some item of cognizance. But now, it *would* be possible to shift our stance a bit and begin speaking about the predicate assumptions of various theoreticians who describe the motions of rocks and raindrops through a theory of gravitational force. All theorists do not embrace the same predicate assumptions concerning the nature of gravity (Einstein and Whitehead had conflicting assumptions in this regard; see Palter, 1956). We could certainly examine the predications of such alternative formulations, and come to appreciate why our two physical theorists differ as they do whether or not their differences in outlook lead to different empirical predictions concerning falling rocks or raindrops (Einstein and Whitehead made essentially the same predictions concerning physical reality). In other words, just looking at the 'left-to-right' or 'antecedent-consequent' flow of observable physical events could not make it clear to us why our two theoreticians had their dispute in the first place. We would have to examine the 'broader-to-narrower' trend of meanings being affirmed by our disputants in order to understand what was going on here (thus, Einstein and Whitehead proceeded from contrasting philosophical, theoretical, and mathematical predications vis a vis the reality they both 'looked at').

Of course, there was a time in the history of thought when explanations of rocks, falling or rolling down hills *were* accounted for in a kind of predicational explanation. It seems utterly stupid to wonder what the rock's predications are, as it rolls down the hill, or what a leaf may be framing into premises encompassing predications as it aligns itself to provide shade for the fruit on the branches of the tree to which it is attached. But Artistotle (1952a) believed that 'nature,' as a whole, was such an intelligently predicating entity, that it worked for a purpose in orchestrating how events took place (pp. 276-277). Aristotle (1952b) also described human beings as predicators, as when a doctor applies certain remedies based on his/her assumptions concerning the nature of an illness or an architect designs a home based on certain assumptions regarding what such a domicile should look like (pp. 161-162).

In the 17th century, with the rise of natural science, British philosophers like Bacon, Hobbes, and Locke thoroughly discredited such predicational ascriptions to 'nature.' Bacon (1952) in particular noted how it did not add to our understanding of leaves to say that they 'had the purpose' of shading fruit on trees (p. 45). And with the rise of Newtonian science, the purely mediational accounting of rocks rolling down hills with predictable regularity greatly simplified the Aristotelian account, in which nature's design was supposedly bringing things of a similar substance closer together - the 'earthy' substance of the rock seeking to get closer to the heart of the earth itself. The Aristotelian teleology was dismissed as a superfluous and non-instructive animism, vitalism, and anthropomorphism (Rychlak, 1984a).

Is Predication Theory Superfluous in Human Description?

Although the dismissal of predicational theorizing in physical accounts made great sense, there is a problem when we return to the example of the physician and the architect. Is it true that an examination of predications in light of *their* behaviors adds nothing to our understanding of what they do and why they may vary in what they do? In the same way that our conflicting physicists disagreed over gravity, we can find many physicians even today who disagree over the diagnosis and treatment of an illness. The same holds for architects, who do not find the meaning of a 'house' to represent precisely the same kind of domicile. I think we would all agree that the Baconian criticism no longer holds in this case, because the only sense we can make of such differences is through a predicational analysis. This salvages a degree of the Aristotelian teleology. In fact, even Bacon would have to agree at this point because he assigned a place for predicational analysis in such realms of knowledge as metaphysics, ethics, and aesthetics, which are teleological disciplines of the first order. It is when we are faced with understanding why certain options were selected or judged to be more worthy than others that we are necessarily drawn to the examination of our predicate assumptions. This style of analysis is always introspective (Rychlak, 1981, p. 27). We have to look through the conceptual eyes of the reasoning intelligence that opted one way or another. Rocks, raindrops, and leaves do not require such an analysis, but people do.

Unfortunately - at least, I find it to be unfortunate that psychology emerged as a discipline in the latter half of the 19th century, when the anti-teleological criticisms of Bacon had long been institutionalized as an aspect of Newtonian science. Properly in search of scientific status, the early psychologists took it as an unquestioned 'given' (in other words, as a predicate assumption) that the same mediational explanations describing rolling rocks and shading leaves must suffice for describing behavioral events, human or sub-human. When John Watson (1924) said "let us try to think of man as an assembled organic machine ready to run" (p. 216) he was asking that his colleagues abandon predicational theorizing for mediational theorizing even as he was framing a grand Newtonian (mechanistic) predication regarding the human being. Any psychologist interested in purpose, choice or intentionality was henceforth to be considered an anthropomorphizer, a non-scientific theorizer. And so we have moved in psychology over the 20th century from one machine metaphor to another, from the earlier muscle twitches to the current clicks of electronic gates. The resiliency of the machine metaphor and its mediational portrayal of behavior is nothing short of astonishing.

And yet, the anthropomorphic side to behavior has never quite gone away. Colleagues who would like to theorize in the vein of mediation theories frequently claim that those of us interested in a predicational model are persisting in a kind of medieval urge to retain spirits and deities in our world view (see Rychlak, 1984). Yet, the truth is that anyone who looks at the continuing trend of our experimental findings in psychology, or who appreciates the vast gaps in our explanations of a cybernetic or information-processing nature *must* arrive at the conclusion that the mediational form of theorizing is in serious difficulty. I cannot go into the many reasons to support this contention, but for anyone interested, a good beginning is to read Brewer's (1974) classic paper on the role of awareness and cooperation in both classical and operant conditioning experiments. The entire thrust of this vast survey of empirical research on conditioning is that we psychologists do *not* manipulate human beings in a machine-like fashion. We can 'condition' them only when they have some reasonable predication of the task confronting them, and are willing to go along with what this requires them to do.

And when we look at the *formal* cybernetic models of behavior today - which are supposed to simulate human reasoning - we find some whopping holes in the presentation. Although the teleologist may be branded as dealing in 'mysteries' (see Maze, 1986, p. 198), the truth is that some pretty mysterious things are going on in the computer model - or rather, outside the computer model. Who does the 'encoding' that is often 'selectively attended' to in the computer model (Cherry, 1953)? Selective attention strikes me as a predicational activity, but there is no such process or device in the computer model. Why is it that intention is more important to retention in long term memory than merely repeating what is to be retained in rote fashion (Craik & Watkins, 1973)? Machines do not intend, so how appropriate is the machine as a model for this feature of human memory? And why are plans, scripts, and schemata so important to an understanding of artificial intelligence (Miller, Galanter, & Pribram, 1960; Schank & Abelson, 1977)? A mediating process need have no sense of the over-all plan of action; all it must do is go through 'this or that' gate - the one that is signalled or opened for it (which was the point of Searle's (1980) notorious 'Chinese Room' example).

Now, concepts like attending, selecting, intending, and framing plans are to be seen in use throughout the cognitive literature (Howard, 1983). Yet the *formal* theory of computer processing or information-processing involving a sensory register, a short-term memory, a long-term memory, and feedback capacities makes *no* allowance for such, what I think we can agree, are concepts devolving from predicational theory. As a result, even those psychologists who embrace computer models are forced to admit that there is something like a 'homunculus' in the machine apparatus (see, e.g., Johnston & Dark, 1986, p. 43). The homunculus is necessary because Watson's machine 'ready to run' is without a predicate assumption as to where to go, what to do, and why to do it. Machines as motor cars and computers need drivers or programmers.

I would like to short-cut this explanatory process by formalizing the homuncular teleology from the outset. I think this would make us more honest in our portrayal of what we are finding in our empirical research.

Since the machine metaphor has to rely on informal homuncular embellishments, why not take the bull by the horns and state from the outset that "A human being is a homunculus." What this would come down to, of course, is that human behavior must be understood as predicational. People do not behave 'in response to' or as 'outputting information previously input.' People 'take a position' on lived experience, they behave 'for the sake of' reasons, purposes, and intentions. Our empirical findings continue to press this conclusion on us in the face of a century of concerted effort to drum such talk out of our professional lexicon. All this repression has succeeded in doing is to drive agential or teleological description underground, where it continues to influence psychological description informally.

A Predicational View of the Person

We are back now to the sort of person I had in mind in my opening comments, the one sitting here today, trying to make sense out of what I am saying by bringing to bear precedent concepts of a wider compass, and subsuming what I have to say in light of these predicated formulations. You are not responding to my stimuli or inputting information that I am outputting. I am not expressing 'information' in any true sense, because what I have to offer here is a point of view, a suggestion that is not as clear as I would like it to be even in my mind. I am taking a position, but precisely where it is directing me, and whether or not I will go the whole route with it is still up in the air. I am struggling to understand. And I do this just the way you do, by arranging some broad meanings within which to order and differentiate my cognitions. So, I draw two broad categories - mediational versus predicational theorizing - and proceed to see how well these predications can order my understanding as I reason along with you, subsuming this or that theoretical outlook by my wide-ranging meanings. And, of course, all of this effort is itself framed intentionally by my even broader predication of wanting to understand the human behavior that I see about me at this conference.

You do not input everything I send your way. You do not mechanically respond to my stimuli. You have to frame these signals and cues in some way, and putting them together in light of your presumption as to what I am driving at, render them meaningful. Depending upon where you position yourself in relation to the point of view I am espousing you can actually hear the very opposite of what I am saying even as I am saying it. Human beings reason oppositionally, so that unlike machines they are always cognizant of what they did not do, what they do not believe, and why they might have done or believed otherwise. So, as I am framing my argument here, if you do not care for its drift, you can be framing meanings in direct contradiction to mine. You will be, so to speak, inputting what I am *not* outputting. I don't believe you are merely mediating here, utilizing early inputs that your psychology instructors placed in your long-term memory years ago to automatically counter what I am saying about human behavior today. I think you are a factor in what you believe, and you have always been a factor - even when your instructors were teaching you a mediational view of human behavior. You believe what makes sense to you. And what makes sense to you is what fits into your fundamental predications or 'basic outlook,' something that you have been working on for a long time now.

But I would bet that at least some of you have found the mediational style of theorizing uncomfortable, if not downright unacceptable when it comes to the description of human behavior. To you, I would say, take heart. There *is* an alternative. There are others in psychology poised to make, if not a Kuhnian paradigmatic shift then at least a modification favorable to predicational theorizing. After all, as I suggested at the outset, we already do talk about our theoretical predications in selected situations. It is but a short step to view all people in terms of ourselves. Possibly then we will shift from the study of artificial to real human intelligence, from the characterization of the machine to the characterization of the programmer of the machine, who ever sets the predications within which the machine must operate. I am encouraged that with the current move to cognitive theorizing in psychology we who favor teleological explanations of behavior will find support for a view of the person, not as 'a machine, ready to run,' but as 'a predicating organism, ready to take a position' on life experience.

References

Aristotle (1952a). Physics. In R. M. Hutchins (Ed.), *Great books of the western world* (Vol. 8, pp. 257-355). Chicago: Encyclopedia Britannica.

Aristotle (1952b). On the parts of animals. In R. M. Hutchins (Ed.), *Great books of the western world* (Vol. 9, pp. 159-229). Chicago: Encyclopedia Britannica.

Bacon, F. (1952). Advancement of learning. In R. M. Hutchins (Ed.), *Great books of the western world.* (Vol. 30). Chicago: Encyclopedia Britannica.

Brewer, W. F. (1974). There is no convincing evidence for operant or classical conditioning in adult humans. In W. B. Weimer, & D. S. Palermo (Eds.), *Cognition and the symbolic processes* (pp. 1-42). Hillsdale, NJ: Erlbaum Assocs.

Cherry, E. C. (1953). Some experiments on the recognition of speech, with one and with two ears. *Journal of the Acoustical Society of America, 25*, 975-979.

Craik, F. I. M.,& Watkins, M. J. (1973). The role of rehearsal in short-term memory. *Journal of Verbal Learning and Verbal Behavior, 12*, 599-607.

Howard, D. V. (1983). *Cognitive psychology: Memory, language and thought.* New York: Macmillan Publishing Co.

Johnston, W. A., & Dark, V. J. (1986). Selective attention. In M. R. Rosenzweig & L. W. Porter (Eds.), *Annual review of psychology* (Vol. 37, pp. 43-75). Palo Alto, CA: Annual Reviews, Inc.

Maze, J. F. (1986). The composition of the ego in a determinist psychology. In W. J. Baker, M. E. Hyland, H. van Rappard, & W. W. Staats (Eds.), *Current issues in theoretical psychology* (pp. 189-199). Amsterdam: North-Holland.

Miller, G. A., Galanter, E., & Pribram, K. H. (1960). *Plans and the structure of behavior.* New York: Holt, Rinehart and Winston, Inc.

Palter, R. (1956). Philosophic principles and scientific theory. *Philosophy of Science, 23,* 111-135.

Rychlak, J. F. (1981). *A philosophy of science for personality theory* (2nd ed.). Malabar, FL: Robert E. Krieger Publishing Co.

Rychlak, J. F. (1984). Logical learning theory: Kuhnian anomaly or medievalism revisited? *The Journal of Mind and Behavior, 5,* 389-416.

Schank, R. C., & Abelson, R. P. (1977). *Scripts, plans, goals, and understanding.* Hillsdale, NJ: Erlbaum Assocs.

Searle, J. (1980). Minds, brains and programs. *Behavioral and Brain Sciences, 3,* 417-457.

Watson, J. B. (1924). *Behaviorism.* New York: Norton & Co.

SKINNER'S PHILOSOPHY AND METATHEORY:

A METATHEORETICAL ANALYSIS

K. B. Madsen

The Royal Danish School of Educational Studies
Copenhagen, Denmark

SUMMARY: This paper presents a metascientific study called ***systematology***. The frame-of-reference, or the metatheory of systematology is briefly presented. It is then applied in an analysis of Skinner's philosophy and metatheory. Skinner's philosophy is found to be a version of ***materialistic monism*** and ***radical empiricism***. Hence, Skinner's metatheory precludes the application of ***intervening variables*** (or hypothetical constructs) of any kind. However, Skinner does use some intervening variables (without surplus meaning), the so-called 'response probability'. But in accordance with his radical empiricism he is using the intervening variable very economically, and his theory is found to have the highest degree of testability.

Introduction

Skinner's article 'Behaviorism at fifty' (Science, 1963) contains a concentrated version of his philosophy and metatheory. The article is thus a convenient object for a metatheoretical analysis and discussion of these points. Therefore, we shall refer mainly to this article in the following pages, and we will regard it as a representative of Skinner's philosophy and metatheory as expressed in his entire work.

Before we begin an analysis of the article, we will place it in a classification of Skinner's production. In order to do that, it is convenient to briefly present our frame-of-reference.

A Metascientific Frame of Reference

Metascience. We regard an analysis of a scientific text - such as what we are doing now - as part of *Metascience*, which is the comprehensive science about sciences. Metascience includes three levels of abstraction:

1. Philosophy of Science: a part of philosophy in general - closely related to epistemology.

2. Metatheory: theory about theories. 'Metatheory' is used in a broad sense - equal to the German 'Wissenschafttheorie' - which includes Methodology, too.

3. Empirical Metascience: various empirical studies of science, such as the History of Science, the Psychology of Science, and the Sociology of Science. In addition to these well-established disciplines, there may be other, lesser-known disciplines. The present author has suggested the name 'Systematology' for a metascientific discipline consisting of the comparative study of scientific texts (see, for example, Madsen, 1984; 1985).

Metatheory. Based upon comparative studies of about 50 psychological theories (see Madsen, 1959, 1973, 1974, and 1975) we have created a general *metatheory*; i.e., a theory about theories. This metatheory conceives of a scientific text (= 'theory' in the broad sense) as composed of three levels of abstraction:

1. The Metalevel: This is the part of a scientific text that contains 'Metatheses'; i.e., philosophical, metatheoretical and methodological propositions. The 'Metalevel' is more or less equal to Kuhn's 'Paradigm'.

2. The Hypothetical level: This is the part of a scientific text that contains *hypotheses* and explanatory *models*. This is '*theory*' in the narrow sense.

3. The Data-level: This is the part of a scientific text that contains '*Data theses*'; i.e., specific and general descriptions of observed facts. In addition, the Datalevel contains '*pragmatheses*'; i.e., descriptions and prescriptions of praxis (including technical applications of science).

If we apply this metatheory to a classification of Skinner's whole production, we will find books and articles on all three levels. Thus, Skinner's book 'About Behaviorism' (1974), as well as 'Behaviorism at fifty' and others is on the Metalevel. Most of the books, such as 'Science and Human Behavior' (1953) and 'Contingencies of Reinforcement' (1969) belong to the Hypothetical level, as do some articles. The Datalevel includes such books as 'Schedules of Reinforcement' (1957) and 'Technology of Teaching' (1968), as well as several articles.

The present author has made a comparative metatheoretical (= 'systematological') study of Skinner's early production (see Madsen, 1959), as well as a later, similar study of representative books from Skinner's total production (see Madsen, forthcoming).

In the remaining part of this paper, we will concentrate on Skinner's Metatheses as they are presented in 'Behaviorism at fifty'.

Skinner's Metatheses.

In the former section we defined the 'Metalevel' as that part of a scientific text (or whole production) that contains 'Metatheses', which are the philosophical, metatheoretical and methodological propositions functioning as presuppositions of a text (or whole production).

In the following sections, we shall analyse Skinner's *philosophical* metatheses and his *metatheoretical* metatheses. However, we leave out methodological metatheses as Skinner does not deal with empirical methods in 'Behaviorism at fifty'.

The philosophical theses can be classified into two main categories:

1. Ontological ('metaphysical') theses about the world in general.
2. Epistemological theses about knowledge in general.

Skinner gives explicit formulations of both these categories of metatheses in 'Behaviorism at fifty'.

Skinner's Ontology. The most important ontological problem for psychologists is the *psycho-physical problem* (the 'Mind-Body' or 'Brian-Consciousness'-problem). Skinner's solution of this problem is presented in connection with his discussion of 'private and public' events, where he writes (p. 5):

> An adequate science of behavior must consider events taking place within the skin of the organism, not as physiological mediators of behavior but as part of behavior itself. It can deal with these events without assuming that they have any special nature or must be known in any special way. The skin is not that important as a boundary. Private and public events have the same kinds of physical dimensions.

This is a clear statement of a *monistic* ontology, and it can be further specified - on the basis of Skinner's whole production - as a *materialistic (physicalistic) monism.* We postpone discussion of this in a later paragraph.

Skinner's Epistemology. Skinner formulates his epistemology in 'Behaviorism at fifty' in this way (p. 5):

> For one thing, a scientific analysis of behavior has yielded a sort of empirical epistemology. The subject matter of a science of behavior includes the behavior of scientists and other knowers. The techiques available to such a science give an empirical theory of knowledge certain advantages over theories derived from philosophy and logic.

This quotation reveals that Skinner has both *an empiricist and an empirically based epistemology* Skinner has elaborated on this fact further in his autobiographical description of the evolution of his production over the years (see Skinner, 1959).

The present author will not argue with Skinner about his ontology or his epistemology, because *my* philosophy is that these philosophical presuppositions are consciously selected - more often, unconsciously preferred - of a scientist as the foundation for his whole production. And the justification of these philosophical Metatheses should be based upon their consequences or 'fruits', among which is the metatheoretical theses to which we now turn.

Skinner's Metatheory. As mentioned earlier, 'metatheory' is used here as equivalent to the German 'Wissenschafttheorie', which includes metatheory in the narrow sense: 'theory of the construction and structure of scientific theories' as well as 'empirical methodology'. As the empirical methods are not dealt with in 'Behaviorism at fifty' we concentrate on Skinner's metatheory in the narrow sense. There is a metatheoretical problem he has especially focussed on; namely, the problem of the use of 'intervening variables'.

Intervening Variables. A big part of Skinner's article is used on an argument against the use of intervening variables (or 'way stations' as he calls them in his paper) in theory construction. Thus, he writes (on p. 11): "The mental state seems to bridge the gap between the dependent and independent variables, ..." He continues (on p. 13):

> Complete causal sequences might, of course, include reference to way stations, but the fact is that the way station generally interrupts the account in one direction or other.

Thus, Skinner is strongly against the use of intervening variables, especially those with mentalist 'surplus' meaning.

The critical argument against *mentalist* intervening variables is a logical consequence of Skinner's *ontological* (and epistemological) metatheses. From a physicalistic ontology (and an empiricist epistemology) it follows that mentalist explanatory concepts should not be used.

However, there is another kind of intervening variables: *physiological* intervening variables. Skinner calls them 'physiological mediators' (see our first quotation from p. 5 in Skinner's article). The physiological intervening variables are *not* in conflict with his physicalistic ontology, nor are they in conflict with his empiricist epistemology, if they are kept free of any *transempirical* (i.e., 'hypothetical') 'surplus' meaning.

There is a third kind of intervening variables: *the 'neutral' intervening variables.* They could also be used without being in contradiction to Skinner's physicalistic ontology and empiricist epistemology - at least, they could be used if they are operationally defined and without any transempirical, 'surplus' meaning. However, it must be admitted that it is very difficult to make a sharp distinction between neutral, intervening variables without 'surplus' meaning and transempirical, *hypothetical con-*

structs with 'surplus' meaning, established by analogy from a *model* (as for example Freud's 'lenze-model' of the 'mental apparatus'). Such hyothetical constructs are in contradiction to a radically empiricist epistemology such as Skinner's.

However, Skinner is not in conflict with his own philosophical presuppositions, as he uses only intervening variables of the neutral kind - those without transempirical 'surplus' meaning. Skinner's most commonly used intervening variables is "response-probability", which appears in many of his books and articles. However, Skinner does not mention this kind of intervening variables in "Behaviorism at fifty", and that is a serious omission.

We can thus conclude, that Skinner's argumentation against intervening variables is unnecessarily strong, because some kinds of intervening variables - physiological and 'neutral' ones - are *not* in conflict with his philosophical presuppositions. It is only the intervening variables with transempirical 'surplus' meaning that contradict his own philosophical metatheses.

The present author thinks, that it has *heuristic value* to use intervening variables, because they serve an *information-economical function* by reducing the number of relationships in a theory. This is very convincingly demonstrated by *N. E. Miller* (see Miller, 1959). However, that leads to our last problem.

Hypothetical Relationships.. The problem with the use of intervening variables is the temptation to *overuse* them. If there are more of them than necessary to explain the data, then there will be *hypothetical relationships* between two or more intervening variables. This decreases the *testability* of the theory involved.

However, although Skinner uses intervening variables himself, he does not overuse them, and the testability of his theories is very high.

The present author has created a formula to express *a quantitative estimation of the testability of a theory*. The formula is used for the calculation of a 'Hypotheses Quotient' (H.Q.) in this way:

$$H.Q. = \frac{\Sigma(H - H)}{\Sigma[(S\text{-}H) + (H\text{-}R)]}$$

In the upper part of the formula is the sum of complete hypothetical relationships between intervening variables in a given theory ('H-H'), while the lower part is the sum of the partly empirical relationships between independent and intervening variables (S-H) and between intervening and dependent variables (H-R). The H.Q. is constructed so that *the lower the H.Q. the higher is the testability* (see Madsen, 1984).

The present author has calculated the H.Q. for 30 psychological theories. They vary between 0.09 (the H.Q. of R. B. Cattell's theory) and 2.00 (the H.Q. of Freud's theory in Chapter 7 of 'The Interpretations of Dreams'). However, *Skinner's theory is exceptional. It has an H.Q. of 0.00 and thus shows the highest possible testability.*

Conclusion. The present metatheoretical analysis has demonstrated that Skinner's theory is quite consistently empiricist. We have also shown it to be more restrictive of intervening variables and transempirical hypotheses than necessary - even from the point of view expressed in Skinner's own philosophical metatheses.

References

Ferster, C. B., & Skinner, B. F. (1957). *Schedules of reinforcement.* New York: Appleton-Century-Crofts.

Madsen, K. B. (1959). *Theories of motivation.* Copenhagen: Munksgaard.

Madsen, K. B. (1973). Theories of motivation. In B. B. Wolman (Ed.), *Handbook of General Psychology* (pp. 673-706). Englewood Cliffs, N. J.: Prentice-Hall.

Madsen, K. B. (1974). *Modern theories of motivation.* New York: Wiley.

Madsen, K. B. (1975). *Systematology: The comparative study of theories.* Copenhagen: Munksgaard.

Madsen, K. B. (1984). The hypotheses quotient: A quantitative estimation of the testability of a theory. In J. R. Royce & L. P. Mos (Eds.), *Annals of Theoretical Psychology* (Vol. 2, pp. 185-202). New York: Plenum.

Madsen, K. B. (1985). Psychological metatheory: An introduction to volume 3. In K. B. Madsen & L. P. Mos (Eds.), *Annals of theoretical psychology* (Vol. 3, pp. 1-16). New York: Plenum.

Madsen, K. B. (forthcoming). *The history of psychology in metascientific perspective.* Amsterdam: North-Holland Publishing Co.

Miller, N-E. (1959). Liberalization of basic S-R concepts. In S. Koch (Ed.), *Psychology: A study of a science* (Vol. 2, pp. 196-292). New York: McGraw-Hill.

Skinner, B. F. (1953). *Science and human behavior.* New York: Macmillan.

Skinner, B. F. (1959). A case history in scientific method. In S. Koch (Ed.), *Psychology: A study of a science* (Vol. 2, pp. 359-379). New York: McGraw-Hill.

Skinner, B. F. (1963). Behaviorism at fifty. *Science, CXL,* 951-958.

Skinner, B. F. (1968). *Technology of teaching.* New York: Appleton-Century-Crofts.

Skinner, B. F. (1969). *Contingencies of reinforcement: A theoretical analysis.* Englewood-Cliffs, NJ: Prentice Hall.

Skinner, B. F. (1974). *About behaviorism.* New York: A. Knopf.

HAS PSYCHOLOGY EXAGGERATED ITS "NATURAL SCIENTIFIC CHARACTER"?

Remarks concerning an empirical topic and a methodological desideratum of "theoretical psychology"

Wolfgang Maiers

Free University of Berlin
West Berlin, Germany

SUMMARY: This paper deals with current critiques of the 'natural scientific approach' in mainstream psychology. The links to the alleged models of either evolutionary biology or physics are critically examined. The idea of an antiscientism avoiding the metaphysical opposition of 'science' and 'humanities' is sketched out. The paper ends with some implications regarding 'theoretical psychology'.

Critics representing divergent views share the opinion that the distortion of the human subject in traditional psychology is due to the latter's adherence to the model of the natural sciences (for example, Giorgi, 1970; Jüttemann, 1985; Koch & Leary, 1985; Rychlak, 1987). It is my view that this conclusion of a *mistaken 'natural scientificness'* obscures the justified critical position and consequential demands for a non-objectivistic psychological 'human science'. Frequently, it is accompanied by playing off the *concrete understanding* of the *individuality* and *historicity* of psychic phenomena against their *causal explanation* and *lawful generalization.* In doing so, such approaches tend to resurrect the classical dichotomy between the ('nomothetic') '*sciences*' and the ('idiographic') '*humanities*'.

I shall rule out as irrelevant those demarcations that presuppose a *monolithic* natural science and ignore the *complementarity* of epistemic paradigms which have prototypically been associated with classical physics and evolutionary biology. Usually, the distinction in this latter case is acknowledged. Some critics identify the predominant 'nomological psychology' as a natural science along *Darwinian* lines which subsumes psychic development under natural laws and, hence, 'biologizes' the 'cultural' human being. Other critics refer to an inappropriate '*physicotropic*' orientation of psychology.

The Myth of Psychology's Evolutionary Thinking

As for the former view, which was recently affirmed in the research project entitled *Civilizational History and Historical Psychology* (Jüttemann, 1986), I want to point out briefly that neither historically nor systematically can a consistent *evolution-theoretical approach* be held responsible for the continuing hold of *naturalism* on mainstream-psychology.

1. The nomological orientation is illegitimately confounded with biologism, here understood as ideological misconstrual of the social essence of humanity by analogy to organismic adaptation. (Is not a 'sociologistic' nomological psychology equally conceivable?)

2. The exclusive attribution of the quest for generality to the sciences is false. Neither do they refrain from nor are the humanities restricted to singular predicates. This view makes sense only if strong regularities in social history are denied and, instead, confined to an 'eternal' order of nature.

3. Besides implying the *idealistic ontology* of an *ahistorical nature* on the one hand and a *cultural history cut off from nature* on the other, this critical position reveals an untenable view of 'lawfulness' as it *metaphysically opposes the general with the specific.* Moreover, it also involves a *mechanistic reduction of determinism:* first, by identifying lawfulness, linear causation and predictability, second, by ignoring the essential asymmetry that is implied in the interaction of organic matter and can be regarded as the elementary emergence of a subject-object-relationship; and third, by opposing causality to finality. To attach the supposed 'biologization' of human agency to its 'purely factual-scientific' 'de-subjectification', 'de-contextualization' and quantification' (Jüttemann, 1986, p. 8), does not do justice to real-life biology. Biological methods pursue, first, the *qualitative description* of the structure and function of given living systems per se, and, second, an *explanation of their genesis.* In relation to the analytic-reductive (experimental, quantitative) lines of biological cognition, the concern with '*teleonomy*' (Pittendrigh) - which involves a mode of thought alien to physics - is accomplished by evolution theory as integrative, 'truly biological' subdiscipline (Darwin, 1982). That is, biology can teach us how essential aspects of the *dialectics of concrete irreversible processes,* such as system contradiction, subject activity, qualitative leaps, functionality of change, etc. are *generalized to lawful statements* in natural science. To be sure, such moments do not exhaust the intentionality, productive force, or reflexivity of human action. If, however, what Joseph F. Rychlak (1987) summarized as 'telosponsivity' is not to remain a mystery, these specific qualities need to be explained against the background of the causal analysis of teleonomous properties of living nature; that is, different levels must be *genetically mediated.*

Such a *natural history of the psyche* - which, if properly done, leads to the transition from the biological to the social-historical stage of evolution (Maiers, 1987) - would have become an integral part of contemporary psychology long ago, if the latter had *really* been inspired by the paradigm of evolution theory. In fact, even nowadays this is awaiting its fulfillment. The antibiologistic critique is in the grips of the received, but *superficial* historiographical assurance that traditional psychology fits into a Darwinian perspective (see Mackenzie, 1976).

True, the 'historisization' of nature and natural science initiated *psychophylogenetic* research in particular, and promised an *overall developmental* psychology in general. However, neither has become dominant: the endeavour of comparative animal psychology has been carried on by biologists (under the rubric of 'ethology'). How about human psychology?

Wilhelm Wundt (1912, p. 4), for instance, refuted the idea that child psychology could solve the 'puzzle of psychogenesis'. He regarded 'Völkerpsychologie' based on a general phylogeny as 'eminent' developmental psychology. In the U.S. James M. Baldwin (1895) followed the same line of thinking in his 'race psychology'. The idea is also found in Felix Krueger's (1915) *Genetic Holistic Psychology* and in Heinz Werner's (1926) conception of a *General Developmental Psychology,* composed of animal, folk, and child psychology as well as psychopathology. Leaving aside various controversies - for example, Wundt's (1917) reservations regarding Krueger - and overlooking problems surrounding the relation between natural, social, and individual history (the problem of 'psychogenetic parallels'), the fact is that the *prospect of a historically grounded psychology has given way to a specialized 'developmental' subdiscipline* as the straight study of psychic patterns and successions within the time continuum of *ontogenesis* (Stern, 1914, or Bühler, 1918).

Even more than in continental European psychology, the historical view waned in the U.S. with the rise of *functionalism/behaviorism.* The supposed biological basis (van Strien, 1987, p. 338) of these movements is, at best, a diluted Darwinism *à la* Herbert Spencer. Spencer's *positivistic evolutionism* misconceived development as merely quantitative growth or decline of behavioral and mental adaptations, and, by ranking evolutionary continuity above the qualitative differences in development, he promoted a kind of social-Darwinistic (survivalistic) '*adaptivism*'. Accordingly, the functionalists, who analyzed the psyche as a special organ and functional variant of individual accommodations to the environment "dependent upon the particular exigencies and conditions which call them forth" (Angell, 1907, p. 67), did this rather from an *abstract*-biological angle - incipiently *levelling species-specific organism-environment relations and degrading psychic reflection to an epiphenomenon.* This view, together with *empiricist* directives of an objectivistic biology

(Jacques Loeb) and exemplars of animal experimentation (Edward L. Thorndike), were merged in John B. Watson's program. In his *functional scheme* of analysis human and subhuman individuals alike were disregarded as subjects of their respective life processes and instead conceptualized *mechanistically.*

The majority of critics seem to realize that objections to a 'natural scientific model' *cannot seriously point to psychology's imitation of the biological investigation of open, self-active systems.* In contrast, and nearer to the official rhetoric of psychology as exact science on the *via regis* of experimental analysis and statistical evaluation of data, they attribute the objectivistic epistemology of psychology to its *slavish devotion to the 'Galilean principles' of physics.*

Psychology's Lip Service to Exact Science

I shall not dispute the initial model function of (classical) physics. However, I deem it not just a deficit of historiographic precision, but rather a serious *'presentistic' bias* to level the development of psychology since its formal inception such that, say, *Wundt's* and *Watson's* approaches are passed off as indistinguishable examples of the *same scientific model* or of a *continuing scientistic self-misunderstanding.* Let me examine this a little further.

Admittedly, Wundt's dual conception of psychology as experimental and comparative-genetic discipline is no longer ignored, that is, the latter orientation is no longer as marginalized, as it was in previous standard histories of psychology (for example, Boring, 1950, esp. p. 321 - but note the recent echo in Jüttemann, 1986, p. 23). Nevertheless, Wundt's argument for the cultural-psychological ('völkerpsychologische') method is still not fully understood: its crux lies in the conception of *psychological experimentation.* Wundt's approach cannot be identified with the experimental-statistical scheme of modern '*variable-psychology*' - a view that has historically been sanctioned with the triumph of behaviourism and the dominance of positivism from John Stuart Mill via Ernst Mach to the logical positivists. The difference is not just one between respective subject matters, rather it affects *methodological principles.* Moreover, this dividing line does *not* run between behaviourism and the classical psychology of consciousness, but has its *beginnings in internal controversies of the latter about 'introspectionism'.*

Wundt (1896) strictly observed the objective and formal premises of physics *qua* model science: that is, the factual appropriateness of the analytical isolation of natural objects as *closed systems* in order to measure internal exchange processes of relevant system qualities, and hence the *applicability of the technical prescriptions* of exact experimentation (systematic variation, replication, etc.). *Therefore, and in consequence of* the 'actuality', the 'creative synthesis' of consciousness, which he believed to obey *sui generis laws of ' psychic causality'*, he assigned only a *limited* role to experimentation, namely to make *possible controlled observation of the 'immediate experience'* and the analytic abstraction of stable elements from it. Compound psychic phenomena and their connections in 'psychic developments' require complementary methods of *'pure observation'* and *comparative description of individually reflected historical objectifications of the human mind.* Accordingly, he rejected the extensive application of 'introspective' experimentation (and measurement) by his students or contemporaries. In contrast to the induced *'internal perception'* of conscious data which are firmly related to quantified variations of physically strictly definable stimuli, traditional introspective, let alone *retrospective*, reports are incommensurable with the methodology of physical observation (Wundt, 1907).

The classical framework of psychology was undermined by a development started within it which led to a *'variabilization'* of the psychological subject matter.

1. *Methodically,* the unlimited experimental correlation between input-variables conceived *ad hoc* by the experimenter and experiential variables of any sort paved the way for the *'control-scientific'* experiment, that is, the manipulation of (usually) representative samples of untrained and unknowing subjects whose individual responses, in the light of 'error variance', are statistically averaged for predictive purposes.

2. Wundt had regarded the *descriptive classification* of experimental phenomena as only a *first step towards a scientific explication* of psychic causality that uses *hypotheses in irreducible terms about covert processes and entities.* By contrast, Oswald Külpe (1893) was satisfied with orderly descriptions of contingent classes of perceptual givens - in conformity with Mach's postulate that theoretical concepts and laws must not go beyond economic abstractions of, and functional relations between, 'sensations'. This, in its turn, favoured Edward B. Titchener's transmission of a *'positivized' structuralist version* of Wundt's approach to American psychology (see his posthumuous *magnum opus*, Titchener, 1929). Titchener's introspectionism acted as a crucial foil for the eventual behaviouristic focussing of associations of S-R elements as end-terms of analysis described in physical thing language - a formula which is retained in the methodology of contemporary psychological explanation and prediction.

Unequivocal modeling on physics? Indeed, the initial "*extension* of the experimental method to subjective phenomena" (Koch, 1959, p. 784) was concerned with determining invariant relationships between physical and psychical events, these being considered comparable to physical statements on conservation. At first glance, this endeavour remained unchanged when the task of psychology became one of fixing correlations between public observables: the organism/person turning into the empty domain at which S and R processes intersect. Did the scientific model for early behaviourism not mean "the *use* of experimental method exactly as in physics (objectively)" (Koch, 1959, p. 784)? In point of fact, the excessive control *annulled* the character of the scientific "*experimental dialogue*" (Prigogine) - that is, notwithstanding the preeminence of the human subject, a balanced reciprocity of the respective powers of nonhuman and human, intelligent, nature. In behaviourism the *intersubjective mode of relations* is replaced by a conception which banishes 'the other one's' subjectivity into the empirically inaccessible 'black box'. Hence, the subject, albeit a non-agent by definition, is suspected as the central 'disturbing' factor. This compels one, in an endeavour that is both necessary and at the same time hopeless, to 'control away' possible effects of an uncalculable subjectivity, by means of a restrictive, unstable, deceptive - in short, de-subjectifying - experimental setting. This *subjectivist inversion* of the due relation between objective and methodical determinants of the subject matter is *unparalleled* in the alleged physical model.

And where are the *psychological equivalents to the dimensions of physics?* Despite the insistence on objective techniques of observation, the use of systematic variables was anything but precise and consistent. Such ambiguities forced behaviourism to become *neo* swiftly: "We thus get, beginning around 1930, the emulation of natural science's *theoretical* method." (Koch, 1959, p. 784). This attempt too, however, to construct hypothetically complex systems out of fundamental laws *independent* from particular structures and of observational measurements is a misunderstanding of physics. Physicists who rely on *experimentation* for revealing the causality of non-evident, factually possible reactions of nature, do not despise *naturalistic observation as objective method.* Their use of the *operational* mode of definition, which relates them to the perceptual space of classical physics as "protophysics" (Einstein) does not imply the assertion that the *meaning of a concept is the act of its measurement,* and that dynamic determination can do without *non-empirical* terms. Above all, physicists *generalize* invariances from effective structures of matter in which they take in the form of special laws. Neither in theoretical interpretation nor in experimental analysis can physicists, therefore, *abstract* from (that is, omit) such structures.

Thus, I believe Norbert Bischof (1981) to be mistaken when he claims for psychology an unrivalled *triumph of the 'Galilean program', the methodology of which - 'material reduction' and 'homogenization' - he sees evidenced* by uniform tenets such as Guthrie's principle of contiguity, and by the general behaviourist neglect of interspecies differences in organismic capacities, etc. For want of a *natural taxonomy* of significant situations and adjusted activities, and of a *non-positivistic analysis* of their psychic mediation, the behaviourist measurements are *substantially dimen-*

sionless (like 'response rate'), and their relations void. (I note in passing: the 'empty organism' doctrine, although especially evident in Burrhus F. Skinner's ultra-positivism, is by no means abandoned in methodological-behaviourist systems of intervening variables. The post-neobehaviourist program of 'functional definition' perpetuates the failure of 'hyphen psychologists' - to borrow Neal E. Miller's expression - to define their variables independently and meaningfully). The residue of a *metaphysical view* of exact-empirical analytics is the *formalist universalization of variable-functions,* that is, the *reification* of mathematically expressed *pure possibilities* for the behaviour of particular objects. Such formal expressions need to be filled object-theoretically. Indeed they are: in physical theorizing the abstractness of the analytical closure of the respective system, and hence, of the exclusion of irreversible developments - a fundamental prerequisite for quantifying motion in mathematical equations - is explicitly or implicitly, accounted for. By contrast, psychology builds its theories within the variable-scheme on an entirely arbitrary pattern *abstracting from the abstractness* of system closure, this double abstraction changing into *ontological reductionism:* In the mechanistic interpretation of the functional relations in terms of 'conditionality' of human beings the *methodical* requirement of closure turns out an *objective* feature: the *homo psychologicus* as *homo clausus.*

Here it is enough to underscore that in main areas of psychology, the terms experiment, variable, measurement, control, law or theory cannot be regarded as true counterparts to their homonyms in the exact sciences.

Beyond Scientism and Idealistic Antiscientism

The moral of this episode is as follows: One may, albeit provisionally, see the history of mainstream psychology as "very much a history of changing views, doctrines, images about *what to emulate in the natural sciences* - especially physics" (Koch, 1959, p. 784). Myths and false corrections, however, are only avoided, if the *differentiation* hinted at in this formula ('*what* to emulate') is taken seriously, and if one is prepared for an *erroneous* copy of science. With respect to our exemplary case, it should be called to mind that the alleged (co-) initiator of a scientistically misconstrued psychology did indeed think psychology was (also) a natural science, but one having characteristics which virtually *preclude a positivistic reading.* Wundt, despite his view of experience in terms of neutral monism, was no modern John Stuart Mill in Machian dress (Danziger, 1979). The historical fact is that Wundt's methodological prospect of an objective investigation of human subjectivity, *embracing both the 'Galilean principles' of analytical-constructive experimentation and the genetic-reconstructive methods of historical investigation,* was *overlooked* in the development of psychology. To be sure, I do not suggest that a balanced perspective on Wundt's heterogeneous thinking has already been achieved. However, recent attempts at a modest and modified experimentalism in the course of an overall 'historisization' of psychology are well advised to become aware of Wundt as a historical *precursor*, and to reflect carefully on external conditions of Wundt's failure as well as on fundamental shortcomings inherent in his dualistic conception.

Wholesale accusations of 'scientism' which have their roots in *general reservations against an 'ultimately positivistic' natural science* prove untenable *historically*. They oppose *systematic* foundational tasks as well. The *implicit irony* of such a critical position is that it remains in the grip of the very scientism it aims to criticize, as it unwittingly takes the - received image of the - 'exact' (analytical-experimental, mathematized) branches of knowledge as *exclusive* standards of scientific endeavour. Moreover, it is erroneous as it believes that 'nomological psychology' strictly *follows* these principles. It escapes the notice of these critics that *notable scientists* (for example, Boltzmann, Planck, Einstein, or Lorenz) have *doubted the epistemological viability* of the received - logicistic - view of the epistemic practices of physics or of biology, and that *former promoters* of orthodox logical positivism themselves have *recanted* the most defective defining tenets of their philosophy (see Koch & Leary, 1985).

By reducing the criticism to the common denominator of a mistaken or at least exaggerated scientificness, and failing to recognize the mainstream-psychological travesty of scientific method, an *interpretive* paradigm suggests itself as an alternative to experimental science *explaining* facts. In order to avoid the obsolete opposition of an idiographic psychology based on *neo-Kantian historism* to the pure and nomothetic psychology of the *physicalistic 'unified science'* brand, we need a *monistic* foundation of a '*psychological science of the subject*' which radically dismisses the tacit agreement of both antipodes, namely, to *tear apart the concrete unity of science* (the pervading nexus of different cognitive modes), and to *abstract from the historical totality of the natural-social reality of the human subject.* With the present extension of 'historisizing' to the exact branches of science (e.g., physical chemistry), the epistemological perspective of an integrative, since historical, scientific world-view - laid down in Friedrich Engels' (1971/1883) *Dialektik der Natur* - becomes imperative. A perspective, that is, in which human mind, society, and nature are referred to each other as *differentiations of a monism of matter which exists by way of change:* "Development and history are no longer a principle that divorces culture from nature, but are rather their connecting link" (Darwin, 1883, p. 8).

The task is - and here the opposition is fully justified - to realize subjectivity in psychological research, hence, to *rehabilitate 'immediate experience'* as object and means of inquiry. This does not imply a '*her-*

meneutic monism', as it certainly precludes the assumption that the individual is encircled by a world of only interpretable subjective meanings. It simply takes account of the fact that human agents experience in their individual life worlds objective social conditions as meanings which they assimilate as premises of their subjective grounds for action. This I regard as the specifically *human manifestation of causation*: the mediation by the individual's decision to realize action possibilities objectively indicated in social meanings. As this responds to emotionally evaluated necessities of maintaining one's action potence under certain circumstances, it can, in principle, be understood by other subjects beyond mere intuition. In order to secure the scientific character of such a start from 'first person singular' experiential data, we need to explicate a given internal state as an instance of typical constellations of objective situational meanings and subjectively functional modes of action respectively. I sketched out this '*structural generalization*' on a previous occasion (Maiers, 1986), and hence, let me simply point to the fact that it bears similarity with principles of generalization which Kurt Lewin (1931) extrapolated the 'methodology of the pure case' in physics. These methodological principles he paraphrased as a *"Galilean mode of thought" still to make its way against the prevailing statistical frequency thinking of psychology.* (Mind the contrast to the contemporary critics referred to above!) *Conceptually,* the empirical study of concrete-historical subjectivity is based on a thorough *historical reconstruction of psyche as a distinct subjective reflection of objective reality* up to its latest phenomenal qualities of human consciousness. Such an approach under the primacy of historical method - remembering Karl Marx' dictum (1964, p. 143): "History itself is a *real* part of *natural history* - of nature developing into man." - should be able to avoid the impasse of dualism. With respect to the exemplar chosen here, it should preserve in a '*critical reinterpretation*' on *materialistic* grounds the rational elements of Wundt's idea of a *sui generis position of psychology* in relation to the natural sciences and the humanities. The endeavour of Critical Psychology follows this direction - based on the '*Cultural-historical School*' of Soviet psychology, which, interestingly, has recently been acknowledged by Toulmin & Leary (1985, p. 597) as representing 'both sides of the Wundtian heritage: the experimental and the cultural'.

Implications for Theoretical Psychology

The *general 'theoretical-psychological' intention* behind this paper has been to argue that metatheoretical analyses with the objective of formulating a heuristic for future psychological research need an *historical approach to both psyche and psychology.* The appropriateness of new directions depends on a competent historiographical systematization of a present problematic that accounts for the progressive as well as discontinuous tradition of scientific issues and solutions. Otherwise, such attempts run the risk of presenting false alternatives. The revival of historical interests that can be observed in recent debates on psychology's 'crisis', is certainly to be welcomed. In contrast to the traditional historiography, which has hardly affected scientific research itself, this new examination of psychology's past claims to be *systematically contributive.* It meets marked tendencies in modern philosophy of science to undermine the 'cult of empiricism' (Toulmin & Leary, 1985, p. 607) by *acknowledging in historical-empirical studies the real practices of varied scientific disciplines.* They thus offer new potentials to properly classify psychology among the sciences, such that the *reductionist 'unitary scheme'* as well as the *illusion of an incommensurable uniqueness* of branches can be overcome. The decisive steps, however, have to be taken from *within* our discipline. It seems to me, as if too often metacritical inspections of psychology's *status quo* are pursued *without leaning systematically* on such historical research. Provided that my observation is correct, this should be of some significance to the course of 'theoretical psychology'.

References

Angell, J. R. (1907). The province of functional psychology. *Psychological Review, 14*,(2), 61-91.

Baldwin, J. M. (1895). *Mental development in the child and the race: Methods and processes.* New York: Macmillan.

Bischof, N. (1981). Aristoteles, Galilei, Kurt Lewin - und die Folgen. In W. Michaelis (Ed.), *Bericht über den 32. Kongress der DGfP in Zürich 1980*, (pp.17-39). Göttingen: Hogrefe.

Boring, E. G. (1950). *A history of experimental psychology.* New York: Appleton-Century-Crofts.

Bühler, K. (1918). *Die geistige Entwicklung des Kindes.* Jena: Fischer.

Danziger, K. (1979). The positivist repudiation of Wundt. *Journal of the History of the Behavioral Sciences, 15*, 205-230.

Darwin und die Evolutionstheorie [Special issue]. (1982). *Dialektik 5.* Köln: Pahl-Rugenstein.

Engels, F. (1971). Dialektik der Natur. In *Marx Engels Werke* (Vol. 20, pp. 307-620). Berlin (GDR): Dietz.

Giorgi, A. (1970). *Psychology as a human science.* New York: Harper & Row.

Jüttemann, G. (Ed.). (1985). *Psychologie in der Veränderung.* Weinheim: Beltz.

Jüttemann, G. (1986). Vorbemerkungen des Herausgebers. In G. Jüttemann (Ed.), *Die Geschichtlichkeit des Seelischen* (pp. 7-27). Weinheim: Beltz.

Koch, S. (1959). Epilogue. In S. Koch (Ed.), *Psychology: A study of a science* (Vol. 3, pp. 729-788). New York: McGraw-Hill.

Koch, S., & Leary, D. E. (Eds.). (1985). *A century of psychology as science.* New York: McGraw-Hill.

Krueger, F. (1915). *Über Entwicklungspsychologie.* Leipzig: Engelmann.

Külpe, O. (1893). *Grundriss der Psychologie.* Leipzig: Engelmann.

Lewin, K. (1931). The conflict between Aristotelian and Galilean modes of thought in contemporary psychology. *Journal of General Psychology, 5*, 141-177.
Mackenzie, B. D. (1976). Darwinism and positivism as methodological influences on the development of psychology. *Journal of the History of the Behavioral Sciences, 12*, 330-337.
Maiers, W. (1987). The historical approach of critical psychology: another case of "paradigm promotion"? In W. J. Baker, M. E. Hyland, H. Van Rappard, & A. W. Staats (Eds.), *Current issues in theoretical psychology* (pp. 175-188). Amsterdam: North-Holland.
Marx, K. (1964). *Economic and philosophical manuscripts of 1844.* New York: International Publishers.
Rychlak, J. F. (1987). The concept of telosponsivity: answering an unmet need in psychology. In W. J. Baker, M. E. Hyland, H. Van Rappard, & A. W. Staats (Eds.), *Current issues in theoretical psychology* (pp. 247-260). Amsterdam: North-Holland.
Stern, W. (1914/1930). *Psychologie der frühen Kindheit.* Leipzig: Quelle & Meyer.
Titchener, E. B. (1929). *Systematic psychology: prolegomena.* New York: Macmillan.
Toulmin, S., & Leary, D. E. (1985). The cult of empiricism in psychology, and beyond. In S. Koch, & D. E. Leary (Eds.), *A century of psychology as science* (pp. 594-617).
Van Strien, P. J. (1987). Model disciplines, research traditions, and the theoretical unification of psychology. In W. J. Baker, M. E. Hyland, H. Van Rappard, & W. W. Staats (Eds.), *Current issues in theoretical psychology* (pp. 333-344). Amsterdam: North-Holland.
Werner, H. (1926). *Einführung in die Entwicklungspsychologie.* Leipzig: Barth.
Wundt, W. (1896).*Grundriss der Psychologie.* Leipzig: Kröner.
Wundt, W. (1907). Über Ausfrageexperimente und über die Methoden zur Psychologie des Denkens. *Psychologische Studien III*, 301-360.
Wundt, W. (1912). *Elemente der Völkerpsychologie: Grundlinien einer psychologischen Entwicklungsgeschichte der Menschheit.* Leipzig: Kröner.
Wundt, W. (1917). Völkerpsychologie und Entwicklungspsychologie. *Psychologische Studien, 10*, 189-238.

COGNITIVE REPRESENTATION: A PSYCHOLOGY IN SEARCH OF MENTALITY

Leendert P. Mos[1]

University of Alberta
Edmonton, Alberta, Canada

SUMMARY: A critique of representational theory in contemporary cognitive psychology from a phenomenological viewpoint. It is concluded that representational, cognitive, theory as a naturalistic, causal, theory of meaning and reference fails as a psychology of the mental.

Contemporary cognitive psychology *posits* the concept of 'representation' as a theoretical entity whereby a person may be said to refer to an object in the precise manner that the representation 'refers' to it and in no other. As such the concept of representation is *nonintentional* for it refers to an object by virtue of being a *re-presentation* of it. However, for a representation to be intentional, it would need to be *interpreted* as being a representation of the referred to object. The representation cannot itself be the bearer of intentional reference![2] Indeed, a cognitive theory that posits an internal representation would also have to posit an intentional act (having the representation as its 'intentional object') of interpretation, were it not for the fact that a representation is *assumed* to be an *interpretation,* on some contextualist or constructivist account, of a particular object. Thus a representation is tacitly construed to be an internal state of meaning, an *intensional* entity which is, however, within cognitive psychology, causally or extensionally conceived of as a re-presentation of an external state-of-affairs.[3] My claim is that this notion of

[1]My thanks to Andy Giorgi and Larry Davidson who led me to make changes in this paper and, more importantly, who taught me about phenomenology.

[2]More generally, a mental state is individuated by specifying a particular cognitive content, a representation, and a relation, a propositional attitude, that a person may be said to have one to another (see Fodor, 1982). While on this account the relation qualifies the content, how it does so is far from clear (in any case, the relation is conceived of as *externally* related to the content - the mode in which the content is entertained, see Rozeboom, 1972), but it is definitely not the case that the relation, or propositional attitude, is an *interpretation* of the content. My point is that cognitive psychology defines its generalizations over relations between representations and external causes and, hence, belongs to what Smith & McIntyre (1982, Ch. 2) have called 'object' theories of intentionality.

[3]This intensional interpretation of the concept of re-presentation needs to be distin-

representation derives its impetus from Gottlob Frege's (1892/1966) semantic distinction between *Sinn* ('sense' or meaning) and *Bedeutung* (that 'referred to', or referent) and that this distinction, while fundamental to the logic of semantic theory, is not an account of intentionality and, hence, is not an account of the mental. Of course, it was never Frege's intent to propose a theory of mind which would be essential if the notion of intentionality is to have any meaning and the concept of *Sinn* is to be understood as a *cognitive content* by virtue of which a person refers to a referent or *Bedeutung*. Hence, insofar as the concept of representation within a *psychological* theory of cognition reflects Frege's concept of meaning as logically distinguished from reference, it fails to capture the phenomenon of intentionality, or *aboutness,* which is characteristic of the mental.

As has often been pointed out, a representation cannot refer any more than a picture can refer to its original except insofar as the picture is *interpreted* as representing its original. If it is argued that a representation is an internal state of meaning, an intensional entity or a cognitive content, then one might ask concerning the 'bearer' of this meaning. Or, if the internal representation is conceived of as an inner language, its intentionality is like the intentionality of any other sign and would minimally require a second, meaning, representation. Whatever the conception of representation (and this would also include representations which are computationally or formally defined - see footnote 3), without a sufficiently rich notion of the mind it will not do as an account of intentionality and, hence, the mental.

The dilemma faced by representational cognitive theory is fairly straightforward. A cognitive theory that invokes the concept of representation sets as its task to explain the intentionality of consciousness, the intentionality of mental acts, within a naturalistic or *causal* framework.

---

[3](cont'd) guished from the computational view which holds that representations are not semantic (that is, not defined in terms of reference, truth, or meaning), but defined formally or syntactically. On the computational view, mental states are individuated only in terms of *formally* distinct representations. I am not directly concerned here with the computational view (formal processes defined over representations) as computations are just processes by which representations have their causal consequences by virtue of their *form*, and hence, would need to be adumbrated by a naturalistic theory of reference if they are to be truly distal. Indeed, Fodor(1982) suggests that cognitive theory ideally would merge a representational theory (of intensional, semantic, or content-distinct representations) with a computational theory (of form-distinct representations) so that the former can have causal consequences in virtue of their form). Of course, Fodor is sceptical about the possibility of a naturalistic theory of reference and, hence, of such a merger, and maintains that the only possible cognitive *psychology* is a computational one which holds to an opague construal of mental acts. While his rationalist account is a strong antidote against a naturalistic, representational, cognitive theory and, indeed, limits the range of the 'psychological,' it also does not provide an account of intentionality.

While cognitive theory need not commit itself to a neuroarchitecture, the thrust of the enterprise is at least implicitly reductionistic. But whether agnostically functionalist or explicitly physicalist, cognitive theory claims to be able to explain what is phenomenally exhibited as intentionality. Such a cognitive account of intentional experiences attempts to explain those experiences by causally correlating them to internal states of the body where the latter are caused by events external and internal to the body. Thus, the claim is that intentionality, or the phenomenal property of *aboutness,* is captured psychologically by the concept of representation which, in turn, is to be subsumed by a bio-physical account. On this view, representational cognitive theories are in principle no different from neo-behavioristic accounts of meaning or action.

While various objections may be raised to this attempt at reductionism, my claim is simply that if human mentation is causal as cognitive theory would have it, then intentionality has no place in it, if for no other reason than that such a theory fails to distinguish between the object of intentionality *qua* object and the object *qua* cause. In fact, cognitive psychologists customarily give only lip service to the notion of intentionality, and even those who seriously take their starting point in folk-psychology quickly abandon intentionality in favour of causal, processing, talk. Perhaps most striking however, is that a representational or causal explanation of intentionality is incompatible with an explication of the phenomenon of intentionality, for these accounts belong to different domains of discourse. A causal account is only possible because it presupposes the *possibility* of *referring* to those entities, theoretical or otherwise, which it invokes in an explanation. Intentional discourse may yield causal discourse, but nothing like intentionality need occur within causal, representational, discourse.[4]

The purported incompatibility of intentional and causal discourses is not resolved by a representational theory derived from, or analogous to, a semantic theory in the tradition of Frege. Fregean *Sinne* are either timeless entities to which we have access only through language, or else they are *cognitive contents* in the same sense of representations. As timeless entities *Sinne* are meanings of linguistic signs in virtue of which those signs may be said to refer. As cognitive contents, meanings are what one *grasps* when one understands an expression for such meanings also contain their mode-of-presentation of the object referred to. But the difficulty for Frege is like that faced by any contemporary, cognitive theory of representation, namely what are we to make of such *cognitive contents*

[4]For example, Mohanty (1981) writes "[I]ntentionality and causal theory are compatible, not in the sense that they supplement or complement each other, nor in the sense that the former is the phenomenal explanandum while the latter is the theoretical explanans, but rather in the sense that the two belong to two different levels of discourse" (p. 14).

without a theory of mind (or a psychology of acts!)? For just as meanings or senses, on Frege's account, are meanings or senses of linguistic signs, just so representations are re-presentations of objects or events, *externally* related to the mental acts that grasp these meanings or intend those objects or events. Indeed, Frege had no conception of intentionality. His *Sinne* are senses of appropriate signs, not of mental acts; just as representations are re-presentations of objects, not meanings of mental acts. Even if it is argued that a mental act grasps such meanings or re-presentations in some particular attitude, those meanings or representations are not *cognitive contents.* Rather they are '*intentional objects,*' concrete or abstract, of mental acts which are themselves bereft of any notion of intentionality. What we require is some conception of the *structure* of a mental act, not only some conception of *structure* which the mental act grasps. For it is the *structure* of a mental act which presumably can account for the act's *directedness* towards a particular of object, concept, or meaning. Thus, while both Frege and contemporary cognitive theorists address problems associated with intentionality or aboutness, neither have a concept of intentionality.

We must be clear just what Frege's intensional theory is a theory of. He maintains that an expression's relationship to its referent is determined by the expression's meaning. Or, that the meaning determines the expression's referent precisely because the meaning contains the mode-of-presentation of the referent, so that every meaning determines its referent in a particular way. Hence, different expressions may have the same referent and yet differ in their reference - in the way these expressions refer to their common referent. Therefore, the meaning of an expression *mediates* the reference of an expression and is not the object of that expression. Thus, the mental act of presenting Venus as the morning star does grasp Venus as the morning star. But it is not the *mental act* of presentation which does this. Rather, it is the expression 'morning star' which, through its sense or meaning, refers to Venus as the morning star. The intentional act of presenting Venus as the morning star is made possible because the expression 'morning star' has that sense and reference in the first place.[5]

Indeed, on Frege's account, meanings belong *neither* to the world of ideas ('psychologism') nor to the world of perceptible things. (In fact, neither do representations although cognitive theorists would be loath to assign them a unique ontological status - hence, the implicit reductionism.) But while meanings are not mind-dependent, they are

[5]This clarification of Frege's concept of *Sinn* derives from Mohanty (1981, p. 17). Both he and Smith & McIntyre (1982, p. 75ff.) point out that Frege assumed that intentional verbs refer to ordinary relations, relating persons to intensional entities, which are governed by principles of extensionality.

mind-related, for every meaning determines its referent in a particular way, under some conception. For, as Frege would have it, meanings or Sinne are intensional entities accessible through language which mediate the relation between expression and referent. But the question not addressed by Frege is how such *intensional* entities enter into the *intentional* relation of any mental act to its object. It is unacceptable to suggest that intensional entities are intentional objects (just as representations are not the objects of mental acts) for then the intentional relation is not directed towards a transcendent object but towards a meaning or representation.[6] So that while Frege's intensional theory of meaning and reference is able to account for referring to non-existent objects (Frege's theory of 'indirect/ reference') and of referring to the same object by way of different meanings, it neither provides an account of intentionality, nor an account of how a *mental act* can be truly directed towards a distal object. The whole point of Frege's semantics was to provide a logical theory which can give an interpretation of reference by way of meaning. While such an account is valuable as a theory of semantics, it remains committed to extensional principles, namely those that characterize a naturalistic or causal framework. Frege's distinction between meaning and reference was introduced precisely to save these extensional principles, and not to provide either a psychological explanation or explication of the mental in terms of the phenomenon of intentionality.

Perhaps, the problem faced by a representatonal, cognitive, theory in the Fregean tradition can be more readily appreciated from within the context of Franz Brentano's (1874/1973) original formulation. Brentano's proposal was simple, and yet radical. He held that the defining characteristic of the mental is *intentionality,* namely that mental acts are always directed towards some object. This formulation immediately presented two questions: first, what is this relation of directedness, or *aboutness,* and second, what is the nature of the *object* towards which the act is directed? Brentano wavered in his answer to both these questions. At first (1874), the relation of directedness is conceived of as an *ordinary* relation holding between a person and an 'intentionally inexistent' object. Later (1911), Brentano adopts a more conservative ontology and rejects intentionally inexistent objects in favour of concrete particulars and, with it, the relational character of intentionality - which becomes merely a surface, grammatical, *quasi*-relation - thereby rejecting the notion that mental acts are *relational* at all. What is quite evident here (between 1874

[6]Of course, on Fodor's (1982) account, cognitive psychology ***ought*** to pursue, as a research strategy, 'methodological sclipsism,' which construes representations opaquely, that is to say independently of the way the world is. For as Fodor so clearly recognizes, there is no prospect for a naturalistic psychology of 'organism/environment transactions' (p. 298ff).

and 1911) is that the phenomenon of intentionality gives way when it is defined in terms of its *object,* especially when that object is taken to be a concrete particular. Theories that take the phenomenon of intentionality to be an *ordinary* relation holding between a two predicates must postulate 'intentional objects' (intensional entities, meanings, or representations), or else they must deny that acts of consciousness, mental acts, are intentional at all! Brentano, like contemporary cognitive theorists, did neither. Rather, Brentano maintains that consciousness is intentional, but that it is non-relational. By doing so, he avoids postulating 'intentional objects' or denying intentionality, but the price he pays is that he severs our intentional relations to ordinary objects (for an extensive discussion of this point see Smith & McIntyre, 1982, pp. 57 - 61).

It is, of course, in this sense that cognitive theory is also wanting. Certainly, on the computational view cognitive theory is methodologically, at least, solipsistic (see footnote 6), but even on the representational view which is explicitly formulated within a naturalistic, causal, framework, the *intended* representations are but re-presentations of objects. Of course, as the behaviorists knew even before the cognitivists did, the problem with this conception of representation is that there is simply no *canonical* way of referring to generalizations defined over environmental events and mental states. Hence, the hopelessness of a representational theory conceived of within a naturalistic framework.[7] Thus, while recent psychological theorizing has come to recognize the role of human subjectivity which was by-passed by its behavioristic predecessors, it has understood this subjectivity entirely in *naturalistic* framework. On such a psychological account there is nothing about the human mind, including that last vestige of the mental, namely intentionality, which cannot be explained in naturalistic, causal, terms.

---

[7]Fodor (1982) opts instead for a computational psychology wherein mental states are opaquely individuated. On such a computational account, "... we can try to say what the mental representation is, and what the relation to a mental representation is, such that one believes that the Morning Star is F by virtue of bearing the latter to the former. And we can try to say how that representation, or that relation, or both, differ from the representation and the relation constitutive of believing that the Evening Star is F" (p. 303). In fact, Dreyfus (1982, Introduction) suggests that Husserl's ***noema*** theory as proposed in ***Ideas*** (1931/1913) corresponds to Fodor's computational theory of representations, whereas Husserl's ***content*** theory which dates from ***Logical Investigations*** (1970/1900-1901) is more like the representational theory criticized here. While I am sympathetic with this suggestion, it is just controversial to suggest, as Dreyfus (1982) does, that Husserl thought of noemata as "complex formal structures" for Husserl was adamant that we must have direct and indubitable access to our noemata if they the structures of our mental acts and, therefore, the way our intentional contents are realized. And whereas we appear to have access to our ***meanings***, we certainly do not have access to our ***computations***.

It was this naturalistic interpretation of the human mind which Immanuel Kant and Edmund Husserl, among others, questioned under the auspices of transcendental, or foundational, philosophy. Transcendental philosophy seeks to understand the world, including our experience, in terms of human subjectivity which is taken to be the *source* of all our ordering, meaning, and interpreting. Transcendental philosophy was not so much an argument, and certainly it was not an explanation of facts, as it was the quest to establish the *preconditions* of objectivity, a quest to show that experience and knowledge are constituted in and through human subjectivity. It was Husserl who held that psychology was to play a foundational role in this endeavor (phenomenology as 'descriptive psychology'). For in spite of his anti-psychologism - his rejection of a naturalistic interpretation of the mental - he evolved a conception of psychology which had as its task to describe ('phenomenological psychology') the peculiar intentionalities proper to each type of mental act and to search out the noesis-noema correlations that characterize mental life.[8]

By way of contrast, Frege held that mental life consists of private particulars and, hence, that psychology as the descriptive science of mental life was to be inductive and statistical. As such, Frege was eager to reject the intrusion of psychology into the domains of logic and mathematics, for the former, as a natural science of the mind, had to rely on the principles of logic and mathematics to carry out its task. But then Frege had no conception of intentionality; his view was merely that mental acts have objects. But Brentano's thesis pertained not only to inexistent objects, but also to the *relation* of intentionality by virtue of which the mental act is directed towards an inexistent object. It was Husserl's

[8]Husserl's rejection of psychologism which is what he called an empirical, genetic, and associationistic psychology, led him to propose, from the transcendental standpoint, an eidetic, descriptive, and intentional psychology. The transcendental critique served to radically undermine the identification of the mental with the psychological and, hence revived the 'mysterious' problem of the relationship between the "subjectivity of knowing and the objectivity of the content known" (see Mohanty, 1985). In fact, Husserl labored long and hard over the relationship between transcendental philosophy ('phenomenology') and psychology. At first, he viewed phenomenology as a 'descriptive psychology,' later he viewed them as parallel endeavors, still later phenomenological psychology was viewed as a hybrid discipline, naturalistic with regard to consciousness, transcendental with regard to the objects of consciousness. However, this last formulation was also eventually rejected for it retained a naturalistic sense of subjectivity - 'transcendental psychologism' - which he found lacked an adequate foundation. Husserl came to doubt the possibility of psychology as a positive science; there being only a transcendental psychology which was identical with transcendental philosophy. Yet he reserved a role for psychology: psychology first informed by the transcendental - a transcendentally constituted subjectivity - which would then permit, by way of a phenomenological psychology, a return to a positive science of psychology. On this account philosophy and psychology became complementary disciplines (see Davidson, in press).

contribution to give an explicit account of the *structure* of intentionality of the mental act in terms of the noema.[9] The noema determines its reference precisely because to grasp the meaning - the noesis-noema correlation - is to know what sorts of experiences (objects) would satisfy it. By contrast, Frege's account began with signs that had senses which then explained how the sign referred to whatever it is a sign of. Mental acts, on Frege's conception, are intentional only because they grasp the senses of the corresponding signs. So what Frege's account of intentionality amounts to is the recognition that the mental act grasps an object; what neither he nor Brentano had, but Husserl did have, was an account of the *sense of a mental act.*

Similarly, it is my contention that cognitive, representational, theory, while providing an account of how a word or meaning refers to whatever it is a word or meaning of, fails to provide an account of how the person by way of a mental act *refers.* And this is because cognitive theory has no account of the concept of intentionality, or aboutness. Frege rightly rejected psychologism for on that view the mental was private and, of course, logic was not. Cognitive theory has modelled the private as a *re-presentation* of the public within a causal account, but has only succeeded in pushing the private further 'inward' without in any way explicating Brentano's defining characteristic of the mental, namely intentionality.

It is perhaps instructive to see how Husserl dealt with the threat of psychologism; how he could speak of the subjectivity of mental life and yet not lose the objectivity of meaning or cognitive content. For no matter how vehemently either Frege or Husserl rejected psychologism, the relationship between the subjective and the objective remained a challenge to both of them. Husserl tried to bridge this relationship by means of the concept of intentionality which, within the context of a philosophy of transcendentalism, was first and foremost a theory of the *constitution* of 'objectivities' in mental acts which present those objectivities as *given.* But then just what was the psychologism that Husserl tried to ward off? Mohanty (1985) maintains that, on Husserl's account, psychologism is the view that phenomena of mind appear in a person's life as *products* whose *production* takes place step by step following well-defined rules.[10]

[9] Briefly, Husserl maintains that all mental acts have correlative noemata or senses which intend the object under a particular description. It is the noema of an act which makes reference possible (and defines the act as intentional), of which truth and falsity are predicated and, as contrasted with the noesis, the noema is non-temporal, intersubjectively available thereby making communication possible. Noemata are not like Fregean *Sinne* however, for while noemata are linquistically expressible, they are but implicitly conceptual and can be raised to a level of conceptual meaning *only* in an act of reflection.

[10] This way of defining psychologism is reminiscent of the computational view (see foot-

These phenomena are then given a naturalistic *interpretation*. But the notions of product and of production are very misleading for what is *produced* in a mental act is not a material entity, but a meaning - with the same claim to reality as things in the world - which can be intersubjectivity identified, recognized, and re-identified. The problem with 'production' language is that the mental becomes identified with the psychological; the mental is thematized within the causal order of nature. But the *mental* as such is not *psychological*. Once this is recognized, the notion that there are various types of discourse, each thematizing the mental in a certain way, becomes intelligible. What Husserl, and earlier Brentano, resisted was the identification of the mental, of intentionality and meaning, with the causal framework of the psychological.

What both psychologism and anti-psychologism have in common is that they share a conception of the mental which is tied to a naturalistic, causal, discourse. To overcome psychologism however is not to reject it (as Frege did), but to recognize that it is an interpretative framework that passes for the material, the ontologically material. The question we must pose is whether this framework is possible and yet grant the phenomenon of intentionality as defining of the mental. Husserl's 'inward turn' was to suspend the psychological framework and ask how it is that empirical, causal, psychological inquiry was possible. Now it must be cautioned that this move, the transcendental move, does not create two worlds: the empirical and the transcendental. As phenomenologists have repeatedly pointed out, there is but one life of consciousness which has both intersubjective and historical reality. It is within this consciousness that all interpretative frameworks are rooted. Only by interpreting the phenomena of mental life as causal products can we come to appreciate Husserl's rejection of psychologism. A natural science of the mind is not to be eschewed, rather it must not be taken as an ontology of the mental. In this sense Husserl challenged the construal of the mental as a private, inner, domain which is to be inserted in, and understood in terms of, a natural, causal, framework. The challenge is not necessarily to be en-

---

[10](cont'd) note 6). The problem with the computational view is that its purported strengths, namely that it has a view of *process* that is both representational (opaquely construed) and is compatible with a materialist ontology, are probably false. First, the notion of process as a digital one may be juxtaposed to process as an analogue procedure which need not stretch the credulity of making semantics into syntax (cognition is not a universal Turing machine at least not on any currently intelligible account). Second, the computational view is not materialist, for the functionalist thesis maintains precisely that its 'descriptions' are not instances of physical laws. Computational representations, which are symbolic and formal, preserve materialism only by playing the mind off against the body. A computational theory could never get off the ground without a meaning-intending theorist. The computational view is like the Fregean and unlike the Husserlian view in that it is extensional (even if it is presented as intensional) and, therefore, it is not intentional (see Pylyshyn, 1980 and Weimer's 1980 Commentary).

gaged in a transcendental phenomenology, it is to be engaged in theoretical psychology: to question the very possibility of a naturalistic, causal, psychology of intentionality.

One need not search far within the cognitive tradition to find clues to an answer. Fodor (1983), near the end of his modularity thesis, asks about the outputs of modules and their relation to further, central, processors. That is, he asks about the level of representation at which the modules interface with central processes. First, we should note that the proposal that there are modules which take transduced information to some representational form which is phenomenologically salient merely moves the problem of intentionality from the distal object to the phenomenologically salient representation. It is as if when we deal with the representation (module output) rather than with the distal object, the problem is made easier. But, of course, it is not any easier since on the psychological model all mental events are private, especially those computational processes within the module which cannot even be brought to awareness through reflection, and the question of the interface between module outputs and higher cognitive processes remains recalcitrant to investigation. Indeed, the major effort in psychology has been to try to demonstrate the *psychological* reality of representations - their efficacy in a processing model - given minimal conditions of input. Or, from within the context of modularity, Fodor poses the question "[W]hat is the most that an encapsulated process should be supposed to compute?" (Fodor, 1983, p. 91), without appeal to central cognitive processes. But since modules are by definition informationally impenetrable (encapsulated) the representations which such systems can effect must be determined solely by the properties of the architecture of the transducers and the object. There is simply no way to determine the *psychological* reality of representations either on the basis of external input or by trying to find the limits of cognitive penetrability. While the purported cognitive impenetrability of modular processes ensures the veridicality of the representations of the module outputs relative to their (worldly) inputs, *the* psychological question, as Fodor clearly recognizes, becomes one of how the person is able to *use* the representational outputs of these modules. And he goes so far as to say that *everything* we know is, in principle, relevant to determining this. Or, on his "First Law of the Non-existence of Cognitive Science," the more isotropic, or global, the cognitive process, the less anyone understands it (Fodor 1983, p. 107). On this assessment it seems rather pretentious, and certainly premature, to cast the 'workings' of the mind into a psychological, causal, framework. Moreover, whatever view one takes of the mental is probably as good as another assuming that its adequacy be assessed not in terms of psychological theory but in terms of the defining characteristic of the mental, namely, intentionality. Fortunately, Husserl provided one such view.

More recently, Fodor (1986) presents the representational theory of mind, and, indeed, the "crucial achievement of the phylogeny of cognition" (p. 14), as the organism's capacity to respond to *non-nomic* properties. When a stimulus property is non-nomic, then that property is one that the *organism represents* the stimulus as having. The nature of this representation which is semantic becomes part of the causal processing chain. So mental representations are introduced to explain the possibility of non-nomic properties which unlike *nomic* properties are not transducer (module) detectable. But it is, of course, the organism's representation of those non-nomic properties which is at issue. Fodor maintains that these non-nomic properties are inferred from (the representations of) modular outputs. The result of this inferring process is what is meant by the representation of a non-nomic property. However, the whole point of talking about the representation of non-nomic properties inferred on the basis of modular, computational, representations is to preserve the causal-like nature of the entire referential process. In fact, Fodor is explicit on this point, namely the transducer-detectable (nomic) properties play the same role in contemporary cognitive theory as the notion of sensory properties did in more traditional accounts. What remains problematic here is what it is for an organism to represent a non-nomic property, except to say that it is *inferred* on the basis of the nomic, transduction-modular, process output. Of course, this will not do for it confronts us with Fodor's own First Law of the Non-existence of Cognitive Science!

The upshot of Fodor's thesis is perhaps most telling with regard to the current status of representational, cognitive, theory. While claiming that the limits of modularity are the limits of our understanding of the mind (given the causal framework), he also maintains that all attempts to develop theoretical models of 'problem solving' have only led to an understanding of input analyses, and that the psychology of thought has proven quite intractable (presumably in a way that the psychology of perception has not). The conclusion is straightforward enough. Mentality is not bound in any way presently understood by either the world or by that part of the world which is its neuroarchitecture. A cognitive, causal, model requires a form-function correspondence and, on this account, there is little that can be expected by way of restraint on the nature of mental acts either from a neuropsychology or cognitive psychology. The cruel conclusion of Fodor's thesis is that there can be no serious psychology of cognitive processes and the reason, on my account, is that the only serious *psychological* model of *meaning* is the representational model and that model fails as an explication of the intentionality of the mental.

References

Brentano, F. (1973). *Psychology from an empirical standpoint.* (Edited by L. L. McAlister and translated by A. C. Rancurello, D. B. Terrell, & L. L. McAlister.) New York: Humanities Press. (Original 1874).

Davidson, L. (in press). Husserl's refutation of psychologism and the possibility of a phenomenological psychology. *Journal of Phenomenological Psychology, 19(1).*

Dreyfus, H. L. (1982). Introduction. In H. L. Dreyfus (Ed.), *Husserl, intentionality, and cognitive science* (pp. 1-27). Cambridge, MA: The MIT Press.

Fodor, J. A. (1982). Methodological solipsism considered as a research strategy in cognitive psychology. In H. L. Dreyfus (Ed.), *Husserl, intentionality, and cognitive science* (pp. 277-303). Cambridge, MA: The MIT Press.

Fodor, J. A. (1983). *The modularity of mind.* Cambridge, MA: The MIT Press.

Fodor, J. A. (1986). Why paramecia don't have mental representations. *Midwest Studies in Philosophy, X*, 3-23.

Frege, G. (1966). On sense and reference. In P. Geach & M. Black (Eds.), *The philosophical writings of Gottlob Frege* (pp. 56-78). Oxford: Blackwell.

Husserl, E. (1970). *Logical investigations.* (Translated by J. N. Findlay.) New York: Humanities Press. (Original 1900-1901)

Husserl, E. (1931). *Ideas: general introduction to pure phenomenology.* (Translated by W. R. Boyce Gibson.) London: Geroge Allen & Unwin. (Original 1913)

Mohanty, J. N. (1981). Intentionality and noema. *Journal of Philosophy, LXVIII*, 706-717.

Mohanty, J. N. (1985). Husserl, Frege and the overcoming of psychologism. In J. N. Mohanty (Ed.), *The possibility of transcendental philosophy* (pp. 1-11). Dordrecht, Holland: Martinus Nijhoff.

Pylyshyn, Z. W. (1980). Computation and cognition: issues in the foundations of cognitive science. *The Behavioral and Brain Sciences, 3*, 111-169.

Rozeboom, W. W. (1972). Problems in the psycho-philosophy of knowledge. In J. R. Royce & W. W. Rozeboom (Eds.), *The psychology of knowing* (pp. 25-93). New York: Gordon & Breach.

Smith, D. W. & McIntyre, R. (1982). *Husserl and intentionality.* Dordrecht, Holland: D. Reidel.

Weimer, W. B. (1980). Cognition is not computation, for reasons that computers don't solve mind-body problems. *The Behavioral and Brain Sciences, 3*, 152-153.

THE CONCEPTUAL DISTINCTION BETWEEN PROPOSITIONAL AND SKILLFUL KNOWING[1]

William E. Smythe

University of Alberta
Edmonton, Alberta, Canada

SUMMARY: A conceptual analysis of the distinction between propositional and skillful knowing is presented, in terms of the technical language of propositional attitude theory. The two types of knowing are shown to differ in important ways with respect to such features as content, objective correlate, Intentional modality, mode of representation, direction of fit, and associated boundary conditions.

Introduction

In this paper I examine the distinction between propositional and skillful knowing, that is, the distinction between 'knowing that' something is the case versus 'knowing how to' do something. Philosophers since Ryle (1949) have made much of this distinction, although it has yet to have a very significant impact on the development of psychological theory. Indifference to the distinction has led to an overemphasis, in contemporary cognitive theorizing, on the more conceptual or 'knowing that' side of cognition, at the expense of understanding the subtleties of the more instrumental form of cognition embodied in 'knowing how'. Thus cognitive theorists have, in the recent past, expended some considerable effort attempting to detail the articulate structure of our conceptual knowledge; and they have done so in at least superficially propositional terms, by appealing to forms of representation that, when not explicitly propositional, are often at least 'sentence-like' in structure. However there is little evident appreciation in this work that much of what we know is, in fact, what we 'know how' to do.

I suggest that a more comprehensive psychological account of what knowledge is and how we use it requires understanding the logical struc-

[1]This work was supported by a Killam Postdoctoral Fellowship and by a Canada Research Fellowship (Award 455-87-0170) from the Social Sciences and Humanities Research Council of Canada. I am grateful for the helpful commentary of Charles Bourassa, Don Kuiken, Leo Mos, and William Rozeboom. An expanded treatment of the ideas in this chapter is to appear in *The Journal of Intelligent Systems*.

ture of skillful as well as propositional knowing. The analysis of skillful knowing that I offer in this paper is basically descriptive and taxonomic. I do not offer an explanatory theory of skills, but rather a descriptive account of some of their more salient features as they arise in everyday sorts of circumstances.

The analysis is structured around three basic sorts of questions that must be addressed in respect to any psychological function that purportedly involves knowing. First: *What* do we know? This is a question addressed to the *content* of the knowledge. Second, is a question that is pervasively confused with the first, namely: What do we know *about*? This question is concerned, not with the content, but with the *reference* of knowledge - with what, in the world, might satisfy some knowledge content, if anything does. This may be characterized in terms of a set of conditions or specifications called the *objective correlate* of the knowledge. Thirdly, and most important for a psychological account, is the question: *How* do we know? By means of what distinctive kinds of psychological acts or states do we grasp or possess various kinds of knowledge? These acts and states constitute the *Intentional modality* for knowing, their most distinctive feature being their *Intentionality,*[2] that is, their directedness or potential for reference to an object, by virtue of which they are said to be 'of' or 'about' something (Brentano, 1924; Searle, 1983).

Propositional Knowing

The top panel of Figure 1 presents what has become the standard philosophical view propositional knowing, as it would be expressed in the present terminology. This view derives from that well established philosophical tradition which analyzes propositional knowing in terms of justified true belief. Although this view has come under increasing criticism as a definition of knowledge, it nevertheless serves the present descriptive purposes quite well.

Content

Propositional knowing is named for its distinctive type of content - a proposition. Paradigmatically, propositional knowing is a matter of knowing 'that *p*' (where the variable '*p*' is a placeholder for some sentence expressing a proposition). Ascriptions of propositional knowledge are not always in this form (as when the content is designated by means of some alternative expression such as a nominal, an interrogative clause, or a descriptive phrase), but may nevertheless always, in principle, be

---

[2]To distinguish this technical usage of the term from the ordinary concept of 'intention', all instances of it have here been capitalized.

translated into it.

In any case, knowing-that-*p* clearly involves more than just knowing some particular sentential substitution for '*p*'. If, for example, John knows that Paul is six feet tall, then certainly he knows more than what is literally contained in the sentence "Paul is six feet tall"; he also knows that Paul's height is six feet, that Paul is twice three feet tall, one foot less than seven feet tall, and so on, ad infinitum. If expressions of John's knowledge do not stand up to paraphrasing in these sorts of ways, then what he knows is not a fact about Paul at all, but merely a string of words. Thus, to say that someone knows-that-*p* in any given instance is to say that he or she knows a proposition expressed by the sentence in question, where 'expressed by' is clearly a one-to-many relation.

Objective Correlate

Propositions must, in principle, have a determinable truth value, either 'true' or 'false'; thus the objective correlate for propositional knowing takes the form of truth conditions. According to the classical two-valued logic of truth, truth conditions are governed by certain requirements. First, it must be possible, by the *principle of the excluded middle,* to determine the truth value of a proposition as either *true* or *false;* and, secondly, by the *law of contradiction,* it cannot be both at once (Scheffler, 1965).

This classical conception of truth imposes some quite definite constraints on propositional knowing. First, and most obviously, one cannot know any proposition that is either false or has an indeterminate truth value. Secondly, the contents of propositional knowledge cannot be as vague their expressions in natural language often seem to suggest. Distinct propositional contents must be well distinguished in terms of their truth conditions. If John's knowing that someone is six feet tall is to be distinguished from his knowing that someone is five feet tall or any other height, for example, then the truth conditions for each proposition must be well differentiated from one other (Goodman, 1976).

Intentional Modality

The relevant Intentional modality for propositional knowing is propositional belief, or believing-that-*p*. Propositional belief may be considered to be the basic psychological condition on expressions of propositional knowledge. To use a sentence, or other communicative device, sincerely to express a proposition just means to use it with the intention of expressing a proposition that one also believes. On the other hand, merely to repeat a sentence in a rote, mechanical way that one fails to believe or to understand does not count as an expression of propositional knowledge, even if the proposition expressed by the sentence happens to be true.

The psychological character of belief is much in dispute at the present time. Difficulties in construal of beliefs as dispositional states are well known (Scheffler, 1965). Moreover, beliefs may come about in a great variety of ways, such as by perception, inference, intuition, indoctrination, and so on; and these all involve a rather complex interplay of other mental acts rather different in character from believing itself. Nevertheless, belief is widely considered to be the common psychological denominator for knowing.

Belief, like Intentional modalities generally, implies a certain capacity for *representation,* in that beliefs represent their associated truth conditions in a certain way. Representation may be most broadly conceived, for the purposes of descriptive psychology, as a kind of selective function, as Searle (1983) and others have recently pointed out. That is, representation is under certain selected aspects or properties from among all those which might actually obtain in some situation. For example, if I believe that there is now a steak in my refrigerator, my belief might represent the steak as 'edible' but not normally as 'dead' material. This form of representation is distinctly *predicative* in nature, inasmuch as it involves explicitly predicating certain attributes or properties of things. For example, from by belief that there is a certain edible object in my refrigerator, it is appropriate to conclude that I believe, *of* that object, *that* it is edible and in my refrigerator. The propositional character of this type of belief is intimately related to the predicative manner in which it represents its associated truth conditions.

Direction of Fit

Another feature which helps to characterize the representational function of belief is *direction of fit.* Beliefs may be said to have the 'mind-to-world' direction of fit, to use a term of Searle (1983). As Searle explains the concept, "if my beliefs turn out to be wrong, it is my beliefs and not the world which is at fault, as is shown by the fact that I can correct the situation simply by changing my beliefs. It is the responsibility of the belief, so to speak, to match the world" (p. 8). Thus to a first approximation, propositional knowing is a matter of having true beliefs that represent their truth conditions predicatively according to the mind-to-world direction of fit.

Boundary Conditions

However, as epistemological theorists have long understood, there is more to propositional knowing than merely possessing true beliefs. Beliefs may sometimes be true for spurious reasons that tend to discount them as bonafide instances of knowing. If, for example, John's belief that Mr. Smith is out to get him stems only from John's paranoid delusion that everyone is out to get him, then, even if it is indeed the case that Mr. Smith is out to get him, John cannot reasonably be said to 'know' it.

Thus a third basic requirement on propositional knowing, beyond the mere possession of true beliefs, is that there be *grounds* or *justification* for the beliefs. This implies, first, that there be adequate reasons, evidence, causes, and so on, for holding the beliefs, and, secondly, that the beliefs be in some way based on these. The grounding or justification of beliefs thus constitutes a set of *boundary conditions*, extrinsic to the representational function of propositional knowing, that must be satisfied in any bonafide instance of propositional knowing.

The topic of grounds or justification for knowledge traditionally has been of more interest to espistemologists than to psychologists; but one point that is of critical psychological importance is the fact that the justification of one's beliefs does not always imply that one can *justify* those beliefs for oneself. The requirement that beliefs be based on something does not imply that this basis is something that the believer himself can always cite. It is possible, for instance, to have good reasons for believing something and for one's beliefs to be based on those reasons, without one being able to articulate or even be aware of the reasons. Children at a certain level of mathematical competence, for example, may be said to have good reason to believe that $3 + 5 = 5 + 3$, insofar as they carry out their calculations consistently with the commutative law of addition, whether or not they know or can state the principle. In other cases, all that may be necessary for the grounding or justification of beliefs is that the beliefs be causally produced in the right way, as in the case of certain perceptually fixated beliefs.

Skillful Knowing

We turn now to the analysis of skillful knowing, that is, the kind of knowing that is manifest in the exercise of skills of various kinds, both motor and mental. Skillful knowing turns out to be analyzable in terms of some of the same general features as propositional knowing; however, as the bottom panel of Figure 1 shows, these features are now instantiated in rather different ways.

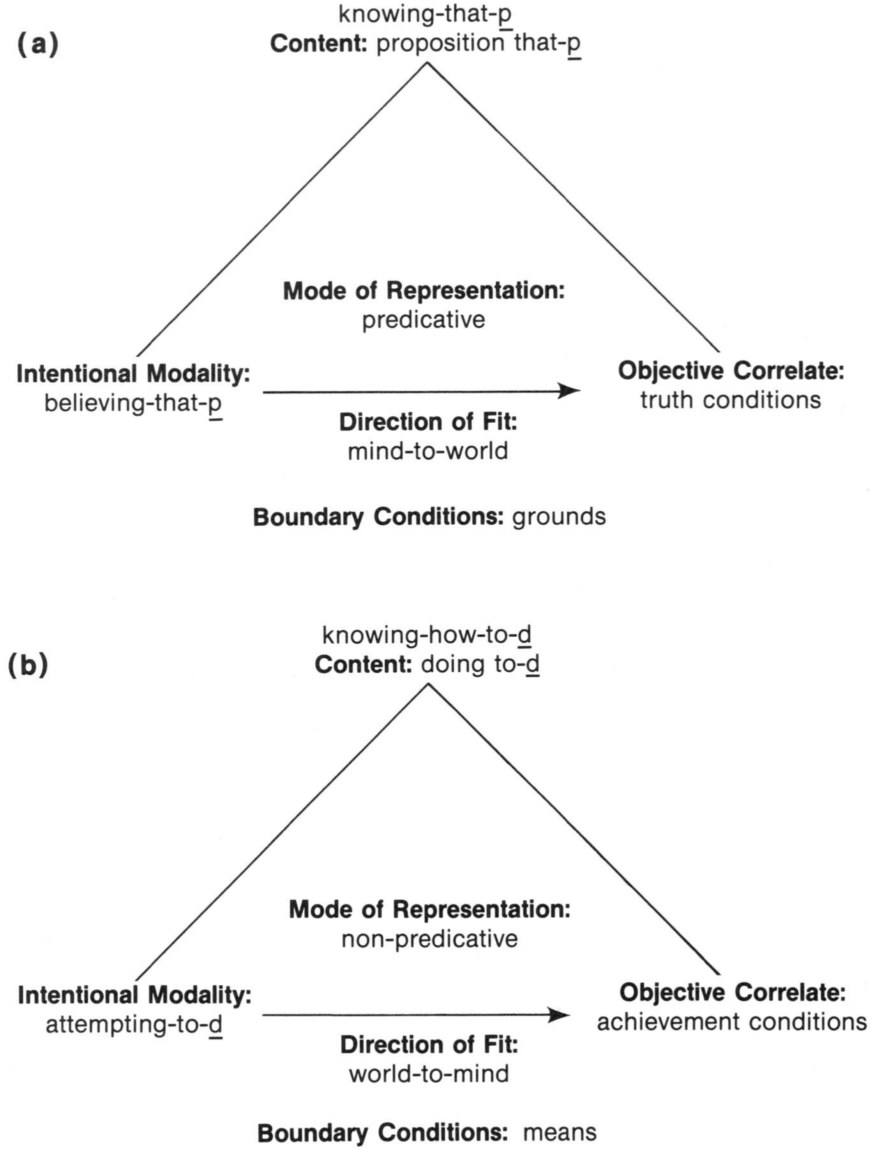

Fig. 1 The basic logical structure of (a) propositional knowing and (b) skillful knowing.

Content

Paradigmatically, skillful knowing is a matter of knowing 'how to *d*', where '*d*' is part of an infinitive construction expressing less than a full proposition. More specifically, '*d*' is a placeholder for an expression referring to some potential skilled activity or achievement such as 'ride a bicycle', 'play chess', 'type', and so on. Expressions of this type are always less than complete sentences and so do not directly express propositional contents.

However, there is a deeper reason for taking the content of skillful knowing to be something basically non-propositional. Unlike designations of propositional contents, the infinitive construction in ascriptions of skillful knowing cannot generally be translated in terms of a that-clause type of expression without a considerable change of meaning. Consider, for instance, replacing the infinitive phrase in the sentence "Joan knows how to ride a bicycle" with a corresponding that-clause, to yield the sentence "Joan knows how *that* she rides a bicycle" (which is perhaps better rendered in English as simply "Joan knows how she rides a bicycle"). Note that this latter sentence by no means ascribes the same kind of knowledge to Joan, for Joan's knowing how to ride a bicycle does not imply that she knows, in any detail, how she or anyone else actually manages the achievement. To use a classic illustration of Polanyi (1962), there is no reason to expect that Joan possesses the sort of analytical knowledge that says she must wind the bicycle along a series of curvatures such that "for a given angle of unbalance the curvature of each winding is inversely proportional to the square of the speed" (p. 50). Conversely, knowledge of this rather esoteric principle of mechanics would not likely be of much use to anyone attempting to ride a bicycle for the first time.

In general, the kind of analytical know-how that is implied by knowing how it is *that* something is done is neither necessary nor sufficient for knowing how *to* do it. The ability to cite the steps of a complex procedure, either linguistically or in some other way, is neither a condition for, nor a necessary consequence of the ability to apply or implement the procedure in a skillful performance. The reason is that much of what we know how to do - knowledge which bridges the gap between the description and the implementation of a procedure - is fundamentally tacit knowledge; our access to it does not often lend itself to any analysis or decomposition into well-defined constituents.

If much in the domain of skillful knowing resists expression in full propositional terms, then, how do we characterize its content? Skillful knowing is addressed to certain potential achievements that an individual possessing the knowledge is capable of. This is a type of content that, for lack of a more suitable term, we shall call a *doing*. Doings, like propositions, are abstract entities. They are not always concretely realized; moreover, they may be designated linguistically in a variety of ways, of which the infinitive construction of the know-how locution is only one. Unlike propositions, however, doings have the logical status of 'unsaturated' rather than 'saturated' predicates (to use Frege's [1952] distinction), which is to say that their reference is not fully determinate in the way that propositional reference typically is. The potential achievement described by 'riding a bicycle', for example, is not specific to the circumstances of an actual achievement in the way that the propositional claim that 'Joan is riding a bicycle' is. This point has important implications for the objective correlate of skillful knowing, which we turn to next.

Objective Correlate

Since the contents of skillful knowing lack full propositional structure, they cannot be said to be 'true' or 'false'. The potential achievements described by 'riding a bicycle', 'playing chess', 'typing', and the like, are just not the sorts of things to which a truth value is meaningfully ascribed. However there are circumstances under which these potential achievements become actualized in particular skilled performances; and so one may speak of *achievement conditions* rather than truth conditions as the objective correlate of skillful knowing.

Like truth conditions, achievement conditions specify the 'objects' of knowledge, but now in the sense of 'objectives' or goals toward which skilled acts are directed. Unlike truth conditions which are, at least in principle, determinate and specifiable, achievement conditions are essentially open-ended and indeterminate. To say that someone possesses a skill is not just to make reference to certain past or current performances under conditions that are readily specifiable, but to the potential for certain kinds of future performances under conditions that may be largely unknown. Moreover, the standards against which skilled performances are assessed tend to exhibit considerable contextual variability, making their achievement conditions inherently fuzzier and less well differentiated than the truth conditions of propositions.

Intentional Modality

Turning now to the Intentional modality for skill, perhaps the most basic psychological condition on expressing skillful knowing is that of attempting to do something. Skilled acts are a form of intentionally directed behaviour, and so one does not speak of skill in cases where achievement conditions are realized entirely by accident as, for example, when an aimless fumbling action fortuitously results in putting a basketball through a hoop, or some other achievement.

Attempting to do something is an Intentional modality that is logically independent of believing something to be the case. In particular, believing that one can do something is neither a necessary nor a sufficient condition on attempting to do it. One may, for various reasons (such as lack of confidence or motivation) fail to do what one readily believes one can do. Alternatively one may sometimes be led to attempt what one does not actually believe one can do, which is not an uncommon practice in the teaching of various skills. There are also certain differences in the way that skilled attempts and propositional beliefs represent their objective correlates. The mental representations that underlie skill are, again, selective to certain 'aspects' but, at least in the case of highly practiced skills, these aspects need not be explicitly predicated of anything. For example, the skilled skier may attempt to traverse different types of terrain by making the appropriate adjustments more or less tacitly and automatically, without explicit awareness 'that' the terrain has particular properties. With respect to these kinds of attributes at least, the form of representation involved in skillful attempting would seem to be distinctly *non-predicative:* One need not attempt *of* a particular patch of terrain *to* traverse it in a certain way, for example, in quite the way that one may, in other circumstances, believe of it that it has certain properties.

Direction of Fit

The direction of fit of attempting also runs in the opposite direction to that of believing. In contrast to the mind-to-world direction of fit of believing, attempting is an instance of what is called the 'world-to-mind' direction of fit. Skilled attempts are aimed at bringing about certain states of affairs in the world to satisfy one's aims, rather than representing any independently determined states of affairs. Thus, when attempts are unfulfilled or unsuccessful, one cannot rectify the situation just by changing one's aims in the same way that one can make amends for one's false beliefs by changing what one believes.

Boundary Conditions

Finally, it is important to point out that skillful knowing cannot simply be equated with the capacity to make successful attempts any more than propositional knowing can be equated with true belief. One tends to withold ascriptions of skillful knowing in cases where attempts succeed by virtue of coincidence or unanticipated side-effects of one's actions. Again, skillful knowledge is subject to certain additional boundary conditions. Generally, these require having at one's disposal some appropriate *means* for achieving one's aims through one's actions.

Means for action implies at least two things: First, the possession of a technique; and, secondly, ability to apply the technique to produce skilled performances. Thus skill involves the active regulation of performance, by way of observing some set of standards or criteria in making one's performances. Moreover, there are a number of distinct ways of accomplishing such regulation. The most transparent one is by explicit step-by-step rule following, a mode which Black (1967) terms *rule-invoking* action. However, rule-invoking actions often lack the kind of free-flowing smoothness of execution that is important for many skills. Thus Black suggests some alternative modes of regulation that are not as rigid as rule-invoking action, yet not as blindly automatic as purely habitual or reflexive behaviour. In one of these modes, termed *rule-accepting* action, the rules or criteria governing an action are not explicitly formulated or referenced by the agent in carrying out the action, but are nevertheless readily accepted by the agent, once they are formulated. In another mode called *rule-guided* action, regulation is provided in an even more implicit fashion by a covert symbolism of 'tips', 'cues', global impression, of 'fit' or 'rightness' of one's actions, and the like, as in the experienced chess player's being able to 'see', without calculation, his best move in some situation.

Black's taxonomy by no means exhausts the possibilities for regulation of skillful behaviour; but one at least begins to see how broad the scope of such regulation might be. The topic of behavioural regulation offers some particularly promising avenues of further inquiry into the psychological mechanisms underlying skill.

Meanwhile the various similarities and differences between propositional and skillful knowing pose a series of more general challenges to cognitive theorists to develop models of mental representation of sufficient breadth of scope to accommodate both.

References

Black, M. (1967). Rules and routines. In R. S. Peters (Ed.), *The concept of education* (pp. 92-104). London: Routledge and Kegan Paul.

Brentano, F. (1924). *Psychologie vom empirischen standpunkt.* [Psychology from an empirical standpoint] (O. Kraus, Ed.). Leipzig: F. Meiner. (Original work published 1874)

Frege, G. (1952). *Translations from the philosophical writings of Gottlob Frege* (P. Geach & M. Black, Eds.). Oxford: Basil Blackwell.

Goodman, N. (1976). *Languages of art* (2nd ed.). Indianapolis, IN: Hackett.

Polanyi, M. (1962). *Personal knowledge* (rev. ed.). Chicago: University of Chicago Press.

Ryle, G. (1949). *The concept of mind.* London: Hutchinson.

Scheffler, I. (1965). *Conditions of knowledge.* Glenview, IL: Scott, Foresman and Co.

Searle, J. R. (1983). *Intentionality.* London: Cambridge University Press.

VALIDITY AND RELIABILITY

FROM A PHENOMENOLOGICAL PERSPECTIVE

Amedeo Giorgi

Saybrook Institute
San Francisco, CA, U.S.A.

SUMMARY: This paper takes up the issue of whether or not the terms 'validity and reliability' can be used in the same sense in logical-empiricism and in phenomenology. Two aspects of phenomenological theory are discussed as they apply to the problems of validity and reliability: (1) the use of the reduction and the effort after essences, and (2) the part of Husserl's theory of meaning wherein he distinguishes among signifying, fulfilling and identifying acts. Both of these strategies lead to a sense of validity and reliability, but a sense that is different from logical-empiricism. Both viewpoints have in common the goal of proper evidence for knowledge claims, but they proceed differently because the meanings of the terms differ.

Introduction

Whatever the ultimate meaning of Kuhn's term 'paradigm' turns out to be, it is at least useful as a provisional descriptive term to differentiate diverse styles of scientific activity based upon different criteria and different frameworks. As one who has spent most of his professional life trying to work within, and articulate, an alternative 'paradigm' I am quite sensitive to the difficulties, theoretical and practical, to which such an endeavor leads. Whatever may be fallible about Kuhn's notion, he was right on target about the difficulties of cross-paradigmatic communication. So often, the same words refer to different things; the same phenomena have different words; the same words have different meanings, and silent but disparate assumptions wreak havoc even if the explicitly articulated matters seem to be harmonious. Unfortunately, this labor is a necessary evil that one has to go through, especially if one is a minority theoretician, in order to communicate with one's colleagues.

An issue that has been looming on the horizon calling for such a labor is the question of the role of reliability and validity in phenomenological psychological research. Ever since interest in qualitative research has been increasing, colleagues and students have been asking me about the validity and reliability of their findings. They want to know whether or not to use judges and how to use them if they have to, or what else they might have to do in order to demonstrate that their qualitative analyses are not merely subjective.

My reaction to these requests has been to go slowly because while I know that the questions of validity and reliability were appropriate for a logical-empirical philosophy of science, I was not sure that these issues could simply be transported to a phenomenological framework without mediation and a possible transformation of sense. This is not to say that some of the issues raised by the questions concerning validity and reliability are not germane for a phenomenological framework. I am only advocating that one should be cautious and one should not assume that the questioning of phenomenologically-based qualitative analyses takes the same form as analyses based upon a quantitative perspective. Two paradigms are involved here and one cannot merely assume that validity and reliability have the same meaning in the two paradigms.

Traditional Meaning of Validity and Reliability

Let me begin with the rationale for validity and reliability as mainstream psychology uses it. Validity, in general, means a correspondence between a proposition and the ability of a referent to match the proposition, and reliability refers to how consistent the match is. More specifically, in psychology, "validity and reliability are values related to measuring instruments used to obtain research data. An instrument is valid if it actually measures the concept it is supposed to measure and the instrument is reliable if it is consistent and gives the same measurement under the same conditions" (Polkinghorne, 1986, p. 129). I shall not go into all of the distinctions surrounding validity and reliability, but rather I'll try to get at the heart of the issue.

What primarily underlies the above understanding of validity and reliability is a logical-empirical philosophy of science and in the following way. Almost all philosophers, including empiricists, acknowledge that the empirical order is contingent and corrigible. Facts and things, the two basic concerns of empiricists, could be other than the way they are. There is a certain robustness and inevitableness to empirical reality, but it is also always constantly changing. Yet, science tries to come up with laws that can comprehend the patterns of change of things and it tries to formulate these laws in as universally a way as possible. Consequently, in order to give to the empirical order a solidity that it does not intrinsically have, the weight of necessity derived from logic and mathematics is brought to bear upon it. Both logic and mathematics, as formal eidetic disciplines, if correctly applied, can guarantee a type of necessity that facts and things as such do not intrinsically have. The extent, then, to which empirical phenomena can be shown to follow the order of number or logic, to that extent they can be said to be valid or reliable. There is certainly enough experience, overall, to show that the application of logic and mathematics to empirical reality can work: the construction of bridges depends upon such application, as do airplane flights, rocket launchings and so on. But there is also sufficient experience to show that such applications are not perfect, and thus the question of the validity and reliability of such an application is relevant. In psychology, of course, the validity and reliability of the instruments or the means of analysis seems to be much less than in other areas of application, but that is another story. The point I want to make is that the use of validity and reliability as critical features of the logic of mainstream psychology is tied to logical-empirical philosophy, with all its assumptions, concepts and interests. Given such a framework, the importance that the questions of validity and reliability receive is understandable.

However, when I work within a phenomenological framework, I find that the necessity for dealing with validity and reliability as I understand them in their indigenous context, is not compelling in the same way. There is something about the mode of functioning of the phenomenologist that makes these concerns seem more remote than proximate, and that is what I hope to clarify shortly. But before doing so, I would like to make explicit in a more direct way the sense in which the questions of validity and reliability concern me as a phenomenologist. Fortunately, for this purpose, I can appeal to an article by Salner dealing with epistemic issues in the human sciences, in which she challenged the relevance of traditional concepts of reliability and validity, and worked out in a way wholly acceptable to me, the sense in which the questions of reliability and validity can weigh upon me with theoretical necessity. I cannot present all of the arguments, but Salner (1986) concludes with the following words:

> We can see from the preceding discussions that the term 'validity' as we have come to understand it in empirical research is too narrow to capture the effort of the human science researcher to present results that can be deemed a contribution to knowledge about human experience. The term 'validity' is bounded by the context of empirical epistemology....Once a correspondence theory of truth is challenged, as it is by human science epistemological arguments, the concept of validity must be defined. From the perspective of human science epistemology, it makes more sense to talk in terms of ***defensible knowledge claims*** than of validity per se (pp. 127-128).

Thus, the issue can be formulated more generically as the issue of the proper evidence for making knowledge claims. The way in which logical-empiricism understands the problem of knowledge, it makes sense for it to speak of validity and reliability the way it does. We shall have to see if we can use the same terms in the same sense for phenomenological research.

In a paper of this length, I can only use theoretical, 'top-down' arguments. Thus, I shall use two aspects of phenomenological theory as ways of showing that the questions of validity and reliability as understood in the logical-empirical framework do not automatically apply to it. In a future work, I shall use a 'bottom-up' argument based upon concrete phenomenological psychological praxis. But before I present my arguments, I want to make explicit some features of phenomenological philosophy that are important for the discussion that is to follow.

Important Features of Phenomenological Thought

For the purposes of this paper, three aspects of phenomenological thought should be made explicit.

1. For phenomenology, consciousness is intentional which means that acts of consciousness are always directed to objects that transcend the acts in which they appear. Sometimes these objects are immanent, which means that the objects belong to other parts of the same unified consciousness to which the acts belong, such as when I reflect on my pre-reflective experience or am present to a particular memory. Sometimes the objects are described as transcendent which means that they are not part of the consciousness to which the acts belong, such as my perception of this room and the people in it.

2. One of the axioms of phenomenology is that there are many ways for consciousness to be consciousness. Important for this paper is the difference between empirical consciousness and ideative consciousness. Empirical objects are always transcendent and Husserl reserves the term 'real' for such objects, which are defined by the manner in which they partake of space, time and 'causality', or perhaps, better, 'regularities.' Ideas and essences are objects that do not have spatial characteristics, and their mode of being temporal and 'regular' also differs from transcendent objects. Empirical sciences are concerned with facts and eidetic sciences are concerned with essences.

3. Phenomenology is a philosophy of intuition. It should be obvious that this has nothing to do with mysticism, romanticism, sentimentalism or any exotic or esoteric attitude. Rather it means the ability of consciousness to present objects determinatively or objectively. Husserl's philosophy also contains a theory of evidence as self-evidence and this is based upon what he calls a primordial dator intuition. He (Husserl, 1962/1913) writes as follows:

> No theory we can conceive can mislead us in regard to the principle of all principles: that primordial dator intuition is a source of authority for knowledge, that whatever presents itself in 'intuition' in primordial form

> (as it were in its bodily reality) is simply to be accepted as it gives itself out to be, though only within the limits in which it then presents itself. Let our insight grasp this fact that the theory itself in its turn could not derive its truth except from primordial data (p. 83).

Evidence, therefore, is not merely a subjective feeling accompanying the experience of certain phenomena. As Levinas (1973/1963) puts it:

> Evidence is a form of intentionality in which an object is facing consciousness *in person* and in the same guise as it was meant. If we say that evidence is the criterion of truth, we do not mean that evidence is only a subjective index of truth; we do not mean that being could appear in such a way as to invalidate the most certain evidences. Evidence is defined precisely by the fact that it is the presence of consciousness in front of being (p. 75).

Husserl (1970/1900 II), himself, in *Logical Investigations* writes:

> If someone experiences the self-evidence of A, it is self-evident that no second person can experience the absurdity of the same A, for that A is self-evident, means that A is not merely meant, but also genuinely given, and given as precisely what it is thought to be (p. 769).

Thus, intuition is related to the presence of meanings and meaning can serve as evidence. Evidence is being present to meaning with insight. Or again, as Husserl (1970/1900 I) says:

> Evidence is to have the luminous certainty that what we have acknowledged *is*, that what we have rejected is *not*, a certainty distinguished in familiar fashion from blind belief and vague opining, however firm and decided, if we are not to be shattered on the rocks of extreme skepticism (p. 60).

I appreciate the difficulties that such expressions may have for empiricists and post-positivists. Kohak (1978) has made the most pointed comments on this matter, as follows:

> Husserl's affirmation of experience as intelligible and intrinsically susceptible to faithful articulation represents both a basic contribution to contemporary philosophy and an affirmation of the most audacious link in the Western Philosophic faith - that the human, simply qua human, is *capax veritatis*.
>
> Husserl presents his conviction that appearance is not a mask but the presence of reality, overt rather than latent, to be *seen* rather than conjectured, the birthright of all humans rather than the privilege of poets, seers, or ideologues (p. 175).

I realize that the above summary of phenomenological thought is wholly inadequate, but it will have to do if I am to get on to my major point, which is to show how modes of phenomenological thinking pose a difficulty for the logical-empirical understanding of validity and reliability.

Meaning of Validity and Reliability in Phenomenological Thought

The first feature of phenomenological thought to be considered for this problem is the use of the phenomenological reduction and the concern for essences by phenomenological researchers. The reduction implies two things: (1) that one brackets or renders non-influential what one *knows about* the phenomenon being experienced in order to be present to it freshly, and (2) that one refrains from saying that the given *is* what it appears to be. In brief, one neither imposes upon a given nor makes existential claims about it. To impose past knowledge upon the phenomenon would risk covering over new aspects that might be discriminated and to make existential claims would risk error because empirical phenomena can never be adequately given. Both phases of the reduction are motivated by the desire to avoid the possibility of error, if at all humanly possible, and still have something left to say. Positively speaking, the motivation for the reduction is because of the concern for proper evidence.

For Husserl, the search for essences means to search for the most invariant meaning or identity that can be assigned to a phenomenon for a given context. These essences do not have to be absolute, especially when dealing with psychological phenomena. The essences or invariant meanings are attained through the process of what Husserl called "free imaginative variation." In this process, one attempts to vary the descriptive features of the given phenomenon in imagination in order to see what the truly invariant - or essential - features of a phenomenon are. If a characteristic is varied that leaves the identity of the phenomenon intact, it is not essential; if a change of the feature transforms the identity, then it would be essentially related to the identity that is guiding the variation. Thus, I can imagine changing the materiality of a chair from plastic to wood and still have a chair, but I cannot remove the seat and still make the same claim. What should be noted here is that using imagined possibilities as a criterion is even more severe than using actually experienced characteristics. I may not have experienced just the back of a chair without a seat, but I can imagine one, and that is sufficient for me to declare a seat as essential for a chair. Thus, in phenomenological procedures, imagined presences are as weighty as actually experienced presences. By articulating essences Husserl hoped to parallel the eidetic sciences of logic and mathematics, but he wanted phenomenology to be more than a formal discipline by attempting to appropriate the sense of content as part of the eidetic realm and therefore hopefully establish a new type of ground for the human sciences. As opposed to Descartes, not only the *cogito,* but the *cogitatum* could also, as essential meaning, be brought into the realm of indubitability.

Now Husserl too, admits that the empirical is essentially corrigible, and thus all of the strategies I mentioned above are ways of avoiding making direct statements about the empirical, but indirectly encompassing them through the description of possibilities and essences. In other words, Husserl limits his statements to meanings and intrinsic possibilities, just as a geometrician can say that a triangle is a three-sided figure whose angles have to have certain characteristics even if such a triangle does not actually exist. Thus, the reduction prevents one from making empirical claims and the search for essences also keeps one from speaking about particulars and directs expression towards the essentials as such. In a word, Husserl seeks secure knowledge by avoiding all contact with the source of corruptibility, the empirical. Yet phenomenology is not just a formal discipline, because, as mentioned, it tries to raise the content of experience to the eidetic level through essential description. If the essential description truly captures the intuited essence, one has validity in a phenomenological sense. This means that one adequately describes the general essence that is given to the consciousness of the researcher If one can use this essential description consistently, one has reliability. But note, this is quite different from applying eidetic certainties to the empirical realm, which is what mainstream psychology wants to do. Phenomenological statements have implications for empirical phenomena, but only as possibilities. These statements say nothing about the empirical as such. For example, eidetically one could say that whatever a chair may ultimately be made of, it must have a seat in order for it to be a possible chair. This statement is not descriptive of any empirical chair, but it sets constraints within which an actual chair can be realized. Thus, eidetic statements as 'pure descriptions' are valid because they are similar to tautologies and analytic concepts, except that they are not purely formal. If used consistently, they are also reliable.

To avoid possible misunderstanding I want to make explicit both that there are grounds for making strong knowledge claims (i.e., phenomenology is not personal opinionating) and that one can err (i.e., phenomenology is non-dogmatic). The strong knowledge claim is based upon all of the precautions taken in trying to arrive at an accurate description; the reduction, the use of imaginative variation, the limiting of the claim to pure possibilities, etc. The possibility for error exists because one can do all that and still describe inaccurately. There are no guarantees, only checks and balances, and primarily the checks and balances come through the use of demonstrative procedures. All one has to do is provide a counterexample to the essential description and it is proven wrong.

Now, then, shall we call these strategies 'validity'? Husserl gains certitude not by applying valid statements to the empirical realm, but by avoiding empirical statements. He draws from the empirical without making a commitment to it. This is how he was able to describe phenomenological psychology as a priori, eidetic and intuitive. By *a priori* he (1977/1962) meant that "this psychology aims first of all at all those essential universalities and necessities, without which psychological being and living are simply inconceivable" (p. 33). He also states that intuition describes for us the source of the *a priori* and then writes (1977/1962),

> The established results, as substantiations concerning essences, can be won only by inner seeing and analysis of the seen, ... These are not conjectured, assumed essential necessities; rather, the necessity and unconditioned universality of their validity become themselves something seen (pp. 33-34).

For something to be valid is to see it as self-evidently true within the conditions he describes. I do caution, however, that Husserl allows for degrees of evidence depending upon the type of object that is given to consciousness and evidence does not always mean absolute evidence. Indeed, the latter is limited and rare.

Again, the principle of validity here is wholly different from mainstream psychology: shall we still call it validity, or shall we use a different term? Perhaps before answering definitively, we should go on to the second example.

The second way Husserl deals with the validity and reliability question, a way that is similar but not identical to that of mainstream psychology, relates to his theory of meaning. Husserl distinguishes many types of conscious acts, and three such distinctions are important for this second point. Husserl (1970/1900) speaks of *signifying acts,* which are the basis for the constitution of meaning, and these acts orient consciousness towards the world; he then describes *fulfilling acts* which are those acts that relate various types of sensory or symbolic fulfillment to the signifying acts; and finally, there are the *identifying acts,* which affirm that the fulfillments meet the criteria of meaning as expressed by the signifying acts. In effect, the acts of identity could be considered to be the basis for validity, and if these identifying acts could be consistently performed, then we would have reliability. At the risk of oversimplification, let's take a mundane example - one that, in fact, frequently happens to me. The signifying act is that I am looking for my glasses; a fulfilling act is that I perceive a pair of glasses, but I also recognize that they are not mine. I see another pair and I recognize them as precisely the glasses I meant. This is the act of identification that relates the realization to the signifying act. Meanings aim at their objects, but intuition reaches them. It is the same object in both cases, one act aiming at it, and the other a direct presentation of it. But this is an *essential identity* of the object, not an existential identity. The object aimed at and the object identified are essentially identical, but the *manner* in which the objects are given is not existentially the same. In the signifying act, the object is emptily present, it is only meant; in intuition it is actually there.

Now the above process should not be confused with the old representational theory of knowledge in which one only knows one's own mental process and then the question becomes one of knowing how the mental stuff relates to the 'outside world.' Nor is it the same as the match between 'theory and data' as mainstream psychology uses these concepts. On one hand, in both cases there is a separation between the two sides that does not exist between a meaning and its fulfillment in an act of identification because of the internal relations that exist among them. That is, the process that takes place from the signifying act through to the identifying act all happens within the intentional relation, the same relation that unites the subject with the world. On the other hand, the meaning that is given in the signifying act transcends the act in which it appears just as much as the glasses in the identifying act do, except that the meaning as object remains immanent. Indeed, one could have the whole process take place immanently, as when one struggles to remember a phone number, rejecting several possible alternatives in the process, and finally settling on the correct one. Consequently, on one hand, the act and the object to which it is directed are constantly distinguished; on the other hand, the primacy of the intentional relation is constantly maintained. Thus, validity and reliability are understood to be achievements of intentionality, and since that relation does not exist in empiricism, the terms cannot mean the same thing.

Well, then, shall we still call these achievements validity and reliability? Or shall we put the term 'phenomenological' before them and call them that? It seems that the latter is the minimum that should be done.

In this paper I have tried to be faithful to Husserlian phenomenological philosophy. The two instances of phenomenological theorizing that I have chosen are sufficiently different from the logical-empirical mode of validity and reliability to make me conclude that they are not the same. What is common is the effort after proper evidence for knowledge claims, but the manner of achieving the evidence is different because of different assumptions which, in turn, inspire different criteria.

References

Husserl, E. (1962/1913). *Ideas.*(Transl.: W. R. B. Gibson) New York: MacMillan.

Husserl, E. (1970/1900). *Logical investigations.* (2 vols., Transl.: J. N. Findley). New York: Humanities Press.

Husserl, E. (1977/1962). *Phenomenological psychology.* (Transl.: J. Scanlon). The Hague: Nijhoff.

Kohak, E. (1978). *Idea and experience.* Chicago, IL: University of Chicago Press.

Levinas, E. (1973/1963). *The theory of intuition in Husserl's phenomenology.* (Transl.: A. Orianne). Evanston, IL: Northwestern University Press.

Polkinghorne, D. E. (1986). Conceptual validity in a non-theoretical human science. *Journal of Phenomenological Psychology, 17*, 129-150.

Salner, M. (1986). Validity in human science research. *Saybrook Review, 6*, 107-130.

THE UNITS OF ANALYSIS PROBLEM IN PSYCHOLOGY: AN EXAMINATION AND PROPOSED RECONCILIATION

James Horley[1]

University of Guelph
Guelph, Ontario, Canada

SUMMARY: The question as to which dimensions or units of analysis should be employed in psychological theory and research is an issue that, despite its crucial nature, has yet to be resolved. In this paper, the many units of analysis that psychologists have to choose from are examined in terms of types. Units concerned with motivation, labelled *A* units, and units concerned with the structure of behavior, labelled *B* units, are suggested as two general unit types. *A* units, such as need or personal construct, and *B* units, such as serial or trait, appear to be employed together in the enterprise of describing and explaining human action. In order to choose an acceptable or adequate pair of analytic units, two sets of evaluative criteria are proposed. Idiothetic focus, integrative emphasis, parsimonious explanation, and stability-change flexibility are proposed tentatively as criteria for judging the adequacy of *A* units; while ecological representativeness, middle-level perspective, operationalizability, systemic relevance, and temporal extension are proposed as evaluative criteria for *B* units. Assumptions and implications of such a unit types and their evaluative criteria are discussed.

Introduction

At a 1957 conference on human motivation, Gordon Allport (1958) posed a question that remains unanswered to date. The question that Allport asked was: What units shall we employ? The question concerns the quest for units that satisfactorily describe and explain people's actions. As Allport noted, a form of the question had been asked over two millennia earlier. Greek efforts to characterize the 'essence of human nature' must be seen as motivated essentially by the same question. Allport's presentation, however, emphasized that the problem was one of utmost importance to modern psychology, and one that had not been resolved in the past two thousand years.

Of course, the search for an adequate unit of analysis is not restricted to the domain of psychology now known as motivation. In

[1]The author would like to thank J. Clarke, G. Morgan, and D. Stout for helpful comment on an earlier version of this paper

another publication, Allport (1985) historically traced social psychology's search for an adequate unit. Also, in an article which was described as a 'revisitation' of Allport's (1958) question, Wallace (1967) argued that personality psychology should look beyond concepts of trait and disposition for an analytic unit to describe the structure of personality. Indeed, all branches of psychology appear to be involved in the search for an analytic unit. The question is: Are all branches searching for the same unit? One might argue that, because we are all involved in the same discipline with the same subject matter, human behavior, we should all require the same unit. Unfortunately, the current state of affairs is not quite so straightforward. First, the domain of psychology is not as clear as one might expect. Although an examination of this question is certainly beyond the scope of this paper, Hyland (1985) and others have suggested that an understanding of psychology as the study of human behavior is insufficient given the variety of meanings of the term behavior. A second point concerns the question of the relationship between a unit of analysis and the theory that posits the unit. Like any concept, an analytic unit intended to describe and/or to explain some aspect of a person carries with it theoretical baggage. Therefore, the description of a unit such as the trait as "theoretically sterile" (Epstein & O'Brien, 1985) is misleading, at best. Our analytic dimensions, however, appear to travel lightly in terms of their theory. Apparently, a single unit is not tied to a single theory. We have a variety of need theories, a variety of trait theories, and even a variety of personal construct theories. In fact, it is precisely this theoretical pluralism that leads one to wonder whether a single unit of analysis is possible within psychology. A discussion of the issue of theoretical pluralism versus theoretical singularism cannot be undertaken here (see Royce, 1978, 1985), but the pertinence of the issue will make some reference to it unavoidable.

Two Types of Analytic Units

In order to simplify the examination of what he described as literally 'thousands' of units of analysis available to psychologists, Allport (1958) suggested that all units could be thought of in terms of two related categories or types: units of motivation and units of personality. Allport seems not to have defined his terms, but he was comparing and contrasting structural or organizational units (units of personality) with motivational or causal units (units of motivation). According to Allport, all units of motivation are simultaneously units of personality, although not all units of personality are units of motivation. He nominated his pet analytic unit, the trait, as one that qualifies as both a personality unit and a motivational unit. The two general unit types, motivation and personality, require some discussion. In particular, the relationship between the two is worthy of attention.

Allport's distinction between the two types of units, personality and motivation, appears to be a useful one. His use of terminology, however, leaves something to be desired. The term 'personality' to describe one type of analytic unit should be rejected as an unfortunate choice of terms, perhaps attributable to a confusion (which still exists) over the precise meaning of personality. Agreement would likely be forthcoming that personality refers to structural or organizational aspects of behavior as well as to motivational or causal aspects. The term 'structure' is perhaps a more useful term to describe the analytic units that refer to organized patterns of behavior. Elsewhere (Horley, 1987), the terms *A* units of analysis and *B* units of analysis have been used to refer to units of motivation and units of structure, respectively. This was done to limit the automatic allegiance among psychologists to the particular terms involved. These terms were also chosen because I am not convinced that 'motivation' and 'structure' are the most appropriate terms to employ.

What precisely are these categories of *A* and *B* analytic units and how are they related? In Table 1, an attempt has been made to exemplify the two types of units by categorizing some specific units. The examples of more specific analytic units represent only a few of the many available, and the order is simply alphabetical. The *B* unit can be seen as an organizing dimension of manifest personality, and, in this sense, it is a unit of analysis. Floyd Allport's (1937) behavior trend, Murray and Kluckhohn's (1953) serial, and the other units listed under dimension *B* units all organize specific acts into larger units. These larger units, however, are not explanatory and, hence, do not address the question 'why?'. The *A* unit can be seen as any analytic dimension that is employed to *explain* behavior. In other words, it describes the motivation for, or the causes of behavior. The *A* unit, however, is not applied to the raw data of behavior. It is used to explain another hypothetical entity, the *B* unit. Thus, we can see that these two types of units might differ in terms of level of abstraction, as suggested by Allport (1958), but that they are both theoretical constructs.

One major point to emphasize is that, although both types of dimensions might be hypothetical, they exist for a different reason. Thus, they cannot be viewed as interchangeable. As noted, Allport (1958) maintained that the trait was a unit that could provide both a behavioral summary *and* an explanation of motivation. He mentioned, however, that some of his colleagues would not agree with him. Indeed, there are few contemporary trait theorists who would. McClelland (1951) argued that human action can be considered in terms of personality traits, but he believed that traits do not explain behavior - the notion of need is required to do so. Even such staunch defenders of the trait as Epstein & O'Brien (1985) have concluded that traits "can contribute little to an un-

Table 1

Categorization of Analytic Units in Psychology

Level:	Behavior	Structure	Motivation
Category Label:	Act	B Unit	A Unit
Specific Unit:	Bodily Movement	Behavior Trend (F. Allport, 1937)	Attitude (G. Allport, 1935)
	Speech Act	Episode (Harré & Secord, 1972)	Drive (Hull, 1941)
		Event (Kelly, 1955)	Incentive (Klinger, 1977)
		Personal Project (Little, 1983)	Instinct (McDougall, 1908)
		Serial (Murray & Kluckhohn, 1953)	Need (Murray, 1938)
		Trait (G. Allport, 1937)	Personal Construct (Kelly, 1955)

derstanding of the personality of individuals" (p. 532), and Epstein has nominated the personal construct as his motivational unit. Not only traits, but all *B* units appear to be more or less explanatorily empty, requiring analysis by an *A* unit. Will any *A* unit suffice? Looking solely at the case of traits, it appears that a variety of *A* units have been suggested as appropriate dimensions to make sense of traits. Inextricable connection between any pairs of *A* and *B* units does not seem to be the case. The selection of analytic units is quite open, with limits placed by general theoretical concerns. These limits appear to be relatively unrestrictive. It may well be that a dispositional *B* unit, like the trait, is incompatible with a situational or behavioristic *A* unit, like the incentive (Wallace, 1967). Other unit pairs, because of theoretical implications, might be complementary (Horley, 1987). As Hyland (1985) described, the notion of complementarity with respect to theory is important but complex. The form of complementarity proposed here, to use Hyland's terms, appears to an 'explanandum-explanans' complementarity, or an overlap between that which describes the data (viz., the *B* unit) and that which explains the description (viz, the *A* unit).

The similar-yet-independent view of *A* and *B* units has implications for claims made by some theorists of 'better' units of analysis. Little (1983), for example, has introduced a new unit which he terms the personal project, and he has described the personal project as a more adequate unit of analysis in personality and environmental psychology. While such a claim may or may not be true, it can only be true within its class, because the personal project is a structural unit that is unable to stand alone. To compare projects or traits to needs or personal constructs is misleading and confusing. This point does raise an important question concerning the two types of analytic units in psychology. How can we judge the adequacy or usefulness of a unit of analysis? On what basis can Little (1983) claim to have a 'more adequate' unit, or how can Allport (1958) describe drives and biological needs as 'wholly inadequate' units? A number of authors (e.g., Staats, 1983) have discussed fashions and fads in psychological theory and research. Fashion may determine the coming and going of analytic units to some extent, but a more 'rational' explanation is also plausible. There must be some criteria - or, more exactly, sets of criteria - to employ as standards against which analytic units are evaluated.

Evaluative Criteria For Analytic Units

Assuming that we all employ criteria to evaluate analytic units, can we take steps to discover and to agree upon an explicit set for use by all psychologists? Such an enterprise would appear well worthwhile, but one with many perils and pitfalls. Whether it can be accomplished at all is perhaps a debatable point. One of the greatest threats to such an undertaking concerns a relationship between units of analysis and psychological theory, and the consequent 'objectivity' of those who might offer criteria for evaluation of units which includes their own chosen unit(s). Even if we accept that they have little theoretical importance, we have to see them as interwoven into our theories. Assaults on the adequacy or usefulness of a particular unit might be perceived as leading to the unravelling of a delicate theoretical tapestry. One must wonder whether such a threatening possibility would be allowed, consciously or otherwise, to occur. Would we be able to propose or to accept criteria that might undermine our pet unit(s)? I suspect that, as individuals, the answer would be 'probably not.' Working as a group, however, the outcome might be different.

The task of generating a set of evaluative criteria for our units of analysis must begin somewhere. I would like to suggest that a set of criteria (or, more precisely, two sets of evaluative criteria) but I would emphasize the tentative nature of the suggested criteria. I would like to think that I can be somewhat objective concerning my chosen units and theory, but perhaps my biases are too well constructed to enable me to see around, over, or through them. Therefore, at best, the criteria that are presented in Table 2 should be regarded as initial proposals to be examined by the larger psychological community before an evaluative status or potential is ascribed to them.

There are two sets of criteria, as mentioned. Consistent with the previous argument, both *A* and *B* units must be considered separately, and it appears that a distinct set of criteria can be generated to apply to each. The first proposed criterion for the evaluation of *A* units (criteria are presented in Table 2 in alphabetical order only) is what might be termed 'idiothetic focus.' The term 'idiothetic,' taken from Lamiell (1981), is intended to capture a concern for both uniqueness of individuals and commonality among individuals. If we are to accept the idea that each individual is, in some ways, like all other individuals, like some individuals, and like no other individuals (Murray and Kluckhohn, 1953), we can conceivably adopt a unit that has such a concern 'built in.' For example, an instinct, at least as proposed by McDougall (1908), would fare poorly against Kelly's (1955) personal construct given this criterion.

A second criterion that might be considered is what might be called 'integrative emphasis.' If we are to accept that the Platonic trichotomy of cognition, affect, and conation applies to all individuals, we should adopt a unit that places an equal emphasis on all three together. Kelly's personal construct theory and his unit, the personal construct, have been assailed as too cognitive (Bruner, 1956) - a charge unlikely to be leveled at the instinct, which seems to emphasize all three functions.

Another, more practical consideration concerns parsimonious explanation. This criterion is borrowed from Royce (1978), who suggested a variety of criteria for evaluating theoretical adequacy. A motivational unit that is unable to provide an explanation of the many expressions of human behavior without growing into an unyielding creation is unlikely to be of use to researchers. Allport (1958) has pointed out that, by the mid 1920's, over 14,000 different instincts had been discussed, and the list was still growing. Rokeach's (1973) value, particularly his notion of terminal value, cannot be criticized on this count.

Stability-change flexibility refers to the ability of the unit to account both for underlying reasons of behavior and change in motivation. The assumption is, of course, that individuals exhibit both stable and different patterns of behavior across time and place. The Hullian drive would likely receive low marks on this criterion, especially relative to the

Table 2

Proposed Criteria for the Evaluation of Analytic Units

Type of Unit	Criterion
A Unit	a) Idiothetic Focus
	b) Integrative Emphasis
	c) Parsimonious Explanation
	d) Stability-Change Flexibility
B Unit	a) Ecological Representativeness
	b) Middle Level Perspective
	c) Operationalizability
	d) Systemic Relevance
	e) Temporal Extension

Kellian construct or the Klingerian incentive.

In terms of the formal evaluation of *B* units, Little (1981) has proposed and discussed a number of assessment criteria guiding the development of his analytic unit, and several of these criteria can seemingly be used to evaluate all structural units of analysis. One of these criteria is what Little has called ecological representatives. A structural unit employed to describe everyday behavioral structure should be recognized as doing so in relevant everyday terms, as opposed to expressions that appear irrelevant. Murray and Kluckhohn's (1953) serial, for example, would necessarily be seen as ecologically representative because specific acts are expressed in relevant, personally meaningful terms. On the other hand, one might view the trait, or certain trait terms, as largely irrelevant.

Another criterion apparently suitable to *B* unit evaluation is what we might term 'middle level perspective.' Little (1981) has argued that some units (e.g., the personality type) are pitched at a macro level, while other units are expressed at a micro level. Units such as Harré and Secord's (1972) episode and Floyd Allport's (1937) behavior trend appear pitched at a middle level of analysis.

In a recent article, Little (1983) has suggested a further, more practical criterion for judging the adequacy of the unit: operationalizability. Murray and Kluckhohn (1953) serial was presented as a well conceived unit, but one that has failed to appear in assessment technique. Whether this is a shortcoming of the unit per se, or whether such a result is due strictly to happenstance, is questionable. Operationalizability may be largely dependent on the satisfaction of a majority of existing (implicit?) criteria at the time of its 'showing.'

Systemic relevance is a further criterion discussed by Little (1981). This criterion assumes that we accept Bertalanffy's (1956) general systems theory, and its view that individuals are dynamic organisms who are a part of, and have to deal with stimuli from a variety of biological and environmental systems. Accepting a systems theoretical perspective, the serial or the personal project that takes into account the social and physical environment is seen as a more adequate unit than the trait or the instruct that largely ignores such systems.

A final criterion to be presented here is temporal extention. Murray and Kluckhohn (1953) describe behavior as occurring over time and, therefore, an acceptable analytic dimension should take the time factor into consideration. Murray and Kluckhohn's nominee, the serial, is a temporally extended unit - and very different from a temporally frozen unit such as the trait.

Assuming that some sets of evaluative criteria can be generated to satisfy the psychological community, we are still faced with the problem of use. Will they be differentially weighted, as in a multiple regression equation? If so, how will the weights be determined? Will they all be given an equal weight? If so, how will 'ties' between units be decided? These and other questions - questions similar to those faced by Royce (1978) who developed a broader set of evaluative criteria for psychological theory - must be answered before this exercise can produce tangible rewards.

Summary and Conclusions

The importance of the choice of units of analysis for all psychologists, experimentalist and clinician alike, cannot be overemphasized (Mancuso & Adams-Webber, 1982). Such a choice is complicated by the plethora of units currently 'on the market.' Therefore, if for no other reason than lessening professional confusion, any effort to clarify the situation with respect to units of analysis within psychology must be recognized as an important step forward. Perhaps one of the first formal attempts to bring some order to this confusion was made by Allport (1958). Allport's classification of analytic units in psychology into units of personality and units of motivation was a useful proposal, but one not to be accepted without ammendment. The choice of terms, for example, appears ill-advised, and the relationship between the two types of unit seems ill-defined.

Elsewhere (Horley, 1987) and in this paper, two categories or types of analytic unit have been proposed. Units whose purpose is to describe the structure or organization of human behavior have been simply and unimaginatively referred to as *B* units; while units whose purpose is to explain the reasons for behavior, or really the motivation behind structured behavior, have been referred to as *A* units. Although all units can be seen as personality units, the relationship between the two proposed types is more independent than the relationship suggested by Allport between his types of units. *A* units and *B* units appear distinct and somewhat independent, with *A* units necessary to explain *B* units.

All units of analysis seem to carry some theoretical baggage, and this relationship between analytic unit and theory appears to have implications for evaluating the adequacy of *A* and *B* units. Royce (1978, 1985) has argued that theoretical pluralism is an obstacle to the progress of psychology as a discipline. He has proposed a set of criteria by which theory can be evaluated as one step toward the achievement of theoretical singularism. Whether we can or should evaluate entire theories is an issue not addressed here, but it is argued that we can and should evaluate aspects of theories, our units of analysis. Two sets of evaluative criteria, one for *A* units and one for *B* units, have been proposed for assessing unit adequacy. Such criteria would unquestionably require updating or revision as our understanding of people changed, but at least some standards by which we could judge the usefulness of our units of analysis would be in place. Our inability to stand back and be 'objective' concerning aspects of our theories appears to be a stumbling block to such a proposal. Because of this, the evaluative criteria proposed in this paper must be viewed as tentative suggestions, unquestionably betraying the biases of the author. If a set of acceptable criteria is possible, it can only be achieved by a concerted effort from the entire psychological community. Staats (1983) has called for a cooperative effort in the attempt to overcome what he sees as psychology's crisis of disunity. There surely is disunity with respect to our analytic units. We have neither a quantum, as does physics, nor an element, as does chemistry. Whether we can limit the numbers of our units in psychology appears to depend very much on our ability to overcome group differences and to suspend personal gain in favour of common goals and collective progress.

References

Allport, F. H. (1937). Teleonomic description in the study of personality. *Character and Personality, 6*, 202-214.

Allport, G. W. (1937) *Personality: A psychological interpretation.* New York: Holt.

Allport, G. W. (1935). Attitudes. In C. M. Murchinson (Ed.), *Handbook of social psychology* (Vol. 2, pp. 798-844). Worcester: Clark University Press.

Allport, G. W. (1958). What units shall we employ? In G. Lindzey (Ed.), *The assessment of human motives.* (pp. 239-260). New York: Rinehart and Winston.

Allport, G. W. (1985). The historical background of social psychology. In G. Lindzey & E. Aronson (Eds.), *The handbook of social psychology* (Vol. 1, pp. 1-46). New York: Random House.

Bertalanffy, L. von (1956). General systems theory. *General Systems, 1*, 1-10.

Bruner, J. S. (1956). A cognitive theory of personality. *Contemporary Psychology, 1*, 355-357.

Epstein, S., & O'Brien, E. J. (1985). The person-situation debate in historical and current perspective. *Psychological Bulletin, 98*, 513-537.

Harré, R. & Secord, P. F. (1972). *Explanation of social behavior.* Oxford: Blackwell.

Hyland, M. E. (1985). Theoretical pluralism and complementarity. In K. B. Madsen & L. P. Mos (Eds.), *Annals of theoretical psychology* (Vol. 3, pp. 317-324). New York: Plenum.

Horley, J. (1987). The construal of events: Personal constructs versus personal projects. In F. Fransella & L. Thomas (Eds.), *Experimenting with personal construct psychology.* (pp. 357-366). London: Routledge and Kegan Paul.

Hull, C. L. (1943). *Principles of behavior: An introduction to behavior theory.* New York: Appleton-Century-Crofts, Inc.

Kelley, G. A. (1955). *The psychology of personal constructs (Vol. 1).* New York: W. W. Norton & Co.

Klinger, E. (1977). *Meaning and void: Inner experience and the incentives in people's lives.* Minneapolis: University of Minnesota Press.

Lamiell, J. T. (1981). Toward an idiothetic psychology of personality. *American Psychologist, 36*, 276-289.

Little, B. R. (1981). *Georgian measurement: Toward a psychology of personal projects.* Paper presented at the Fifth International Congress on Personal Construct Psychology, Brock University, St. Catherines, Ontario, August.

Little, B. R. (1983). Personal projects: A rationale and method for investigation. *Environment and Behavior, 15*, 273-309.

Mancuso, J. C., & Adams-Webber, J. R. (1982). Personal construct psychology as personality theory: Introduction. In J. C. Mancuso & J. R. Adams-Webber (Eds.), *The construing person.* (pp. 1-7). New York: Praeger.

McClelland, D. C. (1951). *Personality.* New York: Holt, Rinehart, & Winston.

McDougall, W. (1908). *An introduction to social psychology.* London: Methuen.

Murray et al. (1938). *Explorations in personality.* New York: Oxford University Press.

Murray, H. A., & Kluckhohn, C. (1953). Outline of a conception of personality. In C. Kluckhohn & H. A. Murray (Eds.), *Personality in nature, society and culture.* (pp. 3-49). New York: Alfred A. Knopf.

Rokeach, M. (1973). *The nature of human values.* New York: The Free Press.

Royce, J. R. (1978). How can we best advance the construction of theory in psychology. *Canadian Psychological Review, 19*, 259-276.

Royce, J. R. (1985). The problem of theoretical pluralism in psychology. In K. B. Madsen & L. P. Mos (Eds.), ***Annals of theoretical psychology*** (Vol. 3, pp. 297-315) New York: Plenum.

Staats, A. W. (1983). ***Psychology's crisis of disunity: Philosophy and method for a unified science.*** New York: Praeger.

Wallace, J. (1967). What units shall we employ? Allport's question revisited. ***Journal of Consulting Psychology, 31***, 56-64.

MEANING HORIZON, PARAPHRASE, AND PHENOMENOLOGICAL INVESTIGATIONS IN PSYCHOLOGY

Don Kuiken and T. C. Wild

University of Alberta
Edmonton, Alberta, Canada

SUMMARY: The integration of recent developments in philosophical phenomenology with those in discourse analysis may contribute to clarification of phenomenological methods in psychology. We argue that (1) the phenomenological analysis of implicit (horizonal) meanings enables precise identification of paraphrasing statements within discourse, (2) paraphrasing statements within discourse form natural, hierarchically arranged meaning units, and (3) the relations between such meaning units, although largely implicit, correspond to the structure of subjectivity.

Introduction

Recently there have emerged several innovative approaches to the study of linguistic descriptions, including task analysis in cognitive psychology (Ericsson & Simon, 1984), account analysis in social psychology (Marsh, Rosser, & Harré, 1977), and phenomenological analysis in general psychology (Giorgi, 1985). A guiding assumption underlying these approaches is that linguistic descriptions of personal experience can contribute significantly to our understanding of various psychological phenomena. However, the history of research guided by this assumption (e.g., introspection, content analysis, etc.) justifies a certain amount of skepticism about the potential of these recent innovations. Their contribution may depend upon whether, compared to their predecessors, contemporary investigators more effectively address two persistent conceptual/methodological problems in studies of linguistic descriptions. First, linguistic descriptions are so complexly structured that it is difficult to specify an appropriate unit of analysis. Units chosen for study are typically either ambiguous (e.g., a theme) or arbitrary (e.g., a simple sentence). Second, the meanings of linguistic descriptions typically extend beyond their explicit, conventional significance, requiring investigators to rely upon implicit meanings. Interpretation of implicit meanings (e.g., affective connotations) is frequently unreliable, whereas exclusive reliance upon explicit meanings (e.g., dictionary definitions) is often psychologically sterile.

The integration of recent developments in philosophical phenomenology (cf. Smith & McIntyre, 1982) with those in discourse analysis (cf. Longacre, 1983) may provide a fresh perspective on these familiar problems and contribute to the development of phenomenological methods in psychology. We propose that a phenomenologically based understanding of discourse (1) enables articulation of natural, hierarchically arranged units of analysis in linguistic descriptions and (2) clarifies the types of implicit meanings present within linguistic expressions.

To develop these points, we will: (1) review the phenomenological conception of implicit meanings in linguistic acts, (2) relate this conception of implicit meanings to the functions of paraphrasing statements within sequences of linquistic acts (i.e, within discourse), (3) indicate how paraphrasing statements may be used to form natural units of analysis within discourse, and (4) suggest that relations among meaning units within discourse, although largely implicit, correspond to the structure of subjectivity.

Individuating and Horizonal Meanings of Linguistic Acts

Within the phenomenological analysis of linguistic expressions, mental acts and linguistic expressions share the same basic intentional structure. Consequently, some distinctions among the meanings of mental acts also apply to the meanings of linguistic expressions. Two of these distinctions provide a foundation for the conception of paraphrase which we regard as pivotal in the systematic study of linguistic expressions. The first is a distinction between the individuating and contingent meanings of a mental (or linguistic) act. The second is a distinction between meanings which are explicit in a mental (or linguistic) act and those which are implicit in such an act. We will review these distinctions and then demonstrate their role in an analysis of paraphrase.

Following Husserl (1900/1970; 1913/1931), acts of linguistic reference are intentional in the same sense as the mental acts which they express. A mental act, or its linguistic expression, intends an object if and only if the act entertains a certain meaning and that meaning prescribes the object. One basic type of mental act is perception of a natural object. The linguistic act corresponding to an act of perception is reference to such a natural entity. Mental acts which prescribe the identity of natural objects are of the form:

$$S \text{ intends that } O \text{ is (conceived as) } X_I$$

E.g., I perceive that this is an apple

Such a mental act may receive linguistic expression in a statement of the form:

O *is (conceived as)* X_I

E.g., "This is an apple"

In mental and linguistic acts of this kind, 'O' is an indexical component ('this') that prescribes (or points to) the intended object as sensuously present to the perceiver in a certain location. 'Is (conceived as) X_I' is a simple or complex predicate ('is an apple') prescribing the property or properties by which the subject, 'S', individuates the intended object, or, in other words, the property or properties by which the subject conceives the identity of the object. Natural individuals are perceived as identical only if they are conceived as being of the same kind across time. Thus, in individuating mental acts of perception and in their corresponding linguistic expressions, the indexical component and the natural-kind predications together prescribe the intended object.

Similarly, mental acts which prescribe the non-individuating or contingent properties of previously individuated objects are of the form:

S *intends that* O *(conceived as)* X_I *is* X_{NI}

E.g., I perceive that this apple is dusty

Such states of affairs may receive linguistic expression in statements of the form:

O *(conceived as)* X_I *is* X_{NI}

E.g., "This apple is dusty"

In this form, 'is X_{NI}' is a simple or complex predicate ('is dusty') indicating the contingent property or properties which the subject conceives the previously individuated object ('this apple') as having.

Thus, perceptual acts - and linguistic acts expressive of perceptual acts - may prescribe individuating (identifying) or non-individuating (contingent) properties of intentional objects. However, according to Husserl, there is always more to the object of a perceptual act than its indexical component and its *explicit* individuating or contingent predications. The individuated object is transcendent; that is, any particular perspective through which the object is intended necessarily prescribes only a few of the object's properties. A transcendent object intended in any particular act may be understood in relation to a manifold of additional acts intending the same object. For example, perceiving 'this' as an 'apple' that is 'dusty' may be seen in relation to other actual or possible acts, such as perceiving 'this' as a 'physical thing', perceiving 'this' as 'red', imagining 'this' as 'tasting sweet', and so on. One aspect of the transcendent object is explicitly intended in a particular perceptual act, but other aspects of the intended object are *implicitly* intended in the act.

Husserl referred to this background of implicit predications as the horizon of the act's intended object. The horizon of a natural object includes both internal and external components. Internal predications prescribe properties of the individual object itself. For example, the internal horizon of 'this apple' includes predications that further individuate the intended object by prescribing it as a 'physical thing', as 'more-or-less spherical', and so on. Also, the internal horizon of 'this apple' includes predications that prescribe contingent properties, such as that it is 'bruised' or 'worm-holed'. In contrast, external predications prescribe the intended object's relations with other objects. Examples of external horizonal predications might be that 'this apple' is 'on the table', that it is 'smaller than a watermelon', and so on.

In summary, the manifold of background predications implicit within the meaning of a single mental (or linguistic) act includes (1) some which are individuating and others which are contingent and (2) some which are about the object *per se* and others which are about about its relation to other entities. These horizonal meanings are present in the meaning of the mental act but not as an explicit part of the predication that characterizes the act. Thus, the implicit meaning of 'This is an apple' will include numerous compatible predications such as 'This apple is a physical thing', 'This apple is bruised', 'This apple is on the table', etc.

The Explication of Horizonal Predications in Discourse:

The Concept of Paraphrase

It follows from the preceding that phenomenological explication of the transcendent objects of mental acts *in principle* requires consideration of implicit horizonal predications. Further, since linguistic expression of complex, affective, or otherwise ineffable mental acts is not always possible, the importance of implicit predication is even more evident for linguistic acts than for mental acts. But, how can the explication of implicit meanings occur in investigations of linguistic descriptions?

Extension of the phenomenological analysis suggests that discourse provides a context within which certain implicit meanings are made explicit. Smith and McIntyre (1982) argue that the horizon of an intended object may be construed as a disposition to intend the object according to compatible background predications (p. 254). If so, the horizon is empirically explicable to the extent that conditions for eliciting linguistic expression of horizonal predications are available. Such conditions are available in discourse when a sequence of statements intend the same transcendent object.

When two or more statements intend the same object, their horizons overlap, and what is implicit in one statement may be explicitly expressed in another. The result is a form of monologic discourse on the intended object, that is, a multiplicity of compatible statements intending the same object. For example, 'This is an apple; it is a physical thing; it is bruised; it is on the table' may be regarded as a brief monologic discourse in which a single transcendent object is intended by each of the separate statements. The predications 'is a physical thing', 'is bruised', and 'is on the table' may be understood as explications of what was implicit in the initial statement individuating 'this' as an 'apple'.[1]

The minimal requirement of horizonal predications is that they be compatible, that is, they must be consistent with the principles of individuation appropriate for the kind of natural object intended (Smith & McIntrye, 1982). For example, the principles of individuation appropriate for apples include their status as physical things, their possession of species-defining genetic material, etc. All other predications about apples must be within the constraints set by these individuating principles. Thus, of the several types of horizonal predication possible (individuating vs. contingent, internal vs. external), individuating horizonal predications are fundamental because they set minimal requirements for the compatibility of all other horizonal predications.[2]

When two or more statements individuate the same object, their relationship to each other is that of paraphrase, where paraphrase is defined as: a statement which prescribes individuating properties of a transcendent object which has already been individuated by another statement within the discourse (e.g., 'This is an apple; it is a physical thing'). Statements which prescribe the individuating properties of the same transcendent object are fundamental because collectively they prescribe the

---

[1]The present analysis may suggest that explication of implicit or horizonal meanings is possible only within monologic discourse. However, although monologic discourse has become the 'data' for task analysis, account analysis, and phenomenological analysis, a conceptually compatible alternative is dialogic discourse in which another person presents an individuating paraphrase of the subject's explicit predication, and the subject either assents or dissents. Analysis of dialogic discourse requires consideration of somewhat different issues than analysis of monologic discourse and will not be attempted here.

[2]Individuating predications are typically about the intended object *per se*, i.e., they are internal. However, this is not a requirement in principle. An important but largely unanalyzed class of individuating predications is external, i.e., prescriptive of properties relating the intended object to other entities. Here we will limit our discussion and examples to internal individuating predications.

subject's conception of the kind of entity the intended object is. By prescribing that conception, the interpretation of other statements prescribing contingent or external horizonal properties of the same entity may be constrained.

It may be useful to clarify present the definition of paraphrase by considering examples of greater psychological interest and complexity. Consider, for example, some hypothetical variations on a monologue by a young woman participating in Marsh, Rosser, and Harré's (1977) study of students in trouble at school. In the following adaptation of that discourse, a young woman describes her affections for her father as follows:

> I don't like my Dad very much.
>
> I get on all right with him, but I hardly
> ever feel like being affectionate with him.

Taking the first statement and the second contrastively structured statement as separate linguistic acts, the second is compatible with the first, given the assumption that feelings of dislike entail a readiness to act in corresponding ways. However, compatibility is insufficiently precise to describe the relation between these statements. More specifically, the predication in the second statement further individuates her conception of her feelings by prescribing as a property of those feelings a readiness to act in particular ways. Thus, the second statement elaborates the first by providing an *individuative paraphrase,* a paraphrase that prescribes an additional individuating property of the intended object.

Individuative paraphrase is continuous with *equivalence paraphrase,* where the latter is understood as a restatement of the individuating properties of the intended object in roughly synonymous terms. Consider this hypothetical variation:

> I don't like my Dad very much.
>
> I don't care for him a great deal.

Because terms are never completely synonymous, strictly speaking there are no equivalence paraphrases. However, the concept of equivalence paraphrase may enable reference to statements which provide minimal individuation beyond that found in the original statement.

A third form of paraphrase is the *contraction paraphrase* in which individuative detail is deleted to derive the gist of the original statement. Consider this hypothetical variation:

> I don't like my Dad very much.

Yeah, I don't like him.

The contraction paraphrase exemplified in the second statement is differentiable from individuative paraphrase only when the order of statements is considered. For some purposes, order may be ignored and the first statement may be regarded as an individuative paraphrase of the second.

Other relations between statements in discourse (e.g., Longacre, 1983; Mann & Thompson, 1986) allow further articulation of the present conception of paraphrase. Consider the use of illustration in this excerpt from the young woman's monologue:

> He couldn't care less what I do as long
> as he knows where I am.
>
> I mean, you know, if I said I was going
> to an orgy, he'd say, "Oh all right, as long
> as I know where you are."

The second of these tightly structured statements constitutes a hypothetical event, a miniature story illustrating the belief that her father is uncaring. This illustration further individuates her belief by specifying a lack of caring in moral matters. Thus, her illustration is a non-discursive form of individuating paraphrase according to the criteria used here.

Another relevant relational concept is simile, as indicated by the following hypothetical variation:

> He couldn't care less what I do as long
> as he knows where I am.
>
> He's like an ostrich with his head in the sand.

The simile elaborates on the meaning of the preceding statement by emphasizing that, not only does the father not care 'what I do', but he also does not want to know 'what I do'. By prescribing this property of not caring, the young woman's simile is also a non-discursive form of individuating paraphrase.

In summary, paraphrase is a particular relation between statements refering to the same transcendent object. This relation is one in which the predications of one statement prescribe individuating properties which are implicit or horizonal in the individuating predications of another statement. By highlighting the importance of individuating paraphrase and by differentiating paraphrasing relations from other relations in discourse, several aspects of phenomenological studies become clearer. First, statements that paraphrase each other may be grouped to form coherent meaning units within a discourse. Second, separate attention may be directed to the non-paraphrasing relations that often implicitly structure monologic discourse.

Paraphrase and Units of Analysis in Phenomenological Studies

Statements that paraphrase each other cohere because they prescribe the individuating properties of the same intended object. Collectively, paraphrasing statements prescribe the subject's conception of the identity of the intended object - at least to the extent that the subject's conception is available within the discourse. Thus, clusters of statements which paraphrase each other form coherent units ('meaning units') within discourse. For example, in the following adaptation of the excerpt from Marsh, Rosser, and Harré's (1977) study, similarly superscripted statements form meaning units because of coherence due to paraphrase relations:

> I don't like my Dad very much.[a]
>
> I get on all right with him, but I hardly ever feel like being affectionate with him.[a]
>
> He couldn't care less what I do as long as he knows where I am.[b]
>
> I mean, you know, if I said I was going to an orgy, he'd say, "Oh, all right, as long as I know where you are."[b]

The segmentation of discourse in empirical phenomenological studies may proceed quite systematically according to this criterion. In doing so, the type of paraphrase uniting the expressions is irrelevant. Expressions related to each other as equivalence paraphrase, contraction paraphrase, or individuative paraphrase are all candidates for inclusion within a meaning unit. Despite this formal egalitarianism, the depth of meaning explication within a discourse will depend upon whether the statements within it provide richly individuating paraphrases of each other.

The formation of meaning units according to paraphrase coherence may require prior analysis of lower level relations among statements. For meaning unit[a], " I get on all right with him" and "I hardly ever feel like being affectionate with him" are separate statements at a lower level of analysis. Their contrastive conjunction in the form, " I get on all right with him, but I hardly ever feel like being affectionate with him", provides a higher order statement which *then* may be related as individuative paraphrase to the assertion, "I don't like my Dad very much". In meaning unit[b], even more complex structuring of lower order statements constitutes (1) the discursive statement regarding lack of caring and (2) the illustrative story that paraphrases it. Despite such complexity, paraphrase analysis provides a systematic principle for determining natural meaning units within discourse. It not only provides a fairly explicit criterion for discerning the transitions in meaning, as in the preceding example; it also provides a criterion for discerning groups of related statements even when those statements are separated by intervening segments of discourse.

Non-paraphrasing Relations and the Structure of Subjectivity

When meaning units are defined using paraphrase analysis, relations between expressions that do not involve paraphrase may be set apart and separately analysed. Note the following example:

> I don't like my Dad very much.
>
> I think that he is uncaring.

One noteworthy feature of the relation between these two meaning units is that it is not one of paraphrase but of justification: "That my Dad is uncaring *justifies* that I don't like my Dad very much". The justification relation involves contingent rather than individuating horizonal predications. That is, the "I think that he is uncaring" statement expresses a mental act which is contingently related to the mental act expressed in "I don't like my Dad very much". Although it refers to a perceived condition within which parental dislike is justified, it does not refer to an individuating property of that dislike.

A second feature of this relation is that it is external.[3] That is, the "I think that he is uncaring" statement expresses a mental act which is related to a separate mental act expressed as, "I don't like my Dad very much". This is analogous to the situation in which 'the apple' is positioned on 'the table'. However, instead of the spatial structure of the relation between two physical objects, the justification structure relates mental acts within the mental life of the young woman.

Consider the following similar example:

> I don't like my Dad very much.

---

[3]Our experience suggests that contingent predications are typically external, although they are not necessarily so. Our examples confound these distinctions for clarity, and space limitations preclude further development of this notion.

I would like to sit down and really sort things out.

In this case, too, the second statement is not related to the first as a paraphrase. Instead the second statement provides a *solution* to the problem of 'not liking Dad very much'. The solution relation is also within the external horizon of the initial statement.

The justification and solution relations are two types of non-paraphrasing relations within discourse (cf. Longacre, 1983; Mann & Thompson, 1986). If the relational structure of discourse corresponds to the relational structure of underlying mental acts, careful classification of relations among meaning units in discourse may provide a vocabulary for describing for the structure of experience. This vocabulary for relations among meaning units can be clearly differentiated from the vocabulary for paraphrase relations by which the meaning units are defined.

However, as indicated by the examples of justification and solution relations, it is common for these relations to remain implicit in discourse (Mann & Thompson, 1986). For example, seldom will a subject explicitly say, "That my Dad is uncaring justifies that I don't like him very much." Without such explication *within* the discourse, the implicit relations referred to as justification, solution, and so on, must be inferred by the phenomenological investigator. Perhaps the classification of relations within discourse is a first step toward the specification of those which can and those which cannot be consistently identified. A meaningful account of human experience - mental acts and their relations - may depend upon our ability to identify both meaning units and relations among such units in linguistic descriptions.

References

Ericsson, K. A., & Simon, H. A. (1984). *Protocol analysis: verbal reports as data.* Cambridge: MIT Press.

Giorgi, A. (1985). *Phenomenology and psychological research.* Pittsburg, PA: Duquesne University Press.

Husserl, E. (1900/1970). *Logical investigations.* New York: Humanistic Press.

Husserl, E. (1913/1931). *Ideas: general introduction to pure phenomenology.* London: George Allen & Unwin.

Longacre, R. E. (1983). *The grammar of discourse.* New York: Plenum.

Mann, W. C., Thompson, S. A. (1986). Relational propositions in discourse. *Discourse Processes, 9,* 57-90.

Marsh, P., Rosser, E., & Harré, R. (1977) *The rules of disorder.* London: Routledge & Kegan Paul.

Smith, D. W., & McIntyre, R. (1982). *Husserl and intentionality: a study of mind, meaning, and language.* Dordrecht, Holland: D. Reidel.

ON HISTORY AND SYSTEM, AND SOCIAL PSYCHOLOGY

Hans V. Rappard

Free University
Amsterdam, The Netherlands

SUMMARY: This paper deals with the question of how the history of psychology might be brought to bear on theoretical psychology. The theoretical problem that is addressed in particular is the systematization rather than unification of psychology. It is argued that essential to any system is an organizing ontological perspective. Next, this concept of perspective is clarified by going into a modern interpretation of the phenomenological concept of essence as founding definition of a knowledge domain. Finally, the possible fruitfulness for systematization of founding definitions is suggested by an illustration from the history of social psychology.

> *In its darkest moments, contemporary psychology trades perspective for technique and applies the latter with such mechanical devotion as to exclude itself from the balance of the history of ideas .... There is a tendency away from the judgment that a system of psychology is an ambitious undertaking and toward the radically different notion that it is merely chimerical. I believe this is a notion to be resisted.*
>
> *D. N. Robinson (1979, p. xi).*

Introduction

It's not by accident that in the title of this paper the word 'system' is used instead of the plural systems. I will not be concerned with the many psychological systems (if systems they are) but, indeed, with History & System, that is, with the relation between history and *the* system of psychology. But psychology is lightyears away from being a system, you will object and that is entirely right: at best, the discipline constitutes an array of micro-theories and disconnected empirical research. But this need not be mentioned here, of course, since especially in North America the 50-odd year old positivist dream of unified science seems to be making a remarkable come-back.

Whatever you may think of this endeavor, both the pursuit of unity, and its rejection as hopelessly doomed to failure would seem eminent problems for theoretical psychology. However, I am not thrilled by the word 'unity'. One reason for not wanting too much to do with the monolithic unity of psychology is found in its massively holistic overtones; the kind of immutable holism that has recently been attacked by Larry Laudan's (1984) deconstruction of the concepts of paradigm, research programme, and even his own research tradition. In various versions of his schematic outline of theoretical psychology as metapsychology, Madsen (1987) has called history of psychology "the oldest and most well established discipline" within theoretical psychology, provided that history contributes to meta-theory or 'systematology'. By systematology is meant the comparative study of psychological theories. However, in the background of the concept of systematology can very clearly be seen Sigmund Koch's (1951) plea for integrative theory. It is my contention, therefore, that systematology may be understood, to some extent at least, as 'creating system' or systematization' and this explains part of the title of this paper. Systematization, that is, the pursuit of a measure of organization of the field seems to me a more realistic option than 'unification'. As a first step towards this goal I may perhaps refer to the multi-level ordering of the various psychological perspectives that Sanders and Rappard (1985) sketched in the third volume of the *Annals of Theoretical Psychology.*

System

What should be understood by 'system'? Interestingly enough several authors on history and systems (Marx & Hillix, 1973; Robinson, 1979) felt the need to go into this question in the introductory chapters of their volumes. Robinson (1979) noticed three essential ingredients in the concept of system.

> ...first, a set of universal propositions from which can be deduced all the events occurring in that part of the universe to which the system is applicable; second, a delineation of what counts as an event; third, the stipulation of which portion of the universe is to be embraced by the system (p. 2).

In regard to the second and third ingredients it is important to note that the author continues saying, "a discipline cannot come into being until a stand is taken on questions of ontology. There must be general agreement on what is to count as an event, on what is to be taken as having real existence. The first stage in the development of any discipline involves ontological legislation." And further, "the very notion of a system implies an organization and codifying perspective (pp. 3-4).

In the selection of these quotations, epistemology has been deliberately glossed over. Often however, ontology and epistemology are mentioned by Robinson in one breath. Indeed, epistemology is named as the fourth ingredient of the concept of system. Nevertheless, ontology seems by far the most important of the two since it is the ontological stance that provides the grounding assumptions of systems. Sure enough, epistemology is closely connected but, as the author himself admonishes, one should not fail to distinguish between ontological and epistemological claims (p. 4). In what follows then, I borrow from Robinson the view that essential to any system is an 'organizing and codifying perspective', plus the contention that such a perspective involves as a first step an 'ontological legislation'.

Essence of Definition

It has already been mentioned that the topic of this paper is the problem of how history may be brought to bear on the theoretical task of the systematization of psychology. I have hinted at my particular view of that task and it was also suggested that in this endeavor an important part may be played by an organizing ontological perspective.

I would now like to spend some time on the further clarification of the idea of such a perspective. I intend to do so by going into a reinterpretation of the phenomenological concept of ground or essence.

In a recent paper the Amsterdam philosopher Theo De Boer (1985) made an attempt to solve certain problems that plagued phenomenology - especially the ontological status of essence. His reinterpretation finds its starting point in Heidegger (and that's one reason why it's called a hermeneutical interpretation). According to Heidegger, essences are not to be thought of as entities - not even 'ideal' ones as seems to be the case in Husserl - but rather as ways of experience. Not ordinary experience but an awareness of the mental activities in which knowledge domains are opened up. Intuiting essence does not entail (outer or inner) perception but instead a reflection on our modes of experience. This view concurs with Kantian philosophy which, starting out with empirical knowledge tried to work its way back to the conditions of this knowledge. Intuition isn't abandoned however, since Heidegger allows for the actual experience of these transcendental conditions which, of course, is not the case in Kant. In short: it is possible for us to reflect on the ways in which we open up or stake out regions of reality, namely, ontological regions.

If the intuition of essence is understood thus, it may be reinterpreted in terms of 'rules'. These rules may be likened to the rules of a game, as Wittgenstein would have it, or to the rules that, in hermeneutical terms, govern the various kinds of human practice. Although this part of De Boer's reinterpretation is not essential to my argument, it does illustrate something important, namely that two categories of rules should be distinguished at two different levels: constituting rules and internal rules. The rules that are fundamental to the game of chess provide an example of constituting rules since they set the very possibility of that game. Internal rules on the other hand are rules that pertain to the actions that are possible once the framework has been constituted.

Constituting rules are always implied by internal rules. They are found at a fundamental level or at a deeper level in any case than the internal rules. There's a host of metaphors for consciousness in which the same difference can be noted. Hume, Wundt, James, and Husserl, to name but a few spoke of the stream of consciousness. More importantly, Brentano distinguished between content and activity of consciousness as did many of his contemporaries. In these metaphors a difference of level is found between some kind of fundamental 'ground-level' and the more superficial 'figures' that depend on that ground-level for their very existence.

With this general figure-ground metaphor in mind, De Boer's hermeneutical reinterpretation of essence may be summarized as follows: Essence is found in the categorial framework or in the constituting rules, that is, in the characteristics or rules that define and thus found knowledge domains. Seen in this light, essence seems to provide the 'ontological legislation' that was mentioned by Robinson. What this 'legislation' would amount to in actual practice, is a definition of the object or field of psychology. "The key problems facing psychology are the very definition and understanding of what a psychological phenomenon is and how to gain proper access to it", the phenomenological psychologist Giorgi (1984, p. 26) writes. And in the Koch and Leary volume *A century of psychology as science* (1985) he argues, in the first part dealing with *The systematic framework of psychology,* that "Whoever can describe the scope of psychology and specify its proper object can on that basis discover its principle of coherence" (p. 58).

It may be objected that this recipe for overcoming psychology's crisis of 'dyssystem' hardly provides grounds for optimism. Already back in the 1930's McGeoch (1933) observed (and was quoted approvingly by Marx & Hillix, 1973).

> Modern psychologists are likely to be casual about the definition of psychology. They recognize that boundaries of fields are always shifting and that new disciplines arise along the boundaries as fields become more specialized. Certainly few psychologists would refuse to study a promising new problem simply because it didn't look like 'psychology' (p. 66).

A brief survey of the history of social psychology may demonstrate the far-sightedness of McGeoch's observation.

Lessons from the History of American Social Psychology

In 1981 Albert Pepitone published an article entitled *Lessons from the history of social psychology.* Among the several lessons that history taught the author, the one of particular relevance here is that throughout the development of the discipline two basic perspectives can be noted: an individualistic perspective and a relatively social one. Both can already be pointed out in the definitions of the object of social psychology of McDougall and Ross, respectively - and even earlier in the French mass psychologists Tarde and LeBon for that matter.

There is a handful of contemporary authors who arrived at basically the same conclusion. Ivan Steiner (1974) distinguished the individualistic from the 'groupy' orientations and maintained that social psychology became much less groupy in the 1960's than it had been two decades earlier. In an article entitled *Contempory social psychology in historical perspective,* Cartwright (1979) pointed to the deep cleavage between psychological social psychology and sociological social psychology. And Gergen (1982) sketched the history of social psychology as a zigzag course between what he called, the exogenic and endogenic worldviews. Although not perfectly, this distinction roughly matches the one between the discipline's 'individualism' and 'social-ism'.

It is possible to further differentiate the social perspective. In 1977 James House wrote on *The three faces of social psychology,* which were (1) psychological social psychology, that is, the individualistic stance; and (2) symbolic interactionism and (3) psychological sociology comprising the social perspective. Recently, Paul Secord (1986) painted yet another kind of social social-psychology into this picture. Thus giving the discipline four faces.

Sticking to the painting metaphor, three or four faces may well strike you as Dadaïsm but perhaps having only two faces is already problematic. In any case, however interesting these further distinctions may be, the basic dichotomy is, it seems, between individualistic and social social-psychology. Neglecting some of the finer details, the two perspectives may also be set up against each other under the captions of 'behavioral' and 'action' psychologies, respectively. The use of these labels prepares the mind for the most important characteristics of the two social-psychological mainstreams. An essential difference between the two stances is that while the behavioral one puts method first, the action perspective stresses substance.

From the methodological point of view. House (1977, p. 163) observes that social psychology "embodies the tradition of experimental, behavioral research which has increasingly characterized all of psychology since the 1920's." Steiner (1974) tried to lay bare the theoretical basis of the connection between individualism and experimentalism. In his view, the individualistic or behavioral perspective takes its point of departure in observable behavior and then tries to move on to the unobserable traits, states or processes within the individual. Hence, the individualistic perspective is bound from the outset to conceive of the person as a self-contained unit or monad and of action as a mere reflection of the events within that monad. In short, Steiner (1974) says

> instead of dealing with long sequences of collective action that move in whatever direction nature may dictate, let us create our own short sequences that won't get out of hand .... The conclusions we reach ought to be reliable because we have carefully controlled the events to which our subject is responding ... our subject has only to fill in the blanks we have left for him. He tells us how a tree will behave in the forest we have contrived. But it is a one-way process; we don't learn how the forest reacts to the tree, or whether forests ever behave the way our programmed subjects have (pp. 99-100).

That the individualistic perspective is closely linked to experimentalism is also Sheldon Stryker's (1977, p. 155) contention. "A major problem of the typical social psychological experiment is that it 'unroots' the person. The psychological focus on the individual leads to the design of experiments which take people out of important social context and treat them in essential isolation from others who are important to them."

On the basis of these few quotations, which could easily be augmented, it may be seen that the individualistic or behavioral perspective is inherently connected to a peculiar kind of - with apologies to Fodor - methodological solipsism. I would not dare to speculate on which came first: methodology or solipsism/individualism. But in any case it can be said that there are methodological reasons behind the individualistic perspective. The very nature of experimental research seems to entail proximal causes, that is, causes that are close in the causal chain and adjacent in space and time to the behavior that is to be explained. Individualistic social psychology operates on the basis of what may be called, quite literally, 'micro' units of analysis.

Naturally, things are different when seen from the social perspective. In this case more distal explanations are sought. Behavior or rather, action, is conceived as a larger unit: it is attributed to events that may be a long distance from the acts to be explained, in terms of both the causal chain and space and time. As Steiner (1974) put it.

> ...the individual is presumed to be an element in a larger system, a group, organization or society. And what he does is presumed to reflect the state of the larger system and the events that are occurring in it. Consequently, one looks for causes that are located outside the individual himself, in the collective actions of others, or in the constraints imposed by the larger system (p. 96).

As might be expected because of its sociological orientation, the action stance sees the object of social psychology as "the processes through which individuals interpret situations and construct their actions with respect to each other" (House, 1977, p. 167). Since, in this case, social behavior is alleged a certain degree of spontaneity, research under the controlled conditions that only the laboratory is able to provide is "actively eschewed" (House, 1977, p. 167). Having outlined a pivotal dichotomy in social psychology, one may well ask if history teaches us anything about the relation between the behavioral and action perspectives.

Gergen's (1982) picture of the development of the discipline as a zigzag course between the endogenic and exogenic worldviews provides a first approximation of an answer to this question. Social psychology seems indeed to have oscillated between the individualistic scylla and the social charybdis. But two cautions should be made here. The first is that during what Cartwright (1979) called social psychology's second 40 years, this zigzag course seems far less pronounced than it may appear when the first 40 years are also taken into account. As I see it, since WW II the pendulum has made one real swing only, notably from the social perspective that characterized the Lewin era to the individualistic perspective that became increasingly dominant since the death of the master and which was strengthened tremendously by the emergence of the cognitive shift in neighbouring psychological disciplines.

The second caution is closely related to the first. Since in my view there is less of a swing of the pendulum than Gergen (1985) would welcome, I find it hard to agree with his prediction that it is bound to stop swinging and going to remain at socio-rationalism or, as it is now called, social constructionism. The history of social psychology seems to be the history of the individualistic or behavioral perspective, the alternative characteristically being eclipsed by the former and hence living a shadowy life. "In retrospect, it appears that the group was never in very good health", as Steiner (1974, p. 101) put it. And, incidentally good reasons why this should be so can easily be found in the context of American culture (Smith, 1986).

In the context of this paper dealing with History & System the question to be asked now would seem to be: Does the bias of social psychology towards the individualistic or behavioral perpective have something to do with its apparent lack of systematization? As argued before, the behavioral stance puts method before substance. Know-how is stressed at the cost of know-what. It can easily be grasped that questions about the precise object of investigation and its relation to the objects of neighbouring disciplines may not be in particularly high esteem when the emphasis is squarely on the methodological tool-kit. According to several authors, the discipline has indeed neglected substantive questions at the price of being exposed to what would seem a natural consequence of this, notably faddism.

A typical example of faddism that is often cited in the literature is the Kitty Genovese murder in 1964 that triggered a spate of research and theory on altruism, bystander intervention etc. In connection with this,

Shaw & Costanzo (1982) note.

> Although theory and research being derived from current events is not necessarily bad ... in the 1960s cognitive consistency theories dominated social psychology ... numerous theories of this type were proposed and became the prevailing theoretical approach in social psychology (at least in frequency of invocation). At the present time, attribution theories are in vogue and are most frequently employed as explanations of behavior. (Would the reader care to predict the next fad in social-psychological theorizing?) (p. 416).

Carl Backman (1980) also sees the discipline as largely determined by faddism. Since little if any attention has been paid to questions of theoretical structure and coherence, the choice of research topics tends to follow the current craze. Another reason for the 'topical fickleness of the field', and one that is of particular relevance here, is found in the reliance on the laboratory experiment as the all-important source of data. This has allegedly led to a general trivialization of the research topic. As described by Backman (1980, p. 166). "either the original substantive problem is transformed into a methodological one, or, more often, into a substantive problem quite different from and almost invariably less significant than the phenomenon of initial interest." What's described here is, in other words, the almost total eclipse of the know-what by the know-how. The late Jos Jaspars summarized this as, "It is not just a question of restricting research to what can be studied by particular methods, but of methods becoming the model for the issues they are supposed to study" (1986), p. 13).

More authors could be quoted giving more reasons for social psychology's faddism (see Backman, 1980, p. 167). But should it suffice for the purpose of this paper that some of them attribute much of the fragmentation of the field to the preoccupation, nay, the 'obsession' with method and technique. "The discipline", Cartwright (1979, p. 87) says, "has become divided along methodological lines rather than by substantive problems."

Conclusion

Keeping the lessons from the history of social psychology in mind, one might hypothesize that an emphasis on substance might help turn the tide of faddism and fragmentation.

Even though the label 'social psychology' is very much in use, according to Cartwright's (1979) diagnoses of the ills of the discipline, we are not sure "where the boundaries of the field should be drawn" (p. 90). Should this diagnosis fail to ring a bell, the prescription surely won't.

> It would be paradoxical if social psychology were ever to abandon the very task that constituted its original ***raison d'etre*** and were to accept either of these (individualistic or social, H.V.R.) approaches as the sole basis for defining its proper subject matter. But if this unfortunate eventuality is to be avoided, we must have a clear conception of the discipline's basic mission, or ***master problem, which will provide an organizing principle for all of social psychology. We need, in other words, a definition of the field*** that places the study of psychological processes within a proper social context" (p. 91, emphasis added).

In view of what was said in an early part of this paper, it may be concluded that Cartwright argues for an 'ontological legislation' - the ontological legislation that Robinson sees as a first step towards the development of a system.

References

Backman, C. W. (1980). Promises unfulfilled - the premature abandonment of promising research. In R. Gilmour & S. Duck (Eds.), *The development of social psychology* (pp. 163-179). London/New York: Academic Press.

Boer, Th. De (1985). Van wezensschouw naar hermeneuse (From intuition of essence to hermeneutics). *Algemeen Nederlands Tijdschrift voor Wijsbegeerte, 77*, 36-59.

Cartwright, D. (1979). Contemporary social psychology in historical perspective. *Social Psychology Quarterly, 42*, 82-93.

Gergen, K. J. (1982). *Toward transformation in social knowledge.* New York/Berlin: Springer.

Gergen, K. J. (1985). The social constructionist movement in modern psychology. *American Psychologist, 40*, 266-275.

Giorgi, A. (1984). The unfinished business of psychology. In D. P. Rogers (Ed.), *Foundations of psychology, some personal views.* New York: Praeger.

Giorgi, A. (1985). Toward the articulation of psychology as a coherent discipline. In S. Koch & D. Leary (Eds.), *A century of psychology as science* (pp.46-59). New York: McGraw-Hill.

House, J. S. (1977). The three faces of social psychology. *Sociometry, 40*, 161-177.

Jaspars, J. (1986). Forum and focus: a personal view of European social psychology. *European Journal of Social Psychology, 16*, 3-15.

Koch, S. (1951). Theoretical psychology 1950: an overview. *Psychological Review, 58*, 295-301.

Koch, S., & Leary, D. E. (1985). *A century of psychology as science.* New York, NY: McGraw-Hill.

Laudan, L. (1984). *Science and values.* Berkeley: University of California Press.

Madsen, K. B. (1987). Theoretical psychology: a definition and systematic classification. In W. J. Baker, M. E. Hyland, H. Van Rappard, & A. W. Staats (Eds.), *Current issues in theoretical psychology* (pp. 165-174). Amsterdam: North-Holland.

Marx, M. H., & Hillix, W. A. (1973). *Systems and theories in psychology.* New York: McGraw-Hill.

McGeoch, J. A. (1933). The formal criteria of a systematic psychology. *Psychological Review, 40*, 1-12.

Pepitone, A. (1981). Lessons from the history of social psychology. *American Psychologist, 36*, 972-985.

Robinson, D. N. (1979). *Systems of modern psychology.* New York: Columbia University Press.

Sanders, C., & Rappard, H. V.(1985). Psychology and philosophy of science. In K. B. Madsen & L. P. Mos (Eds.), *Annals of theoretical psychology* (Vol. 3, pp. 219-295). New York: Plenum.

Secord, P. F. (1986). Social psychology as a science. In J. Margolis, P. T. Manicas, R. Harré, & P. F. Secord (Eds.), *Psychology-designing the discipline* (pp. 128-164). Oxford: Blackwell.

Shaw, M. E., & Costanzo, Ph. R. (1982). *Theories of social psychology.* New York: McGraw-Hill.

Smith, M. Brewster (1986). Review of R. N. Bellah a. o. , Habits of the heart: individualism and commitment in American life. *Contemporary Psychology, 31,* 173-174.

Steiner, I. D. (1974). Whatever happened to the group in social psychology? *Journal of Experimental and Social Psychology, 10,* 95-108.

Stryker, S. (1977). Developments in 'two social psychologies': toward an appreciation of mutual relevance. *Sociometry, 40,* 145-160.

UNDERSTANDING THE COMPLEX DYNAMICS OF HUMAN STABILITY AND CHANGE[1]

Brian L. Mishara

Université du Québec à Montréal
Montréal, Québec, Canada

SUMMARY: Faced with the inherent complexity of changes in human development over time, psychologists have sought relatively simple laws and theories to try to make sense out of the flux of human behavior in a changing world. The search for simple laws may be based upon their desire to emulate the physical sciences, as exemplified in the orderly domain of Newtonian physics. However, such a desire for simple universal laws 'as in physics' may be outmoded; the physical sciences have changed in recent years. Physics has gone beyond Newtonian laws for the study of equilibrium in closed systems to explore the complex dynamics of irreversible phenomena in open systems where linear explanations break down and complex structural changes can occur. This paper presents a model for conceptualizing the processes of complex changes over time based upon the theory of irreversible phenomena in the physical sciences developed by Ilya Prigogine, Grégoire Nicolis and their colleagues. The reader is invited to suspend traditional ways of viewing change and development and embark on an exploration of the usefulness of some alternative mathematical and theoretical perspectives which are based upon recent theory and research in the physical sciences. The overall goal is to present a way of conceptualizing and exploring highly complex developmental phenomena without oversimplifying the complex nature of the processes of behavioral changes over time in the real world.

Modeling Changes Over Time

In simple laboratory or field experiments we are often able to control sufficient numbers of variables to develop models of change over time. Wohlwill (1973) describes several models for studying developmental dimensions which "are homogeneous enough to represent unidimensional continua while still being attuned to significant facets of behavioral

[1]This research was supported in part by a grant from the Canadian Social Sciences and Humanities Research Council. The author thanks Prof. I. Prigogine and his colleagues at the Université Libre de Bruxelles for their inspiration, comments and help, especially G. Nicolis and A. Goldbeter. Also, thanks to C. Braun and P. Cowen for their critical reading of the paper. Nonetheless, the author is fully responsible for the content of this paper.

development" (p. 81). Flavell and Wohlwill (1969) argued that qualitative changes, as proposed by developmental stage theorists, such as Piaget, may have both qualitative and quantitative aspects: the qualitative aspects relate to the form or nature of the behavior being studied; whereas the quantitative aspects relate to questions concerning the consistency or efficiency of a given structural mechanism.

Theorists who stress qualitative changes may emphasize discontinuity to such an extent that the quantitative aspects of research seem to have relatively little importance. Furthermore, qualitative oriented theorists tend to use concepts such as 'structure' which certain empirically minded psychologists look upon with disdain.

It is beyond the scope of this paper to venture too far into past debates over the relative importance of qualitative versus quantitative developmental changes. The approach presented here integrates the qualitative and quantitative aspects of changes over time in an unique manner: using models derived from the physical sciences, we show how qualitative changes in highly complex systems may develop as higher order structures which incorporate their past in a non-linear manner and whose form may be highly complex yet stable entities.

In the physical and biological sciences, complex structural changes can occur when the state of the system is far from equilibrium. Even seemingly 'simple' systems may change their structure in very dramatic ways (Nicolis & Prigogine, 1977). These behavioral-structural changes can range from simple periodic behavior, as in the case of chemical clocks or biological rhythms, to complex aperiodic changes, referred to as, 'chaos'.

There are many examples of how complex structural changes can develop in what seem to be simple systems. For example, in physics, Benard described a curious phenomenon around 1900. An example of the Benard-type phenomenon can be observed if a fluid at rest is maintained between two horizontal plates, with the bottom plate being hotter than the top plate. As the heat of the bottom plate is increased, we first observe the fluid to remain uniform, with heat being conducted from bottom to top according to simple principles of conduction. However, when a crucial level of temperature differential is reached in the bottom plate, the 'system' ceases to be uniform and becomes organized into roll shaped convection cells, with adjacent rolls rotating in opposite directions. At this critical temperature value the system ceases to behave in a simple manner with only quantitative changes as a linear function of the heat applied. Instead, qualitative changes occur and structure develops as the fluid is organized into convection cells. This simple example shows how quantitative variation in a single variable can produce qualitative structural changes in the organization of a system as a whole.

Other examples of the development of structure in the physical and biological sciences by nonequilibrium transitions include the forming of snow flakes, the precipitation patterns of certain sedimentary rocks, chemical waves and spatial structures arising in embryonic development (Gaspard & Nicolis, 1986).

Prigogine and his colleagues (Nicolis & Prigogine, 1977; Prigogine, 1980) addressed the question of how complex organized structures can develop from simple deterministic systems. They found that, in systems far from equilibrium, highly organized qualitative changes can occur in which 'dissipative structures' arise. Dissipative structures develop from unstable situations and persist in time as stable entities. Their nature and very existence is not predictable from the components that lead to their appearance. However, once formed (after a brief period of instability at a bifurcation point), the new organization, or dissipative structure, remains a higher order stable entity until new bifurcations take place.

According to this approach, chance events play an important role near a developmental structural change, or bifurcation.[2] Thus, there is an inherent ambiguity as to the nature of developmental change at certain critical points. Although development can result in remarkable reorganizations and re-structuring, there is no single unidimensional direction of development, as postulated by Werner (1957) and other developmental theorists with a teleological bent. Once established, a structure need not work well to survive, it just needs to resist the forces that menace it (Allen, 1985).

In complex systems operating in elaborate environments, such symmetry-breaking qualitative changes which result in the development of dissipative structures are often present. In the following sections we present some models of regimes which may develop as a result of processes involving symmetry breaking structural changes.

Viewing the Dynamics of Development in Phase Space

Before beginning our theoretical examination of the dynamics of behavioral change, we need to conceptualize complex systems in a particu-

---

[2] The use of the term, 'bifurcation', suggests the work by the French mathematician, René, Thom (e.g., 1981; 1985). Thom developed a highly theoretical 'idealized' mathematical theory which was subsequently used by some social scientists to explain social phenomena. This use of Thom's abstract theories to explain social and biological phenomena was highly criticized as lacking foundations in experimental data (e.g., Sussman & Zahler, 1978). The approach presented here does not presume any superordinate mathematical scenario, such as in Thom's catastrophy models. Rather, we present several concepts which have been used in theoretical work and experimental research in physics, chemistry and biology. The theory and concepts presented here are firmly linked to actual phenomena which have been researched.

lar mathematical manner which allows us to describe certain properties of change over time. The complex system, in this instance, consists of human behavior and may constitute any particular sub-set of human activities we happen to be interested in. The system exists in a complex environment with which it is continually interacting. The system may be described mathematically by a rather large number of state variables (x_i) which may describe the system as a whole at a macroscopic level. Similarly, there exist a large number of parameters through which the system is affected by its environment (λ). Changes in all the x_i state variables over time constitute the development of the system as a whole. If one were mathematically inclined, one could write an algorithm which describes changes in the state variables of the system as a function of various initial conditions and the various environmental parameters. A mathematical expression of the development of the system over time would be:

$$\frac{dF}{dt} = F\,(x_i \ldots \lambda\, j \ldots .) \qquad \text{(Eq. 1)}$$

The fact that one could theoretically conceive of the evolution of a system in such a manner seems logical and simple. However, when we are dealing with complex behavior (for example, changes in the emotional reactions of a person), the state variables and parameters through which the system is affected by its environment are usually so diverse that they are essentially unknowable or at least impossible to measure completely. Even if we could measure them all, the environmental and state variables would have propably changed by the time our measurements were concluded.

We introduced the convention of describing the development of a system in terms of changes in state variables (x_i) which are related to environmental parameters (λ) in order to help introduce a concept which will be used in later discussions, the concept of 'phase space'. Phase space is a multidimensional space whose dimensions constitute all of the variables needed to completely describe the system as a whole. For example, if we could describe all properties of the behavior of a system by two variables, a and b, the phase space would consist of a two dimensional space (in this instance, just a two dimensional phase plane) whose x axis would include all possible values of a, and whose y axis would include all possible values of b. Thus, each possible instantaneous state of the system would be represented by a single point and each point in the phase space corresponds to one and only one state of the system. In our simple example, each possible combination of a and b would be represented by a point in the two dimensional phase space. Each point constitutes a possible solution to our equation (Eq. 1), which corresponds to a mode of behavior of the underlying system at a given point in time. Changes in time of the state of the system can be viewed as the trajectory obtained by connecting the points which represent system states in phase space at different times.

Although it is impossible to visualize phase space portraits of systems which are highly complex and may need hundreds or thousands of variables to describe the system as a whole, we can use the concept of phase space to model development. Furthermore, as we shall see later, with the help of computers and a few mathematical tools, we can use phase space analyses to describe important properties of the development of complex systems, even when we are unable to identify all the various state variables involved.

In the following sections we describe some models of change over time, as portrayed in phase space. Then, we discuss the implications of these models for conceptualizing developmental change and suggest some theoretical and research implications based upon this approach.

In the phase space portrait of any system, as we have seen, all possible combinations of variables participating in the dynamics of the system are represented by points in this multi-dimensional space. Although any of the combinations of variables representing instantaneous states of the system are possible, the *actual* trajectory of a system over time is represented by a much more limited set of points. Not all areas in a phase space will be occupied during the development of a system. If, in a phase space trajectory, the probability of finding a point is equal in all areas of the phase space, we are dealing with a situation of random changes over time. In this instance what happens developmentally is not organized in a meaningful manner and we can say nothing about the developmental process other than stating that the processes underlying changes over time are essentially indeterminate. In this case, the phase portrait of the system would be equivalent to the phase space trajectory of a signal consisting of white noise.

However, if over time the phase space trajectory is such that there is a tendency toward a certain sub-area or certain sub-areas of the phase space, then we are describing a deterministic system. In this instance, there is a tendency over time toward occupying a certain portion of the phase space. We refer to this portion of the phase space as an 'attractor'. The following sections describe certain types of attractors in a developing system.

Equilibrium Models

When a system tends toward a state of equilibrium, whatever the initial conditions, the trajectories will eventually evolve toward one unique fixed point (see Figure 1a). This point represents the combination of state variables which constitute an invariant goal in development, whether or not that goal is reached in the lifespan of the system.

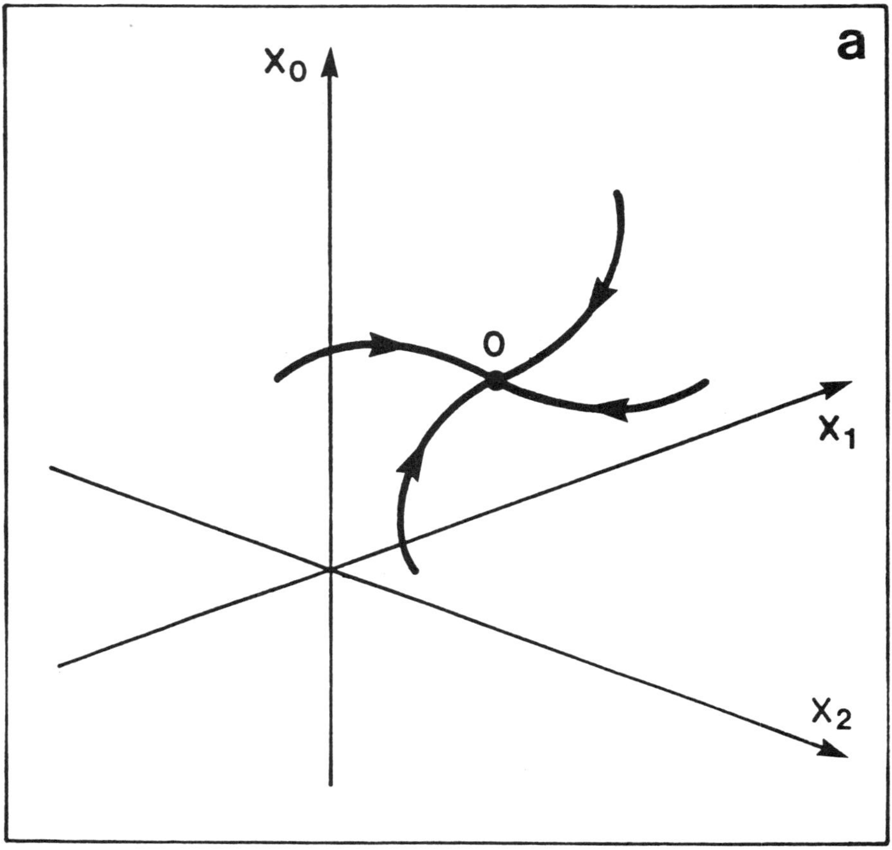

Fig. 1a Phase space portrait of equilibrium models.

Approaches to equilibrium need not be direct. The trajectories toward the point representing the state of equilibrium may, for example, be spiral rather than monotonic (see Figure 1b). Such spiral trajectories may result in approaches to equilibrium which take an indirect path involving damped oscillations, sometimes seeming to be heading elsewhere, but inevitably proceeding towards the unique equilibrium state.

Equilibrium theories have been quite popular in psychology, and they are so diverse in nature that they range from the Freudian psychoanalytical theory of intrapsychic dynamics to theories of homeostasis at the bio-chemical level. In this paper we follow the approach of Prigogine and his colleagues in suggesting that although equilibrium models offer nice descriptions in carefully controlled laboratory situations, they fall short of explaining the dynamics of complex open systems interacting

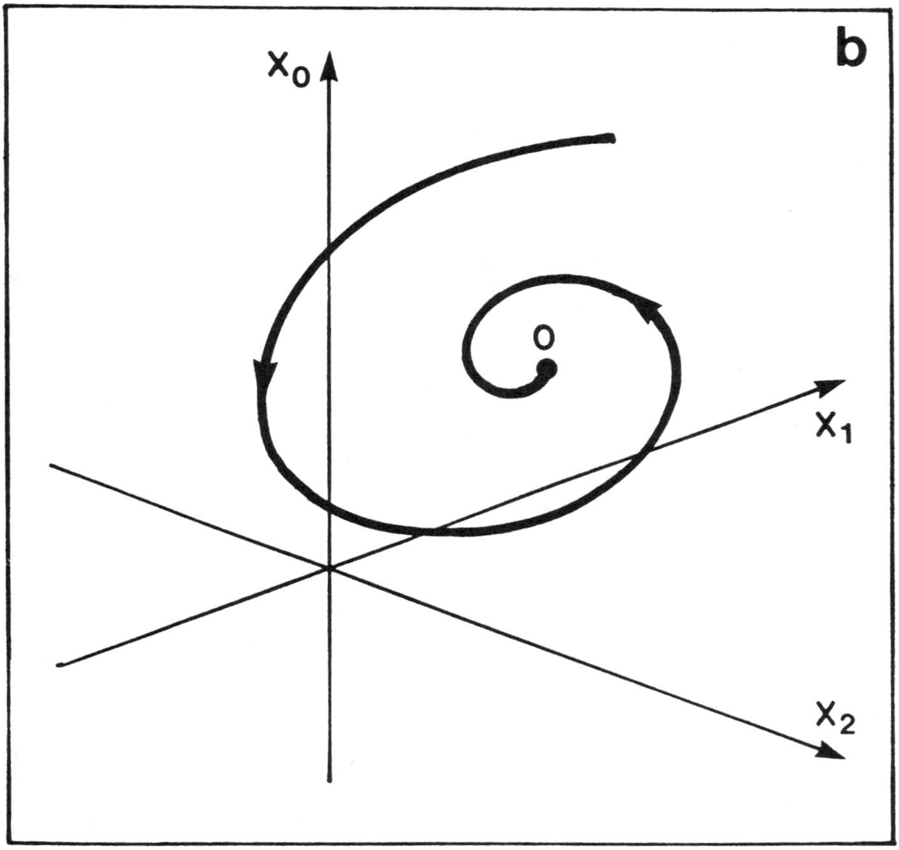

Fig. 1b Phase space portrait of equilibrium models.

with complex environments along multiple dimensions. In this regard, we concur with Riegel's (1976) assessment that the instabilities in life in non-equilibrium situations may offer more interesting insights into developmental issues.

Periodicity

If, rather than tending toward a single point, phase space trajectories tend toward a closed line, the system develops toward a periodic regime (see Figure 2). Periodic attractors can be used to describe periodic behavior such as biological rhythms, chemical oscillations, self-pulsing in lasers. Also, certain electronic circuits may be modeled as periodic attrac-

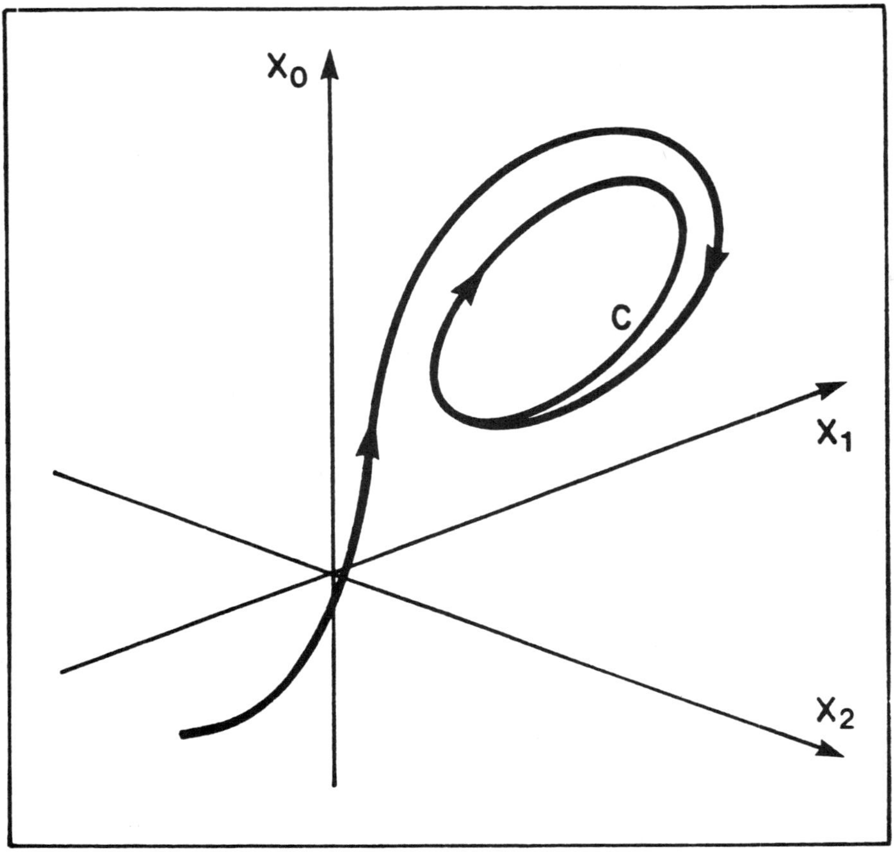

Fig. 2 Phase space portrait of development toward a periodic regime.

tors. An example of periodicity studied in psychology would be diurnal rhythms as related to behavior.

It is also possible to model quasiperiodic motions with two or more incommensurate frequencies. Such quasiperiodicity could be described by surfaces in the form of tori. In a highly speculative vein, one could view certain processes which psychologists such as Riegel (1979) call, dialectic' in terms of models of quasiperiodicity.

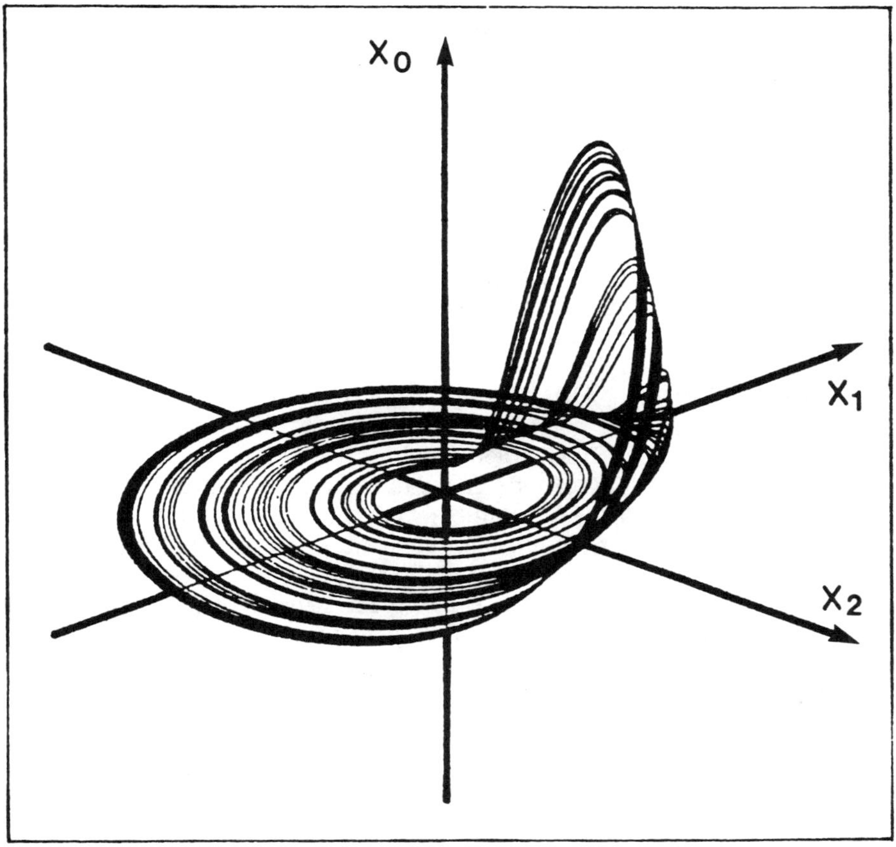

Fig. 3 Phase space portrait of a chaotic attraction: the Rössler attractor.

Chaotic Attractors

Thus far, we have considered attractors which present a fairly simple models of development. In equilibrium models and periodicity, the direction of developmental change is easily described, even though the path towards the developmental goal may be complicated. However, it is possible to have a more complex conceptualization of developmental processes. There may be an attractor which constitutes a sub-area of phase space toward which trajectories develop over time (thus, a deterministic process is occurring), but which combines two antagonistic trends, an instability of motion and a stability of the whole. These attractors are referred to as, 'chaotic' attractors, since they appear to be chaotic in nature. (They were originally called, 'strange' attractors because of their unusual properties.) In chaotic attractors there is both a tendency to go away from a fixed point (that is, instability of motion) and a concurrent tendency to be kept tightly upon an invariant set, thus assuring a stability of the whole. The Rössler attractor constitutes one example of a chaotic attractor. Figure 3 shows a model of the Rössler attractor in a three dimensional phase space.

Empirically determined chaotic attractors may not be as visually impressive as the Rössler attractor. However, all chaotic attractors share certain essential characteristics. First, they have a dimensionality which is different from that of a line or surface; their dimensionality cannot be described by integers, but are fractal in nature, in the sense of Mandelbrot (1983). For example, a chaotic attractor may have a fractal dimensionality of 3, 2 or 6.7. Although several dimensionalities have been suggested to characterize the geometry of a chaotic attractor, the correlation dimension proposed by Grassberger and Procaccia (1983 a, b) seems particularly useful in that it can be calculated from realistically obtainable data sets. The smallest whole number which exceeds the fractal dimensionality of a chaotic attractor constitutes the minimum number of variables needed to fully describe the attractor.

With chaotic attractors, there is a great sensitivity to initial conditions. Two nearby points will have diverging fates over time. In chaotic dynamics, unpredictability enters the picture and only probabilistic description is possible. If human development is conceived in terms of chaotic dynamics, behavior is determined by such variables as experience, history and initial conditions. However, despite the fact that events have direct deterministic links to behavior, the predictability of future states of the system is limited by the very nature of the process of developmental change.

The behavior of several complex systems can be understood in terms of chaotic attractors. For example, turbulence was construed in the 1940's as a quasi-periodic regime which develops only after an infinite number of bifurcations. Later conceptualizations of turbulence showed that turbulence may arise as chaotic behavior evolving after just a few bifurcations from a reference state (see Gaspar & Nicolis, 1985). The dynamics of the thermal convection rolls in the Benard-type phenomenon (described previously) can be understood in terms of chaotic dynamics. This phenomenon can also be used to understand more general situations, such as modeling the earth's atmosphere.

One of the amazing characteristics of several chaotic attractors found to represent experimentally observed situations is their relatively low dimensionality despite their outward appearance of complexity and confusion. For example, a chaotic attractor of climatic variations on the earth over the past million years (Nicolis & Nicolis, 1984) was determined on the basis of climactic data obtained from oxygen isotope analysis of deep sea bed samples at 500 year intervals. Upon casual inspection, the raw data in this study appear very much like white noise, with no obvious pattern. The researchers tried to determine whether the climate on earth is a random system, determined by stochastic processes such as solar variability, or if the earth's climatic changes indicate the presence of a deterministic dynamical system possessing an attractor. They found that the chaotic attractor which describes the climactic variability on earth over the past million years has a relatively low fractal dimensionality, of about 3.1, indicating that deterministic dynamics are present with a relatively low dimensionality.

The Development of Chaotic Attractors: Complexity from Simple Processes

Prigogine, Nicolis and their colleagues (e.g., Nicolis & Prigogine, 1977) have been studying the dynamics of open systems which are far from equilibrium and which exist in complex environments. Their research in physics, chemistry, biology and animal ecology show that by varying certain parameters, the same system may change from an equilibrium regime to a system where new attractors are born. They refer to the mechanism by which new attractors are born as bifurcation. According to their approach to bifurcation theory, if the state of a system is plotted against some constraint, at a certain critical value of the constraint, changes may occur in the system at a critical point of instability.

Such changes may transform the state of the system in remarkable ways, as in the case of the Benard instability described above. In the Benard instability, at a critical point in the increase in temperature differential of the heating plates, the fluid is organized into structures which are referred to as, convection cells. This organized behavior of the system develops when the system is moved away from a state of equilibrium by varying a certain parameter (or parameters). The new structure is qualitatively different from the nature of the system before the bifurcation, and its nature may not be seen in the system prior to bifurcation, although the structure is determined by the history of the system.

Another example in the physical sciences of the development of complexity is the Belousov-Zhabotinski reaction in chemistry (the B-Z reaction). In traditional chemsitry (the type of chemistry most readers of this article probably learned in school), neat reversible equations described what happens when several substances are mixed together. Time and spatial structure are not to be found in traditional chemical equations, and processes are generally reversible - they can go in either direction with time. However, in the B-Z reaction, a simple combination of chemicals results in a radical temporal and spatial reorganization of the system. In

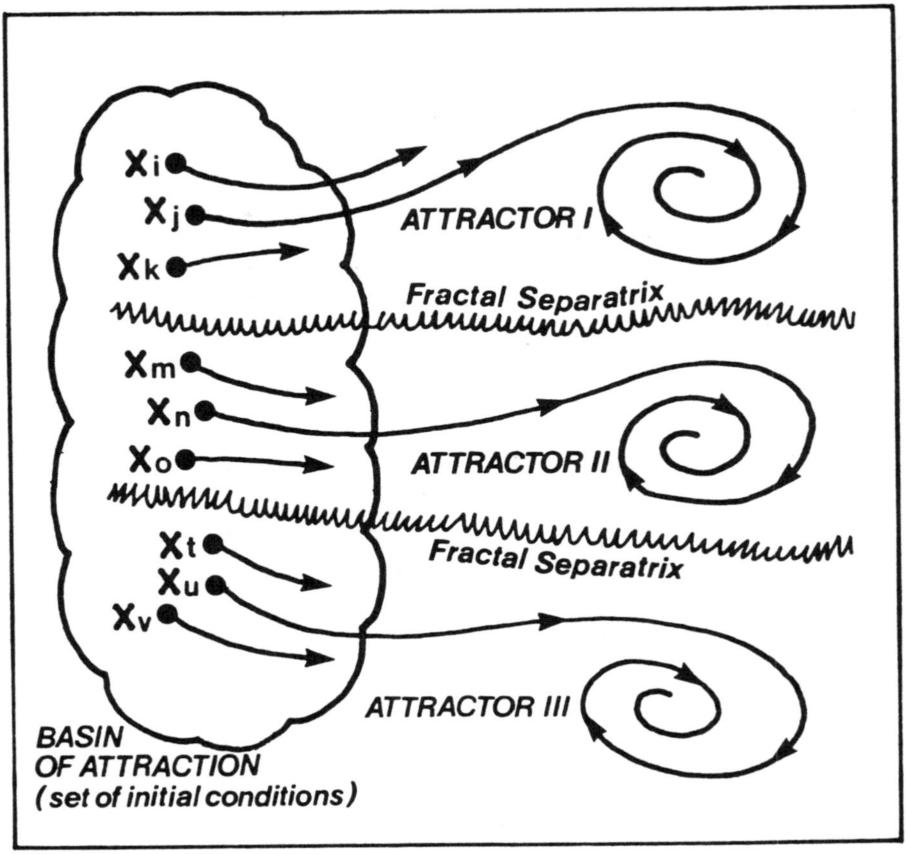

Fig. 4 A model of multiple attractors.

the B-Z reaction three substances are combined in a container. The mixture then organizes itself spatially forming bands of red and blue. In a variant of the B-Z reaction, temporal periodical changes in color occur.

There are several possible models of the development of chaotic attractors (Eckmann, 1981; Gaspard & Nicolis, 1986). One model for the development of chaotic attractors is the Feigenbaum cascade (Feigenbaum, 1980). Here, the development of deterministic chaos is seen as a result of cascades of bifurcations over time. In this model, a sequence of doubling bifurcations develop periodic orbits which increase in length up to a critical value of a parameter after which the system becomes dynamically unstable and the orbits become non-periodic. Here, chaotic dynamics are a natural consequence of multiple bifurcations. Although chaotic dynamics may appear random, they derive from deterministic processes whose history has been lost over time.

Multiple Attractors

In order to simplify the presentation, we have limited our discussion, thus far, to systems having a single attractor. However, it is possible that multiple attractors co-exist in a system (e.g., Nicolis, 1985). When multiple attractors co-exist, each has its own basin of attraction identified by sub-areas in phase space (see Figure 4). The basins of attraction of different attractors are separated by manifolds in phase space which are known as fractal separatrix, and these separatrix emanate from a point in phase space which is called the saddle point.

The areas in phase space which separate different attractors are areas of instability of motion. However, once in the basin of attraction of an attractor, stability of motion is evident as the developmental trajectory is held on the attractor. When multiple attractors co-exist, the developmental trajectory will depend upon where in phase space the trajectory began. New attractors may be born through parameter changes.

Learning about Complex Phenomena from Simple Observations: Limits of Predictability

What can one do with a theoretical perspective which considers development in terms of trajectories in a phase space? In the complex world of humans developing, calculating the dimensionality of attractors in phase space may seem a moot point, since the phase space involves the full set of variables participating in the dynamics of the system. The number of possible contributing variables may be so great that it seems practically impossible to attempt to empirically determine the phase space trajectory. In other words, given our limited capabilities in human scientific observations, is it possible to determine the nature of attractors and phase space trajectories without having to measure all the many variables which participate in the dynamics of a complex system in human development?

Fortunately, with the help of some mathematical tools, it is possible to describe the nature of attractors and make some interesting statements about developmental trajectories without having to try to identify or measure all of the many variables participating in the dynamics of a system. If we can accurately observe a time series sample of a signal which is a product of the dynamics of the system, it is possible to reconstruct the phase space developmental trajectory of the system and make some interesting statements about the existence and nature of attractors. On the basis of one experimentally determined variable, it is possible to determine whether the signal results from an essentially deterministic process or whether the signal contains irreducible random components. For example, in the previous example of the earth's climate over the past million years (Nicolis & Nicolis, 1984), by calculating some time consuming autocorrelation functions with a computer, it was determined whether the climatic variations were just random in nature, or if they represented an attractor. Then, the fractal dimensionality of the attractor was assertained. In this manner, it was possible to take a signal of climatic variation which appeared highly disorganized and random from initial inspection of the data, and find that deterministic processes describe the underlying dynamics; processes which may be described by a fairly low dimensionality.

Besides determining the existence of an attractor and its dimensionality, other interesting information may be obtained empirically about the dynamics of complex systems operating on an attractor. This information may be obtained from a complex signal resulting from the system's developmental dynamics. For example, Lyapounov exponents may be calculated which describe the limits of predictability of the long term behavior of the system. In chaotic dynamics, the very nature of the system's development is such that nearby points have diverging fates over time. Lyapounov exponents describe these limits of predictability. In the case of chaotic dynamics, because of their inherent unpredictability of motion, only probabilistic predictions are possible. Calculations of Lyapounov exponents would help determine how far ahead in time one can predict from initial data.

Conclusions

A few decades ago, it was the hope of behavioral psychology to reduce human behavior to basic laws and predict behavior on the basis of past learning. In the model presented here, simple processes (such as described in classical learning theories) can play a deterministic role in shaping behavior. However, these simple processes develop complex qualitative changes which result in higher order organizations into what Prigogine called, "dissipative structures." In chaotic dynamics, the nature of development is such that the predictability from these simple processes is severely limited by the very nature of the dynamics of the system as it evolves over time. In this model, the origins of complex developmental structures are lost over time. The system forgets its past and the past does not know what is to occur in the future. Nevertheless, past and future are linked in a deterministic manner.

According to this approach, the basic laws which one studies in carefully controlled laboratory experiments are valid for predicting behavior within the confines of the near equilibrium closed system experimental situation. These basic laws may be essential components of a system, just as the bricks which form the walls of a building are crucial elements in the whole. However, as in the case of the building bricks, they do not necessarily contain information which helps one understand the form of the complex whole. Research on such basic building blocks, such as principles of learning, is still valid and useful within the confines of certain contexts. However, the nature of developmental change may be such that there is an inherent limitation in all such 'bottom up' approaches.

This approach calls for a re-evaluation of how developmental psychologists view causality and determinism in their research and theory. The properties of a system at a given point in time may be entirely determined by various events in its history. However, the information concerning the system's determinants may be lost over time and the determining events may not contain information which allows one to know the nature of the qualitative structural changes which will occur in the course of the system's development.

References

Allen, P. M (1985). Ecology, thermodynamics and self-organization: toward a new understanding of complexity. *Canadian Bulletin of Fisheries and Aquatic Sciences, 213*, 3-26.

Eckmann, J. -P. (1981). Roads to turbulence in dissipative dynamical systems. *Review of Modern Physics, 53*, 643-654.

Feigenbaum, M. (1980). Universal behavior in nonlinear systems. *Los Alamos Science, 1*, 4-27.

Flavell, J. H., & Wohlwill, J. F. (1969). Formal and functional aspects of cognitive development. In D. Elkind & J. H. Flavell (Eds.), *Studies in cognitive development: essays in honor of Jean Piaget* (pp. 67-120). London: Oxford University Press.

Gaspard, P., & Nicolis, G. (1985). *Chaotic Dynamics.* Brussels: Faculté des Sciences de l'Université Libre de Bruxelles.

Grassberger, P., Procaccia, I. (1983a). Measuring the strangeness of strange attractors. *Physica, 9*, 189-208.

Grassberger, P., & Procaccia, I. (1983b). Characterization of strange attractors. *Physical Review Letters, 50(5)*, 346-349.

Mandelbrot, B. B. (1983). *The fractal geometry of nature.* (revised ed.). San Francisco: W. H. Freeman.

Nicolis, C., & Nicolis, G. (1984). Is there a climatic attractor? *Nature, 311*, 529-532.

Nicolis, G., & Prigogine, I. (1977). *Self organization in non-equilibrium systems, from dissipative structures to order through fluctuations.* New York: Wiley-Interscience.

Nicolis, J. S. (1985). Chaotic dynamics of information processing with relevance to cognitive brain functions. *Cybernetics, 14*, 167-172.

Prigogine, I. (1980). *From being to becoming: Time and complexity in the physical sciences.* New York: W. H. Freeman.

Riegel, K. F. (1979). *Foundations of dialectical psychology.* New York: Academic Press.

Sussman, H. J., & Zahler, R. S. (1978). Catastrophe theory as applied to the social and biological sciences: a critique. *Synthese, 37*, 117-216.
Thom, R. (1981). *Modèles mathématiques de la morphogenèse.* Paris: Christian Bourgois.
Thom, R. (1985). *Paraboles et catastrophes.* Paris: Flammarion.
Werner, H. (1948). *Comparative psychology of mental development.* New York: Science Editions.
Wohlwill, F. F. (1973). *The study of behavioral development.* New York: Academic Press.

THE CONCEPT OF TRANSITION IN DEVELOPMENTAL THEORIES

Paul Van Geert

University of Groningen
Groningen, The Netherlands

SUMMARY: A general model of the structure of a developmental theory requires two components. One should be inferred from a general framework for describing the state and sequence model of the theory, the other from a framework for describing the transition model. The aim of the present paper is to make an attempt towards building the latter type of framework. A general framework for types and properties of transition concepts and models in developmental theories may serve several functions. First, it may provide a means for systematic description and comparison of the transition component of various theories. Such description and comparison may facilitate the critical examination of theories by clarifying the nature of their essential components. Second, the success of attempts towards unifying theories greatly depends on the amount of (in)commensurability of theories. The finding of common factors or levels requires a systematic comparison of the variables in which theories may differ. Hence, a framework systematically describing those variables, at least as far as the transition component is concerned, is a necessary tool. Third, the building of new models of development, or the elaboration of existing ones, is facilitated by the presence of a general model specifying the various components of developmental theories.

Developmental theories have two major theoretical functions. First, they provide a rationale for possible developmental state and sequence descriptions. A basic distinction is made between sequences that are the result of identity-transforming operations upon state descriptions (hence, the developmental process is a process of (self)-transcendence), and sequences that are the result of identity-preserving operations. This leads to the distinction between prospectively and retrospectively defined developmental theories. Second, they provide a model of developmental transitions, that is, a model explaining why a developing system actually goes through a specific sequence of states (Van Geert, 1986a, 1987a, 1987d, 1988). The present paper will deal with the second aspect, the transition model. It will try to provide a general framework for studying and comparing such models. This framework will consist of three parameters defining the form of transitions.

Levels of Transition

The first parameter concerns the various levels at which developmental change may take place. One of the basic problems of developmental theory building is that of bridging the gap between various levels of temporal organization (Riegel, 1972, 1977; Nelson, 1983). These levels correspond with distinct transition forms and mechanisms.

Sub-person Time. The lowest or micro level is that of sub-personal (neurophysiological) time. It is the level at which the sub-personal processes of association, cognitive computation and the like take place. These levels are traditionally the field of investigation of psychonomics, and only few developmental models, if any, are explicitly concerned with that level. There is one notorious exception, namely the information processing approach to development, which tries to disentangle the information processing strategies at various stages of development. Interestingly enough, the information processing approach has been accused of not being able to offer a truly developmental model. Most developmentalists confine to paying lip-service to some general model of sub-personal processes. Gal'perin, for instance, a Soviet psychologist whose model is based on ideas from the Cultural-Historical School, adheres to the principles of Higher Neural Activity, which finally go back to Pavlov. There's no particular reason, however, why his model would follow from these principles only and not from the principles of internal computations on representations designed by American cognitive psychologists, for instance (Van Geert, 1987c).

Experiential Time. The second time level is the level of experiential time. It is the level of consciously entertained experiences and activities of the subject. This is the level of intentional processes. It is the level at which we get the most direct access to the developing system, e.g., in the form of teaching or providing the developing mind with formative experiences. All developmental theories must have a model of processes at this level. In Piaget's theory, this is the level of action initiated and structured by the subject. In Gal'perin's theory, it is the level of strictly educationally guided action of learners in a curriculum. In Erikson's theory, it is the level of being concerned, in various ways, with some major developmental theme, such as the learning of intellectual skills or the struggle for personal and social commitments.

It is important to note that developmental models describe the processes at the experiential time level in two different ways, one is the aforementioned intentional level, the other the abstract, structural level. These two modes of description are required in order to solve the question of how the experiential level gets connected with the next level, that of life time. Piaget uses the term 'cognitive conflict' to interpret theoretically the meaning of intentional actions by the child. Not all actions are developmentally relevant. Only those are relevant that instantiate a cognitive conflict, e.g., a conflict among different internal schemes or an internal scheme and an observed state of affairs in the world. It is not necessary that the child experiences the action as a conflict, e.g., that it notices the contradiction between two ways of solving a problem and is in doubt about which way to choose. The tension between intentional and abstract descriptions of activities is likely to lead to conceptual confusions. Take for instance the concepts of 'hypothesis testing' associated with Chomsky's earlier view on language learning or the concept of 'triggering' in Fodor's theory of concept development and Chomsky's recent theory on language learning as parameter setting (Atkinson, 1986). Intentionally speaking, the child may simply imitate a phrase he or she hears or simply see that some liquid is water. On the other hand, the theoretical form of this particular imitating or seeing is 'hypothesis testing' and 'triggering' respectively. Of course, not all imitating or seeing by the child are instantiations of those concepts. The error of saying that children are not testing hypotheses but simply imitating what they hear, is of course easily made. This error refers to the problem of how to decide that a particular imitation is hypothesis testing while another is mere imitation? Such decision depends on our ability to link the event at the experiential level with events at the next level, namely the level of life time or stage time.

Stage and Life Time. Life time is the favoured level of description for developmental theories. Some deal with the entire life span either by viewing life as a continuous process of development, as with Erikson's theory (Erikson, 1963, 1980), or they deal with developments that achieve a final state relatively early in life, such as Piaget's theory. Still others deal with specific aspects, such as language, or the development of particular skills which cover a relatively limited time span.

The majority of developmental theories, especially the classical ones, provide a descriptive framework for the stages of life time. It is usually this stage's framework which forms the most widely spread and known contribution of a developmental theory, although the theories themselves may be primarily interested in other aspects. Piaget, for instance, was primarily interested in explaining the nature of human thought by tracing its development and considered the stage theory as a minor contribution. The rather exclusive emphasis on the descriptive stage framework weakens the explanative power of developmental theories. They should not only describe the possible states and sequences, but explain why actual transitions from one state to another take place. The emphasis on the descriptive part of a developmental model usually coheres with an emphasis on characteristic observables of stages. For instance, a pre-operational child is unable to make a correct conservation judgment, solve a seriation task, etc. However, what is needed in an explanative theory is a description of a stage in the form of a structured, dynamic system, which takes as its input theoretical interpretations of events at the level of experiential time, and has as its output specific shifts of its internal structure at the level of life (or stage) time.

Among the classical models, Piaget's is the most elaborate as far as its internal transition structure is concerned (Moessinger, 1978; Piaget, 1975). It relates the structural model of a stage to the level of cognitive conflicts. By introducing the general principle of equilibration, it explains the self-transcending nature of developmental transitions, that is, the way in which the structural properties of a stage change themselves. The main criticism put forward against Piaget is that the model remains relatively abstract. More precisely, it is difficult to establish the link between the abstractly defined processes and the intentionally defined ones. On the other hand, learning or education based models, such as Gal'perin's (Gal'perin, 1969a, b), and information processing models have the great advantage of providing an internal structure which can be linked with the intentional description level in a relatively easy way. Put differently, it is relatively easy to use those models for teaching purposes. The disadvantage of the models is that they lack the power for explaining self-transcendence in the stage system, that is, the system's property to change its own basic features. As a consequence, those models tend to underestimate or even ignore qualitative changes throughout life time. The present problems are not solely related with the fact that transition models should be capable of explaining relations over distinct time levels. They will be addressed anew when dealing with the next parameters of transition models.

Historical Time. Historical time is the time level at which the chain of life times is located. It is the level of cultural and socio-historical development. This can be development over long periods, as with anthropogenesis or relatively short periods, for instance periods of cultural change that account for cohort differences. It is beyond doubt that the structure of culture and society gets reproduced and transformed through its mapping upon individual subjects (Van Geert, 1986c). Those subjects are not endowed with cultural and social knowledge and skills at birth. Thus, there is a deep relationship between the problems of developmental transition in the subject and cultural transition in society (Featherman & Lerner, 1985). There are three views on the nature of this relationship.

The first is the methodological view. It expresses the idea that much of our present knowledge on development through the life span could have rather limited validity, since it is based either on cross-sectional or on longitudinal methods. In both cases, the effect of historically different conditions of development for different generations is ignored (Schaie, 1979). This view, which is associated with the names of life-span developmentalists such as Baltes and Schaie, separates aspects of cultural from those of individual developmental transitions. However, it does not explain the interaction between both time levels.

The second view is the analogy view. It reflects a very old tradition in developmental studies, namely recapitulationism. Ontogenesis recapitulates phylogenesis or anthropogenesis. In the first case, the recapitulation is explained by biological mechanisms, such as will be dealt with in the next sub-section. In the case of recapitulation or anthropogenesis, the analogy between society and individual is explained on the basis of common abstract transition mechanisms which operate on different time and quantity levels. Such is for instance the position of Piaget. In this view, there is no interaction between the life and historical times, only analogy.

The third view is the conditional view. It has found its clearest expression in the Cultural-Historical School of Soviet psychology. The structures and properties of society are the products of historical evolution in the cooperating, labouring species Homo Sapiens. The developmental task of a child born in a particular age, society and social class, is therefore determined by social-historical conditions. The contents the child should appropriate are deeply determined by their particular historical development. It is the logical structure of this historical development - for instance of mathematical concepts - that will directly determine their appropriation by the child (Gal'perin, 1969b). This determining is not a matter of analogy, but of causality. It is interesting to note that in the psycho-analytic tradition Erikson's model of the Ages of Man, follows the same direction of thinking although far less elaborated and specific (Erikson, 1980).

Biological Time. The level of biological time and of phylogenesis is more than the mere extension of historical time. It is by virtue of the biological transition mechanisms operative at this level, that the individual subject gets endowed with the genetic possibilities for development. Classical theories see the influence of biological time on transition mechanisms at the level of life time in terms of general conditions. In Piaget the dynamic invariants of development, adaptation, assimilation, etc., are of biological origin. In the Cultural-Historical tradition, the nature of the factors that make individual development proceed are those that have resulted from the biological evolution of man and from the particular course of hominization. Recently, several attempts have been made at combining biological, historical and life time into one comprehensive theoretical framework, strongly resembling the mathematical theory of population genetics. One approach emphasizes the biological influence on cultural transmission and vice versa (Lumsden & Wilson, 1981), another primarily focuses on the formal analogies between the distribution of genetic properties in a population and the distribution of cultural achievements through individual cultural transmission and learning (Boyd & Richerson, 1985).

Summary. Although developmental theories are primarily concerned with the scale of life time, explaining transitions requires the establishment of relations with other time levels, especially with the level of experiential time. We have seen that processes over experiental time are described on different levels, namely the level of intentionality, and an abstract, theory-specific level. Our understanding of the relations between life-time transitions, abstractly and intentionally defined experiential time processes is far from complete. Besides, the relations between life time, sub-personal time, historical and biological time, also require much further elaboration in spite of general statements of their fundamental importance made by almost any developmental theory.

The Topology of Developmental Dynamics

The second parameter deals with general dynamic and fluctuation properites of the systems involved in a developmental sequence. The dynamics and fluctuations are defined over a topology which, in the majority of models, is quite simple. Such a simple topology is the classical distinction between a developing system and its environment. The basic fluctuation is the exchange of information and the consequent change of the system in the form of a developmental process.

Fluctuation (A)Symmetry. Although developmental theories aim to explain change in the system, some of them endorse the view that the environment changing the system could be an effect of the system changing the environment (symmetry). A theory such as Piaget's tends to emphasize the asymmetry in the flow of information. Of course the subject is active in the environment and explores particular things and not others. However, it is primarily the mental representation of the environment and not the environment itself that is shaped by the mental structure of the subject.

Theories of infant development, such as Trevarthen's or Brazelton's, have more explicitly appreciated the influence of babies upon their environment. Comparable ideas are Chandler's and Sameroff's idea of transaction in development (Sameroff, 1975), or Lerner and Busch-Rossnagel's conception of individuals as producers of their own development (Lerner & Busch-Rossnagel, 1981). The evolution of educational institutions and practices shows society's growing tendency to adapt itself to those who should be educated. Vygotsky's well-known concept of the Zone of Proximal Development expresses the idea that the environment actively adapts itself to the developing subject (Vygotsky, 1978). That is, information from the subject about its current state of development is the principal factor in changing the subject's environment. Thus, although developing subjects in this view do not directly change their environment, the environment is nevertheless definitely determined by the information available about the subjects' actual state of development.

Selectivity of Pragmatic Information Flow. If we treat the developing subject and its environment as two sub-systems of an overall developing system, we shall see that each sub-system shows a specific degree of openness to specific information from the other sub-system. Theories differ as to the amount of developmentally relevant openness they attribute to the subject. In nativist theories such as Fodor's, the subject is maximally closed. That is to say, the information from the environment that is able to provoke a developmental change in the subject is very narrowly defined and strongly dependent on the current developmental state of the subject.

In traditional conditioning theories the subject is maximally open, that is, there is a very wide range of potential fields of learning during any developmental state. The genuine developmental theories, such as Piaget's, Bruner's or Vygotsky's, take an intermediary stand. There is a fairly wide range of information to which the subject is sensitive but the nature of that information is determined by the developmental state of the subject (Van Geert, 1986a). The openness holds not only for the subject, but also for its environment. In fact, the asymmetry discussed in the previous sub-section is a direct consequence of different degrees of openness between subject and environment.

(In)stability. Irrespective of their position on the open-closed dimension, developing systems can show various amounts of internal stability, i.e., the tendency towards self-caused or self-conditioned change under otherwise similar environmental conditions (Van Geert, 1986a).

It is clear that models subscribing to a high amount of closedness of the developing system have to assume a high level of internal instability in the subject, if they want to arrive at development anyhow. The opposite holds for models with a high amount of openness. The internal instability may be directed either towards higher order and organization, or towards lower order. Piaget's theory, for instance, assumes a strong internal dynamic in the developing system, which is a dynamic towards higher order, whereas traditional conditioning theories assume a low level of internal dynamic which is primarily towards lower order (e.g., forgetting, decay of skill).

Topological Differentiation. In most theories the topological differentiation is confined to the simple subject-environment dichotomy. That is, this simple dichotomy suffices to explain developmental transition. In some theories, the topology is fairly complex. A notorious example is the Freudian model which has elaborated the topology of internal subject structure.

Another example is Gal'perin's model, and several other models from the Cultural Historical School, for that matter. In traditional models, the subject-environment dichotomy coincides with the mind-matter dichotomy. The problem then is to explain how mental content, for instance a concept, captured in a material form, for instance an audible word (matter), gets transmitted to the mind of another person in whom this mental content has been absent thus far. This is a very difficult problem, indeed. Gal'perin has tried to solve it by implicitly distinguishing three dichotomies, the public versus private domain, the domain of awareness versus unconscious domain, and the social-objective versus subjective domain. These dichotomies overlap in such a way that the transmission of a content from 'outside' to 'inside' is maximally canalized and facilitated. That is, there is not a single high barrier to take between matter and mind, but three relatively low ones (Gal'perin, 1969b; Van Geert, 1987c).

Summary. If we combine the four variables we find a relatively complex space within which developmental models may differ. Much of the form of the transitions postulated in various theories amounts to particular positions taken by the theories with regard to the variables which in themselves are relatively simple and not limited to developmental models.

Transition Forms

The third parameter concerns the form of the processes or transformations. In the discussion on the levels-parameter we distinguished several forms of transition, located at different time levels, namely, sub-personal, intentional and structural processes and transitions. Thus, the various levels at which transitions in general may occur constitute the first variable of the form parameter.

Descriptors, Effectors, and Effects. The second form variable concerns the dynamic function of transition forms. Consider for instance the concept of 'differentiation' conceived as a transition concept. The concept can have three different meanings in a transition model. First, it could be a 'descriptor'. That is, given a description of a developmental state, it could function as a conceptual operation that the theorist employs to arrive at a description of a more complex state. For instance, if an infant is able to distinguish vowels from consonants, the theorist may predict the next developmental state by differentiating the set of consonants into a set of voiced and a set of voiceless consonants. The ability to distinguish between voiced and voiceless might indeed be the next developmental state of the infant, but it does not follow at all that the child has arrived at that state by having differentiated the set of consonants (Jakobson, 1947; Van Geert, 1986b, 1987a). Thus, 'differentiation' has been used as a descriptor, as an operation suitable for arriving at descriptions of developmental states. Instead of being an operation of the theorist, differentiation may of course be a transition operation in the child. But then we should be careful not to confuse the effector from the effect-meaning of the term. If differentiation is a form of activity of the developing system, it is used in the effector sense. The problem is, however, that differentiation is a form of activity defined at a rather abstract level. It is not an intentional activity of the developing subject, that is, it is not specified at the level of intentional processes. Nevertheless, it would be incorrect to say that differentiation is the mere effect of processes at a lower level of description. More precisely, differentiation is the form the dynamic processes take at the general systems level, while intentional and structural activity is the form they take at the subject level. Finally, differentiation may be the effect of dynamic processes that are not in themselves of a differentiation form. For instance, the effect of simple addition of components may be differentiation. If differentiation is merely an effect term, it is likely, but not necessary, that it is also a descriptor.

Conflict Versus Agreement. Processes and transformations are either of an agreement type or of a conflict type. If agreement is the major dynamic underpinning, effects are coherent with the nature of the information provided or coherence between information available and information provided causes a developmental effect or transition to occur. The simplest example is the reinforcement principle, or the principle of strengthening associations as a consequence of repetition (in the case of reinforcement, the effect is coherent with the nature of the stimulus provided, e.g., pleasant, thus reinforcing, thus increasing the frequency of the associated behaviour, or unpleasant, thus aversive, thus decreasing the frequency of the associated behaviour). Much more complex is the Vygotskian principle of the Zone of Proximal Development, which holds that an activity a subject is fulfilling with the help of a more competent subject will become an activity the subject will be capable of fulfilling on its own. Bryant's recent concept of agreement - children progress when they realize that two ways of approaching the same problem produce the same result - is another example of agreement, and exactly the opposite of Piaget's conflict hypothesis (Bryant, 1986). The conflict hypothesis holds that progress will occur as a consequence of the meeting of two opposing strategies or the alternation of opposing tendencies. Piaget's theory is the best example of such conflict theory. Another example is Doise's social conflict theory, where the Piagetian intra-psychic conflict is replaced by an inter-psychic one (Doise, Mugny & Perret-Clermont, 1975). Erikson's theory too is a conflict theory: during each stage opposing ego qualities may alternate, and new developmental mile-stones are reached as a consequence of establishing a specific ratio between opposing ego qualities (Van Geert, 1987b). Conflict theories differ also as to the consequence of the conflict. The conflict is either unsolvable, as in

Freud's theory, and to a lesser degree also in Erikson's, or leads to an agreement on a higher level, as in Piaget's theory.

It is important to note that 'conflict' is not similar to 'punishment' or related concepts. Punishment is an agreement type of dynamic factor. The form of the information provided, the punishment, agrees with the target of the information, for instance deviance.

Topological Criteria. We have seen that transitions are defined over topologies which, in their simplest form consist of an interior, the subject, and an exterior, the environment. Also the form of the transition may be defined with regard to that topology. Some theories define their transitions in terms of a relationship between the developing system and itself, e.g., at a previous time. Examples are differentiation, integration and equilibration. The system is more integrated now than it was before, for instance. Others define transitions in terms of a relationship between the system and some other part of the developmental topology, e.g., the environment. For instance, the Soviet psychological concept of the mind as mirroring the structure of reality (Leont'ev, 1974), and the corresponding idea of development as increasing truth and detail in the mirroring, provide good examples of this type of transition. Some theories employ both types. For instance, Piaget's concept of equilibration is clearly intra-systemically defined, while his concept of adaptation is extra-systemically defined.

References

Atkinson, M. (1986). Learning and models of development. In P. Van Geert (Ed.), *Theory building in development psychology* (pp. 105-139). Amsterdam: North-Holland.

Boyd, R., & Richerson, P. J. (1985). *Culture and the evolutionary process.* Chicago: The University of Chicago Press.

Bryant, P. E. (1986). Theories about the causes of cognitive development. In P. Van Geert (Ed.), *Theory building in developmental psychology* (pp. 167-187). Amsterdam: North-Holland.

Doise, W., Mugny, G., & Perret-Clermont, A. N. (1975). Social interaction and the development of cognitive operations. *European Journal of Social Psychology, 5,* 367-383.

Erikson, E. H. (1963). *Childhood and society.* (2nd revised ed.). New York: Norton.

Erikson, E. H. (1980). *Identity and the life cycle.* (Original 1959). New York: Norton.

Featherman, D. L.,& Lerner, R. M. (1985). Ontogenesis and sociogenesis: Problematics for theory and research about development and socialization across the life span. *American Sociological Review, 50,* 659-676.

Gal'perin, P. J. (1969a). Stages in the development of mental acts. In M. Cole & J. Maltzman (Eds.), *A handbook of contemporary Soviet psychology* (pp. 249-273). New York: Basic Books.

Gal'perin, P. J. (1969b). Die Entwicklung der Untersuchungen ueber die Bildung geistiger Handlungen. In H. Hiebsch (Ed.), *Ergebnisse der Sowjetischen Psychologie* (pp. 367-405). Stuttgart: Klett.

Jakobson, R. (1947). ***Kindersprache, Aphasie, und allgemeine lautgesetze.*** Stockholm: Almqvist and Wiksell.

Leont'ev, A. N. (1974). Sensorisches Abbild und Modell unter dem Aspekt der Leninschen Widerspigelungstheorie. In J. Lompscher (Ed., ***Lenins philosophisches Erbe und Ergebnisse der sowjetische Psychologie*** (pp. 70-86). Berlin: VEB.

Lerner, R. M., & Busch-Rossnagel, N. A. (1981). ***Individuals as producers of their development.*** New York: Academic Press.

Lumsden, C. J., & Wilson, E. O. (1981). ***Genes, mind and culture. The co-evolutionary process.*** Cambridge, MA: Harvard University Press.

Moessinger, P. (1978). Piaget on equilibration. ***Human Development, 21,*** 255-267.

Nelson, G. K. (1983). Time in developmental studies: A convergence of the dialectical and phenomenal thought. ***Genetic Psychology Monographs, 108,*** 215-243.

Piaget, J. (1975). ***L'Equilibration des Structures Cognitives. Probléme central du Dévelopment.*** Paris: Presses Universitaires de France.

Riegel, K. F. (1972). Time and change in the development of the individual and society. In H. W. Reese (Ed.), ***Advances in child development and behavior*** (Vol. pp. 81-113). New York: Academic Press.

Riegel, K. F. (1977). Toward a dialectical interpretation of time and change. In B. S. Gorman & A. E. Wessman (Eds.), ***The personal experience of time*** (pp. 59-108). New York: Plenum Press.

Sameroff, A. (1975). Transactional models in early social relations. ***Human Development, 18,*** 65-79.

Shaie, K. W. (1979). The primary mental abilities in adulthood. An exploration in the development of psychometric intelligence. In P. B. Baltes & O. G. Brim, Jr. (Eds.), ***Life-span development and behavior (Vol. 2, pp. 68-115).*** New York: Academic Press.

Van Geert, P. (1986a). The concept of development. In P. van Geert (Ed.), ***Theory building in developmental psychology*** (pp. 3-50). Amsterdam: North-Holland.

Van Geert, P. (1986b). The structure of developmental theories. In P. Van Geert (Ed.), ***Theory building in developmental psychology*** (pp. 51-102) Amsterdam: North-Holland .

Van Geert, P. (1986c). Sociocultural reproduction and individual mental development. ***Cognitive Systems, 1(3),*** 207-231.

Van Geert, P. (1987a). The structure of developmental theories. A generative approach. ***Human Development, 30(3),*** 160-177.

Van Geert, P. (1987b). The structure of Erikson's model of the Eight Ages. A generative approach. ***Human Development, 30(5),*** 236-254.

Van Geert, P. (1987c). The structure of Gal'perin's theory of the formation of mental acts. A generative approach. ***Human Development, 30(6),*** 355-381.

Van Geert, P. (1987d). The concept of development and the structure of developmental theories. In W. J. Baker, M. E. Hyland, H. van Rappard, & A. W. Staats (Eds.), ***Current issues in theoretical psychology*** (pp. 379-392). Amsterdam: North-Holland.

Van Geert, P. (1987e). A graph theoretical approach to the structure of developmental models. ***Human Development, 31.***

Vygotsky, L. S. (1978). ***Mind in society.*** Cambridge, MA: MIT Press.

THE INTRODUCTION OF CONSTRUCT VALIDITY TO THE ASSESSMENT FIELD: AN HISTORICAL ANALYSIS

T. B. Rogers

University of Calgary
Calgary, Alberta, Canada

SUMMARY: Construct validity was introduced into the field of psychological assessment during the mid 1950s in response to several pressing problems. This type of validity formalized the requirement that psychological tests be considered instruments of psychological theory. The historical record was reviewed to reveal that the concept was introduced with no formal, open debate. Critical analysis of the idea arrived only after the concept had gained considerable popularity. Despite some telling criticisms, as well as some significant changes in the discipline since the mid '50s, the concept has remained ascendant in the field. It is suggested that this resilience reflects the strength of several metatheoretic assumptions of the field, and that some of the problems plaguing contemporary personality assessment can be traced to the uncritical adoption of the concept of construct validity.

Introduction

Jackson (1973) suggested that the 'modern' era of personality assessment was heralded by the introduction of 'construct validity' about 20 years earlier. This type of validity requires that any personality inventory must be evaluated in terms of the underlying theoretical system into which the test is thought to fit. To quote Jackson (1973):

> If structured tests are to play an important role in psychological assessment, they must be developed on the basis of sound theory, and be validated, not only by empirical means, but by the degree to which they reflect the theoretical construct that they were designed to measure (p. 780).

Thus, the modern era of assessment is seen to have begun when the decision to include theory was taken. Theory, then, is assigned a primary role in the evolution of personality assessment, with construct validity being the primary agent in fulfilling this role.

Viewed in this context, the notion of construct validity is particularly relevant to the study of theoretical psychology. Through construct validity, the introduction of theory is seen as a harbinger of significant changes in the field-thereby ascribing highly important causal powers to theory. In fact, the value accorded theory has undergone several vacillations within the assessment domain, and the pendulum swing back to theory, signalled by construct validity, is a particularly interesting case history in the tension between 'hard' and 'soft' headed orientations. Discussion provides access to several observations about how we go about the business of trying to understand human behaviour and the role played by theory in these efforts. The present essay offers a brief description of the factors which lead to the emergence of construct validity, followed by discussion of how it was introduced, accepted and, eventually, criticized. Following this an interpretation of aspects of this history will be provided.

A Brief History of Personality Assessment

The classic era of personality assessment emerged *circa* 1920 in response to developing trends in the measurement of individual differences, combined with clinical concerns. The Woodworth Personal Data sheet, released in 1920, is generally considered the first personality inventory. It was concerned with identification of soldiers emotionally unsuited for combat during the First War and consisted of yes/no questions such as "Are you happy most of the time?" and "Do you find that people understand and sympathize with you?" Recruits reporting many symptoms on the Data Sheet were detained for further questioning. Early inventories such as this were based on rational concerns about what an inventory might measure.

By the late 1930s a considerable number of inventories had emerged, but so had quite a bit of criticism:

> Investigation fairly consistently confirms the low worth of the most widely publicized instruments (Watson, 1938, p. 270).

> Since the scales in current use have not been adequately validated, studies employing them as measuring instruments and accepting the derived scores as measures, cannot be considered as particularly meaningful (Mosier, 1938, p. 12).

> There are some 500 personality tests, most of which are of little or no value as measurement devices. A few, probably not more than a dozen, could be recommended for experimental use in a testing programme (Kornhauser, 1945, p. 9).

Clearly personality assessment was under siege. A number of reasons for the problems in personality assessment were suggested. One of the leading candidates for fault was theory. At a general level, the discipline was expressing the need for less emphasis on theory.

> The outstanding weakness of modern psychology is a scarcity of fact and an oversupply of theory. Heidbreder, for example, in a recent summary of seven so-called 'schools of psychology' makes the disturbing statement that "there is not enough fact in the whole science of psychology to make a single solid system" (Ross, 1936, p. 200).

In relation to personality assessment, Meehl (1945) argued that the problem was the use of *a priori* assumptions to construct personality inventories. By this Meehl meant theoretical expectations about the universe of content being addressed by the inventory. To quote Meehl (1945):

> Associated with this approach to structured personality tests is the construction of items and their assembling into scales upon an *a priori basis*, requiring the assumption that the psychologist building the test has sufficient insight into the dynamics of verbal behavior and its relation to the inner core of personality that he is able to predict beforehand what certain sorts of people will say about themselves. The fallacious character of this procedure has been shown by the empirical results....It is suggested tentatively that the relative uselessness of most structured personality tests is due more to *a priori* item construction than to the fact of their being structured (p. 297).

But this criticism did not come out of a vacuum. Rather, it was launched from a strong operationist position that favoured tests such as the MMPI. This test was concerned with the assessment of psychopathology and used empirical means to assign items to sub-scales. For example, the schizophrenia scale of the MMPI was made up of all of the items in the test that showed a statistically different response pattern between people in general and diagnosed schizophrenic patients. The 550 unique items on the MMPI were selected from printed materials in the field of psychopathology. This was an elegantly simplistic way of constructing personality tests in that no theoretical or *a priori* assumptions were necessary; rather, the data made all of the difficult decisions about which item belonged where.

The MMPI became immensely popular, gathering a large following in both the clinical and academic fields. It is estimated that over 3500 research studies dealing with the MMPI have been published and that some 300 new scales have been developed from the original item pool.

But the MMPI encountered problems. A major drawback of empirically-keyed instruments like the MMPI, and their attending reliance on criterion-oriented validity, was the need to demonstrate test-criterion correlations for virtually every situation in which the test was to be used. Clinicians were unhappy about this as it restricted the diagnostic use of tests such as the MMPI. They wanted the test to provide access to their own theoretical ideas and clinical wisdom. The academic community was unhappy as well, as the strong operationalist philosophy embodied in the approach was under attack on several fronts (e.g., Carnap, 1953) and pressures were being felt to re-legitimate theoretical constructs. But through all these changes the desire for scientific legitimacy by adhering to the canons of the empiricist-positivist position remained - what was needed was a creative solution that would allow for the re-introduction of theory, at the same time retaining the desirable qualities of the empiricist-positivist position.

The Emergence of Construct Validity

The creative solution was construct validity. The term was introduced in the APA 'Technical Recommendations for Psychological Tests and Diagnostic Techniques' published in 1954. While never explicitly defined in the Recommendations, construct validity involved viewing the test as an indicator of an underlying theory. The traditional techniques of scientific inquiry were felt to be appropriate to the task of establishing this type of validity.

A year later Cronbach & Meehl (1955) published a detailed exposition in which they were quite explicit about the benefits of adopting the idea - particularly how it would free the investigator from the inherent situation-specificity of the prevailing view:

> Construct validity must be investigated whenever no criterion or universe of content is accepted as entirely adequate to define the quality to be measured ....Such interpretations (as enabled by construct validity) permit the clinician to predict performance with respect to criteria which have not yet been employed in empirical validation studies (p. 282, entry in parentheses added).

The 1955 paper discussed procedures for establishing construct validity (e.g., group differences, correlations and factor analyses, studies of internal structure, change and process), followed by the introduction of the concept of the *nomological network.* 'The laws in a *nomological network* may relate (a) observable properties or qualities to each other; or (b) theoretical constructs to observables; or (c) different theoretical constructs to one another.' According to Cronbach and Meehl for a construct to be scientifically admissible it must occur in a *nomological net,* and at least *some* of the laws must involve observables (pp. 290-291). Clearly the nomological network serves a central function in the idea of construct validity and strongly affirms the role of theory in the personality assessment enterprise. Loevinger(1957) argued that the other forms of validity (criterion-related content) were essentially *ad hoc* leading to the conclusion that "construct validity is the whole of validity from a scientific point of view" (p. 641).

This new form of validity was adopted into the field of assessment with considerable speed, being an accepted part of the literature by 1960. For example, Clark (1959) lists studies examining the construct validity of 8 current tests. She also mentions 7 areas of psychological inquiry as involved in construct validation work. In 1960, 'Validity/construct' became a heading in *Psychological Abstracts* and in 1961 eight tests were listed. In summary, then, the notion of construct validity was rapidly accepted in the assessment field and very soon became an important and fundamental concept for researchers and practitioners in the field, and remains so today.

The introduction of construct validity was a radical and highly important shift in the way tests were viewed. For researchers, it elevated the testing enterprise from its status as a mere technology to a scientifically legitimate enterprise, fully integrated into the prevailing approach to doing psychological science. This is nicely revealed in the concluding statement of Clark's (1959) review:

> As this review has pointed out, the work of construct validation is arduous but rewarding to the test developer interested in being part of the main stream of the philosophy of science and behavioral sciences (p. 100).

As well, construct validity gave clinicians freedom to use tests to access their intuitive theories, as tests could now be thought of as indices of theoretical entities, rather than restricted to situations where empirical test-criterion correlations had been demonstrated. It freed test users and designers from the restrictive tenets of what Cronbach (1960) has since called 'exhaustive-definitional-operationism'. It was a highly emancipatory idea, one that was ripe for its time, and one that solved some very real problems for the assessment psychologist in the mid-fifties.

In historical perspective, the actual introduction of construct validity reveals something quite unusual. This is signalled by Loevinger's (1957) comment about the "rather sudden appearance of construct validity" (p. 636). In fact, the historical record indicates that the whole idea of construct validity was imposed upon the field by a committee. It was not the result of a grassroots movement of researchers involved in the area. Nor was it the result of an extraordinary scientific development or breakthrough which clearly demonstrated the utility of the idea. Rather, the introduction of construct validity was achieved by an APA committee, which itself attributes it to a subcommittee of two members.

While there was some indication that the APA committee did consult the literature, and a preliminary draft of the recommendations was published discussing the notion under the name of 'congruent validity' -

this significant change was endorsed and published by the APA, the major legislative body of the discipline. Construct validity became 'law' without so much as one word of open debate in the literature.

Critical Appraisals of Construct Validity

It wasn't until 1959 that published criticism of construct validity emerged (Bechtoldt, 1959). The idea had already gained acceptance in the field by then, witness Clark's review in the same year, and I'm sure that even a more eloquent and telling critique than Bechtoldt's would not have changed things at that point. Perhaps sensing that some debate was in order, Cronbach (1960) rebutted criticisms of construct validity. In an unusual preface to these rebuttals he indicated:

> A primary source (of the criticisms about to be rebutted) has been informal conversations with hardheaded psychologists who have failed to see the need for the concept (of construct validity) or who have felt that they disagreed with it (p. 550, entries in parentheses added).

The literature didn't exist for Cronbach to rebut so he drew on his interpersonal experience - a clear symptom of the need for open debate.

Since 1960 some criticism of construct validity has emerged. There appear to be five lines of attack. (1) Some have argued that construct validity is just another name for procedures that are part of every-day science, hence the term is not justified (e.g., Bechtoldt, 1959); (2) Some logical problems with the procedures of establishing construct validity have been noted (e.g., Meehl, 1978); (3) The idea of validating constructs is in conflict with Popperian notions of falsifiability, suggesting that the term has endorsed a specific philosophical position - one which encourages the reification of traits (e.g., Sarbin, 1968); (4) construct validity assumes a specific philosophical position regarding the nature of 'facts' thereby being in the service of a strong realist position (e.g., Leahey, 1980, provides a strong argument regarding operationism which is readily applied to construct validity); and (5) a renewed concern about the true empirical base of the assessment enterprise has been noted. This latter point requires some embellishment. Gergen (1987) suggests that assessment of psychological states, using tests, may not depend upon publicly observable acts as much as we believe it to be. For example, the publicly observable event in personality assessment is the check-mark or button press that the respondent makes to an item. We have virtually no interest in this behaviour *per se*. Its only interest to us is once it has been interpreted as an indicator of a disposition. In other words, even though the starting point of the assessment process is publicly observable (i.e., the behavioural indication of a response choice), the behaviour in and of itself is seen as virtually irrelevant. Rather, the salient factor is the meaning *we* attribute to it (i.e., as an indicator of a specific disposition). For example, the item 'I would like to travel freely from country to country' is interpreted as evidence of the construct 'autonomy' - and the interpretation is our focal concern, not the response per se. This line of argument weakens the purported empirical base of the assessment exercise, as what we are dealing with is interpretation, not empirical observation. It appears, then, that the fundamental base of the assessment domain is the interpretation not *per se* the behaviour.

This problem is exacerbated when we realize that the same interpretative process is applied to the behaviours we attempt to predict using the test. For example, we *interpret* a person choosing not to attend an office party as autonomous behaviour using the same fundamental interpretive schemata that we used in assigning items to the autonomy scale. This prompted Gergen (1987) to comment: "the definitional system for psychological terms is essentially self-contained" (p. 122). To the extent that the assessment of a trait is interpretive, and the behaviours used to reflect the trait are likewise interpretive, the entire system is closed and observed relationships can be seen as fundamentally linguistic, not anchored in observation. This criticism, of course, has implications that transcend the notion of construct validity and call a number of foundational assumptions underlying personality assessment into question.

In summary, the foregoing review of criticisms indicate significant foundational problems for the concept of construct validity. The idea was introduced in the mid 1950s with virtually no critical analysis, and was accepted unquestioningly by the field. Since then a number of significant critical problems have been noted, and it is indeed somewhat surprising that the concept has survived without formal revision.

An Interpretation

From an historical perspective there are a multiplicity of reasons why the notion of construct validity was introduced. Among these were" (1) the need to liberate testing from strict operationism; (2) the wish to re-admit theory into the discipline; (3) a desire to bring assessment into contact with the prevailing approaches to science; (4) a hope that more rigorous validation standards would help rid the area of questionable tests; and (5) increased movement toward professionalization of the discipline by enhancing self-regulatory process. Some of these (1, 2 above) were trends and pressures being felt across the entire discipline in the 1950s. Others (3, 5, 5 above) were specific to the area, representing the extension of trends established earlier. The confluence of these factors was the uncritical acceptance of the concept of construct validity.

Pre-theoretical issues were also a significant part of the acceptance of construct validity. The integration of assessment with theory, as was being practiced in most of science at the time, was an overt symbol of scientific legitimacy. I believe that this need to demonstrate 'proper' scientific practice was a particularly significant factor in the acceptance of construct validity. It became a talisman, resistant to critique, a seemingly self-evident truth and accepted without debate (see Leahey, 1980, for an excellent and equivalent analysis regarding operationism).

This acceptance can be traced to several historical factors. Morawski (1987) has argued: "With few exceptions, psychologists modeled their epistemology, not after physical science *per se,* but after the ***philosophy*** of physical science" (p. 159). This put psychology in the position of having to continually defend itself as a science because aspects of the subject matter were inherently different from the natural sciences (e.g., reactivity and reflexivity). Methodological canons which provided us with scientific status were valued - leading to accepting and sustaining notions such as construct validity.

Based, as it is, upon a view of science from the 1950s, the idea of construct validity is clearly out-of-date. The so-called cognitive and neuropsychological revolutions have, indeed, had significant impact on how we do science. As well, a number of developments stemming from Kuhn's (1962) insightful analysis of how scientists actually do their work suggest that the 1950s view is clearly out-of-touch with how things are done. If the goal is to evaluate psychological tests in terms of prevailing approaches to doing science, then it is clear that the concept of construct validity is dated and in need of revision.

More importantly, though, construct validity represents a formalized requirement that demands a specific approach to doing science. To the extent one can argue that this approach is in need of revision (as many authors in this volume have demonstrated), it is clear that revision to construct validity is, likewise, required. As the assumptive base underlying construct validity fades into history, so too will the tests that hang on demonstrating this criterion. In the most recent *Annual Review* chapter on personality assessment, Rorer and Widiger (1983) have argued that this *fading* has already begun:

> It is no secret that personality assessment has been in big trouble as it has come under attack from both expert and lay critics. Assessment takes up a decreasing portion of the professional practitioner's time, occupies a place of decreasing importance in the university graduate curriculum, and has been legally outlawed in many selection situations (p. 433).

While Rorer and Widiger's view may be overly pessimistic, and there are more factors than construct validity involved in this fading, an implication of the present analysis is that the time is ripe for a radical and wide-spread re-appraisal.

There can be little doubt that alternatives to construct validity are available. Re-orientations of thinking toward positions such as social constructionism, scientific realism, contextualism, the interpretive sciences, and communication all lead to radical re-alignment of the criteria one might use to evaluate specific tests and the overall assessment enterprise. The foregoing analysis of construct validity indicates, rather clearly, that such a re-evaluation is badly needed. Hopefully, this time, it will be accompanied by public debate.

The major conclusion of the present historical analysis is that theory was used as a rhetorical device to promote the positivist-empiricist programme when construct validity was introduced in the mid-1950s. Couched in apparently neutral, scientific language, the notion of construct validity served to strengthen a particular way of approaching the problems facing psychology. While this orientation made sense in the 1950s, it is in drastic need of revision in the late 1980s. Perhaps it is time that theory be emancipated from its position as handmaiden to the empiricist-positivist programme and be given its own head to facilitate the development of more effective approaches for psychology.

References

American Psychological Association (1954). Technical recommendations for psychological tests and diagnostic techniques. *Psychological Bulletin, 51*, 201-238.

Bechtoldt, H. P. (1959). Construct validity: A critique. *American Psychologist, 14*, 619-629.

Carnap, R. (1953). The interpretation of physics. In H. Feigl and M. Brodbeck (Eds.), *Readings in the philosophy of science* (pp. 309-318). New York: Appleton Century Crofts.

Clark, C. A. (1959). Developments and applications in the area of construct validity. *Review of Educational Research, 29*, 84-105.

Cronbach, L. J. (1960). Recommendations for APA Test Standards regarding construct, trait, or discriminant validity. *American Psychologist, 15*, 546-553.

Cronbach, L. J., & Meehl, P. E. (1955). Construct validity in psychological tests. *Psychological Bulletin, 52*, 281-302.

Gergen, K. J. (1987). The language of psychological understanding. In H. Stam, T. B. Rogers & K. J. Gergen (Eds.), *The analysis of psychological theory: Metapsychological perspectives* (pp. 115-130). New York: Hemisphere.

Jackson, D. N. (1973). Structured personality assessment. In B. B. Wolman (Ed.), *Handbook of general psychology* (pp. 775-792). Englewood Cliffs, NJ: Prentice-Hall.

Kornhauser, A. (1945). Replies of psychologists to a short questionnaire on mental test developments, personality inventories, and the Rorschach test. *Educational and Psychological Measurement, 5*, 3-15.

Kuhn, T. S. (1962). *The structure of scientific revolutions.* Chicago, IL: University of Chicago Press.

Leahey, T. H. (1980). The myth of operationism. *Journal of Mind and Behavior, 1*, 127-143.

Loevinger, J. (1957). Objective tests as instruments of psychological theory. *Psychological Reports, 3*, 635-694.

Meehl, P. H. (1945). The dynamics of "structured" personality tests. *Journal of Clinical Psychology, 1*, 296-303.

Meehl, P. E. (1978). Theoretical risks and tabular asterisks: Sir Karl, Sir Ronald, and the slow progress of soft psychology. *Journal of Consulting and Clinical Psychology, 46*, 806-834.

Morawski, J. G. (1987). After reflection: Psychologists' uses of history. In H. Stam, T. B. Rogers & K. J. Gergen (Eds.), *The analysis of psychological theory: Metapsychological perspectives* (pp. 157-174). New York: Hemisphere.

Mosier, C. I. (1938). On the validity of neurotic questionnaires. *Journal of Social Psychology, 9*, 3-16.

Rorer, L. G., & Widiger, T. A. (1983). Personality structure and assessment. *Annual Review of Psychology, 34*, 431-463.

Ross, C. C. (1936). A needed emphasis in psychological research. *Psychological Review, 43*, 197-206.

Sarbin, T. R. (1968). Ontology recapitulates philology: The mythic nature of anxiety. *American Psychologist, 23*, 411-418.

Watson, G. (1938). Personality and character measurement. *Review of Educational Research, 8*, 269-291).

ON PAYING ATTENTION[1]

Warren Thorngate

Carleton University
Ottawa, Ontario, Canada

SUMMARY: Six principles of ***attentional economics*** are developed and employed as a means of understanding the possible relations between information produced and information consumed. It is argued that because available information far exceeds available attention, decisions about allocating attention become increasingly difficult and increasingly arbitrary. The consequences of this trend are explored in the context of psychological research, the marketplace of ideas, and the consequences of attentional errors.

Everybody lies. It doesn't matter. Nobody listens.
(Anon.)

Times change, even in the abstracts. The first volume of *Psychological Abstracts* was published in 1927, contains 2,730 abstracts appearing in about 250 periodicals. The 73rd volume of *Psychological Abstracts*, published in 1986, contains 31,592 abstracts of articles published in about 1,350 periodicals. Currently, about 121 new psychology articles are published each working day. *Psychological Abstracts* will publish its 1,000,000th abstract sometime before 1990. Over half of these will have been published since 1975.

These astonishing statistics are indicative of a general and ominous trend in most advanced societies of the world: information of all kinds is proliferating at an enormous rate. It is now generally agreed, for example, that the amount of published scientific and technical information alone is doubling every 5-15 years. Because the population of the earth is doubling at about one fourth this rate, a little mathematics will show that if current trends continue, within 300 years every person on earth will literally be buried in scientific and technical publications.

This explosion of information has been recognized and discussed sporadically at least since the turn of the century, and has been a major concern of librarians for almost 40 years (e.g., see Gore, 1981; Stayner,

---

[1]I with to thank Ruth Currie and Barbara Carroll for their assistance and comments in the preparation of this article. Reprint requests should be sent to Dr. Warren Thorngate, Psychology Department, Carleton University, Ottawa, Ontario, Canada K1S 5B6.

1983). The explosion is certainly not limited to scientific and technical areas, as anyone inundated by junk mail or home entertainment options can easily surmise. To my knowledge, however, the psychological effects of information proliferation are rarely discussed by psychologists (but see Milgram, 1970). Perhaps this is because so many psychologists view information as little more than fodder for the cognitive processes in which they are now so engrossed. Perhaps it is because psychologists are as prone as most contemporaries to believe that information is a Good Thing, an antidote to ignorance, a necessary ingredient of wise choice. More is better. Enough said.

Yet significant changes have occurred in our psychological reactions to information growth. We have long passed the era when most available information was accorded at least some polite attention, and new information was eagerly sought. In contrast to many of our academic predecessors, for example, most of us now spend considerable time eschewing information. We toss out book catalogues unopened, shelve journals unread, give away unexamined introductory texts, wipe up spills with tech reports, use theses to prop up answering machines. We invent excuses to miss meetings, avoid colloquia, skip office hours, stay home. And we are not the worst offenders. Politicians hire small armies of secretaries and sychophants to defend them against unwanted mail, phone calls, constituents, and opinions. Editors of trade publications regularly reject manuscripts simply because they are unsolicited, and don't bother to read or even open them. Some granting agencies now insist that applicants do not provide a detailed account of their proposed work or even a listing of previous publications; instead, they resort to publication counts, and require applicants to do the counting!

These and similar reactions to information growth appear to originate in the limits of our attention. Information is supposed to be that which informs, but nothing can inform without some attentional investment. Alas, there is no evidence that the rate at which a member of our species can spend attentional resources has increased to any significant degree in the past 10,000 years. As a result, competition for our limited attention has grown in direct proportion to the amount of information available. Because information has been proliferating at such an enormous rate, we have reached the point where attention is an extremely scarce resource, so scarce that extreme measures - from telemarketing to terrorism - have proliferated as fast as information just to capture a bit of it. No longer can we believe that information is always an asset, that seeking or consuming it is preferable to ignorance. As Simon (1978) has noted,

> In a world where information is relatively scarce, and where problems for decision are few and simple, information is almost always a positive good.

> In a world where attention is a major scarce resource, information may be an expensive luxury, for it may turn our attention from what is important to what is unimportant. We cannot afford to attend to information simply because it is there (p. 13).

In the pages to follow I should like to outline a conceptual framework for analyzing our reactions to the attentional scarcity resulting from information proliferation. I should then like to consider the potential of this framework for understanding three diverse phenomena: the trajectory of psychological research, the changing marketplace of ideas, and the consequences of attentional errors.

An Outline of Attentional Economics

Because most of us were raised with the expression, when we 'pay attention' we rarely stop to think about its metaphorical implications. Yet attention is exactly what we 'pay' for information; it is the primary currency of exchange in our Information Age. The scarcity of attention relative to the amount of information available provides both necessary and sufficient conditions for the development of an attentional economy. It is an economy governed by principles somewhat different from those governing the usual economies of goods and services (cf. Linder, 1970). At least six of these distinguishing principles are worthy of note.

The principle of *Fixed Attentional Assets* states that attention is a finite and a non-renewable resource. Attention takes time, and thus is ultimately limited by the time we are given to 'spend' during our lives (cf. Sharp, 1981). While the young may be blissfully ignorant of the limits of their lifetime, those of us past our halfway points are acutely aware that the time we spend paying attention does run out and can never be recovered. Someone who lives 75 years will be blessed (or cursed) with about 657,000 hours of temporal assets. About one third of these assets will be spent on sleep leaving less than 444,000 hours to spend on wakeful activities. Much of the remainder will be devoted to daily chores of living. For example, a daily 10 minute shower will consume about 4,500 hours or six months of one's life by age 75; eating may consume another 20,000 hours or over two years of that time; almost one year of life may be spent washing dishes; about six months will be spent in WCs. Obligations will also deplete large amounts of attentional assets. A typical worker will be obliged to pay about 80,000 hours or ten years of attention to maintain a secure job, if lucky enough to find one. While awaiting such a job, about 10,000 hours will be spent attending school and another 2,000 hours attending university for a total attentional investment of about 1.4 years. Perhaps no more than 15 years of life's attentional assets will be spent on truely discretionary activities. A two-hour dose of television each day will consume one-third of this; a half-century of bedtime reading will consume less than one attentional year.

The principle of *Singular Attentional Investments* states that attention can, in general, be invested in only one activity at a time. It is certainly possible to engage in a few activities simultaneously. However, most intellective tasks require some amount of singular attention, if for no other reason that most such tasks must be done in different locations and we still cannot be in two places at the same time. We are thus forced either to finish one task before beginning another, or to alternate between them. In either case we pursue most activities serially rather than simultaneously (Simon, 1957), and invent all manner of means to do in succession what we cannot do at once. Included are tactics of setting priorities, following schedules, meeting deadlines, juggling calendars, handling interruptions, and developing patience. Included also is an impressive array of social inventions that divide attentional labours across people rather than time. These are the inventions that produce sufficient conditions for the development of social organization, the growth of specialization, and arguments over who should attend to what.

The principle of *Diminishing Attentional Returns* states that the more attention we continuously invest in only one thing, the less it is likely to continue holding our attention. The principle insures that even though we may invest attention singularly, we will not invest attention exclusively. Instead, we will develop the attentional equivalent of a mixed portfolio. The diminution of attentional returns is usually experienced as habituation or boredom, and appears to regulate our susceptibility to new information and to interruptions. It has obvious survival benefits. Most animals must engage in at least two important activities to survive: they must find meals, and they must avoid becoming meals. If an animal devotes exclusive attention to only one of these activities, it will die either of predation or starvation. Some mechanism is thus necessary to insure that attentional switching will occur. It is this mechanism that exhibits the phenomenon of diminishing attentional returns.

The principle of *Expected Attentional Revenues* states that attentional investments are generally made in expectation of future rewards. When possible, we generally invest attention in stimuli expected to be pleasant or interesting, and divest attention in stimuli expected to be unpleasant or boring. When we do pay attention to the latter, it is usually with hope the investment will sooner relieve us of an attentional burden, or later allow us to attend to more pleasant or interesting stuff. Often our expectations go unfulfilled. When this occurs, we eventually take our attentional assets elsewhere. Unfortunately, it is difficult to determine in advance what will be interesting or pleasant. It is thus almost tautological to declare that interest draws attention, or that one tends to attend to pleasant things. Even so, it is worth noting that what is interesting need not be pleasant, and that what is pleasant can be dull. It is thus possible for unpleasant but interesting stimuli to capture more attention than pleasant but boring alternatives. Exploitation of this possibility has made very tidy sums for those who produce tabloid and television news.

The principle of *Exploratory Attentional Expenses* states that whenever we search for and choose attentional investments, the acts of searching and choosing themselves require attentional investments. The investments will be minimal when habits dictate our choices, or when obligation or circumstance constrains our attentional alternatives. They may become laughable whenever we invest far more attention choosing what we attend to than in attending to what we choose. Between these extremes we will often seek to reduce our attentional expenses by attending to signs, symbols or summaries in order to decide whether to divert our attention or continue the investment (see Bruner, Goodenough, & Austin, 1956). In response to this exploratory tendency, the proliferation of information has been accompanied by a proliferation of information synopses (e.g., abstracts of articles), of synopses of the synopses (e.g., *Psychological Abstracts*, of synopses of the synopses of the synopses (e.g., the index of *Psychological Abstracts*). Such are the consequences of information proliferation that most news media provide only these higher-order synopses and never provide access to the real thing.

Finally, the principle of *Balanced Attentional Budgets* states that attention paid should equal attention received. Often the rewards we hope to receive from our attentional investments themselves take the form of attention, and in particular the attention that others pay to us. At times the attention others pay us is necessary for survival. Sick infants, for example, can rarely survive without a fairly large investment of someone else's attention. Even for healthy adults, attention received is usually rewarding, and arguably necessary for continued mental or physical well being. From the perspective of attentional economics, human interaction is the exchange of attention. Indeed, it may be argued that human interaction exists primarily because of the rewards of attention received (Derber, 1979). The exchange may be reciprocal, as happens in good conversations. It may be serial, as happens when as children we receive attention from our parents only to pay for it by attending to children of our own. Yet attention need not be divided equally amongst individuals, and rarely is. As a result, many individuals may become attentionally rich (famous), while others remain attentionally impoverished (lonely or obscure). Inequalities of attentional distribution can reach staggering proportions. Many people live and die in solitude. Yet in a one hour televised performance, a popular singer can attract an audience of over ten million - the hourly equivalent of 15 lifetimes.

I cannot claim that the above six principles of attentional economics are exhaustive or even fundamental. They do, however, define a perspective from which we may examine some important psychological and behavioural consequences of information growth. Their joint effects on individuals and groups seem to insure that for any given level of information load or overload certain predictable reactions will occur. I wish to concentrate on reactions to situations where the amount of information that should be attended vastly exceeds the amount of information that can be. I must acknowledge, however, that many people live for long periods with an abundance of unused attentional resources. Indeed, on a global scale these people may be far more common than those with scant attentional resources. Curiously, the amount of one's discretionary attention seems to be inversely related to one's material wealth, a phenomenon discussed at some length by Thoreau and associated ascetics. Societies that are rich in both material goods and information can thus be expected to have particularly acute problems of attentional allocation. It is to these societies, and especially to their scientific and intellectural subcultures, that my attention will now turn.

Attentional Economics and the Growth of Psychological Research

To illustrate some of the consequences of attentional economics and information growth, consider some of the responses associated with the growth of research information in psychology. It follows from the principles of Fixed Attentional Assets and Singular Attentional Investments that the volume of information anyone can absorb in a given time will remain relatively constant. I know of no colleague, for example, who claims to read on average more than one new research article every working day. Most, myself included, read considerably less, in part because we choose to pay attention to other information from other suppliers. When *Psychological Abstracts* began publication, someone who read psychology research articles at the rate of one per day could hope to absorb about 10% of the year's published output. Today, someone reading at the same rate can hope to absorb significantly less than 1% of this year's published output. Our individual ignorance, according to one definition of the term, has thus increased more than ten-fold.

Of course, not all information is created equal, and one might think that because a psychologist now has the dubious luxury of ignoring over 99% of all published information available in the discipline only the very best would be chosen for consumption. Alas, there is no necessary connection between the number of alternatives available and the optimality of choice. Indeed, the principle of Exploratory Attentional Costs suggests that, as alternatives multiply, the attention required to make sagacious attentional choices will quickly reach a point of diminishing attentional returns. As a result, one is more likely to become whimsical, arbitrary or confused about one's choices than to become rational or optimal

(Einhorn, 1978; Simon, 1957; Thorngate & Carroll, 1987; Thorngate & Plouffe, 1987). The task of choosing what to attend to from the glut of information now available is now so difficult that we willingly, even eagerly, leave most of it in the hands of fallible others, history, or chance. For example, most of us at one time probably relied on academic advisors to tell us what could escape our attention and what should not. As a result, we probably did not read the works of Vico, Wundt, Fechner, Münsterberg, Bechterev or other such scholars, presumably because our advisors had themselves not read these works or because they decided the works were not worthy of our limited attention.

In the name of attentional conservation, and the reduction of exploratory costs, we continue to allow a host of others to make our attentional decisions for us. Most of us cling to the moot belief that publication of funded research is a minimal test of attentional worth. We thus permit granting agencies, university administrators, publishers, editors, reviewers, and librarians to set a good part of our attentional agendas. We do this knowing full well the often tragic limitations of these agents of selection, limitations such as low interjudge reliability, personal favouritism, preferences for topical fads and fashions all compounded by declining financial support. And for what do we conserve our attention? Often it is to publish more ourselves, to ignore the information produced by others in the expectation that they will attend to ours! In this way we illustrate the principles of Balanced Attentional Budgets and Expected Attentional Returns.

But publishing does not guarantee attention, and the history of most disciplines, including psychology, has given us a litany of often ingenious and occasionally pathetic tactics to extract attention from the uninformed. It all started reasonably enough. Book chapters sprouted titles instead of numbers, then tables of contents, then indices - aids for those who wished to find something in a hurry, minimize exploratory attentional costs, and meet other attentional obligations. By the end of the 19th century publications had become so numerous that clever titles and lavish illustrations began to appear in abundance, in part for their competitive advantage as attention attractants. Shortly after World War One, writers began to insert abstracts in the front of their articles and references in the rear. The former allowed readers to attend only to the main points or conclusions of an article without attending to its arguments. The latter assisted readers in finding additional information, and allowed writers to avoid the reproduction of arguments that might make their work longer, less interesting, and thus less read.

As psychologists, universities, and journals began to multiply between the wars far beyond anyone's attentional budget, it became necessary to develop methods of selecting which publications in which journals should be attended or ignored. Reliance on the reputations of authors or their institutions as attentional selectors was soon supplemented by reliance on media prestige. By World War Two, a well established status hierarchy of journals had emerged to aid in attentional decisions. Journals such as *Psychological Review, Psychological Bulletin, Journal of Experimental Psychology,* and later the *Journal of Personality and Social Psychology* were deemed to be 'high quality' or 'prestigious', in part because of a bandwagon effect: a lot of people devoted their attention to them. Lacking the attentional assets necessary to assess the quality of journal offerings, psychologists decided to judge a journal by its cover, and simply headed for the good journals when looking for the right stuff. Lesser journals, for example, those with small circulation or those requiring payment for publication, were easily if wrongly dismissed as repositories of the works of the incompetent or vain.

By mid-century it became obvious that further efforts were needed to increase the ratio of information consumption to information production within recognized attentional constraints. One such effort was focused on the nature of articles themselves, particularly their length and organization. In order to decrease the length and increase the organization of research articles, the American Psychological Association published its first manuscript preparation guidelines in 1952. Journal articles within its domain were supposed to be clear, concise, and follow a standard format - once again to decrease the amount of attention (also known as 'inconvenience') necessary to find and consume information. In subsequent editions of the *Publication Manual,* special attention was given to preparing the abstract of a manuscript. The second edition (1974) notes that "[an] abstract allows readers to survey the contents of an article quickly" (p. 15). The third edition (1983) is more blunt: "A well-prepared abstract can be the single most important paragraph in the article...[it] will increase the audience and the future retrievability of your article" (pp. 23 & 24). Ironically, despite recognition of the abstract's importance, the third edition reduced its recommended length from 175 to 150 words. Yet attention had at least been officially acknowledged as a scarce and coveted resource. Indeed, so coveted had attention become, that the *Manual's* stylistic advice on how to capture and retain it had expanded from 136 pages (1974) to 208 pages (1983).

Style, format, abstracts, and journal prestige still could not keep the demands for attention under control. The increasingly rapid growth of psychological research information after World War Two once again pressed the limits of attention, and generated a need to consume even more predigested and summarized information. In 1950, the popular services of *Psychological Abstracts* were supplemented by publication of the *Annual Review of Psychology*. The *Annual Review* became indispensable to those who were willing to trust the selective attentions of reviewers as supplements to, if not replacements of, their own. No longer was one obliged to examine and reflect on abstracts of the articles in order to decide if we should examine and reflect on the articles themselves. Now one could rely on reviewers to judge what was hot and what was not, and save attention for other presumably more important matters.

Even the *Annual Review*, however, had its limitations. As successive volumes appeared, an increasing proportion of reviewers admitted they had given up hope of providing a comprehensive account of their chosen areas, and were instead discussing what they thought was interesting. In addition, so many topics were eligible for review that the editors drew up Master Plans to stagger several topics across successive volumes and eschew many others. Some psychologists who believed that psychology could not progress in such a patchwork way contributed to what was perhaps the last great encyclopedic effort in the discipline, *Psychology: A Study of a Science* (Koch, 1959-1963). However, by far the more common response to the selection of topics eligible for selective reviews was the establishment of a number of multi-volumed books reviewing ever smaller topics in ever increasing detail. Many of these hard-bound periodicals were entitled 'Advances in...' or 'Progress in...' or 'Contemporary...' almost as boasts to their readers that scant attention would be paid to 'old' research (usually meaning more than five years of age). In the name of attentional conservation, one presumably had license to engage in all manner of historical pruning.

It is perhaps inevitable that the proliferation of research in psychology would be followed by the proliferation of reviews of research in psychology. Yet some of the results now border on the absurd. In the name of attentional economy, *Contemporary Psychology* sometimes publishes reviews of books that review articles that review research that summarizes data. And in a noble attempt to collect statistics on the use of published information, the *Social Sciences Citation Index* publishes box scores of the number of times articles and their authors are cited. Several universities now employ these box scores to judge the merit of their faculty. The practice of counting publications to assess faculty merit has been augmented, if not replaced, by the practice of counting references to publications. Criteria of merit have thus shifted from information production to audience production.

The scarcity of available attention relative to available information implies that the competition for attention will be relatively severe. Those of us who produce information as well as consume it are thus faced with an increasingly difficult task of selling our products in a buyer's market. Two consequences are apparent. First, we have become increasingly sensitive to the needs, desires, and preferences of those with disposable attention - our potential customers. Second, we have become increasingly sensitive to the activities of our competitors. In psychology, the first has led us to devote more of our efforts to producing topical (read 'applied') research, not because it is inherently more important than the 'pure' alternatives, but because it is more likely to pay attentional dividends. The second has led us not so much to a direct confrontation with competitors in a race to increase the quality of our information, but to a frantic search for our own specialized market niche. In today's informational marketplace, one captures more attention by being new than by being improved.

These two consequences have manifested themselves in several ways. Psychology, like most others, has become a fissiparous discipline, a congeries of specialties. It has divided into hundreds of small topical niches, each with its own jargon, folklore, dominant figures, favored granting agencies, publications, conferences, and controversies. I hazard a guess that each of these niches can support no more than 100-200 researchers; when they become more populated, further division or migration occurs. Of course, it is rare that researchers occupying the same topical niche work in the same organizational niche. Psychology departments thus devolve into mere collections of offices housing conceptual strangers, rather like modern high rise apartment buildings. Colloquium attendance declines because invited speakers are unable to communicate with more than a few departmental members. Travel and telephone budgets soar as each specialist seeks a few distant colleagues who would attend to, consume, perhaps even digest his or her informational offerings.

Other manifestations of specialization are often noticeable. Specialists attack generalists not because they threaten to invade and conquer a specialist's niche, but because they threaten to overlook or ignore it. Competition for students increases because they provide a captive audience for specialized informational products. Debates over curricula become impossibly tangled as specialists jockey for their share of the captive attentional market. Comprehensive exams become anything but comprehensive as graduate students strive only to comprehend their chosen specialties. Course descriptions in university calendars become increasingly vague in order to maintain general discipline divisions while allowing different professors, especially young ones, to teach only their chosen specialties. Graduate students are required, or at least encouraged, to take increasing numbers of courses in methodology and statistics rather than substantive areas of their discipline, a tacit admission that in an era of informational abundance process is product, means are ends.

Attentional Economics and the Marketplace of Ideas

Unfortunately, the little pathologies that develop in psychology departments and other corners of academia in response to the competition for attention are indicative of far more disturbing trends beyond our ivory towers. It's an informational jungle out there, now ruled by those who have discovered and exploited the secret of attracting discretionary attention: *packaging*. In the competition for attention, competitors who are not distinct become extinct. Thus, to attract attention, one's information package must be different than those of competitors in some immediately noticeable way. As implied by principle of exploratory attentional expenses, exteriors have a competitive advantage over interiors in this regard simply because the former captures attention first. The result is a triumph of container over content, medium over message, percept over concept, style over substance, symbol over referent, logo over logic.

As attentional competitors do their best to make their informational products distinct, the combined result is a cacophony of mixed messages arguably indistinguishable from noise. As implied by the principle of diminishing attentional returns, a common reaction to this result is habituation. Those with attention to pay soon come to ignore all but the most spectacular of stimulants. This, in turn, rewards spectacle, and sustains an escalation in levels of stimulation. Extremes thus flourish, often with sad consequences. It is unfortunate, for example, that because so many good causes now exist in the world we are prone to ignore them if they are not accompanied by human interest stories, good visuals, or new world records of suffering. It is tragic that attention is rarely paid to social or political movements until their leaders have abandoned reason for violence, and thus become eligible for 60 seconds of the 6 o'clock news.

The principle of expected attentional revenues suggests that as we choose to pay attention, so too do we choose to stop payment. Those who wish to sustain attention must therefore concern themselves with more than just capturing it. As suggested by the principle of diminishing attentional returns, they must also worry about unpleasantness and boredom. Under conditions of information abundance, consumers of information need never be upset or bored because they are increasingly free to change their attentional loyalties - to 'turn the channel' - without notice. By exercising this degree of freedom people today have become astonishingly fickle in their attentional allegiance. Attention paid to all manner of information now waxes and wanes at a rate approaching that of popular music. The products of science have become particularly susceptible to the trend. For many consumers science is now just another form of entertainment, and not nearly as entertaining as the science fictions it inspires. This is why fewer people are apt to attend a lecture on pollution than a movie on Star Wars.

As previously noted, we have long conceived of information as that which informs, reduces uncertainty or ignorance. It is worth noting now that these are distinctly cognitive, scientific conceptions, and though they have been quite useful, we must realize that other conceptions are possible and useful too. In particular, it seems useful to conceive of information from an emotional perspective, to view information not as that which informs but as that which excites or arouses (cf. Davis, 1971). To speak of information as a source of emotion is to embrace a conception that has a long and distinguished history in the arts and humanities. It is broadly speaking an aesthetic conception, and though often manifested in unaesthetic extremes, it is particularly well suited to any analysis of current attentional preferences.

Perhaps in the best of all possible worlds, truth and beauty really would be indistinguishable, and we would never be faced with a choice between them. Alas, we live in a good world but not a great world, one in which it is possible to be informed without being excited, and to be excited without being informed. As information multiplies, so too do the necessities of choosing between ugly, boring facts and pretty, exciting fictions - between information that however true or important is unable to hold our attention, and information that however false or trivial is able to captivate it. Ironically, under these conditions it is the lasting truths that are most susceptible to attentional decline. When attention was more plentiful, information was consumed as a raw ingredient, and truth considered a durable good. In our age of attentional scarcity, preferred information has become a precooked perishable, a fun food, a jar of Gee Whiz. Lasting truths repeated without variation have become boring old clichés. Everybody knows to everything there is a season. So what's new?

In promoting their informational products, psychologists have yet to recognize many of the practical implications of the shift in criteria of attentional choice. In times past psychologists pursued timeless truths under the assumption that once found they would automatically attract attention. Recent increases in the pursuit of more timely truths have not compensated for the failure of this assumption. Many psychologists have recently attempted to attract the attention of others with a proliferation of studies on domestic violence, depression, the effects of pornography, and other topics of contemporary concern. While the topics seem to attract more attention than, say, verbal learning or the size-weight illusion, the studies do not. This is largely because the studies, attempting to establish truth by scientific method, produce results that are either disturbing or dull.

Though we are trained to believe otherwise, it is difficult for most people to be enthralled by the discovery of yet another complex social problem, or mesmerized by the calculation of yet another complex statistical interaction. Our interest in alleviation of suffering, like our pride in production of numbers, is just not widely shared. By combining the two in our well-meaning efforts, we almost guarantee small and diminishing audiences. Why should an audience risk exposure to information that will induce feelings of guilt or ignorance when there are so many alternatives that won't? We may wish to answer in terms of moral obligation. But in an age of information abundance there are so many conflicting morals that an audience is free to attend only to those justifying its choice of blissful ignorance.

Causes and Consequences of Attentional Error

Of the many standing committees in my Department that grudgingly occupy the attentions of my colleagues, by far the least prestigious is the Library Committee. Its original purpose was to advise the library on new purchases and subscriptions. Now there is virtually no money for new books, and a fixed budget for journals, so as publication costs rise, the Committee is frequently asked to advise what should cease to be acquired. Since 1980 about six psychology journals have been eliminated from the library subscription list each year. It would be of some comfort to know that those now gone had been carefully scrutinized and judged inferior. In fact, almost none had been scrutinized, which is probably why they had been eliminated. The *Polish Psychological Bulletin* is now on the chopping block. It seems that very few North American psychologists reference the *Bulletin*. Soon, even fewer will. This is unfortunate, for the *Bulletin* (published in English) contains reports of some of the best psychology research done anywhere in the world.

I mention the library problem and the *Bulletin* to illustrate that in reducing attentional options, we stand to increase our errors of attentional choice. Of course, it can be argued that there is no such thing as an attentional error simply because, like a tree that falls in a philosopher's unattended forest, it never makes a sound. Yet for those of us who have unknowingly recreated a good old idea (e.g., compare Gergen, 1973 or Thorngate, 1976b with London, 1946), or who have devoted months of attention to a bad one, the errors are embarassingly real. And they increase in direct proportion to the difference between the growth of our attentional investments and the growth of information competing for these investments.

Attentional errors appear to be of the two standard types: errors of commission or *false alarms* (attending to something we shouldn't), and errors of omission or *misses* (overlooking something we shouldn't). When information exceeds our fixed attentional assets, our desire to minimize exploratory expenses will insure that we shall never be able to eliminate these errors. We can, however, regulate their relative frequencies to some degree by adjusting our criteria of attentional choice. At extremes, for example, we can refuse to read anything and thus never read anything that would waste our time, or try to read everything and thus have no time for anything else. Between such extremes, we often attempt to develop criteria we hope will maximize our attentional 'hits' and 'correct rejections' with minimal exploratory attentional investment. These criteria define our interests, and the working parts of our epistemologies.

Unfortunately, as the late Hillel Einhorn (1978) has shown, there is one factor that has a pernicious effect on any criteria we develop to separate the informational wheat from the bran: information growth (see also Thorngate & Carroll, 1987). In an article that has ironically been almost totally ignored, Einhorn demonstrates how the growth of 'applicants' for a fixed resource can defeat any attempt at valid discrimination. In addition, he demonstrates that the growth will affect misses much more than false alarms. Compare, for example, the following two cases.

Case 1. Suppose that in one month you can afford enough attention to read 20 articles, and must choose them from a list of 100. Suppose, also, that had you read all 100 you would have judged you would have found only 20% of them worthwhile. If you choose the month's 20 at random, you can expect four to be worthwhile and 16 to be worthless. But suppose that your choice criteria, though fallible, are sufficient to increase your hit rate from 20% to 75%. As a result, you can expect to read 15 worthwhile articles and 5 worthless ones. Five of the 20 worthwhile articles (25%) will go unread, but 75 of the 80 worthless articles (94%) will be correctly rejected.

Case 2. Now suppose that several years later you must choose your monthly attentional allotment of 20 articles from a list of 1,000. Suppose that the production rate of worthwhile articles has remained constant, so that 200 on the list are worthwhile, and 800 are not. You apply your time-honoured criteria, and once again read 15 worthwhile articles and 5 worthless ones. In doing so you correctly reject 795/800 or 99% of the worthless articles. Note, however, that you have failed to read 185/200 or 92.5% of the worthwhile ones. Thus, by increasing your attentional options 10-fold you have increased the ratio of misses to false alarms 37-fold (from 5/5 to 185/5). By randomly selecting 20 articles from the list of 1,000 you could expect 196 misses. Your criteria will thus reduce your misses by only (196-185)/196=6%. From this perspective it seems perfectly reasonable to question whether it is worth the attentional investment to employ the criteria at all.

The above numbers may be somewhat arbitrary, but Einhorn's principles are not. It is often said that there is too much bad research in psychology. But as we have sought to eliminate bad research, so too have we witnessed the growth of the good. Einhorn's results suggest that psychology now suffers from a surfeit of good research, research that should not be ignored yet cannot be attended. By sampling an ever decreasing proportion of worthwhile articles, we stand an ever increasing chance of overlooking those that just may provide us with a long sought insight, a needed correction in our thinking, a new direction for research. Because of our attentional limits, even the most sagacious criteria of attentional choice may not noticeably reduce the proportion of good information we ignore. Indeed, the sheer number of worthwhile articles can overwhelm our discriminatory powers (Thorngate & Carroll, 1987). We then become suggestible, and thus allow our attentions to be directed more by social forces than by intellectual ones.

Perhaps as information consumers, the criteria we employ to direct our attentions should be of little concern as long as we consume a high proportion of worthwhile information by maintaining a high ratio of hits to false alarms. For producers of this information, however, concerns can be quite another matter. Recall the principle of balanced attentional budgets: attention paid should equal attention received. We often invest vast quantities of attention in producing worthwhile information, and rarely do so without some expectation that attention will accrue to both the product and producer in return. As a result, producers are not so much concerned with false alarms as with misses. Under conditions exemplified by Case 1, producers are sure to benefit from the reduction of false alarms simply because without them there will be no misses. In contrast, under conditions exemplified by Case 2, the reduction of false alarms does little to increase the proportion of hits to misses. In this case, even if there were no false alarms, a producer of worthwhile information would still have 90% chance of being ignored.

What then happens to the 180+ individuals in Case 2 who produce good information that is not consumed? Many are likely to cease production either because they lose interest in being ignored, or because their employers, noting low attentional sales, lose interest in them. Others may attempt to produce even more either to increase their chances of a hit, or to indulge compulsions sustained by job fears or partial reinforcements. They will, however, compete with those who produced the original hits, and who are likely to continue producing with competitive advantages accrued from their original attentional rewards. If the original hit producers cannot be beat, the rest may join them, either by producing accessories for their products (all those little follow-up studies), or packaging and distributing their products for local consumption (as teachers often do). In time, the aggregated result is likely to be an increase in market concentration. Like the automobile, food, communication, and computer industries, the information industry may become dominated by a few famous producers who are unwittingly able to drive out or direct the attentional competition. Their good ideas will thus flourish, and rightly so. But under conditions of attentional scarcity, many more equally good ideas will become extinct.

I am prone to believe that the above possibility has been developing for some time. In psychology, one need only examine the journals of, say, 1927 and 1986 to realize that with the enormous increase in topics addressed has come an enormous decrease in the ways we address them. Cognition, in particular, has so come to dominate the attentions of psychologists in all fields that it has become a de facto explanatory standard. This 'cognitive revolution' may be viewed by some as an indicant of scientific advancement, a desirable consequence of culling inferior behavioural, motivational, normative, dialectical, or other competing explanations. I suspect, however, it indicates only that we have tacitly agreed to ignore phenomena that are better explained by the competitors because (a) they cost more attention to research, (b) they are less likely to attract attention when researched, and (c) we wish to protect our attentional investments.

These suspicions may be unfounded, even unfair. But I hope they further illustrate several important empirical questions inspired by the concept of attentional economics. How do people spend their attention? What are the criteria used in making attentional choices? And what are the consequences of using these criteria? Attention was once a central concept in psychology. It is still, I believe, of vital importance in helping us to understand the production and consumption of information. Perhaps we should no longer ignore it.

References

American Psychological Association. (1974). ***Publication manual*** (2nd ed.). Washington, DC: Author.

American Psychological Association. (1983). ***Publication manual.*** Washington, DC: Author.

Bruner, J., Goodnow, J., & Austin, G. (1956). ***A study of thinking.*** New York: Wiley.

Davis, M. (1971). That's interesting! ***Philosophy of the Social Sciences, 1,*** 309-344.

Derber, C. (1979). ***The pursuit of attention.*** Oxford: Oxford University Press.

Einhorn, H. (1978). Decision errors and fallible judgment: Implications for social policy. In K. Hammond (Ed.), ***Judgment and decision in public formation*** (pp. 142-169). Denver, CO: Westview Press.

Gergen, K. (1973). Social psychology as history. ***Journal of Personality and Social Psychology, 26,*** 309-320.

Gore, D. (1981, November). Curbing the growth of academic libraries. ***Library Journal.*** 2183-2187.

Koch, S. (Ed.). (1959-1963). ***Psychology: A study of a science*** (Vols. 1-6). New York: McGraw-Hill.

Linder, S. (1970). ***The harried leisure class.*** New York: Columbia University Press.

London, I. (1946). Some consequences for history and psychology of Langmuir's concept of convergence and divergence of phenomena. ***Psychological Review, 53,*** 170-188.

Milgram, S. (1970). The experience of living in cities. ***Science, 167,*** 1461-1468.

Sharp, C. (1981). ***The economics of time.*** Oxford: Martin Robertson.

Simon, H. (1957). ***Models of man.*** New York: Wiley.

Simon, H. (1978). Rationality as process and as product of thought. ***American Economic Review, 68,*** 1-16.

Stayner, R. (1983). Economic characteristics of the library storage problem. ***Library Quarterly, 53,*** 313-327.

Thorngate, W. (1976a). In general vs. it depends: Some comments on the Gergen-Schlenker debate. *Personality and Social Psychology Bulletin, 2,* 404-410.

Thorngate, W. (1976b). Possible limits on a science of social behaviour. In L. Strickland, F. Aboud & K. Gergen (Eds.), *Social psychology in transition* (pp. 121-139). New York: Plenum.

Thorngate, W., & Carroll, B. (1987). Why the best person rarely wins: Some embarrassing facts about contests. *Simulation and Games, 18,* 299-320.

Thorngate, W., & Plouffe, L. (1987). The consumption of psychological knowledge. In H. Stam, T. Rogers, & K. Gergen (Eds.), *Metapsychology: The analysis of psychological theory* (pp. 61-91) New York: Hemisphere Press.

LUDWIG VON BERTALANFFY'S CONTRIBUTIONS TO THEORETICAL PSYCHOLOGY

T. E. Weckowicz

University of Alberta
Edmonton, Alberta, Canada

SUMMARY: This paper discusses the contributions to theoretical psychology of the late Professor Ludwig von Bertalanffy, a prominent biologist. Von Bertalanffy proposed open systems theory to explain life phenomena. Open systems, living organisms are examples of such systems, do not follow the second law of classical thermodynamics. They are characterized by negative entropy. This property explains organismic growth, differentiation and increasing complexity. It also explains goal directness, purposefulness and complexity of both human and animal behaviours. Consequently, von Bertalanffy has rejected reductionism and 'atomism' which have characterized both the American Behaviourism and orthodox psychoanalysis. Instead, he has emphasized the organismic and holistic approach. He has also emphasized the unique peculiarities of human behaviour such as symbolism and creation of values. Symbolic and value systems have played a more important role in human motivation than biological drives. The influence of von Bertalanffy's general systems theory has gone beyond biology, it has extended to psychology, psychiatry, sociology, cybernetics and philosophy. Using the general systems theory framework von Bertalanffy has attempted to reconcile the natural scientific approach to human behaviourism with the humanistic one.

It is in keeping with the role of a professor emeritus like myself to dwell on the past and to write about the history of our discipline. The topic of this paper is the late Professor Ludwig von Bertalanffy (1901-1972), a distinguished biologist, and about his contributions to theoretical psychology. The reason why I have chosen this topic is the fact that towards the end of his life von Bertalanffy was a professor of theoretical biology at the University of Alberta, that is, from 1962 to 1968. He left Alberta to join the staff of the Institute of Systems Theory at the University of Buffalo, N.Y. where he died in 1972.

While at the University of Alberta, von Bertalanffy, in keeping with his interdisciplinary approach to the problems of human knowledge held a joint appointment among the departments of Zoology, Psychology, and Philosophy. In addition, he was one of the founding members of the Center for Advanced Study in Theoretical Psychology. The contributions and influence of von Bertalanffy went beyond biology and extended to psychology, psychiatry, sociology, cybernetics, history and philosophy.

Ludwig von Bertalanffy was born in Austria where he studied biology and philosophy at the universities of Innsbruck and Vienna. One of his teachers of philosophy was Moritz Schlick, the leading spirit of the Vienna Circle of Logical Positivists. However, von Bertalanffy rejected the philosophy of logical positivism, the reductionism associated with it, and the *Weltanschauung* of "scientism." He insisted that since there were no 'immaculate observations' the *konstituierende*, (constituent) statements of the protocols of scientific experiments, were influenced by preconceived ideas, presuppositions, and by explicit or implicit theories of the observer. Briefly, by the observer's whole *Weltanschauung*.

Von Bertalanffy's Ph.D. thesis was on the philosophy of Theodor Gustav Fechner, the founder of psycho-physics and experimental esthetics. Its topic was: Fechner and the problem of higher order integrations (von Bertalanffy, 1926). This topic foreshadowed the author's future lifelong commitment to the idea of holism in biology and psychology. This commitment resulted in his becoming a leading exponent of organismic biology.

Von Bertalanffy was for many years a *Dozent* and later a professor (1934-1948) of theoretical biology at the University of Vienna. In 1948 he left war ravaged Vienna for the American continent where he held several research and visiting appointments in Canada and in the United States.

Ludwig von Bertalanffy is mainly remembered as the originator of the open systems theory in biology. This theory rejected both the mechanistic and the vitalistic explanations of life processes. According to the Mechanists life processes could be fully explained by the laws of physics and chemistry within the framework of classical thermodynamics. According to the Vitalists, these processes could not be so explained. The latter assumed that in addition to physical forces, a specific factor was involved which was only present in living matter. This factor was called *entelechy* by Hans Driesch, an influential German biologist at the turn of the century, who carried out experiments on the development of the sea urchin, an *echinoderm.*

Some other terms, such as *elan vital* (Bergson), or *horme* (MacDougall), were also used to denote the putative vital force. This specific factor, the life force, was, according to Vitalists, responsible for organizing and directing the physico-chemical processes in living organisms. It was also responsible for *sui generis* life phenomena such as the plasticity of living forms, their adaptation, their growth and differentiation; generally, for the purposefulness of life processes.

In the thirties, von Bertalanffy proposed a generalized version of the theory of thermodynamics which was applicable not only to closed systems, but also to open systems (von Bertalanffy, 1951). The classical theory of thermodynamics was concerned with closed systems, such as the running down universe. Closed systems were characterized by increasing equalization of energy distribution, accompanied by increasing randomness and disorganization of the system. Briefly they were characterized by positive entropy. Von Bertalanffy's generalized theory of thermodynamics was applicable to both closed and open systems. Living oganisms exemplified open systems. They incorporated energy and matter from the external world, and utilized them to maintain a steady state of systemic organization. Open systems could even increase the complexity of their organization and attain a less probable state than the original. Briefly, open systems were characterized by negative entropy.

Von Bertalanffy believed that the open systems theory resolved the long lasting controversy between Vitalism and Mechanism. The generalized theory of thermodynamics could explain *sui generis* life phenomena in terms of laws of physics and chemistry without recourse to such mystical vitalistic concepts as *entelechy* or *elan vital.* The vitalistic and mechanistic theories were superceded by the organismic theory. Von Bertalanffy (1962) became the leading proponent of the organismic approach to biology. The organismic theory stressed the holistic properties of living organisms, their organization, their growth and increasing differentiation. An organism was more than a sum of mechanically interacting parts, which was the case with man-made machines. The function of the parts showed plasticity and was determined by the organization of the whole. The growth and development of organisms was characterized by equifinality, which meant that the final stage in the development of organisms was, within certain limits, independent of the starting point. The development of living organisms was directed, as it were, by Aristotelian *telos,* which could however be explained by the laws of contemporary physics and chemistry.

The open systems theory was not only applicable to individual growth and development. It was also applicable to the evolution of species. Von Bertalanffy (1960) rejected the mechanistic interpretation of the Darwinian theory of evolution, which attributed the emergence of new life forms to accidental gene mutations and to the environmental pressure of natural selection. Instead, von Bertalanffy believed that, in addition to the accidental genetic mutations and the pressure of natural selection, there were intrinsic forces of organization which were responsible for the direction the evolution took in different species. Thus in addition to the environmental fitness there was the fitness of organismic design. (Shades of Goethe I suppose.)

The organismic theory assumed that biological systems were stratified, presented a hierarchy of levels of organization. At the lowest level of the organizational hierarchy were complex protein and DNA molecules. At the higher level there were cells, then at the next higher one, organs.

Finally, there was the whole organism, which was an important unit of biosphere. However, the hierarchy of systems organization did not end at the boundary of the individual organism, but proceeded further to animal and human societies. It could be discerned even in the ecological systems of the biosphere.

The idea that organisms were dynamic, highly organized systems led von Bertalanffy to reject the notion that organisms reacted mechanically to the environment in the manner of passive automata or robots. Stimuli did not evoke responses in otherwise inert systems. They only modified spontaneous activity of organisms which were autonomous. Consequently von Bertalanffy (1956, 1959, 1967) became critical of psychological theories which, conceptualized human behaviour in terms of reflexes and homeostasis: e.g., the S-R units, reduction of drive or reduction of tension. On this score he criticized both S-R behaviourism and orthodox psychoanalysis. He also objected to the reductionism characterizing these two theories. Behaviourism tried to reduce human behaviour to that of animals, while orthodox psychoanalysis tried to reduce the behaviour of mature human beings to that of infants. They tended to disregard symbolism, the most important characteristic feature of human behaviour. Man was *homo symbolicus.* Human behaviour could not be adequately explained in terms of conditioned reflexes, or in terms of a few simple biological drives such as hunger, thirst, sex, parenting, and aggression. Man's behaviour was controlled by systems of symbols and values which were created by him. However, once created, symbols possessed dynamisms and inertia of their own. They could take control of man's behaviour. Symbols were not arbitrarily imposed by the contingencies of environmental events in the way in which signs and conditioned stimuli were imposed. They were created by man and were posited by him to stand for and denote external objects or events. They could also connote emotional experiences associated with certain objects or events. In the latter case they constituted value systems. The capacity to create symbols and to posit them to stand for external objects and events was unique to the human species. Man lived in the world, or worlds of symbols, which he interposed between himself and the world of things.

In his thinking about the importance of symbolic systems for human beings, von Bertalanffy was influenced by Ernst Cassirer's philosophy of symbolic forms (Cassirer, 1953-1959) and by the language theory of Karl Buehler (1934). The latter was a professor of psychology at the University of Vienna. He, as well as his wife, Charlotte Buehler, were close friends of von Bertalanffy. Charlotte Buehler was a humanistic psychologist interested in the developmental and clinical psychology. She emphasized the importance of values in the development of adolescents and in psychotherapy. She believed that value disorientation played an important role in psychopathology. Von Bertalanffy emphasized also the importance of value systems in shaping human behaviour. Human behaviour was controlled by systems of symbols and values to a greater extent than by biological drives. The symbols and values could become powerful motives and could take precedence over the drives, as illustrated by martyrs dying for their faith. Men were known to prefer death to their dishonour. The most noble deeds of heroism and altruism as well as the most cruel atrocities were motivated not by biological instincts such as sex, parenting or aggression, but by value and symbol systems.

Symbolic systems although internalized by human beings had a degree of autonomy, were subject to their own logic of intrinsic rules, and showed developmental trends. Language was the best example of such a symbolic system with a considerable degree of autonomous existence. Thus, although man originally created symbols, the symbolic systems once created could take control of human behaviour and could dominate it. Cultures, religions, and ideologies, were such symbolic systems which often determined human fate. These systems had a logic of their own, moreover they were not static but were developing in certain directions. von Bertalanffy believed that the laws of development of open systems applied not only to biological systems, but also to the development of symbolisms, cultures, and societies. He called the extended version of the open systems theory - the general systems theory. Similarly to living organisms, artistic styles and forms of music tended to become increasingly complex, to reach a zenith, then to become stereotyped, to decline, to lose artistic vigor, and finally to be superceded by new styles and forms.

Von Bertalanffy rejected Wilhelm Dilthey's and Wilhelm Windelband's anti-historicistic notion that history was an idiographic science. He believed that it was a nomothetic science, and that there were laws of historical development which could be conceptualized within the framework of general systems theory. On the issue of historicism he sided with Giambattista Vico, Karl Marx, Oswald Spengler and Arnold Toynbee, Bon Bertalanffy (1924) was a particular admirer of Spengler's historicistic theories.

The consequences of the fact that man was a symbolic animal were, according to von Bertalanffy, enormous. Biological evolution based on genetic changes was superceded by the cultural history based on the accumulation of experience handed down from one generation to another, which was also influenced by the intrinsic development of symbolic systems. Consequently the time scale of historical periods in which the changes of human society were measured, replaced the time scale of geological epochs in which biological evolution was measured. Also the trial and error learning by association was replaced by reasoning based on the manipulation of symbols according to certain rules. The latter procedure was much faster and more efficient. In addition, symbols could represent anticipated future goals which could guide present behaviour. According to von Bertalanffy, acquisition of symbolic behaviour was the basic factor in *anthropogenesis.*

As mentioned earlier, von Bertalanffy was critical of both American behaviourism and of orthodox psychoanalysis because of the reductionist philosophy subscribed to by these two schools. Also because they presented an unflattering, mechanistic image of man, man as robot. Von Bertalanffy's ideas were based on the Leibnitzian concept of man rather than on the Lockean. This was the concept of man as an active, creative, striving agent, rather than the one which viewed man as passive, reacting to and reflecting the environment. However, the creator could sometimes be dominated by symbolic systems produced by his creations.

These factors made von Bertalanffy more sympathetic to the 'third force', Humanistic psychology which was trying to remedy the shortcomings of the behaviouristic and psychoanalytical schools. Humanistic psychology presented a more dignified image of man. It emphasized the totality of personality, rejected reductionism, and put stress on the uniquely human psychic manifestations. However, von Bertalanffy was wary of the idea that human behaviour could be explained in terms of the self-actualization of one's unique potential. This could be true of certain historical periods such as the Renaissance, but was not true of other periods such as the Middle Ages. Humans sometimes sacrificed their personal interests and goals to become parts of a super personal symbolic system, actualizing some impersonal ideals. They tended to efface their individuality and at times their identity as unique human beings. The medieval European and the Asian Buddhist monks provided a convincing example.

Von Bertalanffy was a real Renaissance man whose interests went far beyond biology. He was interested in, and made important contributions to psychology, psychiatry, cybernetics, sociology, anthropology and history. He believed that the general systems theory which proposed a conceptual schema outlining the orderly change and increasing complexity of organization was applicable to all disciplines concerned with man. An organism was a system of complex biochemical reactions. A society was a system of communication pattern and institutions, while a culture was a system of symbols. As many of his contemporaries and predecessors in German-speaking countries, von Bertalanffy attempted to build a bridge between *Naturwissenschaften* (natural sciences) and *Geisteswissenschaften* (humanities). He believed that the conceptual framework of the general systems theory, which was applicable to several disciplines, provided such a bridge. The fact that it was applicable to both physiological and psychological phenomena pointed to the basic isomorphism of these two kinds of events. Von Bertalanffy (1964) rejected the Cartesian doctrine of body-mind dualism. According to him the Cartesian doctrine was a product of the particular categories of thinking adopted by Western culture (such as the Aristotelian category of substance adopted also by Descartes). The hard line separating the physical from the mental disappeared when one considered the experiences of children, the experiences induced by psychedelic drugs or those of schizophrenics. It disappeared also when one stepped outside the ambit of Western culture and considered the experiences of people from other cultures. Also modern physics showed the relativity of many common sense categories such as matter, energy, space and time. Von Bertalanffy (1955) believed that the categories of thinking were relative, that reality could be contemplated from different perspectives. In adopting the position of perspectivism, and in denying that categories of thinking were absolute, von Bertalanffy followed in the footsteps of Nicholas of Cusa (1401-1464), a renaissance scholar and a precursor of general systems theory, on whom he wrote a book (von Bertalanffy, 1928). Cusanus believed that absolute truth could not be known. Such a knowledge could be only approached from different perspectives providing apparently contradictory appearances of reality, which nevertheless complemented one another *(coincidentia oppositorum).* Von Bertalanffy found the conceptualizations of Cusanus very useful in his dealings with the problem of mind-body relation. They were also in keeping with Bohr's principle of complementarity between wave and quantum mechanics.

Von Bertalanffy died in 1972, fifteen years ago. One can ask what is the status of his contributions to psychology today? I am not qualified to judge his technical contributions to biology. His writings as far as psychology was concerned, were of a programmatic nature, they did not amount to a definite theory, but offered some ideas and metaphors. However, they drew the attention of both behaviouristic and cognitive psychologists to the danger of creating a human psychology not only without mind, but also without man, and even without an animal.

There are two kinds of thinkers and scientists. The first are 'trail blazers', who propose new revolutionary ideas, point in the new directions for scientific developments, create new paradigms of science, and leave the details to others. The second are those who follow the new trail, carry out careful experimentations within the established paradigm, and work out the precise formulations of theories. Ludwig von Bertalanffy represented the first kind, he was a 'trail blazer'.

It is too early to decide whether the general systems theory amounted to a 'Kuhnian revolution' in science and humanities. The verdict will be passed by future intellectual historians and future historians of science.

Finally, a few remarks should be made about the impact of von Bertalanffy's theories on the discipline of psychology. As it has been stated earlier von Bertalanffy rejected atomism, stressed holism and also the importance of organization. In earlier years he felt a strong affinity with Gestalt psychologists who rejected associationism and stressed the importance of organization of total experience. He was sympathetic to Kurt Lewin's topological theory of personality and to Kurt Goldstein's organismic theory. Von Bertalanffy's interest in the growth and development of organisms made him very receptive to Heinz Werner's theory of orthogenesis. He was also sympathetic to Piaget's theory of mental development because the latter had earlier than others rejected mechanistic associationism. In America his impact was perhaps greater on psychiatry than on academic psychology. Two leaders of American psychiatry in the post-war period Karl Menninger and Silvano Arieti found von Bertalanffy's system theory very relevant to psychiatry. Karl Menninger based his theory of 'vital balance' on von Bertalanffy's ideas. Silvano Arieti stressed the importance of the disorder of symbolic systems as the essence of schizophrenia. The present cognitive psychology which constitutes the main stream of the discipline can be described as a shift away from associationism to structuralism. This shift has been associated with a growing interest in information processing, in the encoding and decoding of symbols, and also in psycholinguistics. Although these developments cannot be attributed directly and entirely to the impact of General Systems Theory, they represent a reaction to the same deficiencies of the discipline of theoretical psychology with which von Bertalanffy was preoccupied.

References

Bertalanffy, L. von. Einfuehrung in Spenglers Werk. *Literaturblatt Koelnische Zeitung.*

Bertalanffy, L. von. (1926). Fechner und das Problem der Integrationen hoeherer Ordnung, Doctor's thesis, University of Vienna.

Bertalanffy, L. von. (1928). *Nikolaus von Kues.* Muenchen: G. Mueller.

Bertalanffy, L. von. (1951). *Theoretische Biologie.* Bern: A. Francke A. G.

Bertalanffy, L. von. (1955). An essay on the relativity of categories. *Philosophy of Science, 22,* 243-263.

Bertalanffy, L. von. (1956). A biologist looks at human nature. *Scientific Monthly, 82,* 33-41.

Bertalanffy, L. von. (1959-1954). General system theory and psychiatry: In S. Arieti (Ed.), *American handbook of psychiatry, Vol. 3, 5.* New York: Basic Books.

Bertalanffy, L. von. (1968/1949). *Problems of Life.* New York: Harper Torchbooks.

Bertalanffy, L. von. (1962/1928). *Modern theories of development* (J. H. Woodger, trans.). New York: Harper Torchbooks.

Bertalanffy, L. von. (1964). The mind-body problem: a new view. *Psychomatic Medicine, 24,* 29-45.

Bertalanffy, L. von. (1967). *Robot's men and minds.* New York: Braziller.

Bühler, K. (1934). *Sprachtheorie: Die Darstellungsfunktion der Sprache.* Jena: Fischer.

Cassirer, E. (1953-1957). *The philosophy of symbolic forms.* New Haven: Yale University Press.

CATEGORY MISTAKES IN ACT* AND GAPS:[1]

Remarks on Anderson's Adaptive Control of Thought and Tulving's General Abstract Processing System

R. J. Jorna

University of Groningen
Groningen, The Netherlands

SUMMARY: In this article two theories of human cognition will be discussed, those of Anderson (1983) and Tulving (1983). It is claimed that in these theories category mistakes can be discerned, because of the fact that various levels of description and also various forms of representation are confused. The instruments for analyzing the levels of description and forms of representations have been borrowed from Dennett (1978) and Arnheim (1971). It is stated that in order to study mental representations the different features of mental codes (or symbols) should be investigated.

Introduction

If one accepts the line that the human brain is capable of processing information, then it follows that one should question the form and the structure of this information as well as the rules and procedures necessary to process such information. In cognitive psychology these questions are mainly answered by doing experimental research and by formulating simulation models and psychological theories. The aim of both the cognitive theories I will discuss here, is to explain human cognition and human memory. The assumption is that mental processes are a real domain for investigation. Within this domain mental representations, having particular properties, can be defined and postulated. The processing of information, carried out by human individuals, means that operations on mental representations are being executed. Another assumption is that mental representations and the operations upon them are causally connected with behaviour. In this article I will not question these assumptions of cognitive psychology. Instead I will accept the view that in our cognition we have at our disposal mental representations which are caus-

[1]Preparation of this article was supported by Grant 560-269-009 from the Dutch Organization for Scientific Research (Z. W. O.). For comments on an earlier draft, I would like to thank J. L. Jackson and J. A. Michon.

ally connected with overt behaviour.

I will discuss two theories within cognitive psychology and I will look at their internal consistency as well as at some of the concepts they use. The theories I will focus on are the ACT* theory (Adaptive Control of Thought) of Anderson (1983) and the GAPS theory (General Abstract Processing System) of Tulving (1983). The evaluation of the internal consistency and the theoretical assumptions will be based on two criteria. The first of these is borrowed from the philosopher Dennett (1978). He proposes three stances that could be used in examining psychological theories: a physical stance, a functional stance, and an intentional stance. The advice Dennett puts forward, is that we should try neither to confuse nor to merge these stances.

The second criterion is borrowed from the psychologist Arnheim (1971). He states that signs, symbols, and pictures have different levels of abstraction and indicates that these levels should be discerned in the case of representing something.

My article will be divided into three parts. First, I will review Anderson's ACT* theory and Tulving's GAPS theory. Second, I will discuss the three different stances proposed by Dennett and the different functions of signs, symbols, and pictures, as proposed by Arnheim. Finally, I will try to show that much confusion exists about fundamental notions in theories of mental representation, such as those put forward by Anderson and Tulving.

Two Theories of Mental Representation

Anderson's Adaptive Control of Thought: In the last version of ACT*, Anderson (1983) gives an account of his theory as a unified theory of the human mind. The starting-point involves the use of production-rules, consisting of IF-THEN statements in which, if certain conditions are fulfilled, an action is carried out. Anderson says that the ACT* production-system consists of a working memory, a declarative memory, and a production memory (see Figure 1, from Anderson 1983, p. 19).

Furthermore, a distinction can be made in the declarative and the procedural part of representations. Declarative representations consist of tangled hierarchies of cognitive units which may vary in nature, whereas procedural representations refer to processes such as encoding, storing, retrieving, and matching.

Declarative representations form the knowledge base and this knowledge (or knowledge representation) consists of cognitive units, such as propositions, temporal strings, or spatial images. The knowledge representation has a hierarchical structure in which propositions, temporal strings, and spatial images are tangled (see Figure 2, from Anderson 1983,

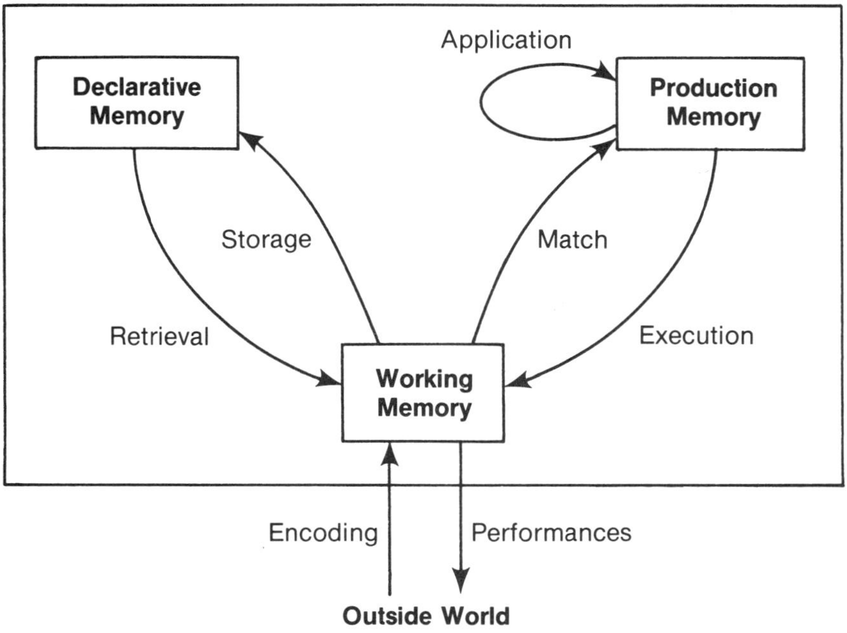

Fig. 1 A general framework for the ACT production system, identifying the major structural components and their interlinking processes.

p. 25). In fact all three knowledge representations are stored together and side by side in the long term memory. In his ACT* theory Anderson discusses the following features of propositional, temporal strings, and spatial image representations. Within temporal string representations the information is encoded in the form of strings in order to fix the sequential structure of events. Strings are not only involved in the succession of events, but also in the understanding of a sentence, since words are also perceived successively. The most important aspect of temporal string representations is that they preserve the ordinal structure of information.

Spatial image representations keep the configuration of elements in a visual field. For example, because of the fact that in the perception of a face the mouth is below the eyes, the mental representation of the face will maintain the orientation between mouth and eyes.

In case of propositional representations, the abstract information of verbal assertions is encoded. For example, in the sentence "Peter sells John a bike" "selling" is encoded as a triadic relation, which takes three arguments. It does not matter whether the sentence was of the form just mentioned or that it had the form "The bike has been sold by Peter to

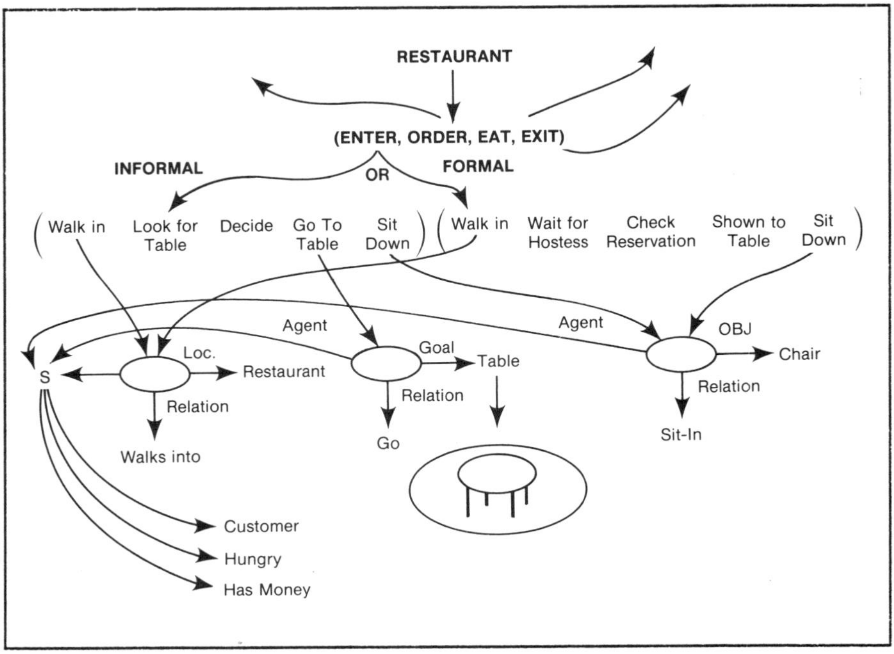

Fig. 2 An example of a tangled hierarchy formed from cognitive units.

John."

According to Anderson the storage and retrieval of the three knowledge representations is an all-or-none matter (p. 62). Irrespective of their nature, cognitive units are wholes and will be processed as such. The main difference between the types of representation lies in the fact that both images and temporal strings represent the structure of the environment more directly, whereas propositional representations are more indirect.

There are two interesting points in the description Anderson gives of knowledge representations. The first point is that propositions form traces in memory, but in fact the other representations do so as well. The question is what does he mean by trace? The second point is that it does not matter which notation is used for the different types of knowledge representation. The reason for this is that notation is a matter of convenience (p. 71). I think that Anderson does not give sufficient attention to these aspects of representation since different representations can reflect different levels of abstraction. I will return to this point below.

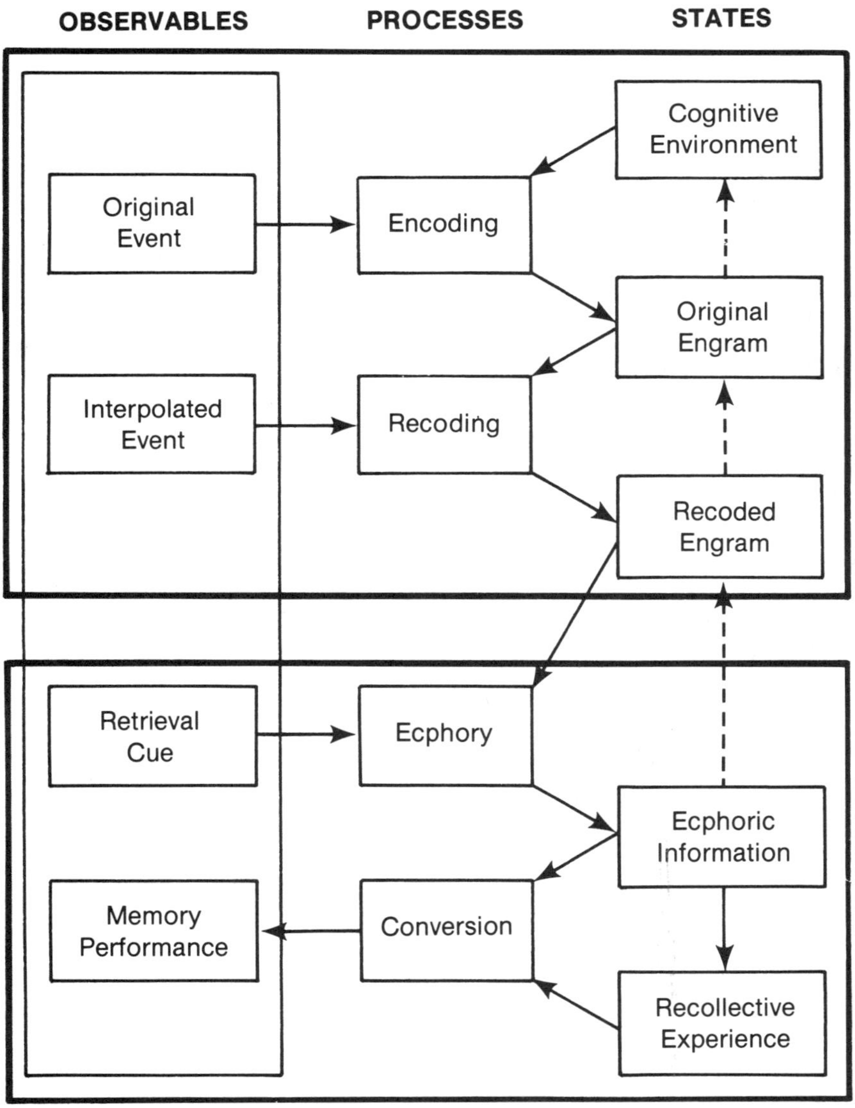

Fig. 3 Elements of episodic memory and their relations.

The combination of declarative and procedural representations is explained by a mechanism of activation. According to ACT*, activation and the spreading of it can be considered as the energy by virtue of which the "cognitive machinery" runs (p. 86). A pattern of activation originating from a stimulus activates a node in the network and spreads along the connections and, hence, the other concepts associated with it. The working of the spread of activation in the cognitive system is supported by reference to the neural system, which also operates by means of nodes, networks, and patterns of activation. Anderson illustrates this in the following way. "Activation spreads through the declarative network along paths from original sources to associated concepts" (p. 86). By means of degrees of activation-spread, information runs from declarative memory towards working memory and so on. Furthermore, mathematical rules are formulated, according to which the activation and its spreading grows and declines. So, with the help of the mechanism of the spreading of activation many kinds of empirical and experimental phenomena, such as priming, fact retrieval, and the nature of working memory can be explained.

Tulving's General Abstract Processing System: In GAPS, Tulving makes a strong distinction between episodic and propositional representations. With respect to the information in episodic memory he claims that its source is perception, that the cognitive units consist of events or episodes, and that the organization of episodic memory is temporal. These features are contrary to those of propositional memory which he claims have their origin in understanding that the cognitive units are facts, concepts, and ideas, and that their organization is conceptual or semantic (Tulving, 1983, p. 35).

Concerning the units in the episodic system Tulving states the following: "The prototypical unit of information in the episodic system is an *event* or an *episode*. An event is something that occurs in a particular situation. It always has a beginning and an end in time, and the interval between the two temporal boundaries is filled with activity, frequently but not always by one or more 'actors'" (Tulving, 1983, p. 37). In the episodic system, events as well as actors are encoded and their encoding is more direct than in the case of propositions, since, according to Tulving, propositions are represented in memory symbolically.

If we look more closely at GAPS (see Figure 3; from Tulving, 1983, p. 135) we see that it is a framework for the storage and retrieval of information in the episodic system. GAPs combines several features of memory. In the first place there is the encoding of the original event as well as of the retrieval cue. In the second place GAPS accounts for the matching of new information within the existing cognitive environment. In the third place the storage in memory is realized in the form of memory traces or engrams. And finally it distinguishes the retrieval process, which Tulving calls the ecphoric process, from the conversion process, whereas, the combination of both leads to a memory-based performance.

Let me illustrate GAPS by means of an example. Suppose someone asks me about the landing of my plane in Calgary. In Tulving's terms the following would have happened in my memory system. The landing of the plane is an original event which has been encoded in my memory system. The encoding is adjusted to my cognitive environment - an environment, which is very restricted on the subject of flying - and leads to a memory trace; what Tulving calls an original engram. Eventually another event occurs after the landing; an event which is closely related to flying, for example, waiting for my luggage. I will encode the interpolated event and, together with the original event, both will combine into a recoded engram.

In this example encoding and recoding can be considered as processes, whereas the cognitive environment, the original and the recoded engram are (mental) states. In my opinion the most intriguing aspect of this model is the engram; what does Tulving mean by engram? On the one hand he says that an engram is the difference before and after stimulus input. But on the other hand the notion is borrowed from biology, and the concept presupposes a physiological foundation.

Furthermore, at the engram level both functional and structural features can be distinguished, but Tulving is not very clear about either of them. In fact, an engram can be everything, as witnessed by the following quotation (Tulving, 1983) "Whether we think of engrams as information stored about past events as a record of operations, attunements, or dispositions, or even as pictures, images, copies, propositions, analogue representations, feature bundles, or as particularly marked parts of associative networks, makes relatively little difference to our understanding of how memory works, [...]" (p. 160). Clearly, Tulving is not very precise here concerning the features of instantiations of engrams, because, according to him, images, pictures, copies and propositions are all interchangeable. It my opinion these instantiations of engrams do have different functions and different aspects, but these will be discussed in the next section.

Let me now return to the example of my landing in Calgary. Up until now only the storage aspect has been discussed. What about the retrieval of information in GAPS? In Tulving's view the question of the landing as verbal statement can be seen as a retrieval cue. This cue starts an ecphoric process, which in combination with the recoded engram leads to an interim report. Tulving calls this report ecphoric information.

Finally, by means of a conversion process this ecphoric information is translated into a memory performance. In the example of my landing, the ecphoric information would consist of a combination of the represented question about my landing and the digging up of the recoded engram of the landing experience. My memory performance could have consisted in answering the question, for example by saying: "the landing was nice and quick, but collecting my luggage took a long time."

In fact, the retrieval process consists of two parts, an ecphoric part and a conversion part. According to Tulving, this makes it possible to understand the difference between recognition and recall. These two memory tasks differ as well in retrieval cues, which leads to a difference in ecphoric information, as in memory performance, which is the result of a difference in conversion processes.

About Stances and Levels of Abstraction

After this somewhat brief description of Anderson's ACT* and Tulving's GAPS models I will proceed to critically examine both theories. To do so, I will refer to Dennett's three stances in explanation and discuss the various aspects of representations (or images) suggested by Arnheim.

Three Stances on Explanation. Dennett (1978) mentions three stances one can adopt in explaining and predicting the behaviour of intelligent systems. In the first place there is the physical stance. In this case one predicts and explains behaviour on account of the actual physical or physiological state of the system according to the laws of nature. Most times we only use this knowledge when the system fails or when it does not behave properly. An instance of a prediction from the physical stance is, according to Dennett (1978), "If you turn on the switch you'll get a nasty shock" (p. 5).

In the second place there is the design stance. In giving design or functional descriptions, it is necessary to know what the design of the system looks like. In that case the parts of the design are being conceived of as relatively independent and as properly functioning units in the system. As Dennett (1978) remarks: "The essential feature of the design stance is that we make predictions solely from knowledge or assumptions about the system's functional design, irrespective of the physical constitution or condition of the innards of the particular object" (p. 4). An instance of a prediction from the functional stance is: if I turn on the switch of my computer, the system will start.

Finally there is the intentional stance. When a system is so complex that we cannot make predictions on the ground of knowledge of the laws of nature or the design of the system, we could ascribe intelligence to the system. In that case we ascribe beliefs, desires, and rational knowledge to the system, and we make predictions by considering that the system might want to win, or want to survive or some such thing. But, as Dennett (1978) remarks "we should remind ourselves that in adopting an intentional stance we are taking out a loan of intelligence and this loan must eventually be repaid" (p. 12).

The conclusions we could draw from Dennett's stances for cognitive psychology are the following. When we mix up the stances, we get category mistakes. These mistakes can arise in at least two ways. First we could confuse a physical stance with a functional stance and in this case we are using physical or physiological characteristics in a functional explanation (or discription). The second lesson Dennett teaches us is that we should be careful in adopting an intentional stance. If we want to describe and explain thinking and reasoning by using rationality, then normally we should not accept as part of the explanation the thing we want to explain.

Aspects of Various Forms of Representations: Let us now turn to the views of Arnheim (1971). His remarks on the different functions of representations are directly applicable to the Anderson and Tulving theories of mental representation because in both these cognitive theories symbols, pictures and signs occur. It should be stated, however, that Arnheim uses the term image, but this term has the same meaning as representation (or symbol system).

Arnheim proposes three forms of representation, representations as signs, representations as symbols, and representations as pictures. Arnheim's starting point is that representations reflect dyadic relations. This means that in the case of representations as relations, the relation takes two arguments, the represented thing and the result of representing. (However, Goodman (1981) has argued that a representation need not necessarily be a dyadic relation; it could also be a categorization or classification.)

It is normal that a representation does not automatically have an interpretation for the interpretation depends upon the context. I will take Arnheim's own example of a triangle to illustrate the different functions of representations; that is to say, that a triangle can be a sign for danger, a picture of a mountain, or a symbol for a hierarchy.

A representation can be seen as a *sign* if it reflects none of the visual characteristics of the thing it represents. This is the case in the triangle as a sign for danger. Another example of a representation as a *sign* is the alphabet. None of the characters in the alphabet - at least not in the English alphabet reflects visual characteristics of the things for which the letters stand.

A representation can be seen as a *picture* when the thing it represents is located at a lower level of abstraction than the representation itself. If someone sees a triangle as a representation of a mountain then the representation functions as a *picture*. The road-sign with crossing bars also represents a *picture*, but, at the same time, it is also a *sign* to pay attention.

Finally, a representation can be seen as a *symbol* when the thing it represents is located at a higher level of abstraction than the representation itself. Someone who thinks that a triangle stands for hierarchy uses the representation as a symbol.

Sign, symbol, and picture indicate different aspects of representations. However, it is not so easy to say whether a representation is a symbol, a sign, or a picture, since both the context as well as the perceiver decide on the actual use or function of the representation. Nevertheless, it is conceptually useful to maintain a distinction among these three functions in order to avoid category mistakes when we deal with representations.

Conclusions

In my opinion we can draw several conclusions from Dennett's three stances on explanation and Arnheim's three aspects or functions of representations which are relevant to an evaluation of the cognitive models presented by Anderson and Tulving. First I will apply Dennett's analysis to ACT* and GAPS and then I will apply Arnheim's distinctions.

In both ACT* and GAPS propositional traces and engrams are proposed as part of the explanation. Furthermore, Anderson accepts the principle of the spreading of activation as a working mechanism in human cognition. The concepts of engram, trace, and spreading of activation are borrowed, as Anderson and Tulving explicitly state, from the physiology of the human nervous system. However, both authors are also explicit in their claim that theories in cognitive psychology are formulated on a functional level. According to Dennett's functional stance on explanation, explanations of human cognitive behaviour in ACT* and GAPS should be formulated independently of physiological considerations. I think that my review of ACT* and GAPS shows that part of the functional description of both these theories is supported by such physiological concepts as engram, propositional trace, and spread of activation.

For example, Anderson's description of the strength of a trace seems to depend on the physical parameters of traces (Anderson, 1983, pp. 35 and 173), although production system traces are conceived of functionally. The problem in this case is that the terms which have been defined physically are being used metaphorically in the functional descriptions. This means that the physical parameters are being used in a more or less loose, but suggestive way to provide explanatory power in a functional explanation. After Dennett and Ryle, I would merely point out that this mingling of stances on explanation leads to category mistakes and, perhaps, consequently to incomplete theories.

There is, however, another conclusion to be drawn from Dennett's distinctions. He suggested that in adopting an intentional stance one takes out a loan on intelligence. One adopts an intentional stance if one uses intentional notions such as signal *reading,* event *encoding,* and message *understanding* in one's cognitive theory (Dennett, 1978, p. 12). Within ACT* and GAPS all sorts of concepts are used in the explanation of the intelligence of cognitive systems, which presuppose, instead of explain, intelligence. It remains unclear whether this loan taken out on intelligence will ever be paid back.

If we now consider Arnheim's distinction among three functions of representation, we see that while both ACT* and GAPS grant a central role to the concept of representation, neither model can account for the different aspects of functions of representations. Neither Anderson's three types of knowledge representation, namely spatial images, temporal strings, and propositions, nor Tulving's distinctions between episodes on the one hand and concepts and facts on the other, can even begin to account for Arnheim's functions of representations. Nowhere in these theories can an indication be found which accounts for the different aspects or functions of representations.

From Arnheim's distinctions among sign, symbol, and picture we may conclude that we are dealing here with at least three different forms of representations each with their own characteristics and features. Subsuming symbols, propositions, pictures, etc. under a single concept of representation violates their different functions and features. The differences in the functions of symbols, pictures, and signs contradicts the easy interchanging of 'representations' that has been explicitly defended by Anderson and presupposed by Tulving in his definition of events. My conclusion is that we have here another category mistake, but this time at a different level. For as both Arnheim and Goodman (1981) have shown, it really does matter whether we deal with pictures, symbols, signs or propositions.

Indeed, Tulving's distinction between episodic and propositional representations is entirely uninformative if, on Arnheim's terms, all sorts of 'representations' are confused in an event.

My overall conclusion has to be that at least the ACT* and GAPS theories in cognitive psychology include category mistakes at various theoretical levels. This not only diminishes their explanatory power of the empirical findings but also reduces their conceptual lucidity and, hence, theoretical value.

Finally, I will explicitly state that my claim is not to stop cognitive psychology. What I have tried to do is to point out some difficulties in two current theories of cognitive psychology. As a consequence of my criticism, I urge that more time should be spent on conceptual analysis. Especially on conceptual research pertaining to the nature of mental codes or mental symbols (see Goodman, 1981; Kolers & Smythe, 1979) as well as on the translatability of one (mental) code into another.

References

Anderson, J. R. (1983). *The architecture of cognition.* Cambridge: Harvard University Press.

Arnheim, R. (1971). *Visual thinking.* London: Faber & Faber.

Dennett, D. C. (1978). *Brainstorms.* Montgomery, ALA: The Harvester Press.

Goodman, N. (1981). *Languages of art.* Brighton: The Harvester Press.

Kolers, P. A., & Smythe, W. E. (1979). Images, symbols, and skills. *Canadian Journal of Psychology, 33(3),* 158-184.

Tulving, E. (1983). *Elements of episodic memory.* Oxford: Oxford University Press.

Tulving, E. (1984). Précis of elements of episodic memory. *The Behavioral and Brain Sciences, 7,* 223-268.

ON OBJECTIVE AND SUBJECTIVE ANCHORING OF COGNITIVE ACTS: How Behavioural Valence Modifies Reasoning Schemata

Maria Lewicka

University of Warsaw
Warsaw, Poland

SUMMARY: The controversy between constructivistic and realistic views of human cognition can be reconciled by introducing the notion of the anchorage of cognitive acts. Objectively anchored cognitions serve to identify necessary conditions of outcomes and are therefore functional mainly for processing negative and non-intended occurrences, while subjectively anchored cognitions help to identify sufficient conditions of outcomes and are employed mostly to process positive and intended phenomena. Human deviations from normative models of rational judgment are the result of preoccupation with sufficiency at the expense of necessity and, hence, by the prevalence of subjectively over objectively anchored cognitions.

Realism-Constructionism Controversy in Psychology

Epistemological assumptions which underlie theorizing in psychology are by no means unified. One of the major epistemological controversies, bearing on the shape of contemporary psychological theories of cognition, is the old 'realism vs. idealism' philosophical question. The question will be rephrased here as that of *an anchoring* of human cognitive activity, which theories of cognition may either locate *outside* an individual: in external objective phenomena whose properties are *reconstructed* by a subject in a cognitive act, or *within* the subject and his or her capacity to *construct* subjective conceptions of the world. Those who tend to accept the first, realistic, position are also inclined to view cognitive activity as externally constrained: extrinsically motivated, restricted to objectively imposed demands, but also often as inadequate and fallacious. Within this point of view a subject is a reality tester, gradually approaching truth, in the process of which, however, he or she is bound to err and be susceptible to numerous illusions. Proponents of the other, constructivistic point of view tend to ascribe to humans considerable interpretive freedom, while suspending judgment on the validity of its outcomes, and to view cognitive activity as intrinsically motivated and constrained only by limitations of cognitive potential and by individualized content of cognitive schemata.

Both points of view are idealizations and are therefore viable to easy criticism: rushing trains and falling bricks which create obvious limitations to human freedom in theorizing about the world form favourite arguments of 'realists', while the apparent differentiation of everyday phenomena is the gist of commonsense argumentation provided by 'constructivists'. Both sides are therefore willing to make concessions, due to which contemporary realists depart as much from Locke's formulations as do constructivists from those of Berkeley's. This convergence, however, when it comes to explicit stating of philosophical assumptions, is often superficial and the profound gap separating the two points of view is not easy to bridge, as witnessed for example by a number of papers presented in this volume (cf. Gergen; Tolman).

In contrast to theoretically-minded psychologists, research-oriented ones are not always aware of epistemology which guides their theoretical predictions. Moreover, they would frequently deny any merits coming from philosophical reflection for solution of their own theoretical or empirical dilemmas. Perhaps this is the reason why empirically oriented areas of the recent 15 years have been manifesting obvious convergence of the two epistemological positions, unlike the preceding years of research in cognition. Facts from the post-war history of research in social cognition and judgment under uncertainty are good examples.

A considerable portion of studies in social cognition from the 50s and the 60s (for instance, research in cognitive consistency or early research in attribution) has never been referred to by researchers in decision making and judgment under uncertainty, not because the two areas had nothing in common, but because the first were taking constructivistic, (see Sampson, 1981 for review and criticism) while the latter, realistic epistemological positions. It is only with the gradual switch of decision researchers from normative models which specified criteria of valid judgment, to a descriptive analysis of what the judgmental process really looks like, that the two lines of research have become to converge (cf. Montgomery, 1986). Due to the very same evolution, cognitive social psychology has incorporated a vast amount of findings collected by decision researchers. Markus and Zajonc's chapter on social cognition in the last edition of the *Handbook of Social Psychology* (Markus & Zajonc, 1985) is almost entirely devoted to a detailed listing and description of numerous cognitive biases, most of them identified in the area of judgment under uncertainty. This was made possible by the constructivists' easy assimilation of the notion of judgmental heuristics as the major explanatory construct introduced by Kahneman and Tversky (Tversky & Kahneman, 1974; Kahneman, Slovic, & Tversky, 1982). (For a good demonstration of the easy assimilation of the concept of judgmental heuristics by social psychologists see Nisbett & Ross, 1980).

The integration of the two research domains has not only been influenced by the fact that previous realists have come to accept constructivistic positions but perhaps even more so by the reverse movement. When H. H. Kelley (1971) introduced the post-Millian model of inductive inference into the until then constructivistic area of attributional reasoning, this led to identification of numerous errors in social judgment (deviations from the validity criteria), reinterpreted by specialists in probabilistic judgment as further examples of already known judgmental fallacies (Nisbett, Borgida, & Crandall, 1976). External criteria of judgmental validity and, hence, realistic assumptions, have also been built into experimental paradigms employed to study illusion of control (Jenkins & Ward, 1965; Alloy & Abramson, 1979; Langer, 1975), covariation assessment (Shaklee, 1983), or stereotype formation (Hamilton, 1976). This movement towards realism has been reinforced further by experimental social psychology undertaking traditional clinical problems, since it is very difficult to remain a constructivist when for instance faced with obviously distorted cognitions of a depressed patient.

On the whole then, it seems as if in empirical psychology we have been facing a convergence of both positions, with perhaps previous constructivists yielding more to the realistic point of view than the other way round. Does this mean that the last word in this controversy is a simple compromise, crowned with a worn-out cliche that any cognitive act is double-anchored, both in the object cognized and in the cognizing subject?

A word of warning is needed here. It is well known that any mechanistic compromise usually leads to eclecticism. And indeed, when studying the contemporary literature in social judgment one cannot escape a strong impression that quite a number of its generalizations bear a strongly eclectic character. The picture of a person who evolves out of this research is that of a nice, although intellectually somewhat crippled, creature committing judgmental errors whose severity however, is not that alarming as to call it an emergency.

What I would like to suggest instead is to propose a hypothesis, which although compromising, seems to escape eclecticism. I will hypothesize that human beings are both realists and constructivists, but that they are rarely both at the same time. Hence cognitive acts performed by an individual are either anchored in the cognized object, thus leading to realistic assessment of its properties, or in the subject, favouring freedom in construction of its diverse interpretations. The two types of anchorage would correspond to a difference in cognitive perspective a subject may take: objective, external anchorage would underlie a perspective of *an observer* while subjective, internal anchorage, that of *an actor*. Since simultaneously holding both the actor's and the observer's perspective is fairly difficult (one could call it a 'psychological version' of Heisenberg's principle), irreconcileability of the realistic and constructivistic positions in one single cognitive act becomes understandable.

Positive and Negative Behaviour and Subjective vs. Objective Anchorage of Implicational Schemata

From what has been said so far two main research problems may follow. One concerns the nature of reasoning schemata activated under actor and observer perspectives; the other regards the conditions triggering them. Answers to both questions are intertwined and, as it will be postulated in this paper, are rooted in the distinction between two general classes of behaviour: approach (an act of affirmation of an object), and avoidance (an act of its negation). I will suggest that the main function of cognition is to identify conditions enabling execution of both types of behaviour. Since, however, the logical structure of conditions favouring efficient approach and avoidance differs, so the reasoning schemata employed for this purpose will also be different.

Let us start from a trivial stance. Notice that in order to approach an object it is enough to trigger one of its sufficient, even if not necessary, conditions, but that in order to avoid it, it is indispensable to negate at least one of its necessary, even if not sufficient, conditions. It follows from the logical canons of induction (Mill, 1843; Ajdukiewicz, 1955) that reasoning schemata employed in identifying sufficient and necessary conditions differ, and require different anchorage of assumed cognitive acts. It will be postulated here that it is this very difference which constitutes the gist of the distinction between the actor and observer cognitive perspectives.

In logical terms this may be depicted as a difference in focus on either of the two terms of a logical implication: one which stands for a hypothesis held by a subject, for instance a hypothetical condition of an outcome, while the other depicts evidence for the hypothesis, that is, the outcome itself. After Klayman and Ha (1984), the former term will be symbolized by 'H' (hypothesis), the other by 'T' (target). Independent of the fact that there is usually a fixed temporal order of succession of the two terms, since the hypothesized condition (H) precedes in time the ensuing outcome (T), logically both terms may stand in a function of either an antecedent or a consequent of the implication.

It will be assumed here that cognition may be viewed as processing implications and, hence, a cognitive act may be presented either as processing of the '$H \rightarrow T$' implication or of the reverse '$T \rightarrow H$' implication. Since the antecedent of an implication is logically defined as a sufficient condition of the consequent, and the consequent as a necessary condition of the antecedent (cf. Ajdukiewicz, 1955), it may be easily noticed that processing of the $H \rightarrow T$ implication leads to identification of sufficiency of hypothetical conditions H, while processing of the 'T → H' implication leads to identification of necessary conditions for T. I will further postulate that *a cognitive act is always anchored in the antecedent of the processed implication and that, therefore, in the former case the act of cognition is anchored subjectively in the hypothesis held by the subject, while in the latter case the cognition is anchored objectively in the target.* Identification of sufficient conditions of outcomes is thus a part-and-parcel of a subjective cognitive attitude of an actor, while identification of necessary conditions is part of the objective attitude of an observer.

It would further follow that differently valenced outcomes, positive objects which a subject wishes to approach, and negative objects which he or she wishes to avoid, should be ascribed a different epistemological status by a cognizing individual. Positive outcomes which trigger the cognitive perspective of an actor, should be conceived by people as having a more 'subjective' character than negative outcomes which activate the perspective of an observer. This asymmetry find corroboration in a number of empirical findings. For example, it has been shown that people display more interpersonal consensus when evaluating undesirable than desirable states of affairs (Lewicka, 1981; Edwards & Holmgren, 1980), and that they are significantly more accurate and interpersonally congruent when asked to identify objects described with negative than with positive labels (Czapinski, 1986). Let us also note that even on the linguistic level this asymmetry is markedly pronounced: we use the phrase 'approachable objects' as a synonym for positive entities, by which we tend to imply that a subject may but does not have to approach the object, but at the same time we tend to say 'objects to be avoided', and not 'avoidable objects', implying that there is not much freedom involved in our decisions on whether to avoid or not undesirable states of things. Both, the more imperative character of avoidance over approach behaviour and the higher interpersonal consensus on what constitutes negative than positive sides of things, seem to demonstrate that people would consider negativity as more descriptive of reality and hence more objective than the individually differentiated and subjectively less compelling positivity.

Sufficiency and Necessity Reasoning Schemata: Further Theoretical Distinctions

In order to probe deeper into the difference between the two types of inferential schemata, let us refer to the familiar, two-by-two, contingency table, with four logical terms: H, non-H, T, and non-T, where H stands for a hypothesized condition of an outcome T, T for the outcome itself, non-H for alternative non-hypothesized conditions favouring occurrence of T, and non-T for the alternative outcomes (see Fig. 1).

	H	non-H	
T	p (H^T) positive hits (a)	p (non-H^T) false negatives (c)	p (T)
non-T	p (H^non-T) false positives (b)	p (non-H^non-T) negative hits (d)	p (non-T)
	p (H)	p (non-H)	
Sufficiency of H for T: p (T/H) = a/(a+b) Necessity of H for T: p (H/T) = a/(a+c)			

Fig. 1 Two-by-two contingency table.

Marginals of the contingency table correspond to base rate probabilities of all four options and the four cells are filled with probabilities of respective conjunctions.

In line with popular distinctions, let us call the four cells of the table: (a) positive hits, (b) false positives, (c) false negatives, and (d) negative hits.

The two conditional probabilities, describing relationships between two positive terms, H and T, correspond to what we have previously described as sufficiency and necessity relationships. The probability of T given H, p(T/H), reflects a probability that H is as sufficient condition of T, while the probability of H given T, p(H/T), is an estimate of the degree of H's necessity for T. Estimation of sufficiency of H for T requires taking the contents of two cells, (a) and (b), into account, that is, computation of the number of positive hits as compared to the number of false positives. In order to estimate the necessity of H for T, attention should be shifted to the cell (c) and, apart from usual attention paid to the raw number of positive hits, it should also take into account the number of false negatives. We are thus faced with two types of evidence which may invalidate the H - T relationship: one is given by the (b) cell, another by that of the (c) cell.

In line with our previously delineated rationale, we can therefore expect that people should be more sensitized to the false positive disconfirming evidence when testing hypotheses about positive outcomes and to the false negative falsifying evidence when negative objects are targets of their hypotheses. Since tendency to weight false positives higher than false negatives would lead to risk-avoidance while the reverse to risk-seeking behavior, we would expect more risk-aversion for gains than losses, while more risk-seeking behavior is predicted for losses than gains. This is precisely the claim made by Kahneman and Tversky (1979), ensuing from differential shapes of money utility function for gains (concave) and losses (convex). With regard to human cognitive decisions this claim has been empirically corroborated by the 'win-stay-lose-shift' pattern of behaviour, displayed in hypotheses-testing situations (preference of a certain over uncertain option when the experimenter's feedback is "yes" and for an uncertain over a certain one when it is 'no' (see also Klayman & Ha, 1984).

Risk aversion for gains is closely related to the so called 'negativity effect', observed in positive-negative asymmetry research, that is, higher weight is attached to encountered negative than positive information and hence higher impact of the former than the latter on ensuing behaviour (cf. Kanouse & Hanson, 1966; Peeters, 1985; Czapinski, forthcoming). As such, the negativity effect forms a realistic counterpart to the otherwise optimistic attitude of people, displayed in their prior ratings of outcomes probability (Matlin & Stang, 1978; Peeters, 1971; Czapinski, 1985).

Computing the values of the two conditionals, sufficiency and necessity, in terms of a difference in anchorage, plays different cognitive functions: estimating probability of an outcome when its cause is hypothesized to be known (subjective anchorage, sufficiency estimation) is a task of *predicting the outcome from its hypothetical preceding conditions,* while estimating probability that a cause was present when its outcome is known (objective anchorage, necessity estimation) *is a task of explaining the outcome with its preceding conditions.*

The difference between the two types of inferences has been acknowledged in literature as a forward (predictive) and inward (causal) inference (Anderson, 1979) or forward and backward inference (Hogarth & Einhorn, 1985). However, in my opinion, the distinction has not been given sufficient attention in psychology and the qualitative psychological differences in information processing strategies have not become a proper theoretical focus in the psychological literature.

The cognitive act of prediction can thus be defined as an act of establishing sufficiency, while that of explanation as establishing necessity relationships between hypothetical conditions and their outcomes. As such the two types of inferential processes will provide answers to two different questions: the former will answer the question "how to make T occur? Will it follow from H?", while the latter: "Why did T occur? Did it occur because of H?".

In line with the model presented here, we can expect that people would take more interest in predicting than explaining positive outcomes and in explaining rather than predicting negative ones. This claim has received substantial empirical corroboration since the "why?" question was found to be asked significantly more often with respect to unexpected and negative events while the "how?" question was asked more frequently with respect to positive events (cf. Wong, Weiner, 1981; Weiner, 1985; Abele, 1985).

What do Normative Rationality Models Expect of People?

Complaints about irrationality of lay thinking in humans are probably as old as normative models setting criteria of what constitutes valid judgment. Chronologically the first complaints were about errors committed in natural logical reasoning. They usually refer to the tendency to ignore truth-falsehood tables, to incorrectly interpret logical connectives and quantifiers (Braine, 1978; Rips, 1983), and to draw erroneous conclusions in syllogistic inferences (Johnson-Laird, 1983).

The present century introduced into the analysis of human rationality a set of additional validity criteria. Methodological requirements of falsificationism in science, accompanied by the development of inductive logic, provided criteria for correct hypotheses-testing (cf. Evans, 1982), while development of probabilistic calculus has brought a requirement that in everyday life people should also be able to employ textbook definitions of probability and randomness, properly estimate covariation between events, and employ Bayesian formula to compute conditional probabilities (Kahneman, Slovic, Tversky, 1982).

Equally stringent criteria have been imposed upon human causal reasoning. The main target of attack is directed towards a popular tendency to ignore policausality in the perceived determination of events, and to ascribe causal roles to the most obvious and salient factors (Nisbett & Ross, 1980).

The area is now abundant in research and diverse theoretical interpretations, ranging from severe condemnation of intellectual deficiencies of laymen to their hottest apology. As could be expected, the critics of lay performance base their verdicts on an assumption that normative models constitute the only criteria of correct judgment. Advocates of lay judgment, in turn, defend commonsense inferences by either shaking the belief about the imperative character of normative models (Kruglanski,

1983) or by suggesting non-orthodox inferential calculi assumed to fit better the logic of everyday thinking (Cohen, 1977, 1981; Braine, 1978).

I would like to argue in this section that the reason why lay people do not conform in their judgments to normative prescriptions lies in the difference in anchorage of cognitive acts produced spontaneously by people and those prescribed by the models. I will postulate that whereas the majority of normative models require that people simultaneously hold a subjective and objective perspective (and thus focus on both sufficient and necessary conditions of explained and predicted outcomes), the most typical attitude taken by lay people in experimental tasks is subjective, suggesting greater focus on sufficiency than necessity and, hence, the actor's rather than the observer's perspective. This, as it has been argued above, does not mean that people are unable to spontaneously shift to the observer's attitude and to pay at least equal attention to necessity as to sufficiency, thereby conforming more to the requirements of rational judgment. However, this shift would require that the experimenter rephrase an experimental task not as one requiring approach (affirmation of the phenomenon considered) but, rather, requiring avoidance (negation). Apart from the area of research in attribution theory which deals with both positive and negative behaviours, this has rarely been done, for some reason researchers prefer the investigation of 'cool' rather than 'hot' cognitions.

Let us then take a closer look at the structure of experimental tasks typically used in studies on rational judgment. For reasons of space, I have selected only four research domains: Bayesian rule of conditional probability, hypotheses-testing behaviour as exemplified by Wason's 2-4-6 task, H. H. Kelley's model of attributional reasoning, and studies in the structure of natural concepts.

The Bayesian formula can be rephrased as a prescription for how to compute necessity of factor A for factor B from knowledge of its sufficiency: $p(A/B) = p(B/A) \cdot p(A)/p(B)$. The two values are equal only if prior probabilities of both factors are the same since then their ratio equals one. However, this is rarely the case, something to which people seem oblivious, and, hence, the most typical error committed is to neglect the disparity between prior odds and substitute the known value of sufficiency for the unknown necessity.

A classic example of this fallacy is the famous 'cab problem', introduced by Tversky and Kahneman (cf. Kahneman, Slovic, & Tversky, 1982). Subjects are told that two cab companies operate in one town: one company owns blue cars and 85% of all cabs in the city, while the other company owns the remaining 15% of cars which are green in colour. One night a cab was involved in an accident and luckily a witness was present who testified that the cab involved in the crash was green. The witness' credibility was estimated at 80%. The subject is asked to estimate probability that the cab involved in the accident was indeed green.

The typical answer provided by subjects is 80% instead of the proper Baysian estimate of 41%, suggesting that people find it difficult to include in their computations the information on the difference in prior odds of a blue and a green car appearing at some place in the town. The detailed numerical description of the problem is presented in Table 1.

It follows from the table that what subjects seem oblivious to is the fact that since blue cars by far outnumber the green ones, even a highly credible witness would call more blue than green cabs green, thus lowering the estimate of necessity of a car being green for its recognition as green, as compared to the credibility measure (sufficiency of being a green cab for its recognition as green).

Subjects seem to face a similar problem when solving the famous 2-4-6 task, devised by P. Wason (1968). Subjects are asked to guess a rule, known by an experimenter, connecting three different numbers in a string. They are also told that the string 2-4-6 conforms to the rule and are asked to discover the rule by producing any three number strings to which an experimenter would answer that it either does or does not conform to the rule. The catch lies in the experimenter's rule being larger than any hypothesis typically formed by a subject on the basis of the initial 2-4-6 string (the proper answer is 'any three numbers in ascending order' while subject's typical guess goes for 'three even numbers ascending by equal intervals'). The typical subject solves the task by producing several strings which he or she hypothesizes as conforming to the rule (e.g., 10-12-14, 116-118-120, etc.), each time receiving a positive feedback from the experimenter and, hence, gaining increasing certainty that this is the proper rule. What he or she should do instead, is to produce strings inconsistent with the leading hypothesis (e.g., 1-4-15), since a 'yes' answer from an experimenter would then be a cue to enlarge the too narrow hypothesis (what is normatively required is employment of falsification and not confirmation strategy in testing the hypothesis).

It can easily be noticed that what subjects are doing is focusing more on the sufficiency of their hypothesized rule for experimenter's positive answer than on its necessity. The subject's rule, because it is more narrow than that of an experimenter's, is of course sufficient (it will always bring a positive feedback) but it is not necessary. Again, then, the normative prescription underlying the experimental set-up, requires of people to acknowledge both sufficiency and necessity and, again, subjects prefer to focus only on sufficiency of their hypotheses (for analogous interpretation and further data see: Klayman & Ha, 1984, 1985).

A third and similar example of cognitive preference is provided by research on causal attribution. The only normative model of inference in social psychology regarding this issue has been provided by H. H. Kelley (1967), known since then as 'Kelley's cube'. According to this model,

Table 1

Numerical Representation of the "Cab Problem"

	Hypothesized Car Being		
Witness Evidence	Green (H)	Blue (non-H)	
green (T)	.12	.17	.29
blue (non-T)	.03	.68	.71
	.15	.85	

Sufficiency of H for T: p (T/H) = .12/.15 = .80
Necessity of H for T: p (H/T) = .12/.29 = .41

somebody's behaviour will be ascribed to an external (situational) or internal (dispositional) cause, dependent on three types of cues provided: information on behaviour consistency (how common is the actor's behaviour across time and situations), information on behaviour distinctiveness (how common it is across different targets), and information on social consensus (how common it is across different actors). Out of the three types of cues two, behavioral consistency and consensus, refer to the distinction drawn in this paper, since the more consistent the actor's behaviour across time and situations, the more sufficient are the dispositional properties of the actor for producing this behaviour, while the less popular the behaviour across different actors (the lower behavioural consensus), the more necessary are actors' personal dispositions for its occurrence.

One of the best documented phenomena in attributional research is the so called 'fundamental attribution error' (Ross, 1977), consisting of overestimating the role of actor's personal dispositions at the expense of situational factors. It follows from Kelley's model, that dispositional attribution is a product of a combination of two cues: high consistency and low consensus of behaviour. Erroneous overestimation of the role of personal factors would, according to this model, have its source in the subject's judgments being guided almost entirely by the information on consistency and not consensus. This is a finding fairly well documented in attributional research (Nisbett, Borgida, Crandall, 1976; Szmajke, 1984). Since consensus information is nothing other than information on prior probability of the explained outcome (T), an estimate which requires a switch to an observer's perspective, the pattern of data suggests, again, that in this type of task subjects display a strong preference for the cognitive perspective of an actor, and thus sufficiency estimation.

Fundamental attribution error is not the only attributional bias observed by researchers employing Kelley's cube[3]. Another is preference for dispositional attributions of one's own successes and situational ones for one's own failures. As argued above the switch from an actor's to an observer's perspective should be accompanied by giving greater weight to consensus information which, in turn, should facilitate situational attributions. The success-failure asymmetry thus follows closely from the model since it documents that with regard to positive outcomes of one's own behaviour people are willing to accept the actor's, and for negative outcomes, the observer's cognitive perspective.

The fourth and the last research domain to be briefly discussed here is the controversy over the nature of natural categories. Without going into the details of the controversy (for a review see: Homa, 1984), let me mention that the classic normative definition of a concept used to conceive of it as a set of both sufficient and necessary criteria of class membership however, more recent approaches, developed mainly from the investigation of natural categories, have proposed a more heterogeneous structure of the concept. The most popular approach has been that of E. Rosch (Rosch, & Mervis, 1975), suggesting that the structure of a natural category is highly differentiated, with a main core formed by a 'prototype', which is defined as a set of features characteristic of the most frequently encountered exemplars of the concept. Objects are categorized as concept exemplars according to their global similarity to the prototype and not in terms of whether they do or do not possess definitional features. The most frequent example used to illustrate this notion is that of the concept of a 'bird', whose prototype denotes a subset of a set of definitional birds consisting of the most frequently encountered examples of birds (for instance, 'robin' is the prototype bird in America while 'sparrow' is in Poland, both being more 'bird like' than, for instance, chickens or ostriches).

Thus, prototype has a richer, and more concrete connotation than the official definition of a concept. For example, in the case of birds, there are two additional features introduced by people into their lay definitions: the bird's size (small or medium) and its ability to fly (cf.

Rosch & Mervis, 1975). Hence a prototype may be defined as a conjunction of features which together constitute a sufficient but not necessary condition for class membership (robin-like features are sufficient but not necessary criteria of 'birdness').

Allowing that the majority of objects encountered by people in their everyday life are either positively evaluated (for empirical demonstration of the positivity bias in social perception see: Peeters, 1971; Matlin and Stang, 1978; Czapinski, 1985) or neutral and, hence, that they first of all trigger the reaction of affirmation and not negation of their exemplars (a child is usually asked 'point to a bird', and not to 'not to point to a bird'), it is little wonder that the majority of natural concepts have a non-classic, sufficiency-based prototypical structure. What would happen, however, if the concept denoted a class of objects spontaneously triggering the reaction of behavioural or symbolic negation, for example, negative events? If for instance all birds happened to be dangerous, we could expect that people should not find it difficult to draw an equivalence between chicken and robins, thus focusing more on the necessary than purely the sufficient criteria of class membership and, hence, ending up with the concept structure more reminiscent of classic definitions.

The model presented here implies also that identification of necessary conditions is made easier if the prior probability of target occurrence is smaller. We would expect then that cognitive categories employed to denote classes of negative events should be more specific and concrete than broad and heterogeneous categories denoting positive or neutral events. Empirical data corroborating this hypothesis exist and they have been reviewed by Czapinski (1985).

Concluding Remarks

In conclusion, the observed violations of diverse normative models of rational judgment appear to have a common denominator: they are focused on *sufficient* conditions of explained, predicted, or identified phenomena rather than on their necessary conditions. This, in turn, is due to the general prevalence in lay thinking of subjectively over objectively anchored cognitions and, hence, of the actor's rather than the observer's perspective. The reason for this asymmetry is probably two-fold. One is the structure of the most commonly used experimental tasks which mostly trigger the affirmative, approaching rather than negative, avoiding reaction in subjects. The second reason is more fundamental. It appears that the reaction of affirmation is ontologically more primary, than that of negation. It is, of course, logically primary since in order to negate an entity one has first to positively identify it in an act of affirmation. The existent linguistic data also justify the claim of not only logical but ontological primacy of positivity. Ontological primacy of positive evaluations as compared to negative ones is given by the former using significantly more often the semantically non-marked, and the latter the semantically marked, and hence ontologically secondary, adjectival categories (cf. Clark & Clark, 1977; Benjafield, 1983). In another set of studies it has been shown that the notion of semantic markedness may also be valid as applied to verbs. Verbs denoting positively directed behaviour carry a logical structure of affirmation, and verbs denoting negative acts (avoidance or neglect) carry a structure of logical negation (Lewicka, 1986), and, hence, display opposite patterns of behaviour in the logical contexts of disjunction and conjunction (Abelson & Kanouse, 1966; Wyer & Carlston, 1979).

If positively oriented behavior and hence the subjective anchorage of cognition are the most typical states of minds in humans (and perhaps not only in humans), one should not wonder that cognitive researchers should have expended considerable effort in order to devise their tasks in such a way as to break the habitual cognitive set in their subjects and induce a spontaneous switch to the objectively anchored perspective of an observer.

However, this does not mean that 'constructivistic' approaches provide more valid descriptions of people's typical behaviour than 'realistic' ones. On the contrary, the research evidence on positive-negative evaluative asymmetry clearly demonstrates that people are endowed with built-in intellectual tools to efficiently handle negative occurrences and, thus, willingly conform to normative prescriptions of objectively anchored judgment. What the model presented in this paper seems to imply, and what the research on evaluative judgment appears to corroborate, is that people manifest a strong constructivistic tendency to build their own, individualized versions of positivity within, however, boundaries allowed to them by an objective and rationally reconstructed negativity.

Normative models of rational judgment are thus not a whim of scholars but a powerful tool for reconstructing objective properties of the human environment and, as such, they constitute an extension of part of the natural biological equipment of human species. Were it not for this biological equipment our constructive abilities would have to be confined to very tight boundaries. One can therefore look at biological and social evolution as a process of endowing living organisms with more and more efficient tools to handle negativity, thus promoting an increase in the number of degrees of freedom for positively directed behaviour.

References

Abele, A. (1985). Thinking about thinking: Causal, evaluative and finalistic reasoning in social situations. ***European Journal of Social Psychology, 15***, 315-332.

Abelson, R. P., & Kanouse, E. E. (1966). Subjective acceptance of verbal generalizations. In S. Feldman (Ed.), ***Cognitive consistency: Motivational antecedents and behavioral consequences*** (pp. 173-199). New York: Academic Press.

Ajdukiewicz, K. (1955). ***Introduction to F. Bacon's "Novum Organum"***. Warsaw: PWN.

Alloy, L. B., & Abramson, L. J. (1979) Judgment of contingency in depressed and non-depressed students: Sadder but wiser? ***Journal of Experimental Social Psychology: General, 108***, 441-485.

Anderson, N. H. (1978). Progress in cognitive algebra. In ***Cognitive theories in social psychology*** (pp. 103-126). New York: Academic Press.

Benjafield, J. (1983). Some psychological hypotheses concerning the evolution of constructs. ***British Journal of Psychology, 74***, 47-59.

Braine, M. D. S. (1978). On the relation between the natural logic of reasoning and standard logic. ***Psychological Review, 85***, 1-21.

Clark, H. H., & Clark, E. V. (1977). ***Psychology and language: An introduction to psycholinguistics.*** New York: Harcourt.

Cohen, L. J. (1977). ***The probable and the provable.*** Oxford: Clarendon Press.

Cohen, L. J. (1981). Can human irrationality be experimentally demonstrated? ***The Behavioural and Brain Sciences, 4***, 317-331.

Czapinski, J. (1985). ***Wartosciowanie - zjawisko inklinacji pozytywnej. O naturze optymizmu.*** (Valuation - the phenomenon of positivity bias. On the nature of optimism). Wroclaw: Ossolineum.

Czapinski, J. (1986). Informativeness of evaluations in interpersonal communications: Effects of valence, extremity of evaluations, and ego-involvement of evaluator. ***Polish Psychological Bulletin, 17***, 155-164.

Czapinski, J. (forthcoming). ***Wartosciowanie -efekt negatywnosci. O naturze realizmu.*** (Valuation - the negativity effect. On the nature of realism). Wroclaw: Ossolineum.

Edwards, J. D., & Holmgren, R. L. (1980). Normative ambiguity ratings of 120 personality-trait words. ***JSAS, Catalog of Selected Documents in Psychology, 10***, 87.

Evans, J. St. B. (Ed.). (1983). ***Thinking and reasoning.*** London: Routledge & Kegan Paul.

Hamilton, D. (1976). On cognitive basis of stereotypes. In J. S. Carroll & J. W. Payne (Eds.), ***Cognition and social behavior.*** New York: Lawrence Erlbaum.

Hogarth, R., & Einhorn, H. J. (1986). Judging probable cause. ***Psychological Bulletin, 1***, 1-32.

Homa, D. (1984). On the nature of categories. In G. H. Bower (Ed.), ***The psychology of learning and motivation*** (Vol. 18, pp. 49-94). New York: Academic Press.

Jenkins, H. M., & Ward, W. C. (1965). Judgment of contingency between responses and outcomes. ***Psychological Monographs, 79***, 594.

Johnson-Laird, P. N. (1983). ***Mental models.*** Cambridge, MA: Harvard University Press.

Kahneman, D., Slovic, P., & Tversky, A. (1982). ***Judgment under uncertainty: Heuristics and biases.*** Oxford: Cambridge University Press.

Kahneman, D., & Tversky, A. (1979). Prospect theory: an analysis of decision under risk. ***Econometrica, 47***, 263-291.

Kanouse, D. E., & Hanson, L. R. Jr. (1971). Negativity in evaluations. In E. E. Jones, et al. (Eds.), *Attribution: Perceiving the causes of behavior* (pp. 47-62). Morriston: General Learning Press.

Kelley, H. H. (1967). Attribution theory in social psychology. *Nebraska Symposium on Motivation, 15*, 192-238.

Klayman, J., & Ha, Y-W. (1984). *Confirmation, disconfirmation, and information in hypotheses-testing.* Unpublished manuscript. The University of Chicago, Graduate School of Business, Chicago.

Klayman, J., & Ha, Y-W. (1985). *Hypotheses-testing in rule discovery. Strategy and structure.* Paper presented at the Tenth Research Conference on SPUDM, Helsinki, Finland.

Kruglanski, A., & Ajzen, L. (1983). Bias and error in human judgment. *European Journal of Social Psychology, 13*, 1-44.

Langer, E. (1975). The illusion of control. *Journal of Personality and Social Psychology, 32*, 311-328.

Lewicka, M. (1986). Do verbs obey deMorgans' laws? *Polish Psychological Bulletin, 17*,(2), 101-110.

Lewicka, M. (1981). *Evaluative asymmetry of verbal labels.* Unpublished manuscript.

Markus, H., & Zajonc, R. B. (1985). The cognitive perspective in social psychology. In G. Lindzey & E. Aronson (Eds.), *Handbook of social psychology* (Vol. 1, pp 137-230). New York: Random House.

Matlin, M., & Stang, D. J. (1978). *The Pollyana principle. Selectivity in language, memory and thought.* Cambridge, MA: Schenkman Publishing Company.

Mill, J. S. (1843). *A System of Logic.* London: Parker, Son, & Bourn.

Montgomery, H. (1986). *Information search and evaluative processes in decision making: a computer based process tracing study.* Unpublished manuscript.

Nisbett, E. R., Borgida, E., & Crandall, R. (1976). Popular induction is not necessarily informative. In J. S. Carroll & J. W. Payne (Eds.), *Cognition and social behavior* (pp. 115-135). New York: Lawrence Erlbaum.

Nisbett, E. R., & Ross, L. (1980). *Human inference: Strategies and shortcomings of social judgment.* Englewood Cliffs, NJ: Prentice-Hall.

Peeters, G. (1986). Good and evil as software of the brain. On psychological "immediates" underlying the metaphysical "ultimates". *Ultimate Reality and Meaning: Interdisciplinary Studies in Philosophy and Understanding, 9*,210-231.

Peeters, G. (1971). Positive-negative asymmetry: On cognitive consistency and positivity bias. *European Journal of Social Psychology, 1*, 455-474.

Rips, L. J. (1983). Cognitive processes in propositional reasoning. *Psychological Review, 90*, 38-71.

Rosch, E., & Mervis, C. B. (1975). Family resemblance: Studies in the internal structure of categories. *Cognitive Psychology, 7*, 573-605.

Ross, L. (1977). The intuitive psychologist and his shortcomings: Distortions in the attribution process. In L. Berkowitz (Ed.), *Advances in experimental social psychology* (Vol. 10, pp. 173-220). New York: Academic Press.

Shaklee, H. (1983). Human covariation judgment: Accuracy and strategy. *Learning and Motivation, 14*, 433-448.

Szmajke, A. (1984). Oddzialywanie informacji o stopniu dystynktywnosci i interpersonalnej powszechnosci zachowania na dokonywanie atrybucji przyczynowych. (Effect of distinctiveness and consensus information on causal attributions). *Przeglad Psychologiczny, 1*, 125-147.

Tversky, A., & Kahneman, D. (1974). Judgment under uncertainty: Heuristics and biases. *Science, 184*, 1124-1131.

Wason, P. C. (1968). On the failure to eliminate hypotheses ... A second look. In P. C. Wason & P. N. Johnson-Laird (Eds.), ***Thinking and reasoning*** (pp. 165-174). Penguin

Weiner, B. (1985). Spontaneous causal thinking. ***Psychological Bulletin, 97***, 74-84.

Wong, P. T. P., & Weiner, B. (1981). When do people ask why questions and the heuristics of attributional search. ***Journal of Personality and Social Psychology, 40***, 650-663.

Wyer, R. S., & Carlston, E. E. (1979). ***Social cognition, inference, and attribution.*** Hillsdale, NJ: Erlbaum.

PIAGETIAN THEORY RECONSIDERED:

AN INTERPRETIVE READING OF PIAGET

Gary Kose

Long Island University
Brooklyn, NY, U.S.A.

Patricia Heindel

College of Saint Elizabeth
Convent Station, NJ, U.S.A.

SUMMARY: Piaget's theory has been influential in psychological discussions of development and cognition. His theory is commonly considered a structural theory which posits the existence of logical-mathematical structures that direct the way the developing subject comes to know the world. This paper will argue that such a characterization of Piagetian theory is misleading. Instead, it is suggested that for Piaget, the central problem was to explain the formation of cognitive structures, and Genetic Epistemology was his unique philosophic solution to this problem, which stresses the importance of the constructive 'activity of the subject'. In light of this interpretation, the psychological implications of Piagetian theory are considered.

Introduction

In Jean Piaget's long and prolific career he has assumed many roles. In expounding a theory of cognitive development he raised philosophic questions by insisting on the importance of psychological states for explaining matters of epistemology. In accounting for the psychological nature of thought he stressed the influence of biological functions. And, when discussing the relationship between biology and psychology, he argued for the preeminence of logic and objective truth, and committed himself to scientific methodology. This interdisciplinary endeavor resulted in a body of literature that is rich but also ambiguous. It would be mistaken to reduce Piaget to any one role, be it epistemologist, psychologist, biologist or scientist. But how, then, should Piaget's theory be understood? To what field of inquiry does it properly belong, and how should it be evaluated.

The result of the ambiguous status of his theory can be easily seen. Piaget has had a limited impact on the disciplines of biology and philosophy, and among psychologists, many commentators take a narrow view of his work and restrict their critiques to his statements about psychological functioning without giving due consideration to the philosophical aspects of his theory. For example, psychologists who take an empiricist perspective see Piaget as an implicit nativist who posits a rationality, in the form of cognitive structures, within the psychological make-up of the developing subject (see Gelman & Baillargeon, 1983). Not surprisingly, Piaget's theory fails to stand up to the demands of empirical standards in establishing the existence of such non-empirical entities as cognitive structures. From a rationalist's perspective, Piaget is seen as a clandestine empiricist who gives too much credence to the actual experience of the subject in accounting for the development of rational thought. Here, Piaget's theory is rejected for its failure to recognize the need for natively given potentialities (for example see the Piaget-Chomsky debate in Piatelli-Palmarini, 1980). It is important to keep in mind that Piaget clearly intended to argue against empiricism and nativism in proposing his alternative *tertium quid*. There is no question about his intention; the more pertinent question concerns how the unique product of his intention, his Genetic Epistemology, should be understood and evaluated. Piaget's theory cannot be appreciated and critiqued within the confines of traditional empiricist and rationalist epistemologies that are still a part of contemporary psychological discourse; his theory must be approached on its own distinctive grounds.

Piaget and Structuralism

Piaget (1971) has defined Genetic Epistemology as the "attempt to explain knowledge, and in particular scientific knowledge, on the basis of its history, its sociogenesis, and especially the psychological origins of the notions and operations upon which it is based" (p. 1). This very broad definition is at the very least vague and has been described as incoherent (Hamlyn, 1971). Genetic Epistemology seems to accept that fundamental knowledge structures are logical and mathematical in nature, which allow for an objective understanding of the world, free from subjective distortions. Such structures seem to serve the teleological purpose of directing evolutionary and developmental processes. Yet, Genetic Epistemology also tries to maintain that such formal knowledge structures can only be known and understood through a careful examination of the course of individual psychological development. Numerous attempts to understand Piaget's seemingly circular enterprise have often transformed it beyond recognition. In the many attempts to establish empirical methods, replicate his original studies, and produce critiques, the central theoretical importance of Piaget's Genetic Epistemology has been lost. Perhaps the most common distortion of Piaget's endeavor has been to characterize Genetic Epistemology as a variant of twentieth century structuralism (Flavell, 1963; Reese & Overton, 1970; Wozniak, 1975; Broughton, 1981).

Structuralism itself is not easily understood, but it is more familiar than Genetic Epistemology. The roots of structuralism can be traced back to the rationalism of Descartes, and can be clearly seen in Kant's reaction to empiricism (Cassirer, 1953). Kant insisted that what we can know in terms of mental content is generated in an orderly and predictable way by the very structure of the human mind, rather than through reflection on experience. Structuralism can be seen as a reaction against empirical and positivistic approaches to human affairs. There are at least three general characteristics to any structuralist theory (Hawkes, 1977; Riegel, 1975). First, the focus of any structuralist theory is to explain the organizational properties of various types of human experience. For example, linguistic behavior, mathematical knowledge, and social functioning have been typical subjects for structural analyses. Secondly, structuralist theories imply a certain interiority and utilize a kind of dual level method of analysis which attempts to penetrate beneath the directly sensible, ever changing surface phenomenon to reveal latent structures (Wozniak, 1975). Such structures are then defined in terms of a stable system of meaningful relationships and juxtaposition. The third characteristic of structuralist theories is an explanatory value attributed to structures and a de-valuing of surface level experiences. Human activity, whether it is perceptual, motoric or representational, can only occur to the extent to which the activity is a realization of an underlying structure.

Piaget's theory can be placed within the French Structuralist tradition originating with the works of Emile Durkheim and Ferdinand de Saussure, in which social and linguistic reality were understood as a reflection of underlying organizational structures (Broughton, 1981). For example, de Saussure (1959) reformulated the study of linguistics from the encyclopedic task of categorizing the ever-changing features of language usage to a structural science, studying the system of rules underlying individual speech patterns. For de Saussure, language was a system in which isolated elements are arbitrary, and meaning emerges from the systematic relationship between linguistic elements. This underlying system served to generate specific, meaningful communications.

In viewing Piaget as a structuralist, it appears that his theory posits the existence of a system of cognitive structures to explain thought and the growth of knowledge. These structures would be formal and logical in nature, and would be distinct from the surface content of thought and knowledge. The changes in the qualitative complexity of such structures would determine variations in the way an individual encounters and comes to know the world. Many of the recent criticisms of Piaget's theory have been criticisms directed at this view of Piaget as a structuralist. Piaget has been criticized for his use of formal terms in explaining thought and action. He has also been criticized for stressing the logical nature of cognitive structures and for underestimating the importance of the activities and experiences of the subject in the growth of knowledge. And, further, he has been attacked for neglecting the influence of social and cultural factors on performance (see Gellman & Baillargeon, 1983 for a review). In summary, these dissatisfactions with Piaget's theory are dissatisfactions that can be raised against structuralism's tendency to undermine individual action and contextual experience in explaining human affairs and knowledge.

Piagetian Theory Deconstructed

While Piaget's Genetic Epistemology may be understood as a type of twentieth century structuralism, such an understanding obscures several important aspects of his theory. An examination of Piaget's writings reveal that he was a very special structuralist, if he could be considered a structuralist at all. His short work entitled *Structuralism* (1970) can hardly be read as a manifesto. Here, rather than proclaiming allegiance, Piaget distinguished himself from the structuralist movement. Piaget began this work, as he had many other works, by rejecting any attempt to understand human activities through strictly empirical means. In this regard, he recognized the importance of considering organizational structures. In particular, he noted the quality of 'wholeness' as the defining mark of any structure. This distinction was not to deny that structures have elements or segregated parts, but the elements of a structure are subordinate to laws, and it is in terms of these laws that the structure *qua* whole or system was to be defined. However, for Piaget, it was insufficient to merely describe such structures and the laws that define them. Piaget's recognition of wholeness was not intended as a theoretical contribution (as it was for Gestalt Psychology), rather the idea of whole, self-sufficient structures raised a good many problems. Two principle problems which concerned Piaget (1970) were understanding the nature and the formation of structures (pp. 6-10).

These problems came up in Piaget's discussion of logical and mathematical structures. Piaget pointed out the limits of such formal systems to adequately explain their nature, and he argued that logical and mathematical structures are maintained and understood only through their operations or functions. Again, in discussing linguistic structures, Piaget took Chomsky to task for ignoring the question of the formation of his deep level structures by opting for a vague form of nativism. And, in discussing psychological structures, Piaget argued that the Gestalt notion of field theory was inadequate to explain a full array of structural phenomena and ignored the role of the active subject in forming organizational wholes. Thus, it appears that Piaget was not committed to generating another structuralist theory but rather, saw that structuralism posed central problems which required further study and understanding.

To understand Piaget's reaction to these problems, one must come to terms with the distinctive aspects of his Genetic Epistemology. In addition to cautioning against merely describing structures and their internal relationships, Piaget (1970) stressed the necessity to understand "the logical procedures or natural processes by which the whole (structure) is formed" (p. 9). In this sense, Piaget proposed a method for studying systems or structures that was distinctly different from the descriptive method of structuralism. In Piaget's Genetic Epistemology, the methodological stance involves an examination of the formative process involved in the construction of a structural system of knowledge. This method was made familiar through Piaget's developmental studies of the structural domains of time, space, causality, etc. Through the examination of children's awareness of these domains, Piaget hoped to reveal important epistemological findings regarding the formation of these structural domains. However, in addition to this methodological stance, the central tenet of Genetic Epistemology maintains that the transformations that occur throughout the formative process of a structural domain come to define the structure in its most elaborate form. In contrast to structuralism, where structures are defined in terms of the systematic relationships that exist between constituent elements, Genetic Epistemology proposes that structures of knowledge are defined in terms of the transformations and operations that establish such relationships. Piaget (1970) writes, "Were it not for the idea of transformation, structures would lose all explanatory import, since they would collapse into static forms" (p. 12). Piaget goes on to describe how the wholistic, autonomous, self-sufficient qualities of structures are inherent in any set of transformations. And, in essence, it is the transformational acts which define a structure, not the structure which defines the acts. Piaget (1970) writes, "If the character of structured wholes depend on their laws of composition, these laws must of their very nature be structuring: it is the constant duality, or bipolarity, of always being simultaneously structuring and structured that accounts for the success of the notion of law or rule employed by structuralists " (p. 10). In this sense, in Piaget's Genetic Epistemology, a structure is understood as an act that sustains itself and gives rise to the appearance of a wholistic, autonomous and constant structural system. This position seems to be an anathema to the central tenets of structuralism.

The distinctive quality of Genetic Epistemology can be clearly seen in Piaget's description of a very simple example. Piaget (1971) gave an account of how a young child playing with pebbles discovered a characteristic of the number system (pp. 16-17). In this example, the child lines up a row of pebbles and counts them from left to right getting a sum of ten. Then the child, just for fun, counts them from right to left to see what number he would get and is amazed that he gets ten. Next, the child puts the pebbles in a circle and counts them, again getting a sum of ten. The child discovered that no matter how the pebbles were arranged, when he counts them the sum comes to ten. In this way, Piaget described how the child came to know the commutativity of the number system, i.e., that the sum is independent of the order. For Piaget, what was important in this example was not the child's appreciation of the system of relationships existing between the pebbles; although the child could appreciate an aspect of the relationships after his experience. Rather, what was essential for Piaget was the transformational acts performed in arranging and counting the pebbles. It was the repetition of arranging and counting that defined for the child this structural feature of numbers. Further, what was crucial for understanding this aspect of numerical knowledge was not unobservable, formal or deep in any way. In this example, the knowledge of commutativity was immanent in what a structuralist might call the surface level of experience. This knowledge existed in the actions of the child.

So far we have argued that Piaget was not a structuralist. His Genetic Epistemology does not posit structures as an explanation for actions, thoughts or human knowledge. Instead, Genetic Epistemology takes as its theoretical object of study the nature and the formation of knowledge structures. Much of Piaget's work has been directed towards understanding the nature and formation of physical and logical knowledge structures. However, this should not be seen as a valorization of physical or logical structures in determining psychological processes and functions. In fact, the inverse seems to be the case. Knowledge structures, for Piaget (1970), were understood as "simply a system of transformations" whose roots are operational and depend on the formation of instruments of transformation. In concluding his work entitled *Structuralism*, Piaget recognized the relative importance of the structuralist movement. He states, "structuralism is a method ... whose doctrinal consequences have been quite various. Because it is a method, its applicability is limited; ... it admits the legitimacy of other methods. Far from ousting genetic or functionalist studies, it rather implements them by giving them the benefits of its very powerful instruments of analysis" (p. 143). It would seem that Genetic Epistemology provides one such method which is a needed supplement for an understanding of the origins and formation of structures.

Piaget Reconsidered

The argument, that Piaget was not a structuralist, has been presented in a strong form. However, Piaget was concerned with structures. He was concerned with the problems they presented, and also, he found that formal structures were necessary at the level of theoretical explanation (Piaget, 1968). Piaget (1968) maintained that in order to explain intelligent conduct we need constructive, rather than reductive explanations that rely on structural, abstract models. Such models, he stated, "set a certain standard of legitimacy and precision to constructive explanations by stressing the activity of the subject" (p. 181). But what was most fundamental to Piaget's theoretical enterprise was a focus on the 'activity of the subject'. In Genetic Epistemology objective structures of knowledge are examined in terms of their origin and formation in the activity of the subject. And specifically, it is the subject's actions which are crucial in gaining access to such structures. This point about the activity of the subject can be seen at various levels of intelligent conduct, be it the reactions of an infant searching for a toy, the motoric acts of a child arranging and counting pebbles, or the act of deduction used to establish conceptual coherence. For Piaget, this point about the activity of the subject was observed at a psychological level but most importantly, this was an epistemological point that applied in all domains. Throughout his work, Piaget maintained that his primary interest was in the 'epistemic subject' and not necessarily the actual psychological subject. Piaget's observations and writings were directed towards showing how the subject's activities construct knowledge; this endeavor was extended to domains of knowledge, such as logic, that were traditionally thought to be free from subjective and contingent distortions. In this way Piaget's work utilized psychological functioning to make an epistemological point. It is this strange melding of action and knowledge, of the empirical and the rational, of function and structure that makes Genetic Epistemology so difficult to understand; but nonetheless, it is this melding that distinguishes Piagetian theory. As Piaget (1970) wrote, "in order to understand man we must know something of epistemology, and in order to understand epistemology we must have a knowledge of man" (p. 525).

Among psychological theorists, Piaget has long been considered a type of 'enlightenment' figure stressing rational structures of thought and a universal course of cognitive development, in contrast to more functional accounts of thought and knowledge. However, when his theory is freed from the characterization of structuralism and attention is focused on the activity of the subject as a unit of analysis, Genetic Epistemology can be seen in a new light and two vistas, previously ignored, are opened for further consideration. The first concerns the relationship between Piagetian theory and functional approaches to thought and knowledge. Structural and functional theories have been typically viewed as incompatible, and Piaget's theory, when viewed as a structural theory, has been seen as antithetical to any functional approach. However, it has been argued that Piaget has always had a strong commitment to consider the importance of function in understanding the nature of structure (Beilin, 1983). In his last work Piaget (1977) returned to his early emphasis on the polarity between assimilation and accommodation as two aspects of the functional activity of the knowing subject in articulating the notion of equilibration. Also, it appears that the Genevan School has been extending Piaget's legacy in just this direction. As Inhelder (1978) writes, "You will perhaps be surprised that we are moving away from the epistemic subject, which for decades was our concern, in order to further our interests in the psychological subject: the child in his progressive discoveries of means to resolve problems that are indissociable from specific contexts" (cited in Bullinger & Chatillon, 1983, p. 232). In a recent review, Bullinger and Chatillon (1983) present an overview of this recent work examining the functional relationship between thought and practical activity. It would appear that Piaget's studies in Genetic Epistemology implemented and necessitate a thorough examination of psychological functioning.

A second vista concerns an explication of the nature of the 'activity of the subject'. Since the Cognitive Revolution in the 1950s and 1960s, and the decline of behavioral analyses, there has been an emphasis on descriptive accounts of information in thought, memory and perception. Such descriptions have become the *sine qua non* of information processing models. These descriptions typically exclude or make vague reference to the activities of the subject. It would appear that from the perspective of Genetic Epistemology there is a need for a return to the study of action. From what Piaget has written concerning the epistemic subject, action was interpreted in the broadest sense, including everything from the muscular movements of the eye and hand, to the operations of thought. While Piaget's theory stressed the importance of action in thought and knowledge, Piaget did not distinguish types of action, nor did he examine the specific influence of various types of action on knowledge structures (see Beilin, 1977). Furthermore, within the purview of Genetic Epistemology, an examination of action would not be limited to an examination of objective, physical acts. For Piaget, it was the activity of the subject that was crucial in coming to knowledge, that is, actions within the perspective of the subject. Again because of his focus on the epistemic subject, Piaget did not address issues concerning subjective aspects of action, intentionality and consciousness. Despite a theoretical foundation that implicates such issues, Piaget's theory did not address them. As early as 1953, the phenomenologist Aron Gurwitsch recognized that Piaget's work set forth ideas that were essential to attaining an objective understanding of the world; however, he pointed out that Piaget had not provided an account of how such an understanding was experienced in consciousness. For Gurwitsch, what was required was an integration of Piaget's findings with studies in phenomenology. It is interesting that in Piaget's (1977), last work he was concerned with the reality status of his equilibration model, (that is, in terms of psychological functioning), and asked about the child's experience of conflict and disturbances in action and thought. It would seem that an examination of the subjective aspects of action is one way of extending themes in Genetic Epistemology.

Theories very often take on a life and momentum of their own, beyond that of their creators. As a result, a theory may be subjected to a variety of interpretations, and it becomes difficult, if not impossible, to determine which interpretation is correct and true to the spirit of the theory. To the extent that a theory moves beyond any one theoretician, set of studies or historical setting, determining which is the correct interpretation becomes a moot point. Perhaps, theoretical interpretations should be judged in terms of their appropriateness and the extent to which they tap sources of richness from within the theoretical enterprise. This paper has addressed the issue of interpretation relevant to Piagetian theory. It has been argued that, contrary to popular interpretations, Piaget's work does not fit in neatly among contemporary structuralist theories. Structuralist interpretations lead to a host of insurmountable problems and limit the usefulness of the theory. Further, it was suggested that such an interpretation is not consonant with Piaget's writings on structuralism, nor is it consistent with the direction of some of the most recent work that was motivated by Piaget. Characterizing Piaget's work within a structuralist framework has the effect of creating a paper tiger out of the theory and obscuring aspects of the theory that could be influential in contemporary discourse. Instead, it has been suggested that Piaget's orientation, his Genetic Epistemology, is best understood as a post-structuralist theory reacting to problems raised by structuralism. Piaget's methodological orientation was to examine the formative process associated with knowledge structures; and his understanding of such structures was based on an emphasis of actions and transformations. It seems that the primary focus of his endeavor was to establish an epistemological point, but correlatively, his endeavor established a need for psychological investigation and theory. For Piaget, the activity of the knowing subject has consequences for the establishment of knowledge whose truth transcends the experience of the subject. It would seem that this type of interpretation provides a richer context for an appreciation and evaluation of Piaget's Genetic Epistemology.

References

Beilin, H. (1981). Language and thought: Thistles among the sedums. In I. E. Sigel, D. M. Brodzinsky, & R. M. Golinkoff (Eds.), *New directions in Piagetian theory and practice* (pp. 41-71). Hillsdale, NJ: Erlbaum.

Beilin, H. (1983). The new functionalism and Piaget's program. In E. K. Scholnick (Ed.), *New trends in conceptual representation: Challenges to Piaget's theory?* (pp. 3-40). Hillsdale, NJ: Erlbaum.

Broughton, J. M. (1981). Piaget's structural development psychology: Piaget and structuralism. *Human Development, 24,* 78-109.

Bullinger, A., & Chatillon, J. -F. (1983). Recent theory and research of the Genevan school. In P. Mussen (Ed.), *Handbook of child psychology, Vol. 3, Cognitive Development.* (pp. 231-263). New York: Wiley.

Cassirer, E. (1953). *Substance and function, and Einstein's theory of relativity.* New York: Dover Publishers.

de Saussure, F. (1959). *Course in general linguistics.* New York: The Philosophical Library, Inc.

Flavell, J. (1963). *The developmental psychology of Jean Piaget.* New York: Van Nostrand.

Gelman, R., & Baillargeon, R. (1983). A review of some Piagetian concepts. In P. Mussen (Ed.), *Handbook of child psychology, Vol 3, Cognitive Development.* (pp. 167-231). New York: Wiley.

Gurwitsch, A. (1953). *The field of consciousness.* (4th ed., 1982). Pittsburgh, PA: Duquesne University Press.

Hamlyn, D. W. (1971). Epistemology and cognitive development. In T. Mischel (Ed.), *Cognitive development and epistemology* (pp. 3-24). New York: Academic Press.

Hawkes, T. (1977). *Structuralism and semiotics.* Berkeley, CA: University of California Press.

Piaget, J. (1968). Explanation in psychology and psychophysical parallelism. In P. Fraisse & J. Piaget (Eds.), *Experimental psychology: Its scope and methods* (pp. 153-182). New York: Basic Books.

Piaget, J. (1970). *Structuralism.* New York: Basic Books.

Piaget, J. (1971). *Genetic epistemology.* New York: Norton.

Piaget, J. (1977). *The development of thought: Equilibration of cognitive structures.* New York: Viking Press.

Piatelli-Palmarini, M. (Ed.). (1980). *Language and meaning: The debate between Jean Piaget and Noam Chomsky.* Cambridge, MA: Harvard University Press.

Reese, H. W., & Overton, W. F. (1970). Models of development and theories of development. In L. R. Goulet & P. B. Baltes (Eds.), *Life-span developmental psychology: Research and theory* (pp. 116-150). New York: Academic Press.

Riegel, K. F. (1975). Structure and transformation in modern intellectual history. In K. F. Riegel & G. C. Rosenwald (Eds.), *Structure and transformation: Developmental and historical aspects* (pp. 3-24). New York: Wiley.

Wozniak, R. H. (1975). Dialecticism and structuralism: The philosophical foundation of Soviet psychology and Piagetian cognitive developmental theory. In K. F. Riegel & G. C. Rosenwald (Eds.), *Structure and transformation: Developmental and historical aspects* (pp. 25-48). New York: Wiley.

THE PRACTICE OF HEALTH PSYCHOLOGY AND BEHAVIORAL MEDICINE: WHITHER THEORY?

Henderikus J. Stam

University of Calgary
Calgary, Alberta, Canada

SUMMARY: If theories give form to our social activities, then how might one interpret the absence of theoretical foundations in a professional community? Health psychology is a recent case of a scholarly community in search of theory. This paper examines the professional claims made by this area and the social context that has generated these claims. A comparison between health psychology and its unwitting partner, family medicine, indicates that professional status has preceded the development of a theoretical and practical knowledge base. Historically, North American psychology has followed this pattern. I conclude that the absence of theory in health psychology is a strategic act designed to ensure that its understandings of health and illness do not clash with those of the health care professions.

Introduction

This paper will examine the 'emerging' fields of health psychology and behavioral medicine for their theoretical and jurisdictional claims.[1] In doing so I will attempt to demonstrate that health psychology and behavioral medicine have (a) made very weak theoretical claims for their basis as sub-disciplines, (b) that there is a particular social context that has generated these knowledge claims, (c) that these same claims are shared by family medicine, and (d) that there is a similarity between the emergence of psychology at the turn of the century and the current popularity of health psychology. Finally, I wish to examine the implications for both theory and practice of this development of subdisciplines in psychology. The aim is to convince that psychology itself is subject to the conceptual constraints of praxically different historical contexts.

---

[1]Unless otherwise indicated, 'health psychclogy' and 'health psychologist' shall be used broadly to include 'behavioral medicine' and the practitioner of behavioral medicine. Although this violates many of the definitional lines laid out by the two groups, in practice they are not nearly as distinguishable. Furthermore, the arguments in this paper can readily be applied to both areas and both groups of practitioners.

Origins

Several commentators have noted that health psychology is currently one of the fastest growing areas in North American psychology (e.g., Stone et al., 1987). The American Psychological Association division of health psychology was founded in 1978. Shortly thereafter new journals, such as Health Psychology, were founded that devoted themselves entirely to health problems from a psychological vantage point. Dozens of edited books on the subject have appeared in the last decade. The recent publication of textbooks devoted solely to health psychology testifies to its solid establishment as a sub-discipline (e.g., Taylor, 1986).

Likewise, behavioral medicine, health psychology's sometime competitor, sometime co-habitant in the discipline, was launched in February 1977 at a Yale conference. In 1978 the Academy of Behavioral Medicine Research and the Society of Behavioral Medicine were both founded. By that year almost 2500 psychologists (or 5% of the membership of APA) were on the faculties of U.S. medical schools (Matarazzo, 1980).

To what can we attribute this flurry of research in the late 1970's? According to its practitioners, the time was simply ripe: Taylor argued that "our current state of knowledge has virtually demanded the development of the field of health psychology" (1986, p. 3). Matarazzo (1980, p. 814) believed that "it seems obvious to me that as the field which has the longest history of involvement in the study of human behavior, psychology has the scientific knowledge base, the practical applied experience, and the educational institutional supports to begin immediately to make important contributions to health psychology." The proponents of health psychology also mentioned the importance of opportunities in contributing to health care and especially in obtaining grant money and other financial supports (e.g., Weiss, 1982). Runyan, DeVellis, DeVellis, & Hochbaum (1982) exclaimed that "psychologists entering the field of public health are much like the explorers of past centuries landing on new continents" (p. 170). Weiss (1982) proclaimed "if there ever was a time of opportunity for Health Psychology, that time is *now*!...Never in the history of psychology has such a unique opportunity presented itself - the opportunity to develop effective strategies to treat and prevent disease and to promote health - as we have today" (p. 81).

Behavioral medicine has also had its town criers. Gentry (1984), for example asked "why has behavioral medicine surged to the forefront as regards a paradigm for either empirical research or clinical application?" One of the reasons he proffered was "the general maturity of research in the social and behavioral sciences" (p. 6). Lang (1980) too was enthusiastic: "experimental psychology is potentially one of the scientific pillars of modern general medicine, as are now her sister disciplines - physiology, anatomy, and pharmacology" (p. xv).

One can readily multiply the examples. I should like to point to the obvious disparity between these proclamations, the theories supporting them and the practice implied therein. To do this, I will begin by examining how these areas define themselves and from where they derive their theoretical underpinnings.

Theoretical Claims

Health psychologists generally rely on this definition proferred by Matarazzo (1980):

> *Health psychology* is the aggregate of the specific educational, scientific, and professional contributions of the discipline of psychology to the promotion and maintenance of health, the prevention and treatment of illness, and the identification of etiologic and diagnostic correlates of health, illness, and related dysfunction (p. 815).

This definition simply argues that health psychology is any aspect of psychology applied to health and illness concerns. Matarazzo (1980) differentiates this from 'behavioral health', which is the

> interdisciplinary field dedicated to promoting a philosophy of health that stresses ***individual responsibility*** in the application of behavioral and biomedical science knowledge and techniques to the ***maintenance*** of health and the ***prevention*** of illness and dysfunction by a variety of self-initiated individual or shared activities (p. 813).

The rather unusual term 'behavioral health' is obviously meant to include psychological concerns in what traditionally has been the public health domain.

Behavioral medicine, on the other hand, is clearly interdisciplinary in outlook although psychologists were instrumental in its foundation. The term itself was first used in 1973 in the title of a book edited by Birk. It was called *Biofeedback: Behavioral Medicine.* Several conferences in quick succession attempted to define behavioral medicine, with an amended definition proposed by Schwartz and Weiss in 1978 that eventually came to be widely cited. This amended definition was deemed more satisfactory than previous definitions because it explicitly included reference to the notion of the integration of thought and technology. It defines behavioral medicine as

> the interdisciplinary field concerned with the development and integration of behavioral and biomedical science knowledge and techniques relevant to health and illness and the application of this knowledge and these techniques to prevention, diagnosis, treatment and rehabilitation (Schwartz & Weiss, 1978a, p. 250).

There are also several competing terms in the fray. These include 'psychological medicine', 'psychosomatic medicine', 'comprehensive medicine', and 'clinical health psychology' (Matarazzo, 1980; Gentry, 1984). The battles fought over the precise definitions of these terms are not always polite and are reminiscent of psychology's earlier definitional battles over its status as a science at the turn of the century, especially in the United States. One reason that this sparring occurs at all, in my view, is that there is no substantive theory underlying health psychology or behavioral medicine. The level of definition is the level of complexity at which health psychologists debate.

In their various justificationary papers psychologists have attempted to specify the bases for these areas in a more precise fashion. For example, George Stone (1982) argued that health psychology and the health system should be defined broadly and should be directed "not only to the individual whose health is at issue, but to the whole complex of institutions and forces within which the pursuit of health takes place" (p. 2). Aside from the health care system, these latter also include political systems, sociocultural support systems, planning agencies, and third party organizations. He argued that health psychologists should be concerned with the transactions that occur among the different elements of the system - the exchange of various kinds of resources including money, goods, services, information, and regulation.

Behavioral medicine is also viewed as broad and inclusive in its areas of expertise. Virtually no medical or social science is excluded in discussions of behavioral medicine's interdisciplinary thrust. Furthermore, psychology and medicine are viewed as equal status disciplines. Schwartz and Weiss (1978b) suggested a matrix approach for targeting problems in behavioral medicine which emphasizes the respective contributions of various disciplines. It suggests that each of a number of disciplines (e.g., psychology, medicine, sociology, anthropology, physiology, etc.) contributes equally to the understanding of specific medical problems such as myocardial infarction, asthma, and so on.

Although some are unhappy with such a matrix view (e.g., Gentry, 1984), this model is probably a more accurate model of behavioral medicine. It suggests a *multidisciplinary* rather than interdisciplinary approach with each discipline contributing in a somewhat parallel fashion.

Thus far I have said little about the explicit theoretical claims of these sub-disciplines. Although there are occasional references to coping theories or psychosomatic theories (e.g., Stone, 1980), there are in fact only two interrelated positions which are consistently raised as foundational theories for health psychology.

Systems theory. The first is adaptation theory or more generally, systems theory. On this view, health psychologists' should study "the physiological adaptive mechanisms of the body as they respond to challenges or hazards in the form of physical or chemical insults." The theory then "generalizes the principles derived from this study into levels of more complex behavior" (Stone, 1980, p. 67). Some health psychologists have argued that this view allows us to ignore strictly physiological theories since they would fall outside of the purview of health psychology. The systems view is rarely, if ever, applied to actual problems in health psychology however nor has it even been fully developed as a theoretical perspective. Claims made by health psychologists under the system model are typically functional in nature. This is not surprising since the limited application of the systems model to psychological phenomena is in fact functionalist inasmuch as systems conceptions adhere to the three necessary conditions for a functionalist model (Evans-Pritchard, 1951): First, systems are natural phenomena with interdependent levels that serve to maintain the system; second, within systems theory social events are reduced to empirical relationships that are predictable, and third, systems theory is ahistorical about the makeup of systems. In this sense systems theory may not at all be at odds with the biomedical model. Within the context of health and health systems, such functional views espouse a concept of personhood as a well-tuned machine rather than a sentient being (cf. McLean, 1986).

Defining theoretical terms in health psychology is made no easier by claiming one has a systems model. Since functionalism is one of the main theoretical foundations of modern psychology, rooted as the latter is in behavioral and cognitive traditions, it is not surprising to see functionalism appear in health psychology, albeit unannounced. As in psychology generally, theoretical terms in health psychology are functionally defined. The meaning of these terms can be specified by describing a functional role within the theory (Clark, 1983; Putnam, 1975).

But even if one were to overcome such implicit functionalism, could systems theory provide health psychology with a useful perspective? Anthony Giddens (1979) claims that systems technology has as an implicit agenda the placement of human activity within control systems. Giddens has serious reservations about the application of systems theory to human conduct and specifically argues against its use in the social sciences. Instead, he argues that human actors in social systems are reflexive and that their self-regulation is not of the sort that apply to mechanical systems. Even von Bertalanffy (1968) noted that systems theory might lead to a technocratic society and ought to be understood and applied with "humanistic concerns" (cf. McLean, 1986). If health psychology were to adopt systems theory in practice, it is not clear what it would gain in sophistication of analysis beyond its current functionalist bent.

Biopsychosocial theory. The second major position frequently reported as justification for health psychology is the biopsychosocial position. In this case virtually everyone who cites this view refers to a paper by George Engel published in *Science* in 1977. Engel's major concern however was not to develop new theory but to critique the medical model or 'biomedicine'. Only the latter half of his paper concerned itself with the biopsychosocial model and most of this is by way of example rather than a delineation of the model. In fact, he does not even define the term but instead argues that the "model must...take into account the patient, the social context in which he lives, and the complementary system devised by society to deal with the disruptive effects of illness, that is, the physician's role and health care system" (p. 132). He argues that the dichotomy between 'disease' and certain 'problems of living' is clear neither for patient nor physician. As an example he describes the case of grief. It exemplifies, for Engel, a phenomenon in which psychological factors are primary yet it constitutes a discrete syndrome with a relatively predictable symptomatology which includes bodily and psychological disturbances. What is biopsychosocial about this? For Engel, a biopsychosocial model would merely take all these factors into account. "The psychobiological unity of man requires that the physician accept the responsibility to evaluate whatever problems the patient presents and recommend a course of action" (p. 133). In closing his paper however Engel equates the adoption of a biopsychosocial perspective with a 'general-systems' approach. "For medicine, systems theory provides a conceptual approach suitable not only for the proposed biopsychosocial concept of disease but also for studying disease and medical care as interrelated processes" (p. 134).

What could be the possible reasons for the heavy citation of Engel's paper? It is essentially empty of theory and contains vague claims of promise for a model never fully described. Some effort has already gone to clarifying and extending the biopsychosocial model in an attempt to strengthen its foundations and applicability (e.g., Jasnoski & G. Schwartz, G. Schwartz, 1985; M. Schwartz & Wiggins, 1986). Most citations to Engel's paper nevertheless treat it as a conclusive statement. I would argue that its very emptiness of theory is apropos. Without being specific, health psychology can adopt such models as rhetorical devices and as empty jargon.

Health Psychology as Rhetoric - The Social Context

Both Burke (1969) and Shotter (1987) have argued that rhetoric functions to establish commonality. Rhetoric concerns itself not only with the techniques of argumentation or persuasion but with the shared understanding necessary for argumentation to proceed. Hence the importance of establishing topics and the need to specify common objects or topics of discourse. Furthermore, embedded in these sayings and doings are "methods or procedures which work to render the point of our sayings and doings intelligible, both to others and ourselves" (Shotter, 1987, p. 285). On this view, rhetoric concerns itself with "the study of those aspects of language usage aimed simply at 'giving shape or form' to the thought and activity of the human world" (Shotter, 1987, p. 284).

The construction of the common objects or topics of discourse in health psychology is most of what passes for theory. The constitutional problems have thus far preoccupied its adherents. This derives directly from the practices of health psychologists. Present activities are directed into an already structured context. This context is an organized setting created formatively by past activity. This is what Shotter (1987) called the "self-specifying nature of everyday practical activities" (p. 284-285).

What are these past and present practical activities in health psychology? North American psychologists have been involved in health care settings since the turn of the century. In December of 1911, the American Psychological Association established a committee consisting of Shephard Franz and John Watson together with a pathologist and psychiatrists Adolph Meyer and Morton Prince to consider how psychology could contribute to medical education and practice. The three physicians agreed that a psychology, somewhat reoriented from its then current preoccupation with reaction time measurement and introspection, could make essential contributions to medicine. Watson took the position that psychology had much to offer and was not properly appreciated (Stone, 1980). In 1928, Bott surveyed medical curricula from 1912 to 1928. He concluded that there was increasing recognition of the importance of prevention in mental health as well as the growing belief that psychological factors influenced life adjustments pivotal for health (Bott, 1928).

These examples can be multiplied for the remainder of the twentieth century (see Stone, 1980) and illustrate the obvious point that psychologists have had a long-standing interest in health. Health psychology is not proclaiming a new trend in the late 1970's. By 1955, 346 psychologists were employed in medical schools in the United States and in 1964 there were 993 (Stone, 1980). Without the formative activities of generations of psychologists it is unlikely that health psychology would be where it is today. Nevertheless, the emphasis of today's health psychologist is different from his or her predecessor.

There are two events that might be worthy of examination to help explain the rapidity of expansion in health psychology, at least in North America. The first concerns the number of Ph.D's graduating yearly in North America. As recent APA publications and reports have indicated (e.g., Howard et al., 1986), Ph.D.s in psychology were granted at an accelerating rate from 1965 to the early 1980s. (There is currently some levelling in this trend.) New professional schools of psychology opened in the 1970's and competed for students with established universities.

Typically these professional programs produced practitioners rather than researchers or academics. At the same time, traditional job markets (clinical and academic) have shrunk and clinical practice is being shaped by strong marketplace pressures (see special issue, APA Monitor, January 1986).

Coincident with this trend is a fundamental shift in the nature of medicine in the United States. These changes are complex and were initiated by two developments, a larger supply of physicians and improved insurance coverage. This was followed by Medicare-Medicaid reforms which led to increased cash flows and the inevitable emergence of for-profit health care organizations (Ginzberg, 1986; Relman, 1987). Thus it was possible for psychologists to enter health care settings more freely during the 1970's.

In 1968 William Schofield, a professor of psychiatry and psychology at the University of Minnesota, was asked by the APA Board of Directors to examine the potential for psychology of what was then the new health insurance. He interviewed officials of federal health agencies in 1968 and reported in 1969 the "tremendous potential for psychology in the broad domain of health and illness." This was at a time when Schofield himself claimed that "only a smattering of psychologists have interested themselves in clearly medical nonpsychiatric problems" (Fisher, 1986, p. 16).

These practices created the context for the emergence of health psychology in the late 1970's. They also belie the repeated dictum that health psychology had special theoretical and research foundations to offer to the health care system. Obvious structural changes accompanied this emergence; the rhetoric followed. Psychologists were faced with an opportunity to expand their practice; the need to develop models for the new settings led to the hurried and uncritical acceptance of such notions as biopsychosocial medicine. This is of course also consistent with certain views within contemporary sociology wherein professions are construed as modes of occupational control rather than vocations. Professionals in turn attempt to preserve priviledge through the exercise of social closure. A profession's knowledge base is developed not as the disinterested pursuit of 'truth' but instead functions as a strategy of market regulation (Turner, 1986). Hence claims to the validity and significance of psychological knowledge in health care settings are an important determinant in legitimating psychologists' authority. As Turner (1986, p. 274) has argued, "changes in beliefs and practices occur when there is a gap between available social positions and the supply of qualified personnel such that these 'surplus' actors are forced to innovate to secure new markets, clients and rewards." But psychology is not the only profession attempting to expand its influence in health care.

The 'Other' Profession - Family Medicine

In family medicine there is an interesting parallel development to that of health psychology. Consider the following quote:

> In order to deal with many of the problems confronting them, family physicians must accept the idea 'that illness includes a patient's failure on the job, deviant behavior, and unhappiness in addition to pain and organic pathology.' Residents must also develop skills and attitudes 'along the lines of Engel's psychobiomedical model'" (Kunitz, 1983, p. 429-430).[2]

Family medicine, at the same time as psychology, was redefining disease, but for its own purposes, not those of psychologists. Furthermore, it also expanded the definition of family. Rather than accepting the typical conception of nuclear family, physicians in family medicine stated that they ought to be concerned with the 'primary group' which includes the family and any intimate associates. Proclaimed one family physician:

> The ***individual*** can no longer be seen as the only significant object of attention for the family physician or the health care team. Equally deserving of attention are the ***primary groups***, particularly the family. However, roommates, close friends, or intimate associates are also included. The ***primary group*** is an intimate, continuing, personal association on a face-to-face basis determined by degree of intimacy rather than proximity or complementary role status. Intervention at this level, or at other levels, may include any number of physical, psychological, social, or cultural factors involving disease and health (Johnson, 1975, p. 116).

Family medicine has expanded its definition of disease and family not only to claim new territory for itself but also, according to Kunitz (1983), because its practitioners are those that are attracted to this specialty because they already hold such 'liberal' views about the nature of disease. In particular he argues that, for family medicine, specialty status within medicine was achieved before a substantive body of knowledge existed on which to base it. This latter claim could readily be made of health psychology.

The emergence of psychological and social problems as a focus of family medicine shares certain features with psychology's emergent interest in health. In particular, the changing structures of modern medicine prepared both professions for the foray into the psychological and social

---

[2]Interestingly, Engel's term 'biopsychosocial' has been transformed into 'psychobiomedical'. One of Engel's purposes in writing his paper was to dispose of the notion of biomedicine. It is also important to note that most other medical specialties have frowned on Engel's work and have on occasion actively denounced the intended departure from a biomedical model (Smith, 1970; Thomas, 1978).

realms of health care. If anything, the parallel cases of these two disciplines makes obvious the rhetorical function of their proclamations of knowledge and expertise.

Early Twentieth-Century Psychology - The Historical Context

There is a second, perhaps less obvious, parallel case I would like to sketch. An examination of the founding of North American psychology at the turn of the century leads to similar conclusions about the practices of the first psychologists and the use of rhetorical devices to proclaim disciplinary territory. As Danziger has pointed out in his paper on the social origins of modern psychology, American psychologists proclaimed that experimental psychology would "supply the fundamental laws governing all human activity, irrespective of context." (Danziger, 1979, p. 35). It would become the "master science" from which all other social sciences drew their principles. Psychologists themselves were very concerned to provide the technical competence to deal appropriately with the problems of an expanding industrial nation. Universities were largely in the control of business interests or politicians and appointees who represented such interests. The self-definition of these early psychologists and the definition of the nature of their field of action were mutually complementary (Daniziger, 1979).

This brief synopsis of early twentieth century psychology has implications for how we might view the development of health psychology. New scholarly or professional communities, characterized by new intellectual interests, seek legitimation through targeting those groups most immediately concerned with the life or death of the new discipline. Danziger illustrates this in the case of the founding of American scientific psychology by describing the attempts at legitimation through an appeal to the industrial and business interests of the U.S.

How would health psychology fit within such an analysis? Health psychology is heavily dependent on physicians, and the health care system in general, for its legitimation. Without the tacit if not overt approval of these groups, health psychologists would have no access to patients, hospitals or health care settings. Therefore, health psychology's existence must not be threatened by the gate-keepers of medicine. And it follows that health psychologists cannot afford to theorize or proclaim practices antagonistic to these gate-keepers.

Discussion

In order to dispell the notion that the purpose of this paper is entirely negative, I would like to examine several issues which might give shape to further theory. First of all, I would hardly suggest that psychology should *not* be involved in health issues. Psychologists have been, are now and likely will be involved in the health care system in the future. Instead, I would like to focus on the relation between theory and practice in the health care setting. The rhetorical proclamations of health psychologists and the lack of a substantial theory make it virtually certain that medical problems will be viewed by psychologists as precisely that, *medical* problems. Their structure is non-problematic, ahistorical and acultural.

This effect can be observed within most of the areas of health care that psychologists have investigated. I will briefly allude to one area where the focus is obviously psychological, namely, that of physician-patient communication. From a linguistic and sociolinguistic perspective, information exchange in medical settings can be construed as a series of elaborations and condensations. Information is not only elicited by a physician but also negotiated (e.g., Tannen & Wallat, 1986). Psychologists, however, have typically adopted the medical profession's concern with patient-physician interaction, namely an emphasis on the communication skills of the physician and their relationship to satisfaction and compliance (e.g., DiMatteo, Hays & Prince, 1986). The social nature of the relationship is taken as given, that is, as defined by the medical profession.

If anything, the absence of a theoretical foundation guarantees that the practices of psychologists will coincide with those of the health care staff within medical structures. With its focus on adjustment, health psychology considers healthy the patient who has regained the ability to perform. Health is a functional entity and removed from the experience of illness (cf. McLean, 1986). As such it coincides with biomedicine; but that is also its purpose. If psychologists had a substantial theory of health and illness it would almost certainly be at odds with the biomedical model. The likelihood of gaining entry into the medical world would then be very problematic, if not impossible. Perhaps psychologists could take their cue from that small group of medical sociologists who have not allowed the medical establishment to define their priorities. For example, Strauss, Fagerhaugh, Suczek & Wiener (1985) have conducted research in health care settings that has led them to conclude that the work of health care professionals, from physicians to technicians, has been radically and irrevocably altered by the current prevalence of chronic - as opposed to acute - illnesses and the new technologies developing to manage them. However, as a consequence of their theorizing (using a 'grounded theory' strategy) and research, these authors are also explicit about the need for change in the structures within which medical work takes place.

Theories give form to our social activities and substantive psychological theories of health and illness might lead to practices at odds with the medical establishment. If health psychology is to drop its theoretical blinders it would question rather than take as given the nature of health care. But health psychologists may not be willing to accept the consequent change in practices. The absence of theory is a strategic tactic for the health psychologist; the creation of theory might be viewed as a subversive act.

References

Bertalanffy, L. von (1968). *General systems theory.* New York: George Braziller.

Bott, E. A. (1928). Teaching of psychology in medical courses. *Bulletin of the Association of American Medical Colleges, 3,* 289-304.

Burke, K. (1969). *A rhetoric of motives.* Berkeley, CA: University of California Press.

Clark, A. (1983) Functionalism and the definition of theoretical terms. *Journal of Mind and Behavior, 4,* 339-352.

Danziger, K. (1979). The social origins of modern psychology. In A. R. Buss (Ed.), *Psychology in social context.* (pp. 27-45). New York: Irvington.

DiMatteo, M. R., Hays, R. D., & Prince, L. M. (1986). Relationship of physicians' nonverbal communication skill to patient satisfaction, appointment noncompliance, and physician workload. *Health Psychology, 5,* 581-594.

Engel, G. L. (1977). The need for a new medical model: A challenge for biomedicine. *Science, 196,* 129-136.

Evans-Pritchard, E. E. (1951). *Social anthropology.* London: Cohen & West.

Fisher, K. (1986). Joining mind and body to promote health. *APA Monitor, 17(1),* 16-17.

Gentry, W. D. (1984). Behavioral medicine: A new research paradigm. In W. D. Gentry (Ed.), *Handbook of behavioral medicine.* New York: Guilford.

Ginzberg, E. (1986). The destabilization of health care. *New England Journal of Medicine, 315,* 757-761.

Howard, A., Pion, G. M., Gottfredson, G. D., Flattau, P. E., Oskamp, S., Pfafflin, S. M., Bray. D. W., & Burstein, A. G. (1986). The changing face of American Psychology: A report from the Committee on Employment and Human Resources. *American Psychologist, 41,* 1311-1327.

Jasnoski, M. L., & Schwartz, G. E. (1985). A synchronous systems model for health. *American Behavioral Scientist, 28,* 468-485.

Johnson, A. H. (1975). Toward clarification of objectives for family practice and family medicine. *Journal of Family Practice, 2,* 111-119.

Kunitz, S. J. (1983). The historical roots and ideological functions of disease concepts in three primary care specialties. *Bulletin of the History of Medicine, 57,* 412-432.

Lang, P. J. (1980). Foreword: Behaviorism at the bedside. In B. G. Melamed & L. J. Siegel (Eds.), *Behavioral medicine: Practical applications in health care* (pp. xiii-xx). New York: Springer.

Matarazzo, J. D. (1980). Behavioral health and behavioral medicine: Frontiers for a new health psychology. *American Psychologist, 35,* 807-817.

McLean, A. (1986). Family therapy workshops in the United States: Potential abuses in the production of therapy in an advanced capitalist society. *Social Science and Medicine, 2,* 179-189.

Putnam, H. (1975). Philosophy and our mental life. In H. Putman (Ed.), *Mind, language, and reality: Philosophical papers* (Vol. 2, pp. 32-65). Cambridge: Cambridge University Press.

Relman, A. S. (1987). Practicing medicine in the new business climate. *The New England Journal of Medicine, 316,* 1150-1151.

Runyan, C. W., DeVellis, R. F., DeVellis, B. M., & Hochbaum, G. M. (1982). Health psychology and the public health perspective: In search of the pump handle. *Health Psychology, 1*, 169-180.

Schwartz, G. E. (1982). Testing the biopsychosocial model: The ultimate challenge facing behavioral medicine. *Journal of Consulting and Clinical Psychology, 50*, 1040-1053.

Schwartz, G. E., & Weiss, S. M. (1978a). Behavioral medicine revisited: An amended definition. *Journal of Behavioral Medicine, 1*, 249-252.

Schwartz, G. E., & Weiss, S. M. (1978b). Yale conference on behavioral medicine: A proposed definition and statement of goals. *Journal of Behavioral Medicine, 1*, 3-12.

Schwartz, M. A., & Wiggins, O. P. (1986). Systems and the structuring of meaning: Contributions to a biopsychosocial medicine. *American Journal of Psychiatry, 143*, 1213-1221.

Shotter, J. (1987). The rhetoric of theory in psychology. In W. J. Baker, M. E. Hyland, H. Van Rappard, & A. W. Staats (Eds), *Current issues in theoretical psychology* (pp. 283-296). Amsterdam: North-Holland.

Smith, L. H., Jr. (1970). Biomedical research and national policy. *Journal of Clinical Investigation, 49*, 1301-1305.

Stone, G. C. (1980). Psychology and the health system. In G. C. Stone, F. Cohen, N. E. Adler (Eds.), *Health psychology - A handbook* (pp. 47-75). San Francisco: Jossey-Bass.

Stone, G. C. (1982). Health psychology: A new journal for a new field. *Health Psychology, 1*, 1-6.

Stone, G. C., Weiss, S. M., Matarazzo, J. D., Miller, N. E., Rodin, J., Belar, C. D., Follick, M. J., & Singer, J. E. (1987). *Health psychology: A discipline and a profession.* Chicago: The University of Chicago Press.

Strauss, A., Fagerhaugh, S., Suczek, B., & Wiener, C. (1985). *Social organization of medical work.* Chicago: The University of Chicago Press.

Tannen, D., & Wallat, C. (1986). Medical professionals and parents: A linguistic analysis of communication across contexts. *Language and Society, 15*, 295-312.

Taylor, S. E. (1986). *Health psychology.* New York: Random House.

Thomas, L. (1978). Science and the future of medicine: Future prospects. *Transactions of the Association of American Physicians, 91*, 74-75.

Turner, B. S. (1986). Sociology as an academic trade: Some reflections on centre and periphery in the sociology market. *Australian and New Zealand Journal of Sociology, 22*, 272-282.

Weiss, S. M. (1982). Health psychology: The time is now. *Health Psychology, 1*, 81-91.

THE ROLE OF COGNITION IN EMOTIONAL EXPERIENCE

W. Gerrod Parrott

Georgetown University
Washington, DC, U.S.A.

SUMMARY: This paper considers the origins of the phenomenological experience of emotion. It is argued that contemporary psychology unnecessarily restricts emotional feelings to the sensation of bodily changes, despite there being cognitive origins as well. There may be several reasons for this restricted view. It has a long history, from Descartes to William James to the present; it justifies the collection of physiological data; it seems congruent with there being physical causes and effects of moods and emotions; and it seems congruent with a view of cognition as rational and nonbiological. Yet, these reasons are unsound. Thinking also can be affected by physical causes, and it can be primitive and innate as well. There are compelling reasons to temper the historical emphasis on bodily feelings and physiological measures. Consider that there exist feelings states that seem to be primarily cognitive; examples would be certainty, confusion, amazement, and *deja vu*. The existence of such states suggests that cognition could contribute to the phenomenological experience - the feeling - of emotion as well. Such a conception has several advantages to recommend it. It helps account for differences in the experience of cognitively complex emotions that have no known physiological differences, and it aids the conceptual reintegration of cognition and affect.

Introduction

This paper examines one aspect of the relationship between emotion and cognition, namely, emotional feelings and what role cognition may play in creating them. In order to address this topic in some depth it will be necessary to exclude a number of related topics that have been common in recent debate among psychologists and philosophers. For example, much has been written about the role of cognition in *leading* to emotion, for example, about what sorts of assessments are necessary for emotions to occur and about how differing assessments lead to different emotions. Much has also been written about the ways in which emotion affects subsequent cognition, for example, about how memory and judgment are facilitated or distorted *following* an emotional experience. While each of these topics will have some bearing on the present topic, the focus of this paper is the role of cognition in emotional experience itself. It will be argued that there are not only roles for cognition in leading to emotion and in following emotion, but that cognition can play important roles during emotion as well. This position is at variance with the prevalent view in experimental psychology, which posits that emotional feelings are the result of bodily sensations. The problems with this more accepted position, along with the reasons for its continuing popularity, will be examined below.

In discussing these issues, it is unnecessary to answer the question of whether emotions *necessarily* involve a conscious experience of feeling - some authors think they do (e.g., those taking a biologically based position, such as Izard, 1982), others think they do not (e.g., those taking a social constructivist position, such as Averill, 1983), and there are complex arguments between the two positions. But this question falls outside of the present discussion, because there is *no* disagreement over whether emotions *sometimes* may involve feelings - everyone agrees that this is the case at least sometimes. So the argument being advanced may be stated as follows: When emotions do involve feelings, these feelings may be due in part to the cognitions that are occurring during the emotion.

Let me begin with an example. Consider the case of Fred, who is an undergraduate student. Fred is sitting in the library one evening, trying to study for an exam he has the next morning. But Fred is not getting much studying done, because he is emotionally distraught. He is distraught because his girlfriend invited him to a dance at her sorority that evening and he could not go because he had to study for his exam. He knows that his girlfriend is there at the dance without him, and he is terribly afraid that she is having a wonderful time. He is afraid that she is meeting lots of other boys, boys who are charming, who are good dancers, who are handsome, have lots of money, and tell entertaining stories. He is afraid that his girlfriend is the center of their attention, that she is having the time of her life, and that she has not thought of her poor boyfriend in the library a single time all evening. He is thinking that he may no longer seem so special to his girlfriend and that their relationship is less secure than he had thought, and he is dwelling on the implications of these beliefs for his plans and goals in life. In short, Fred is very jealous. Now let us suppose that Fred is aware of his jealousy, that he is in an emotional state and is experiencing emotional feelings, and that this is not a case of unconscious emotion or of a personality disposition or of an attitude toward women or of any other of the problematical cases that crop up in the theory of emotion. What is the source of these feelings?

The prevalent view in psychology is that feelings originate in the body and that they reach awareness much as do sensations - we *feel* these bodily changes just as we *feel* external stimuli. This assumption is present in a variety of current theories, ranging from biological to cognitive. On this account Fred's feelings of jealousy result from his sensing changes that are occurring in his body. His heart is beating more quickly than usual, there is a knot in his stomach, there is tension in certain of his facial muscles. These changes in physiology, says the prevalent view, are the source of Fred's emotional feelings. I have no objection to the claim that such things contribute to Fred's feelings; I merely claim that this view is too restricted. I would propose that there are other sources of feeling as well, sources that are cognitive. Consider Fred: as he tries to study, he finds that his thoughts keep drifting back to his girlfriend, to fantasies of her dancing and laughing and staring into the eyes of other boys. He vascillates between different coping strategies, sometimes wanting to go spy on his girlfriend, and sometimes wanting to force the whole topic out of his mind. Fred tries to keep his mind on his studies, but he must willfully force extraneous thoughts out of his head and pay attention to his textbook, and despite his efforts his thoughts keep returning to the dance at the sorority. Does it not seem plausible that the lack of ability to concentrate, the experience of being unable to control one's train of thought, results in a quality of consciousness that is part of Fred's feeling of being emotional? That having a mind that seems determined to fantasize precisely the scenes that one would least want to occur is a type of experience that is unique to being afraid or anxious? That alternating between different plans of action contributes to a feeling of confusion? That being certain that unseen, uncontrollable events are threatening one's relationship could be part of what it is to feel insecure? These aspects of Fred's thought are symptoms of his jealousy in every sense as his knotted stomach and racing heart are, and the experience of having these thoughts is an emotional feeling in every sense that the experience of sensing muscular tension is.

Emotional Feelings as Sensations

The above claims are at variance with the views of many contemporary psychologists and philosophers, who hold that emotional feelings (like feelings in general) result from physiological changes, not from thoughts. This claim often seems largely a tacit assumption, yet a few suggestive quotations from the current literature can be found to establish the point. For example, C. E. Izard (1984) states his position clearly:

> Biosocial theorists . . . define emotion experience in infancy largely in terms of feeling, and feelings as primarily a function of sensory processes that do not require cognitive transformation in order to change the quality of consciousness and influence perceputal-cognitive processes and behavior (p. 458).

Cognitive theorists, Izard writes, "ignore what many, including William James, have believed to be a very significant part of emotion, that is, 'felt emotion' or feeling" (p. 458). Elsewhere Izard (1982) states:

> Emotion is a form of *feeling*. It seems an easy step to go from joy-feeling or sadness-feeling to joy-meaning or sadness-meaning. But this difference in conceptualization may be important, for [a cognitive theorist] can reason that emotion as meaning changes with human development from infancy through old age, and I argue that emotion-feeling is invariant over the life-span. The *feeling* component of joy in the infant is the same as that in the aged person .... And to fail to come to grips with the emotion state or feeling and its motivational impact on consciousness is to overlook the key process or mechanism in the mediation of emotion-cognition interactions (p. 231).

Thus for Izard the felt quality of emotion is seen as its essence, an essence that is independent of any thoughts that may accompany it.

One sees similar views in philosophy as well. William Lyons (1980) writes in his recent book on emotion:

> An occurrent emotional state will include the person's beliefs about his or her present situation, which may or may not be caused by a perception of some object or event, but which are the basis for an evaluation of the situation in relation to himself or herself. This evaluation in turn causes the wants or desires which lead to behaviour, while the evaluations and wants together cause abnormal physiological changes and their subjective registering, feelings (p. 57).

Thus, for Lyons too, to the extent an emotion involves feelings, it involves 'abnormal physiological changes'.

There are certainly theorists who disagree with this view - Frijda (1986, Chap. 4) being a particularly clear recent example - but they are, I claim, in the minority. The prevalent view is that emotional feelings are physiological; that they originate in the periphery of the nervous system, like sensations; and that they cannot be caused directly by cognitions, which are believed to be essentially different and unable to produce this type of subjective experience.

This view has a long history, of course. The origins of the idea are present in Descartes, whose account of emotion entailed a flow of animal spirits from the body to the pineal gland, resulting in the subjective experience of the activities of the spirits in the body. Emotion, then, was a feeling in the soul based on the perception of changes in the body. This idea was further elaborated by Hume, who thought of emotional experiences as feelings of pleasure or pain, albeit ones that were associated with certain ideas (see Neu, 1977). Thus, for Hume, emotions were feelings in much the same sense that sensations of external stimuli are feelings. Emotional feelings were considered as originating externally to the mind, and thus as not being the product of the mind's cognition. This idea reached its fullest development in the theory of William James, who is primarily responsible for passing it on to contemporary psychologists. It was James who first explicitly identified emotion with such bodily changes as accelerating heart beats and trembling limbs. This idea remains today, having survived the downfall of much of the rest of James' conception. While this view aided empirical study of emotion in some ways, it has caused psychologists to focus on physiology as the sole source of emotional feelings and to fall prey to a variety of problems as a result.

It is well known that this 'Cartesian' view of emotion succumbs to a variety of criticisms. Wittgensteinians have pointed out that this view falls prey to the problems of any 'private language' (Kenny, 1963). Others have pointed out that while emotions can be cited as motives behind behavior, feelings cannot (Bedford, 1957; Lyons, 1980). Likewise, Solomon (1976) shows that emotions can be considered inappropriate, and feelings cannot be that, either. Nearly everyone points out that emotions usually have objects, that they are 'about' something, and feelings are not (see, for example, Kenny, 1963). And then there is the problem that the physiological patterns that presumably underlie each emotional feeling have never been identified (Mandler, 1979). Yet the belief persists that emotional feelings must be sensations.

One reason for this persistence may be that, while these criticisms effectively show that emotions cannot be identified with unique feelings or *qualia,* they do *not* show that emotional feelings come from anything *other* than sensation. So the response to these criticisms, to the extent that psychologists are aware of them and try to accommodate them, has been to develop increasingly sophisticated theories of emotion, theories that carefully acknowledge the importance of beliefs, judgments, assessments, desires, and motives, yet that continue to claim that emotional feelings result solely from the sensation of abnormal physiological changes.

A second reason for this persistence may be that it is comforting to locate psychological phenomena in the body. It is easier to measure things out there, using electromyographs and what not. This is no doubt a false comfort, since it gets rid of none of the philosophical difficulties, but it may be a factor nonetheless.

A third reason may be that some affects seem more biological than others. When cognitively-oriented theorists consider emotion, they tend to take as their prototypes such cases as jealousy or resentment, and with these the need for cognitive complexity is present almost as a matter of semantics. There just is not such a thing as free-floating jealousy or resentment; one must be jealous *of,* or resentful *at,* someone or something. But many psychologists take a more biological orientation, and take as their prototypes something more akin to *moods.* Moods sometimes seem to occur for no apparent reason, and there are numerous instances in which hormones or other physical agents seem to influence their appearance - for example, when sleeplessness or hunger leads to irritability, or lack of sunlight during winter leads to depression. Focusing on these aspects of affect encourages the belief that emotional feelings are physical sensations. This belief may be wrong as well, however, since it is possible that these physical causes affect feeling by affecting cognition first, which then alters feeling. That chemicals affect thinking is not a farfetched idea (see Parrott & Sabini, in press). High progesterone levels in women are associated with dreams having higher maternal content (Baron, 1977); amphetamine overdose leads to paranoid thoughts (Angrist, Sathananthan, Wilk, & Gershon, 1974); and there is some reason to think that antidepressant medications may work by affecting how people think (Simons, Garfield & Murphy, 1984). Yet the biological side of emotion may still cause people to think of sensation as the basis of feeling.

For some reason, cognitions do not strike psychologists as being powerful enough to account for passion. There seem to be several reasons for this. First, there is a tendency for many people to think of cognition as being rational, conscious, verbal, and controlled. Second, psychologists think of emotion as having a long evolutionary history. They think of emotions as being discrete, biological states, much like hunger and thirst are. Hunger and thirst do not seem to require cognition to produce 'feelings' of hunger and thirst, so why should anger, fear, shame, or jealousy? Emotion is thought to be primitive, to be innate, to be present in infants and in animals. Cognition is thought of as contrasting with that. The computer metaphor of cognition is taken more literally than many would suppose. The cortex is discussed as if it were built by IBM, while the emotions inhabit the limbic system, which we share with the beasts of the jungle.

Obviously this is a caricature, but there really is some truth to it. Zajonc's (1980) famous paper on *Feeling and Thinking* argues for the independence of affect and cognition on just the sorts of grounds that I have mentioned above. These grounds are false, however (Parrott & Sabini, in press). Certainly *some* cognition is rational, conscious, verbal, and controlled, but much is not. An excellent example of cognition that occurs automatically and uncontrollably is provided by the Stroop effect, in which people are given the task of naming the color of ink that is used in writing out the names of color words. When the color of the ink does not match the color named by the word that is spelled, people tend to pronounce the word that is spelled, not the color of the ink, despite their efforts to do otherwise. So not all cognition is controllable or the product of a person's will. It is commonplace for thoughts to 'happen' to people, even when the people do not want to have these thoughts or when they are actively trying to prevent these thoughts from occurring.

Equally fallacious is the belief that emotion differs from cognition in being biological, innate, or primitive. That cognition can be innate has been suggested rather persuasively, I believe, by Professor Chomsky. That it is biologically based seems obvious as well - a reading of the ethological literature will convince one that even insects are capable of apparently complex, innately given, calculating abilities. That cognition can be primitive is perhaps less obvious, but consider the following. It is surely the case that not all of our values, biases, and cognitive predilections are known to us, having been examined rationally and adopted because we believe that they are true; surely no one 'knows thyself' thoroughly and has chosen to be all that he or she is. Instead, surely some of our values, biases, and predilections were ingrained at an early age, were passively and tacitly acquired; surely some are unknown to us, and were they to become known we would disavow them. Experience tells us that we are interested in things that we think we should not be, that we disapprove of things that we believe we ought to think are permissible, that we seem not to know our own habits of thought. Therapists report seeing these things all the time. In this sense our cognitions can be primitive.

The Cognitive Component of Emotional Feelings

Thus, a final reason why psychologists believe that cognition is incapable of producing emotional feelings is that they think of the wrong types of cognition when considering the validity of this claim. It therefore seems likely that if psychologists are to be convinced that cognition has a role in emotional experience, it will be necessary to characterize the types of cognition that lead to feelings.

Calhoun (1984) has proposed a distinction between 'beliefs', which she considers to be clear, fully conceptualized and articulated; and what she calls 'cognitive sets', which are unarticulated frameworks for interpreting the world that are largely outside our awareness. She likens the results of cognitive sets to *percepts,* which are experienced directly, as opposed to the results of beliefs, which are known only intellectually. It is 'cognitive set' that often leads to emotion, she claims, and I would add that it is cognitive set that results in certain subjective emotional experiences. A related characterization has been suggested by de Rivera (1985), who applies some work in phenomenology to this problem. He likens feeling to touching in that the person touching is also touched. Cognitions that lead to feeling involve a reciprocity, a loss of the distance of objectification, and a corresponding vulnerability that comes from the possibility of being affected oneself. Suzanne Langer (1967) has also addressed this question of what types of thinking lead to feeling, although her efforts in this direction seem more metaphorical. She postulates that feeling is a 'phase' of organic activity, like steam is a phase of the substance H_2O. But she herself is clearly dissatisfied with this account and more generally with our lack of knowledge about the conditions that lead to conscious feeling.

What can be added to these accounts? It seems likely that for cognition to lead to emotional feelings it needs to be habitual so that it may be automatic and proceed without conscious control (or, for some emotions, despite attempts at conscious control). R. S. Peters' (1962) well-known claim that emotion is characterized by *passivity* would seem to be satisfied by such cognition, since people would experience the thoughts as happening to them, not as something that they tried to think. This characterization is quite crude, unfortunately, and it is almost certainly missing important detail and incorrect in some that it provides. Yet it is enough to argue that some types of cognition can produce the qualities of emotional feeling.

A strong argument for this thesis is a simple existence proof demonstrating that cognition can produce *non-emotional* feelings as well as emotional feelings. Consider such states as feeling certain, confused, interested, amazed, or surprised. These states may be referred to as *cognitive feelings* since they are not emotions (see Fehr & Russell, 1984), yet they seem to be feeling states in a sense similar to that in which emotions are. They seem to be true feelings in the sense that they refer to phenomenological experiences, but they are feelings that, intuitively at least, do not seem to involve sensing bodily changes. These feelings are not well understood. Perhaps they involve some specialized representation of the results of an unconscious cognitive process, perhaps they are a sort of readout of the result of complex cognitive computations (Clore & Parrott, 1987). Nevertheless, the existence of these states suggests that cognition can produce feeling states without sensation of bodily changes, and this phenomenon increases the plausibility that cognition may contribute to emotional feeling as well.

Several objections to this existence proof may be anticipated. One concerns the assumption (made above) that cognitive feelings do not involve bodily changes: It could be asserted that cognitive feelings do involve sensations of bodily change. Now this objection carries some risk. If thoughts of interest or certainty produced bodily changes, one would be hard pressed to imagine any conscious cognition that *did not* give rise to physiological changes, thus risking the fallacy of the excluded opposite: If the criterion that distinguishes conscious cognition from emotion is to be that emotion but not cognition produces physiological changes, one would be forced to conclude that there is no true conscious cognition at all. Even supposing that this problem could be repaired, the debate would descend into the same quagmire that emotion research has waded through ever since William James, with researchers searching for decades for signs of these elusive physiological states. So this objection does not seem very promising.

A second objection might claim that cognitive feelings are really just emotions that occur in response to certain thoughts. For example, feelings of confusion would be depicted not as feelings resulting from a certain cognitive outcome, but rather as the result of bodily changes that were produced by a certain unpleasant emotion that was produced by a certain cognitive outcome. Thus, the gist of this objection is the claim that between every cognition and its putative feeling is an emotion that is the actual cause of that feeling. This objection is perhaps more interesting than the preceding one since it is free of logical difficulties, but it has similar empirical difficulties, namely, those of locating elusive physiological states.

It should be noted that it is not being claimed that there is no difference between emotional and unemotional cognition. There is a very real distinction between experiencing an emotion toward an object and merely contemplating that object, but it is not the difference that most people seem to think it is, namely, the difference between sensation and cognition. Rather, the argument is that there are different types of cognition, some of which lead to feeling states and some of which do not. The types that do may form part of the conscious experience of an emotional episode. There is no *a priori* reason to consider the rapid heartbeat and knotted stomach that accompany jealousy as any more fundamentally part of the emotion than the experience of having thoughts of insecurity and suspicion.

There are definite advantages to conceiving of emotional feeling as deriving from cognition as well as from sensation. One difficulty for biological accounts of emotion is that evolution can account well enough for the physiological differentiation of certain basic emotions, but is at a loss to account for the differences among cognitively complex and subtle emotions present in humans, many of which have no known physiological differences (consider envy and jealousy). Traditionally cognitive accounts, such as Schachter's, have claimed to be able to account for the differentiation of cognitively complex emotions; they claim that the diffuse physiology of emotional states is differentiated by cognitive 'labeling'; but the traditional cognitive theory supplies no account of how cognitive labeling affects the experience of the emotion (Gordon, 1978). One advantage of the account proposed in this paper is that it suggests a mechanism by which specific cognitive content may color affective experience.

Another advantage of the present account is that it tends to dissolve the distinction between cognition and emotion. In contemporary psychological parlance emotion and cognition are depicted as being qualitatively different phenomena, similar to - indeed, derived from - Descartes' distinction between mind and body. This left the study of emotion with the problems of dualism, including the problem of how these two types of phenomena affect each other. The viewpoint advocated here may eliminate some of these difficulties by eliminating the qualitative distinction between cognition and feeling. Cognition and emotion cease to be two completely distinct entities, because cognition is as fully a contributor to emotional experience as is sensation of bodily change. These advantages should encourage future theorizing and research to consider emotional experiences to be the product of people's thoughts as well as of their physiological reactions.

References

Angrist,B., Sathananthan, G., Wilk, S., & Gershon, S. (1974). Amphetamine psychosis: Behavioral and biochemical aspects. *Journal of Psychiatric Research, 11*, 13-24.

Averill, J. R. (1983). Studies on anger and aggression: Implications for theories of emotion. *American Psychologist, 38*, 1145-1160.

Baron, J. (1977). Menstrual hormone changes and instinctual tendencies in dreams. *Motivation and Emotion, 1*, 273-282.

Bedford, E. (1957). Emotions. *Proceedings of the Aristotelian Society, 57*, 281-304.

Calhoun, C. (1984). Cognitive emotions? In C. Calhoun & R. C. Solomon (Eds.), *What is an emotion?* (pp. 327-342). New York: Oxford University Press.

Clore, G. L., & Parrott, W. G. (1987). *Cognitive feelings and metacognitive judgments.* Manuscript submitted for publication.

Fehr, B., & Russell, J. A. (1984). Concept of emotion viewed from a prototype perspective. *Journal of Experimental Psychology: General, 113*, 464-486.

Frijda, N. H. (1986). *The emotions.* Cambridge: Cambridge University Press.

Gordon, R. M. (1978). Emotion, labeling, and cognition. *Journal for the Theory of Social Behavior, 8*, 125-135.

Izard, C. E. (1984). Emotions without feelings? [Review of *Children's emotions and moods: Developmental theory and measurement.] Contemporary Psychology, 29*, 457-459.

Izard, C. E. (1982). Comments on emotion and cognition: Can there be a working relationship? In M. S. Clark & S. T. Fiske (Eds.), *Affect and cognition: The seventeenth annual Carnegie Symposium on Cognition* (pp. 229-240). Hillsdale, NJ: Erlbaum.

Kenny, A. (1963). *Action, emotion and will.* London: Routledge & Kegan Paul.

Langer, S. K. (1967). *Mind: An essay on human feeling* (Vol. 1). Baltimore: The Johns Hopkins University Press.

Lyons, W. (1980). *Emotion.* Cambridge: Cambridge University Press.

Mandler, G. (1979). Emotion. In E. Hearst (Ed.), *The first century of experimental psychology* (pp. 275-321). Hillsdale, NJ: Erlbaum.

Neu, J. (1977). *Emotion, thought, and therapy.* Berkeley: University of California Press.

Parrott, W. G., & Sabini, J. (in press). On the "emotional" qualities of cognition: A cognitive account of some properties of affect. *Cognitive Therapy and Research.*

Peters, R. S. (1962). Emotions and the category of passivity. *Proceedings of the Aristotelian Society, 62*, 117-134.

de Rivera, J. (1985, August). *The concept of feeling and its relation to emotion.* Paper presented at the annual convention of the American Psychological Association, Los Angeles.

Simons, A. D., Garfield, S. L., & Murphy, G. E. (1984). The process of change in cognitive therapy and pharmacotherapy: Changes in mood and cognition. *Archives of General Psychiatry, 41*, 45-51.

Solomon, R. C. (1976). *The passions: The myth and nature of human emotion.* Garden City, NY: Anchor Press.

Zajonc, R. B. (1980). Feeling and thinking: Preferences need no inferences. *American Psychologist*, *35*, 151-175.

A THREE-DIMENSIONAL MODEL OF THE BRAIN AND PSYCHOPATHOLOGY

Lorne T. Yeudall

Alberta Hospital
and
University of Alberta
Edmonton, Alberta, Canada

SUMMARY: As in many areas of concern to psychology, there often has been a dichotomous perspective regarding the conceptualization of normal and deviant behavior. The dichotomy referred to is that of nature versus nurture, or biogenic versus psychogenic. Rimland (1969) suggests that the psychogenic perspective in regard to mental illness has prevailed in the past years, even though there has been little substantive evidence for this view. He further stated that in time, research would demonstrate the important role of biogenic factors in mental illness and eventually the purely psychogenic hypothesis will be abandoned. Indeed, there is now substantive evidence for biological determinants playing a major role in the genesis of most psychiatric disorders. The pendulum has moved from the extreme position of a purely psychosocial etiology to a biopsychosocial model of causation. The impetus for our theoretical and pragmatic approach to the treatment of psychiatric disorders, came from the early formulations of Flor-Henry (1976) regarding the significance of asymmetrical brain dysfunction in psychopathology. the ability to categorize psychopathology in terms of asymmetrical patterns of brain dysfunction promises a possible objective method of differential psychiatric diagnosis, independent of behavioral symptomatology. This chapter presents a theory based on 13 years of neuropsychological research utilizing a multimodal approach in the assessment (neuropsychological, brainstem, subcortical and cortical evoked potential and power spectral EEG) and treatment of psychopathology. The model proposed is multidimensional in nature, and views psychopathology as spectrum disorders with multiple causal factors interacting within a biopsychosocial matrix. The present aspect of the theory focuses on the biological determinants, as they are considered to play the major role in the genesis of psychopathology.

A Three-Dimensional Schema of the Brain

The current model was developed to aid the conceptualization of various clinical disorders and the development of assessment strategies and tools to measure the functional integrity of the central nervous system (Yeudall, Fedora & Fromm, 1987). The three fundamental brain dimensions of the model (left or dominant versus right or nondominant, anterior versus posterior, and cortical versus subcortical) are based on evidence that important functional differences exist between different regions of the brain along these axes (Geschwind, 1965; Luria, 1973a; Ojemann, 1983; Penfield, 1975; Pribram & McGuinness, 1975). We view the brain as being dynamically organized in a multilevel and hierarchical fashion with interactive parallel processing systems for sensory inputs, motoric readiness, motor output and emotional and motivational states. Higher level cognitive processes are assumed to occur at higher levels of brain organization and, in general, are qualitatively different depending on which hemisphere of the brain is involved.

Dominant Versus Nondominant Hemispheric Functions

Neuropsychological and neurophysiological studies indicate that in approximately 95 percent of right-handed and 65 percent of left-handed individuals, the left or so-called dominant cerebral hemisphere plays a greater role in symbolic propositional language functions. The right or nondominant hemisphere, on the other hand, plays a greater functional role in the processing and organization of visual-spatial, tactual, and musicogenic information. Of particular significance, the nondominant hemisphere also plays a greater role in both receptive and expressive functions associated with affective or emotional behavior. At a more global level of analysis, the dominant hemisphere is specialized to analyze information which is fundamentally temporal-sequential in nature and regulates sequential motor behaviors. In contrast, the nondominant hemisphere specializes in the processing of information in a holistic or syncretic manner and is involved in the spatial and rhythmic (emotional) modulation of motor behavior. The degree of functional lateralization varies, depending on the nature of the sensory information, as well as the attentional set and cognitive strategy being utilized by the individual (Luria, 1973a). It appears that the expression of propositional speech becomes completely lateralized to the left hemisphere in the majority of right-handed adults, whereas singing and the affective tone of speech become lateralized to the nondominant hemisphere (Sperry, Gazzaniga, & Bogen, 1969).

In addition to the functional differences attributed to the two hemispheres, there is evidence for neuroanatomical hemispheric differences for specific homologous regions of the brain (Whitelson, 1983). Recent evidence also indicates significant differences in the ratio of neurotransmitter substances found in different brain structures in the two hemispheres (Oke, Keller, Medford, & Adams, 1978; Tucker & Williamson, 1984). The left brain neural systems appear to be more related to cholinergic,

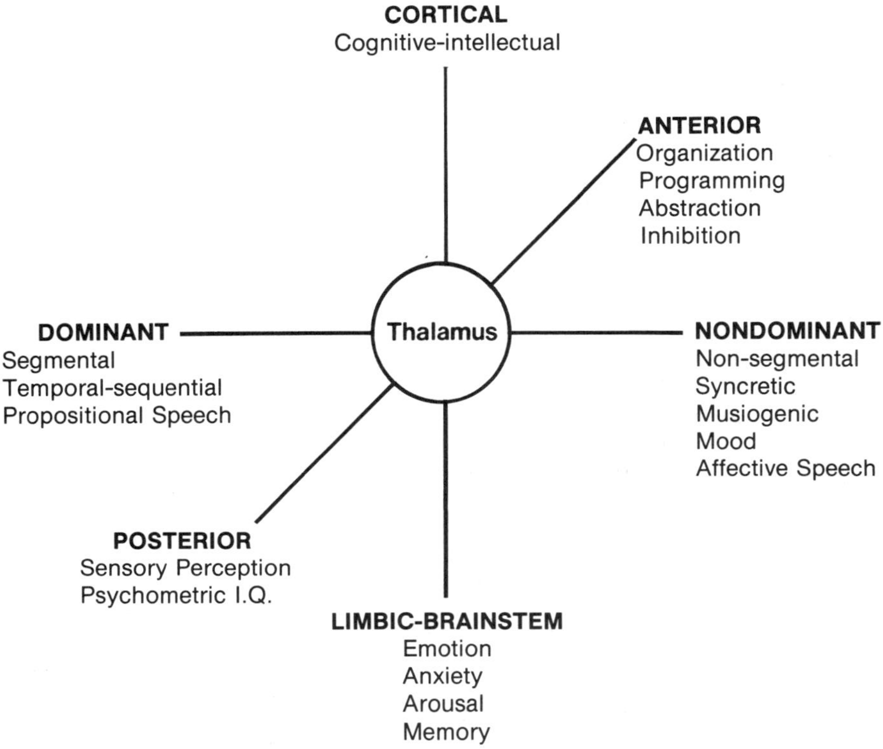

Fig. 1 Functional three-dimensional model of brain function.

dopaminergic, and GABAergic neurotransmitter activity. In contrast, the right neural brain systems are more influenced by noradrenergic and serotoninergic activity (Fig. 2). Flor-Henry (1983, 1985) has reviewed evidence supporting the hypothesis that a functional reciprocal inhibitory/facilitory relationship exists between the two cerebral hemispheres and that this relationship is fundamentally related to the balance of neurotransmitters within and between the two hemispheres. In his hypothesis the left hemisphere has a general inhibitory function and the right hemisphere has a general excitatory function regulating mood, erotic states, and aggressive behavior.

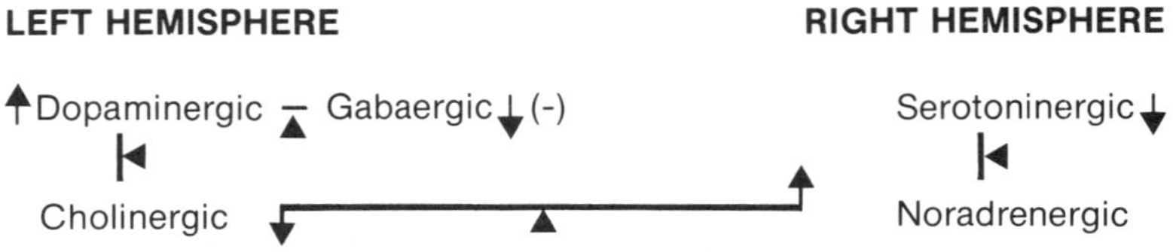

Fig. 2 Neurotransmitter reciprocal relationships within and between the two cerebral hemispheres as proposed by Flor-Henry (1983).

Cortical Versus Limbic or Subcortical

The second dimension of the model differentiates the cortical systems from the subcortical-limbic and brainstem systems. As is the case in the relationships between the two cerebral hemispheres, a homeostatic reciprocal relationship exists between the cortical and subcortical systems. In general, higher brain regions have a regulatory role (either inhibitory or facilitatory) on lower brain systems. The neocortical systems are primarily involved in higher cognitive-intellectual and regulatory functions, whereas the limbic/brainstem systems are important in arousal, integration of emotional and vegetative reactions with the learning process and in the storage of information from different sensory modalities. The stimuli for this integration can be generated both from within the limbic system and from the external environment.

Sensory-input, except for vision and smell, and all motor-output systems flow through the midbrain and brainstem. Dysfunction of these subcortical brain regions can disrupt or distort the transfer of neural information to and from the higher cognitive and emotional regions of the brain, thereby mimicking abnormalities of these higher regulatory structures. In addition, dysfunction of the brainstem and midbrain can result in specific symptomatology related to respiration, sweating, temperature and heart rate, as well as psychic symptoms pertaining to mood, depression, auditory hallucination, motivation, inattention and memory functions (Trimble & Cummings, 1981).

Anterior Versus Posterior Brain Systems

The parietal, occipital, and the middle and posterior temporal lobe regions of the cortex are primarily involved in the processing and elaboration (cross-modality comparisons) of information from the different sensory modalities. In contrast, the anterior regions of the frontal and temporal lobes play a higher level executive function integrating information received from the other regions of the brain (including the limbic system) and regulating ongoing and anticipated future behavior.

Luria (1973b) suggested that the prefrontal regions of the human brain play a decisive role in the formation of plans and intentions and in the regulation and verification of complex behaviors, particularly through the speech mechanisms of the dominant hemisphere. In his view, the frontal lobes "allow for comparison of the effect of action with the original intention." (Luria, 1968, p. 149). Pribram has pointed out that frontal lobe patients can recognize errors made by others as well as themselves, however they cannot utilize this knowledge to control their own behavior (Konow & Pribram (1970). Dysfunction of the dorsolateral convexity of the frontal lobes, in addition to impairments of higher order cognitive functions, also results in decreased attention (selective and sustained), drive, motivation, abstractive reasoning and memory consolidation, and increased behavioral impulsivity and disinhibition. In contrast, dysfunction of the inferior orbital limbic regions of the frontal lobes results in emotional outbursts, change of personality, lack of an indifference to emotional feelings or conflicts (e.g., loss of guilt, shame or remorse) and an increase in sexual and aggressive behaviors. In contrast to the dorsolateral convexity of the prefrontal lobes, dysfunction of the orbital limbic regions has little or no primary effects on higher cognitive intellecutal functions.

The temporal lobes, as in the case of the frontal lobes, also appear to have a functional division between the cognitive-intellectual (dorsolateral convexity) and the emotional or limbic areas (anterior and mesial portions) of the brain. The temporal neocortex is topographically situated such that information from all the sensory modalities systematically converges on the posterior regions of the temporal lobes (Jones & Powell, 1970). Consequently, it is ideally located for the integration of information from the external world with that of existing internal states, including previously learned memories triggered by incoming information.

In contrast to the executive and regulatory functions of the frontal lobes, the temporal lobes are more related to the individual's subjective consciousness and play an integrative role between information from the external world and the individual. Injury lateralized to the left temporal lobe results in disturbances of receptive and expressive language related activities which are manifested as impairments in the comprehension of the written or spoken word, writing, verbal memory, and in logical, analytical, and sequential thinking. Delusions, fear, and auditory hallucinations are also associated with left temporal lobe dysfunction. Damage lateralized to the right temporal lobe more often results in disturbances in processing and recall of and memory for visual, spatial, and kinesthetic information, and qualities of music such as tone and melody. In addition, lesions of the right temporal lobe are associated with visual hallucination, distortions of space and objects, experiences of *deja vu* and *jamais vu,* fear, and disturbances of mood.

Psychopathology Viewed from the 3-Dimensional Brain

The proposed three-dimensional model of the brain is viewed as a functional dynamic interactive system. It follows from the model that the clinician, or theoretician would benefit from having knowledge of the functional integrity of these interactive brain systems when attempting to comprehend or conceptualize the complexity and nature of psychopathology. The genesis of specific psychiatric disorders, which we believe are fundamentally rooted in neurobiology, can be the result of disturbances in more than one of the proposed brain systems, or as a consequence of disturbed reciprocal or regulatory influences between different brain systems involved in specific behavioral functions. Consequently, the etiology and treatment of an individual patient can differ dramatically depending on whether or not abnormal brain function exists, as well as which brain system or systems are abnormal for a given individual. The theoretical and pragmatic significance of the model will be briefly reviewed in the following section.

Diagnosis, Asymmetrical Dysfunction and Medication

The development of objective quantitative assessments as adjuncts to psychiatric diagnosis could be of immense benefit as many individual psychiatric cases typically have overlapping symptoms found in several disorders. This overlap of psychic symptoms increases diagnostic errors and, consequently, time in treatment. It appears from our work and that of others, that there is a remarkably high relationship between psychiatric diagnosis and asymmetrical lateralized dysfunction as measured by spectral EEG, evoked potentials and neuropsychological assessments.

Appropriate treatment of patients with medication based on differential diagnosis has provided evidence for normalization of premorbid abnormal brain activity and cognitive functions in different psychiatric disorders. Goldstein (1977) found significant improvement in schizophrenic patients after their medications were changed following quantitative EEG findings which revealed previously unsuspected asymmetrical dysfunction. In fact Goldstein (1977) and Flor-Henry (1978) have shown that in schizophrenia and affective disorders, psychotropic medication normalizes the previously abnormal hemispheric dysfunction reflected by quantitative EEG activity, and that the remission of symptoms covaried with the normalization of the EEG activity of the two hemispheres. Similarly, cognitive deficits also attenuate or disappear in depressed patients following appropriate chemotherapy (Fromm & Schopflocher, 1984). More specifically, tricyclic antidepressants significantly alter the EEG spectrum of the right hemisphere in normals and endogenous depressed patients: the latter disorder being characterized by greater asymmetrical right hemisphere dysfunction which is normalized by tricyclic medication.

A biochemical basis for the observed relationships between psychopathology, asymmetrical dysfunction, and medication effects on the brain (both in normals and psychiatric patients) is supported by histochemical evidence indicating that several of the major neurotransmitters implicated in psychiatric disorders are asymmetrically distributed in the two cerebral hemispheres of the brain (cf. Flor-Henry, 1985).

Over the past 5 years, we have been utilizing the pattern or topography of brain dysfunction in terms our three-dimensional model of the brain to assist in the differential selection of medication in the treatment of various psychiatric disorders as well as persistent criminality (Yeudall et al., 1987). There is now a large body of evidence supporting asymmetrical left hemisphere dysfunction in schizophrenia, asymmetrical right hemisphere dysfunction in endogenous depression, mania, manic-depressive illness (for a review see Flor-Henry, 1987) and persistent criminality (for a review see Yeudall et al., 1987). In the next section I will briefly discuss the relevance of our brain model to anxiety, atypical depression and the panic attack syndrome.

Anxiety, Atypical Depression and Panic Attacks

There is accumulating evidence that anxiety is fundamentally related to dysfunction of the left hemisphere (Ross & Rush, 1981; Tucker, 1981). Ross and Rush (1981) concluded from the analysis of brain damage patients that depression is primarily a bilateral disorder of the brain and that each hemisphere participates in the expression of depression through the modulation of different symptoms. Their findings indicated that endogenous or atypical depression correlated with right hemisphere dysfunction, whereas they hypothesized that nonendogenous depression originates in the left hemisphere. We also have found atypical depression (masked depression, characterized primarily by anxiety and irritability, and frequently an alexithymic disposition) to be associated with asymmetrical left hemisphere dysfunction. More recently we also have found a significant proportion of individuals suffering from panic attacks associated with and without agoraphobia to have a high incidence of asymmetrical left brain dysfunction as assessed by neuropsychological measures (Yeudall, Schopflocher, Sussman, Barabash, Warneke, Gill, Otto, Howarth, & Termansen, 1983). However, 57% of the panic attack patients had normal neuropsychological profiles, thus implicating normal functioning of the cerebral cortex. In contrast, over 94% of these same patients had abnormal brainstem evoked potentials indicated by asymmetrical interpeak latencies implicating the left hemisphere. Thus if only neuropsychological measures were used to assess cortical functions, approximately 50% of panic attack patients would show no evidence of brain abnormalities and would support a psychological etiology for half of the patients with this disorder. Also of significance, emerging from our three dimensional model of brain function, is the finding that 91% of the panic attack patients with agoraphobia had cortical dysfunction (asymmetrical left = 90% and asymmetrical right = 10%) as implicated by significant neuropsychological impairments. From these results we proposed that agoraphobia develops primarily in those patients because they have impaired cortical or verbal cognitive functions associated with dysfunction of the frontal and temporal lobes. That is, they are unable to comprehend and cope with the devastating nature of their panic symptoms and succumb to avoidance learning pertaining to developing the fear associated with panic attacks. For the majority of patients with atypical or masked depression and panic attacks associated with greater left hemisphere dysfunction we have found monoamine oxidase inhibitors to be the medication of choice. This is consistent with the preliminary evidence indicating that phenelzine (Nardil) has asymmetrical dominant hemisphere effects. The commonality of asymmetrical left hemisphere dysfunction in these disorders suggests a possible reason why monoamine oxidase inhibitors are the drugs of choice for these different disorders in which anxiety predominates the clinical picture.

Conclusion

A heuristic three-dimensional model of brain function is presented in order to conceptualize the symptomatology observed in different psychiatric disorders. It is argued that different brain systems of the left and right hemispheres when dysfunctional result in symptom clusters or complexes which, in turn, covary with specific psychiatric disorders such as schizophrenia and depression. The model also provides the basis for possibly differentiating subtypes of depression pertaining to endogenous versus atypical or masked depression. The theoretical and pragmatic significance of the model is discussed in the conceptualization of the panic attack syndrome. It is also proposed that all three dimensions of our brain model are necessary for an adequate theoretical conceptualization of different psychiatric disorders.

References

Flor-Henry, P. (1976). Lateralized temporal-limbic dysfunction and psychopathology. In H. Steklis, S. Harnad, & J. Lancaster (Eds.), Origins and evolution of language and speech. *Annals of the New York Academy of Sciences, 280*, 777-797.

Flor-Henry, P. (1978). *On certain aspects of the localization of the cerebral systems regulating and determining emotion.* Paper presented at the American Association of Biological Psychiatry, Atlanta, GA.

Flor-Henry, P. (1983). *Cerebral basis of psychopathology.* Littleton, MA: John Wright.

Flor-Henry, P. (1985). Observations, reflections, and speculations on the cerebral determinants of mood and on the bilaterally asymmetrical distributions of the major neurotransmitter systems. In W. G. Dewhurst & G. B. Baker (Eds.), *The pharmocotherapy of affective disorders: Theory and practice* (pp. 151-184). London: Croom and Helm.

Flor-Henry, P. (1987). In cerebral dynamics, laterality and psychopathology. In R. Takahashi, P. Flor-Henry, J. Gruzelier, & Si Niwa (Eds.), *Cerebral dynamics, laterality and psychopathology: A Commentary* (pp. 3-21). Amsterdam: Elsevier Science Publishers.

Fromm, D., & Schopflocher, D. (1984). Neuropsychological test performance in depressed patients before and after drug therapy. *Biological Psychiatry, 19*, 55-72.

Geschwind, N. (1965). Disconnexion syndromes in animals and man. Part II. *Brain, 88*, 585-644.

Goldstein, M. (1977). *Characteristics of EEG hemispheric asymmetries on psychopathology.* Paper presented at the Sixth World Congress of Psychiatry, Vienna, Italy.

Jones, E. G. , & Powell, T. P. S. (1970). Connexions of the somatic sensory cortex of the rhesus monkey: III. Thalamic connecions. *Brain, 93*, 37-56.

Konow, A., & Pribram, K. H. (1970). Error recognition and utilization produced by injury to the frontal cortex in man. *Neuropsychologica, 8*, 489-191.

Luria, A. R. (1968). The complex mechanism of psychological processes. *Impact of Science on Society, 18*, 141-156.

Luria, A. R. (1973a). *The working brain: An introduction to neuropsychology.* London: Penguin.

Luria, A. R. (1973b). The frontal lobes and the regulation of behavior. In K. H. Pribram & A. R. Luria (Eds.), *Psychophysiology of the frontal lobes.* New York: Academic Press.

Ojemann, G. A (1983). Brain organization for language from the perspective of electrical stimulation mapping. *The Behavioral and Brain Sciences, 2*, 189-230.

Oke, A., Keller, R., Medford, J., & Adams, R. N. (1978). Lateralization of norepinephrine in human thalamus. *Science, 220*, 1411-1413.

Penfield, W. (1975). *The mystery of the mind: A critical study of consciousness and the human brain.* Princeton: Princeton University Press.

Pribram, K. H., & McGuiness, D. (1975). Arousal activation, and effort in the control of attention. *Psychological Review, 82*, 116-149.

Rimland, B. (1969). Psychogenesis versus biogenesis: The issues and the evidence. In S. C. Plog & R. B. Edgerton (Eds.), *Changing perspectives in mental illness* (pp. 702-735). New York: Holt, Rinehart, and Winston.

Ross, E. D., & Rush, A. J. (1981). Diagnosis and neuroanatomical correlates of depression in brain-damaged patients. *Archives of General Psychiatry, 38*, 1344-1354.

Sperry, R. W. , Gazzaniga, M. S. , & Bogen, J. E. (1969). Interhemispheric relationships: The neocortical commissures, syndromes of hemisphere disconnection. In P. J. Vinhken & G. W. Bruyn (Eds.), *Handbook of clinical neurology: Disorders of speech, perception, and symbolic behavior* (Vol. 4, pp. 273-290). Amsterdam: North-Holland.

Trimble, M. R., & Cummings, J. L. (1981). Neuropsychiatric disturbances following brainstem lesions. *British Journal Psychiatry, 138*, 56-59.

Tucker, D. M., & Williamson, P. A. (1984). Asymmetric neural control systems in human self-regulation. *Psychological Review, 91*, 185-215.

Whitelson, S. F. (1983). Bumps on the brain: Right-left asymmetry as a key to functional lateralization. In S. J. Segalowitz (Ed.), *Language functions and brain organization* (pp. 117-124). New York: Academic Press.

Yeudall, L. T., Schopflocher, D., Sussman, P. S., Barabash, W., Warneke, L. B. , Gill, D., Otto, W., Howarth, B., & Termansen, P. E. (1983). Panic attack syndrome with and without agoraphobia: Neuropsychological and evoked potential correlates. In P. Flor-Henry & J. Gruzelier (Eds.), *Laterality and psychopathology* (pp. 195-216). Amsterdam: Elsevier.

Yeudall, L. T., Fedora, O., & Fromm, D. (1987). A neuropsychosocial theory of persistent criminality: Implications for assessment and treatment. In R. W. Rieber (Ed.), *Advances in forensic psychology and allied disciplines: An international and interdisciplinary review* (Vol. 2, pp. 119-191). Norwood, NJ: Ablex.

MORAL OBJECTIVITY:

TOWARD A NEW UNDERSTANDING OF INTUITION

William J. Hague

University of Alberta
Edmonton, Alberta, Canada

SUMMARY: This paper maintains that the idea of intuition as a source of moral objectivity merits deeper consideration. By using the core paradigm of Positive Disintegration theory, and thus seeing intuition as a multilevel concept, new richness of meaning is brought out and important distinctions regarding intuition's psychological functioning can be made. A hermeneutic dialogue between individuals at various levels of development offers the possibility of getting at moral objectivity through levels of authentic subjectivity.

Introduction

The quest for objectivity is nowhere more urgent than in the practical domain of morality. How can one know that what one chooses as morally right, actually is so? How can we as human individuals share some communicable standards with other individuals? How can we as peoples and nations share universal standards of behavior that transcend time and place? And, more basically, is moral objectivity even possible, or are we left adrift in a sea of subjectivity that is individual, whimsical and arbitrary.

But perhaps I have already begun to stack the cards against a solution to the problem by implicitly accepting the assumption that objectivity and subjectivity form a dichotomy, the former being a real and rational connection with things 'out there,' the latter a purely personal, emotional and whimsical response to indefinable intra-personal experiences and wishy-washy sensations, somewhat reminiscent of the 70's theme: "If it feels good, do it." Moral philosophy has gone to great lengths to avoid the rigidity of authoritarianism on the one hand and the rampages of sheer subjectivism on the other. Subjectivism has been scorned as whimsical, arbitrary, unstable and entirely unreliable, certainly in the case of individuals and even in the case of group consensus where the 'moral majority' has frequently been found to be not so moral. But this paper hinges on the idea that postulating this very dichotomy between objective and subjective is the root of the problem, particularly when taken in overly-simplistic terms based on the presumption of antagonism, and restricted to a unilevel understanding of subjectivity.

Philippa Foot (1982) laments the fact that moral philosophers have a penchant for leaving gaps in their philosophical understanding of the values of different societies. She attributes this to "conventions that forbid the philosopher to fill chapters with descriptive material about human nature and human life. It isn't supposed to be part of his work to think in a somewhat discursive way that is suitable to reflections about the human heart, and the life of men in society" (p. 165). It is one of the goals of this essay to, in some small way, help fill one of these gaps.

Our approach to the question of moral objectivity will spring from a deceptively simple statement of Bernard Lonergan (1974): "Objectivity is the fruit of authentic subjectivity" (p. 214). Objectivity is not the fruit of just *any* subjectivity, but of *authentic* subjectivity and, as I shall propose, *authentic* subjectivity is related to the level of authenticity within the individual. What immediately needs to be done, with Lonergan's statement then, is to explore the meaning or meanings of "authentic subjectivity." To this task we shall apply the novel core paradigm of the theory of Positive Disintegration - the concept of multilevelness - which holds, not only that there are levels of development in the traditional chronological sense, but that there are qualitative levels within concepts and psychological functions. That there are levels within the concept 'authentic subjectivity' will be offered as a suitable approach to the objectivity question. 'Authenticity' in this sense becomes then neither a static concept connoting a state of perfection in the subject, nor a limitation of objectivity to traditional rational sources. Rather since we are in the realm of morality, mere speculative judgments of value are not enough; it is only in performance, in the pursuit of moral good, that authenticity is found. With decision and choice, one makes oneself an authentic or inauthentic subject. To explore the levels of authentic subjectivity we will return to an old, but recently revitalized word in the psychology of morals - intuition. We will explore intuition as a holistic, multilevel term for understanding the possibility of attaining moral objectivity through 'authentic subjectivity.'

Why Intuition?

In my introduction I mentioned intuition as an old but renewed term in moral philosophy and psychology. One person responsible for the resurrection of the term intuition is Lawrence Kohlberg. Under the influence of his critics (notably Carol Gilligan) Kohlberg (1984a), begrudgingly acknowledge the existence of 'B type' persons who gave Stage 5 'right answers' to his dilemmas, as the result of an *intuitive* understanding of the core reasons for their choices.

> A type B person is someone who intuitively or in his or her 'heart' or 'conscience' perceives the central values and obligations ... articulated rationally by Stage 5 and uses these intuitions to generate a judgment of responsibility ... implied then is the 'Platonic,' 'Kantian' or 'intuitionist' view that conscience can dimly intuit rationally principled justice and act accordingly (p. 63)

One who has only a *unilevel* view of intuition is in danger of giving conscience credit only for *dimly* intuiting. If we have a *multilevel* view we perhaps can credit conscience with the capacity for 'brighter' more objective intuitions. Interestingly, we need go no further than Kohlberg himself to find someone exploring (without using the terminology) the many levels of intuition in pursuit of moral objectivity, and finding that objectivity at higher levels of intuition. Kohlberg's excursions into Stage 7 in 1970 and his recent updatings of his thought (1984b) clearly develop this theme. Fifteen years ago Kohlberg called Stage 7 a metaphor and not really a stage at all. More recently (1984b) he elevated it to a 'soft stage'. Whatever its status, it was meant "to take away from Stage 6 the excessive demands placed on it, the demand that it provide the answer to the problems of the meaning of life" (1970, p. 3). Kohlberg (1981) found in Stage 7 "an emotionally powerful intuitive grasp of reality that a metaphysics can only in a limited way express conceptually." (p. 369). The beginnings of a multilevel approach were expressed by Kohlberg and Candee (1984a) when they said that type B judgments rest on a content-related and teleological intuition of a natural hierarchy among nine universal moral norms and that this hierarchy is "dimly perceived at the type B perspective from Stage 2 onward, but it is only at Stage 5 that the hierarchies become consensual..." (p. 64). Going even further, Kohlberg described Stage 7 as taking the postconventional person beyond the merely rational into the experiential, the religious, and even the mystical where a whole person, not just a cognitive person, is intuitively active in finding a will to meaning and a will to be moral, despite apparent meaninglessness and the immorality of the world as it exists. Kohlberg (1981) has said, "Mystical experiences that are religiously significant are those in which the oneness of being is disclosed and the subject-object duality is overcome" (p. 369). Kohlberg's mature view led him to an appreciation of levels of development that encompassed much more than cognitivism, achieving at higher levels of religious experience an intuitive grasp of objective morality in an experience of life that transcended subject-object dichotomies.

Another of Kohlberg's mature statements relevant to our topic is the result of his relationship with Jürgen Habermas. At the end of a massive chapter, entitled, "The Current Formulation of the Theory" in his *Psychology of Moral Development* (1948b) Kohlberg says:

> We believe in line with Weber (1949), Habermas (1983) and others that objectivity is a "moment" of scientific inquiry; that the essence or "truth" value of objectivity does not reside in some reified, permanent or factual quality inherent in the object of inquiry, but is rather to be found in and understood as a process of understanding which is the changing relationship between the investigator and what he or she observes. We believe that it is this theoretical and methodological orientation aptly expressed by Habermas' notion of "objective hermeneutics" that characterizes our work (p. 319).

It is not surprising to find the presence of Habermas in this issue, given the widespread influence he has had, but it is more interesting and exciting to explore where the ideas of Kohlberg and Habermas in the context of multilevelness might take us.

Some scholars have recoiled from the word 'subjective' when talking of morals because it envisioned a rampant individualism, a rule by personal urge, or at best a rule by the great sweaty masses of the majority. But by looking at subjectivity at various levels of authenticity, we can, I think, propose a subjective approach to moral judgment making that enriches the concept of objective hermeneutics. It also enriches that word 'intuition' by giving it levels of meaning, permitting higher, more authentic levels of intuition. Clearly I am building a case for moral judgment making that portrays not just a series of cognitive stages stretching through childhood and adolescence, but one that usually finds its greater complexities and proliferation of levels in adult life, and its highest refinements in addressing the transcendent, religious, meaning-laden moral questions that permeate the higher levels of development. It takes time to develop from being a 'subject' in the immediate world of unreflected sensations to becoming an authentic person in the adult world of meaning. It is a journey, not an arrival. It is not a static state of perfection. Authenticity means continuously asking questions of self and life, moving from immediate experience to understanding, and beyond understanding to reflection, and through reflection to judgment and, ultimately to questions of worthwhileness - questions of value. It is a process towards higher levels and an entrance into that transcendent domain of ultimate meanings and metaethical questions of value where subject-object dualities disappear. Authenticity, at core, is a process and a function of what questions we ask of life.

What is Multilevelness?

I have so far been using multilevelness as though we all concurred in its meaning, and in a sense we do. But Dabrowski has mapped out some qualitative criteria for levels of concepts. These deserve demonstration here if we are to share understanding of levels of intuition.

In general, Dabrowski's levels are distinguished by a movement from the automatic, and unreflected to the more voluntary and reflected upon. Each new structure is qualitatively different from the preceding. It is more complex, yet more integrated. Forces of self-direction and self-determination emerge, permitting transcendence of the biological life cycle. The movement is from inner experience determined by behavior and external forces, to behavior determined by inner experience. Self direction, autonomy, and authenticity are the forces that give each new level a higher qualitative component.

Dabrowski distinguished five orthogenetic levels of development, which are characterized at each level by the presence of an active shaping force which he called dynamisms. Just as the presence of characteristic dynamisms distinguishes ontogenetic levels, so the active presence of these dynamisms in human activity indicates the orthogenetic level of that behavior. Time does not permit a full exploration of all the dynamisms Dabrowski postulated, and any thorough consideration of the levels of concepts deserves a holistic stance. But perhaps a glimpse at some of the dynamisms most relevant to objective judgment-making would serve our present purpose.

Besides the authenticity dynamism which Dabrowski saw as operative at higher levels of development, he described another high level dynamism particularly relevant to our discussion of moral objectivity. It is the dynamism he called "Subject-Object in Oneself" - an ability he ascribed to higher level persons to see others as subjects and oneself as an object. To my mind it is something much more than identification or role-taking which has long been explored in the psychology of morals. This dynamism includes not only the ability to stand in another person's moccasins, sharing their subjective experience, but to stand outside oneself, to distance oneself from oneself, to assume the unaccustomed role of seeing oneself as an object, and to reflect upon that. The self-objectification will often be expressed in words or other affect-laden images allowing room for distanciation and the objectivity that comes from gaining perspective. Van Gogh's self portrait is as much a personal distanciation as is Hamlet's soliloquy. Dabrowski and Piechowski (1977) report an illustrative passage from a reflection of one of their subjects:

> Thinking appears to me to be one-sided; it has lost somewhere its logical certainty. I am more uncertain and more hesitant, yet at the same time, I find myself richer in my thoughts and feelings. Perhaps loss of certainty in thinking and its closer interdependence with feelings are really tied together with a greater complexity and depth of thinking as a way of knowing (p. 150).

The image is affect-laden. Most often, as in this illustration, it is in words. Sometimes it is in life lived. By imaging oneself in relationship to others, one gains distance, perspective and, ultimately, objective self-understanding. On the other hand, by trying to interpret the affect-laden images (words and actions) of others we engage in hermeneutics, gaining to some extent the other's subjectivity. We will return to this hermeneutical process toward the end of this paper when we address the practicalities of constructing and communicating objective values. For now, the concept of intuition will carry us along our way.

Intuition as a Multilevel Concept

Looking at intuition from a multilevel perspective, we can see it is not something to be summarily dismissed as mere emotional whimsy, nor, at the other extreme something always to be taken religiously as a kind of mystical certainty. At lower levels there are mere hunches, based on little experience and still less reflection where whim and fancy and gratification of instinctual drives are uppermost. These automatic, unreflected responses have frequently been identified with intuition, leaving the concept there in its lowest unilevel sense to be neglected. It is no wonder that intuition in this unilevel sense has been scorned as a source of moral objectivity. But the answer is not to scurry back for more cognitive approaches to objectivity. The most promising approach is to explore the higher levels of intuition, enhancing the concept by combining cognition, affect, imagination, reflection, and the wisdom of experience and sensitivity in a context of care and responsibility. Central to this is another of Dabrowski's dynamisms which he calls, personality ideal. This dynamism causes the individual to be troubled by the gap between what he is and what he ought to be. His personal moral striving is the effort to close this gap. The closure is realized in eminent human beings by the identification to a higher degree between what is and what ought to be. What ought to be and what is have become almost one. This is authenticity at its highest levels.

I have, throughout, been emphasizing the highest levels of development. The most authentic subjectivity is this transcendent realm, where the greatest objectivity is found, but not because these eminent individuals have *discovered* objectivity 'out there.' Rather, they have *constructed* it in lives lived authentically. The subject-object duality is overcome in a personal oneness and in an interpersonal oneness with others at similarly high levels. There is, according to Dabrowski, a remarkable (but not perfect) convergence among eminent persons in their convictions of what is truly valuable and moral. Just as the convergence is not perfect, neither are the lives lived 'perfect' examples of all virtues. Now it is obvious that there are not many Gandhis or Schweitzers around. Eminent people are few in number. But the rest of us at lower levels of development need not be mere passive recipients of their moral teachings as in the tradition of the philosopher kings. If objectivity is a "moment of scientific enquiry" (Habermas) then moral objectivity is there in the 'moment' of each individual's search into not only the verbal teachings, but also the *lives* of eminent individuals. It is there according to the level of authenticity that each individual has attained.

Objectivity, then, is not found in mere subjective feeling, nor in purely cognitive functioning nor in blind conformity to the majority nor in passive acceptance of the teachings of some moral authority. It is the "changing relationship between the investigator and what he or she observes." It is created by relationships among persons where the 'text' to be interpreted is not only the words of a famous moral teacher, but the subject of hermeneutic perusal is also the life lived by that eminent person. The objectivity of this 'moment' is a function of the authenticity of the teacher and the student, the observed and the observer, the 'text' and the level of authentic intuition of the moral 'hermeneuticist.' Traditional authority-centered approaches have depicted the common man as merely a recipient of moral teachings, passively receiving 'truths' from an authority who, for some reason, knows better than he or she what should be done. The approach presented here, however, emphasizes the authenticity of the eminent person as a source of objectivity, but, by stressing the hermeneutic relationship of teacher and student, demands a measure of authenticity at all levels of development. Ultimately, as with most things human, it is relationship and responsibility that guide humans intuitively to an objective morality.

Postscript

Besides the many other biases present in this paper, there is behind it all a whole set of value judgments - most important of which are the value judgments implicit in the term 'higher level.' Some will complain that I am using a circular argument, postulating that an objective value hierarchy can be arrived at by relating to the lives and teachings of eminent persons, while, all the time, the selection of who these eminent persons are is based upon a whole network or heterarchy of values often only implicit. My reply to this is that the consensual validity we seem to have regarding which concrete persons exemplify the best of humanness may well be the most satisfactory foundation we can achieve as a ultimate base for moral judgments. Objectivity is objectivity; it is not certainty; nothing important in life is held together with the bands of certainty.

But, as Plato appreciated, and Whitehead after him, the lives of the best human beings are held together by other 'bands' - the lines of beauty, harmony and relationship. In that beauty is goodness to which, through fineness of feeling, individuals respond intuitively in accord with their level of development.

References

Dabrowski, K., & Piechowski, M. (1977). *Theory of levels of emotional development.* Oceanside, NY: Dabor.

Foot, P. (1982). Moral relativism. In J. Meiland, & M. Krausz (Eds.), *Relativism, cognitive and moral* (pp. 152-166). Notre Dame: University of Notre Dame Press.

Kohlberg, L. (1970). *The ethical life, the contemplative life and ultimate religion - notes toward Stage 7.* Unpublished lecture notes.

Kohlberg, L. (1974). Education, moral development and faith. *Journal of Moral Education, 4,* 5-16.

Kohlberg, L. (1977). The implications of moral stages for adult education. *Religious Education, 72,* 183-201.

Kohlberg, L. (1981). *The philosophy of moral development.* San Francisco: Harper & Row.

Kohlberg, L., & Candee, D. (1984a). The relationship of moral judgment to moral action. In W. Kurtines & J. Gewirtz (Eds.), *Morality, moral behavior and moral development* (pp. 52-73). New York: Wiley.

Kohlberg, L. (1984b). *The psychology of moral development.* New York: Harper & Row.

Lonergan, B. (1974). *A second collection.* Philadelphia: Westminster.

MODELS OF LAYERED STRUCTURE IN PERSONALITY[1]

Desmond Cartwright
University of Colorado
Boulder, CO, U.S.A.

Helene Peckar
Norwich University
Northfield, VT, U.S.A.

SUMMARY: Models of layered structure in personality are examined for conflict, fulfillment, and factor theories. These are compared with a Paradigm Case of layered structure derived from other sciences. Various instances in natural and social science fit the Paradigm Case more or less closely. Among personality models, those of conflict and fulfillment theories fit quite well except for parameters of volume and shape. Factor models vary also in not having homogeneous content in a particular stratum. Possible constructions are briefly suggested for further conceptualization and measurement of layered structure in psychological space. It is pointed out that approaches emphasizing the interaction of person and situation are not exempt from the necessity of understanding and assessing personality structure.

A theory of structure proposes "... a finer grain, different component parts, or other forms of deeper reality than appears to our senses or to previous tools of observation." (Cartwright, 1979, p. 189). Examples include the cell theory in biology and Dalton's atomic theory in physics.

An important concept in theories of personality structure is that of 'layers', and this concept has been widely used in proposing models to account for such phenomena as psychological symptom formation (e.g., glove anesthesia) and differential response to 'subliminal' stimuli (cf. Dixon, 1971; Silverman, Lachman, & Milich, 1982). Rationales for different psychological treatments often rest upon an assumption that "...personality is compartmentalized or layered and that the outer layers may be helped more easily than the inner ones" (Kirman, 1977, p. 21).

Models of Layered Structure in Personality

Following Maddi (1980) the theories to be considered are organized into conflict, fulfillment, and factor types.

[1]We are grateful for the helpful comments on earlier drafts of this paper given by D. Greenland, K. Schlesinger, P. Ossorio, and G. Weisz.

Conflict Models

In Sigmund Freud's topographic theory (Freud, 1900/1953) he distinguished three layers of personality as conscious, preconscious, and unconscious. The preconscious mediated memory and perception in access to consciousness. Censorship was exerted over contents from memory and perception insofar as they triggered associations with ideas of forbidden impulses arising from the unconscious. Ideas related to such impulses sprang directly from the instincts and also from previously repressed materials.

A less well-known but compelling conflict theory is that of Gittinger (Winne & Gittinger, 1973), in which the person has three main kinds of tendencies: Internalizing versus externalizing, regulated versus flexible, and adaptive versus uniform in taking roles. A person is born with a predisposition toward one direction or the other for each of these tendencies, and this constitutes her or his Primitive Response Style. Yet both sides of each pair of tendencies are required for full adult adaptation, and often parents want their children to develop the other side. For example, an internalizing child who likes to sit and think may be urged to be more active, get out and play, be more like other local children. An externalizing child who is too active and noisy for the parents' liking will be admonished to "sit still and be quiet for once!" By adolescence a child will have learned how to behave and will have developed a Compensated Response Style. In many cases the compensation will be quite strong, so that a child who was born an externalizer might become an internalizing adolescent. By adolescence, the compensated personality is usually so well developed that the person is not conscious of his or her primitive tendencies, and the compensated personality is often referred to as the Basic Personality.

Beyond family and school the person still must adapt to the wider culture in work and social life. Further changes in tendencies are required, which lead to the Modified Response Style. An adult who has developed into a particular corporate image (as described by Merton, 1957) offers a good example of the modified personality.

In Gittinger's system a person's tendencies at each of three layers, Primitive, Basic, and Modified, can be assessed using the Wechsler battery of intelligence tests, with the individual profile scored ipsatively. For example, someone getting a very low score on Digit Span, a high score on Arithmetic, and a low score on Information would be classified as Primitive Externalizer, compensated Basic Internalizer, and Modified Externalizer.

David Saunders (1982) has noted that the theory allows for each person to be compensated on none, one, two, or all three tendencies. On a national norm sample he finds the average to be 1.6 for males and 1.5

for females. In a select sample of adults applying to adopt a child, the mean was 2.0. Saunders describes this select sample as acutely defensive, based upon other test data, a result commensurate with the theoretical expectation that "... when the intensity of compensation is great, acute defensiveness, operating at an unconscious level, is likely to be present" (Winne & Gittinger, 1973, p. 20).

In summary, conflict models typically postulate a structure of three layers, with the layers composed of ideas and affects, or of tendencies. At least one layer has been created by repression or compensation.

Fulfillment Models

Carl Rogers' theory of personality has explicit concepts of layering. In considering what it means to become a person, Rogers has written that each client in therapy seems to be asking the question: "How can I get in touch with my real self, the self that is underlying all my surface behavior?" (Rogers, 1961, p. 108). The client progresses by successively discovering, examining, and dropping one false front after another. There are layers of false fronts, facades, or other structures. Peeling off layer after layer, a client may find deeply unacceptable impulses and feelings, such as self-pity, which had been covered by bitterness; or hatred which had been covered by solicitousness.

One woman, quoted by Rogers in his famous address at Oberlin College (1984, p. 5), says: "So... course I mean, I can't verbalize it yet. It's just being terribly hurt! ... And then of course, I've come to ... to see and to feel that over this ..see, I've covered it up. (weeps) I've covered it up with so much bitterness, which in turn I've had to cover up."

What are the contents of layers in Rogers' theory? They are feelings and self-concepts which have been denied or distorted in awareness because they "run contrary to" introjected values, or "conditions of worth" (Rogers, 1959, p. 226). Within the self-concept as a whole one layer of distorted concepts may cover another layer of less acceptable concepts.

Perhaps the layers are best seen as layers of awareness. Vaughan quotes a participant in one of her workshops as follows: "I began to listen to myself for the first time. I realized that there were many layers to my awareness, and I could get in touch with much deeper levels of myself" (Vaughan, 1979, p. 22). Yet another interpretation is that we are dealing with layers of memory, with a whole layer of memories blocked from recall until special procedures remove the block (Seamands, 1985, p. 27). Seeman (1986) and Cain (1986) interpret it as "degrees of being in touch."

In summary, Rogers' model postulates an indefinite number of layers of feelings and self-concepts or of awareness of them.

Factor Models

One well-known factor theory of personality is that of H. J. Eysenck (1984). In this model, factor analysis yields 'descriptive traits.' He contrasts these descriptive traits with 'fundamental traits', which are the neurophysiological processes presumed to be causing variation in the descriptive traits. For instance, scores on a test of extraversion yield measures of that descriptive trait; but each individual's score reflects his or her balance of inhibitory to excitatory potentials in the brain. Thus in Eysenck's model the structure of personality consists of two layers, one descriptive or dispositional, the other neurophysiological.

Perhaps the most explicit example of 'layered structure' in personality is given by R. B. Cattell's theory of strata. The theory rests upon data derived from factor analysis in which the rotations to simple structure are allowed to be oblique, thereby yielding correlations between the first-order factors. Analysis of these correlations yields factors at the second order, and so on. In Cattell's work with the Sixteen Personality Factor Questionnaire (16PF) he has reported eight second-order factors, and five third-order factors (Cattell, Eber, & Tatsuoka, 1970, pp. 111-125).

Cattell's theoretical model assumes that all factors reflect the influence of uncorrelated source traits. Obtained correlations between these source traits are due to other influences. An example is the correlation found between temperature and oxygen partial-pressure when measures are taken over a range of altitudes, so that altitude co-influences the other two measures. Finally Cattell concludes: "... the most likely model for psychological data (so long as we remain in a system recognizing strata) is what has been designated the stratified uncorrelated determiner, or SUD, model" which assumes that factors function independently and "that secondaries are orthogonal to each other and to all primaries - as well as to tertiaries" (Cattell, 1979, p. 308). He orthogonalizes representations of first-order factors on initial variables, of second-order factors on first-orders, and of third-order factors on second-orders. In summary, Cattell's model proposes that source trait influences on behavior exist in several strata. Each stratum consists of one or more independent influences. The influences in a stratum are causally independent of those in other strata. However, one influence at a higher stratum may cause two influences in the next lower stratum to appear correlated.

Models of Layered Structure in Other Sciences

Geology. As the classic instance, a structure of layers in rock may be seen in a stratigraphic column like that found on U.S.24 between Tennessee Pass and Minturn, in Colorado. In the lowest stratum are Precambrian schist and gneiss; next is a stratum of quartzite; then sandstone, dolomite, and so on (Chronic, 1980). These layers vary in thickness and in content. As we see them now they appear to be solid, and fixed in volume and shape. Each layer has mainly homogeneous contents distributed throughout its space.

Atmospheric Science. Tropical, subtropical, and other zones around the earth differ in seasonal pattern, amount of insolation, temperature pattern, and gas content. Concentric layers are the troposphere, stratosphere, mesosphere, and thermosphere, each of which is separated by an area of 'pause,' in which the pattern of temperature change stops (Greenland & DeBlij, 1977).

Clouds are either stratiform or cumulus. Stratiform clouds are blanket-like, cover large areas, and occur at three levels: 'stratus' up to 1.5 kilometers; 'altostratus up to 6 kilometers; and 'cirrostratus' above that. As air layers rise gradually over a stable dense air layer, moisture condenses, forming the temporary cloud layer. Sometimes one layer breaks through another, as when a cumulus cloud rises through a stratiform cloud (Greenland, 1987).

Botany. Trees have seasonal growth of cambium, making the familiar 'rings' (cf. Bannan, 1962). So layers can also have cylindrical shape and have the same kind of contents.

Biology. An animal cell has concentric layers: (1) a cell membrane; (2) cytoplasm layer, consisting of ectoplasm (more viscous) and endoplasm (less viscous); (3) nuclear membrane; and (4) the nucleus. The cytoplasm contains various organelles, such as mitochondria and endoplasmic reticulum; the nucleus also contains important organelles such as chromosomes and the nucleolus (Groves & Schlesinger, 1982, p. 84). Here we find layers with content that is homogeneous except for major discontinuities due to other entities contained in the layer.

Photomicrographs of the retina show four main layers: rods and cones, nuclei of rods and cones, nuclei of bipolar cells, and nuclei of ganglion cells (Gardner, 1958, p. 192). Here we see that two different layers might actually contain different portions of the same contents (inner and outer segments versus the nuclei).

Sociology. Societies are frequently described as having a structure of classes or castes (c.f. Merton, 1957), and Webster's Third International Dictionary gives "a many-layered social structure" as one example of meaning of 'layered structure'. Here a layer has volume only in the sense of a given size of population, and one layer is 'above' another in political or other forms of social power.

A Paradigm Case for Layered Structure

The descriptions of layered structures in other sciences enable a Paradigm Case Formulation (PCF: Ossorio, 1983), in which the Paradigm Case is used as standard, and other cases are introduced as transformations of the Paradigm Case. In PCF, parameters and values are specified for the Paradigm Case, and transformations are expressed as variations on certain parameters. It is obvious that the kind of reality concept involved is of first importance in the representation of real-world phenomena. The possibilities here are given exhaustively by Ossorio (1978) as Object, Process, Event, and State of Affairs. A 'layered structure' is best represented as an Object concept, and so we formulate a Basic Object Unit (Ossorio, 1978, p. 52) for our Paradigm Case, having constituents, and relationships among the constituents.

Constituents. A layer is three-dimensional, having volume and shape, with a particular solid (such as dolomite) distributed througout its volume more or less homogeneously.

However, a layer does not exist by itself. In order to qualify as a layer it must be juxtaposed to at least one other layer having the same shape but from which it is separated and different in some way. One layer differs from another in location and in some feature of content.

Relationships. The Basic Object Unit next requires a list of relationships. The most important relationship in the present case is relative location, one layer being adjacent to one, or at most two, other layers; and one layer being located above or around another layer.

We summarize the Paradigm Case of layered structure as one that has at least two adjacent layers, each having properties of volume, shape, solid contents, and location. The layers are similar in shape but differ in location and contents.

A formation of sedimentary rocks fits the Paradigm Case very well. Layers of the atmosphere vary in not having solid contents. Interpenetrating cloud layers depart in not having separate locations. Tree rings depart in having the very same kind of contents in different rings. Cell layers depart in having far less homogeneity of content. Retinal layers depart in having not different contents, but different parts of the same content. Layers of social structure depart in having no obvious volume or shape.

It is apparent that ordinary scientific usage accepts as cases of layered structure many that depart substantially from the Paradigm Case. Comparing a Paradigm Case to a variant case exemplifies ingenuity in the same way that use of metaphor, simile, or analogy does, namely as a hopefully useful and suggestive means of communicating a new potential description to the variant case (c.f. Black, 1962, p. 44; Schefler, 1979, p. 129; Toulmin, 1953, pp. 38-39; and Young, 1951, p. 31). Of course,

PCF (and scientific model construction in general) goes beyond metaphor into groups of transformations, and standards of appraisal invoke heuristics rather than esthetics.

Discussion of Models of Layered Structure in Personality

We may expect models of layered structure in personality to depart from the Paradigm Case. Indeed they describe layers only in terms of contents (e.g., Primitive versus Compensated tendencies), and relative location (e.g., unconscious impulses are at a deeper level than conscious intentions). Much of the scientific interest of such models resides in their hypotheses concerning the influence of one layer upon another (as in the effect of Primitive Flexibility on the appearance and functioning of Regulated tendencies at the Compensated level). In this way personality models emphasize what is usually not explicit in layered structure models of other sciences, namely the details of relationships between layers. Nevertheless, in other sciences, such details are of considerable interest to specialists (c.f. stress factors in plate tectonics or nutritional relationships in cell biology).

In conflict models the 'deeper' layers are less accessible to consciousness due to one or another mechanism (such as repression) that has adaptational significance. In fulfillment models, similarly, 'deeper' layers are less readily available to awareness, and sometimes also 'more meaningful' or 'closer to the real self'. These comparatives imply distance and space of some kind, hence volume and shape are conceivable properties.

Can suitable theoretical constructions of psychological space be developed? The basic analytic methodology is already in place (c.f. Guttman, 1968). However, it would seem necessary to work at the level of intraindividual measurements, and to ensure that dimensions have a common meaning such that a change in two or three dimensions yields a joint change of the same kind (even as '3 miles north, then 4 miles east' yields '5 miles northeast'; this feature does not characterize present-day 'spaces' derived by typical factor-analysis or multidimensional scaling). It would be profitable to explore fundamental conceptual issues in the analysis of 'space' as used or usable in psychology so that, for example, operational definitions could be offered for segmentation in a 'vertical' dimension such that the layer associated with each segment has its own distinguishable type of content. Some suitable tools have already been devised by Dixon (1971) and Silverman et al. (1982).

The Paradigm case of layered structure has layers with content homogeneously distributed throughout each layer's volume. This feature does not characterize a stratum in factor theory, because the constituting factors are explicitly independent sources of influence of different kinds.

Their only homogeneity is in having been extracted at the given order of analysis. It is doubtful that this is sufficient to satisfy a description of 'homogeneous content'. Moreover, Sells & Murphy (1984) have questioned whether it is profitable to treat factors as existing at different orders. They have suggested that 'higher-order' means 'greater bandwidth' or broader influence, and that it would be possible to calibrate known factors for bandwidth. Thus they would eliminate the layered structure model of personality that Cattell has developed, and which he has defended with vigor. (Cattell, 1972, 1979, pp. 281-313). Possibly the same work suggested for conflict and fulfillment models would yield independent procedures for determining the location of factor strata.

A model of layered structure is indispensable for many theories, such as Gittinger's. Behavioral, social learning, or interactionist approaches to personality may also need to take account of a layered structure as they increasingly recognize the need for person variables. These variables "...refer to products within the person of his or her cognitive development, social learning, history, and genetic endowment" (Mischel, 1986, p. 496). Whether as 'traits' or otherwise (c.f. Cartwright, 1975; Endler, 1982), such 'products' are stable characteristics of persons, hence are suitable subject matter for a theory of personality structure.

Noting that situations tend to have specific (and not general) effects, Mischel (1986) says that "...the impact of particular situations (or 'treatments' in experimental or clinical contexts) depends on the particular people in them" (p. 495). Conflict or fulfillment models would suggest that the impact of a situation depends on the particular layer of personality activated in the particular individual. Rather good clinical and experimental examples of such contingencies are given respectively by Horowitz (1979) and by Silverman, et al. (1982). In summary it seems that studies of situational influences or of interactions between those influences and personality characteristics should be viewed as studies of behavior and its multiple determinants. Studies of personality structure are not only different but also have higher priority, because they alone can provide a proper understanding and assessment of the personality that interacts with situations.

References

Bannan, M. W. (1962). The vascular cambium and tree-ring development. In T. T. Kozlowski (Ed.), *Tree growth*. New York: Ronald.

Black, M. (1962). *Models and metaphors*. Ithaca, NY: Cornell University Press.

Cain, D. J. (1986). *Personal communication*.

Cartwright, D. (1975). Trait and other sources of variance in the S-R inventory of anxiousness. *Journal of Personality and Social Psychology, 32*, 408-414.

Cartwright, D. (1979). *Theories and models of personality*. Dubuque, Iowa: Wm. C. Brown.

Cattell, R. B. (1972). The 16PF and basic personality structure: A reply to Eysenck. *Journal of Behavioral Science, 1,* 169-187.
Cattell, R. B. (1979). *Personality and learning theory, Volume 1.* New York: Springer.
Cattell, R. B., Eber, H., & Tatsuoka, M. M. (1970). *Handbook for the Sixteen Personality Factor Questionnaire (16PF).* Champaign, IL: Institute for Personality and Ability Testing.
Chronic, H. (1980). *Roadside geology.* Missoula, Montana: Mountain Press.
Dixon, N. F. (1971). *Subliminal perception: The nature of a controversy.* London: McGraw-Hill.
Endler, N. S. (1982). Interactionism: A personality model, but not yet a theory. In M. M. Page (Ed.), *Personality - current theory and research* (pp. 155-200). Lincoln: University of Nebraska Press.
Eysenck, H. J. (1984). The place of individual differences in a scientific psychology. In J. R. Royce & L. P. Mos (Eds.), *Annals of theoretical psychology* (Volume 1, pp. 233-285). New York: Plenum.
Freud, S. (1953). The interpretation of dreams. In J. Strachey (Ed.), *Standard edition of the complete psychological works of Sigmund Freud* (Volumes 4 & 5). London: Hogarth. (Originally published in 1900).
Gardner, E. (1958). *Fundamentals of neurology.* Philadelphia: W. B. Saunders.
Greenland, D. (1987). *Personal communication.*
Greenland, D., & Deblij, H. J. (1977). *The earth in profile.* New York: Harper and Row.
Groves, P. M., & Schlesinger, K. (1982). *Introduction to biological psychology* (2nd ed.). Dubuque, Iowa: Wm. C. Brown.
Guttman, L. (1968). A general nonmetric technique for finding the smallest coordinate space for a configuration of points. *Psychometrika, 33,* 469-506.
Horowitz, M. J. (1979). *States of mind: Analysis of change in psychotherapy.* New York: Plenum.
Kirman, W. J. (1977). *Modern psychoanalysis in the schools.* Wayne, NJ: Avery Publishing.
Maddi, S. (1980). *Personality theories.* Homewood, IL: Dorsey.
Merton, R. K. (1957). *Social theory and social structure.* Glencoe, IL: Free Press.
Mischel, W. (1986). *Introduction to personality.* (4th ed.: a new look). New York: Holt, Rinehart, and Winston.
Ossorio, P. G. (1978). *What actually happens.* SC: University of South Carolina Press.
Ossorio, P. G. (1983). A multicultural psychology. In K. E. Davis & R. Bergner (Eds.), *Advances in descriptive psychology* (Vol. 3, pp. 13-44). Greenwich, CT: JAI Press.
Rogers, C. R. (1959). A theory of therapy, personality, and interpersonal relationships, as developed in the client-centered framework. In S. Koch (Ed.), *Psychology: A study of a science, Volume 3.* New York: McGraw-Hill.
Rogers, C. R. (1961). *On becoming a person.* Boston: Houghton-Mifflin.
Rogers, C. R. (1984). What it means to become a person. In *Annual Editions: Personal growth and behavior 84/85* (pp. 195-206). Guilford, CT: Dushkin.
Saunders, D. R. (1982). On Turner's assessment of the Personality System. *Journal of Clinical Psychology, 38,,* 616-623.
Scheffler, I. (1979). *Beyond the letter: A philosophical inquiry into ambiguity, vagueness, and metaphor in language.* London: Routledge and Kegan Paul.
Seamands, D. A. (1985). *Healing of memories.* Wheaton, IL: Victor Books.
Seeman, J. (1986). *Personal communication.*
Sells, S. B. , & Murphy, D. (1984). Factor theories of personality. In J. Mc. V. Hunt & N. S. Endler (Eds.), *Personality and the behavior disorders* (pp. 39-72). New York: John Wiley and Sons.

Silverman, L. H., Lachmann, F. M., & Milich, R. H. (1982). *The search for oneness.* New York: International Universities Press.
Toulmin, S. (1953). *The philosophy of science.* London: Hutchinson.
Winne, J. F., & Gittinger, J. W. (1973). An introduction to the Personality Assessment System. *Journal of Clinical Psychology, Monograph Supplement, 38,* 1-68.
Vaughn, F. E. (1979). *Awakening intuition.* Garden City, NY: Doubleday Anchor.
Young, J. Z. (1951). *Doubt and certainty in science.* Oxford: Clarendon Press.

THE CURRENT DIRECTION OF THEORETICAL PSYCHOLOGY: AN EPILOGUE

Wm J. Baker

University of Alberta
Edmonton, Alberta, Canada

SUMMARY: This paper attempts to present an overview of the current evolution of theoretical psychology as this has been reflected in the 1985 and the current 1987 conferences as well as in other events which have served to make this emerging discipline visible to the field as a whole. It outlines a brief overview of the concrete events such as these conferences, related publications, and the formal establishment of the International Society for Theoretical Psychology (ISTP) as well as the intellectual trends reflected in these events. The most general conclusion to be drawn from all of this is that we are seeking not so much to eliminate the many differences in perspectives that we bring to these events, as that we are attempting to develop a clear and common language in terms of which we can explore and understand these differences.

The Concrete Events

The Center for Advanced Study in Theoretical Psychology, established in 1967 at the University of Alberta, was probably the first formal unit to be devoted specifically to the study of theoretical issues in psychology. It was a clear reaction, in the North American environment, to the "dust bowl empiricism" attitude which actively discouraged exploration of the philosophical presuppositions essential to the discipline as well as critical analyses of the myriad theoretical concepts bandied about, explicitly or implicitly, in the literature. Contacts with scholars sympathetic to the concept of the center, both in North America and Europe, led to the recognition of the need for a journal or some other formal publication to begin to unite the disparate and informal efforts that were found. This was eventually realized in the series generally entitled *Annals of Theoretical Psychology*, published by Plenum Press. The first two volumes were released in 1984 (Royce & Mos, 1984a; 1984b), three others followed these (Madsen & Mos, 1985; Mos, 1986; Staats & Mos, 1987), and three more are in various stages of planning.

Efforts generated by these publications led to extensive contacts with similarly motivated scholars, especially at Plymouth Polytechnic in the UK and the Free University, Amsterdam, which suggested enough interest to consider the establishment of an international society to draw together a much broader range of people to help to define what we were after. An initial conference was organized and held at Plymouth in 1985, attracting 55 participants. The 27 papers presented were published in a volume entitled *Current Issues in Theoretical Psychology* by North-Holland (Baker, Hyland, van Rappard, & Staats, 1987). This is Volume 40 in their general series entitled *Advances in Psychology* which is functioning as an outlet for explicitly theoretical papers. A clear indication that a formal society was in order led to steps in that direction along with the plans realized here for this second conference and the formal establishment of the International Society of Theoretical Psychology (ISTP)[1]

The Intellectual Trends

On the conceptual side, the picture of theoretical psychology that emerges is a hierarchical one whose top-most level is, quite naturally, a broad 'philosophy of science' consisting, at that level, of definitional and methodological constraints which attempt to specify the boundary conditions for what we seem to want to mean by 'doing science.' There is, in this, an interesting shift from the older approach of defining a static entity called 'science' to a concern with the activities of people engaged in this domain. This is, I believe, a direct consequence of the examination, in recent years of the history, sociology, and psychology of scientists which has been triggered by the writings of Kuhn (1970a; 1970b), Lakatos (1978), Feyerabend (1976), and many others.

When this evolving notion of the philosophy of science is directed specifically to psychology, it raises discussions as to whether or not there are issues unique to psychology which can justify the maintainence of psychology as a distinct discipline. Such discussions usually center on concepts such as mind, consciousness, self-awareness, experience, etc. The type of question that is ultimately proposed is: Is there a set of phenomena to be accounted for which is so uniquely different from those addressed by other sciences that a separate domain, with a possibly unique set of its own constraints, must exist? The majority of theoreticians in psychology would appear to answer this in the affirmative, although some radical reductionist positions are still maintained.

The philosophy of science is also used to provide a set of constraints on what we may consider to be 'acceptable' theories. Theories, in general, are distinguished from speculation usually as a consequence of

---

[1]Requests for information about or membership in ISTP may be directed to Dr. Wm J. Baker, Center for Theoretical Psychology, University of Alberta, Edmonton, Alberta, Canada, T6G 2E9 or Dr. Hans van Rappard, Dept. of Psychology, Free University, Trans. 1, P.O. Box 7161, 1007 MC Amsterdam, The Netherlands.

some notion of 'testability.' This latter notion can be explicated in external (empirical) terms or internal (formal or analytical) terms, i.e., testability in terms of external validation, usually against data of some sort, or internal coherence with respect to the terms and relations among terms proposed by the theory. As soon as a particular position is espoused as a 'theory of X,' data constraints become operative. It is essential to immediately specify the scope of the theory, to delimit the set of phenomena to be accounted for by the theory if it is to be treated seriously as a 'theory of X.'

It doesn't seem to matter, in at least one important sense, how we come at these issues, be it 'determinist,' 'materialist,' 'critical realist,' 'constructivist,' or 'phenominologist.' There is a clear recognition among all of us that we have surrendered the utterly naive pursuit of absolute truth within science. I recall a comment by Truman Kelly relative to Thurstone's belief, in the 40's, that factor analysis itself was uncovering the true 'vectors of the mind,' that such a pursuit of "spaceless, timeless, populationless truth" was an utterly futile pursuit. He fully recognized then what appears to be fully conceded now, that all analyses are embedded in the subjects chosen, the variables selected, and the theoretical biases governing the whole enterprise.

While it may be useful, even necessary for the scientific realist, to posit the existence of facts completely independent of our knowing them (that silly tree, falling in the forest, does make a noise, but it doesn't necessarily make a sound), there are no disembodied facts that we can know which are then independent of the idiosyncratic manner in which we come to know them, or of the manner in which we attempt to talk about them. This, in a sense, is the nature of the critical interplay taking place between 'scientific realism' on the one hand and 'constructivism' on the other. The concept of *context sensitivity* is fast becoming an inherent part of almost every point of view we have heard espoused at this conference.

This notion of knowledge being necessarily conditional on other knowledge or facts has been a gradually emerging, but serious issue, more narrowly found in experimental work itself within psychology. It traces back, e.g., to Jenkins' (1974) initially unnerving, but eventually essential conclusion, that the only real finding in psychology, for the interpretation of the meaning of any putative fact, is that "it depends" on a lot of other conditions which constitute the context within which such a fact or event must exist. Deese (1965; 1984), addressing the issue of meaning, especially as encoded in language, saw the futility of ever attempting to reify the topic, to disengage it from the meanings *intended* by particular producers of such language functioning in a specific set of conditions of which both speaker and hearer are aware. Gibson (1979) made a set of radical proposals beginning with the idea that all observation entails not only information about the thing observed but, inescapably, information for the observer about himself relative to that thing. Gibson made it clear that he now held that it was the self-conscious observer who actively seeks information from his world and attaches meanings (e.g., affordances) to the experiences thus engendered, who acts on the world rather than merely being acted upon by it. He probably would not have used the term 'self-conscious,' but it is clearly what he had in mind when he conceded that the observer is necessarily aware of himself as an observer relative to the object observed. The visual array, for Gibson, is real, but the information to be extracted from that array, even in his "direct perception," is necessarily a conjoint function of array and idiosyncratic observer. Psychology, then, can no longer be simply stimulus driven. Any attempt at 'explanation' couched totally in stimulus terms or parameters will either be wrong or simply irrelevant for psychology. Our problems must, in Gibson's terms, be reparameterized, i.e., expressed in terms relative to our observer's world as he experiences it (hence his notions of 'affordances,' etc.).

These immediately preceeding comments have been with respect to our subjects as they participate in our experiments and they emphasize the obvious fact that self-conscious subjects, fully aware of their surroundings, actively assess our experimental conditions and react in their own individual manners to what they believe it all means. What is true of our subjects is, of course, true of us as we act as scientists. This is precisely the issue raised by those recent authors who have addressed the psychology and sociology of doing science. It is all quite relative to the individual scientist himself.

This relativizing of science, combined with the insistence that the scientist himself is inherently enmeshed in his own efforts and analyses, has shifted our attention from a Platonic view of a separately existing thing called 'science' to serious consideration of the behavior of people called 'scientists' and how they react in the context of various 'scientific communities.' But a community exists if and only if a common language exists, and a common language exists only if it is mutually intelligible to all of its members. Much of this is touched upon by other papers in this volume, especially those of Danziger, Gergen, van Hezewijk, Rychlak, Salner, and Terwee.

There is a temptation in this to let the language create the community, but I think that is wrong. Neither culture nor language exist as idiogenic forces, Durkheim (1953) notwithstanding. I don't accept an extreme 'constructionist' position, though Gergen (this volume) would seem to want to. I would prefer to suggest that, from either Tolman's or Giorgi's domains, common *experience* is essential if we are to discover whether or not we use our *language* in a similar manner. Then once we begin to treat the observing scientist as active and responsible for how and why he observes, we make him the essential context within which we are to interpret *his* conclusions, not those of some disembodied, reified 'science.'

Perhaps it is time to persuade journal editors to abandon the pretense of objectivity that is entailed in the insistence on the use of the 'third person' perspective in writing style. In citations we are allowed to say, e.g., "Baker claims that ... ", but Baker himself is discouraged from writing, "I believe this indicates ... " which would make explicit the author's involvement in his conclusions. Seen in this relativized context, and abandoning the silly pretext that, in our writings, we are simply presenting facts or the unvarnished truth, we begin to look at scientific writings as being quite similar to most other forms of writing, simply as attempts to persuade the reader to the writer's point of view.

The remarkable advantage of doing this within a specific scientific community is that the use of language becomes vastly more precise as scientists meticulously work out the boundary conditions for the 'appropriate' use of various terms and expressions, generally by forcing those utterances into experiential contexts which are controlled or experimentally constrained to a degree that will, hopefully, guarantee the same experience for different observers. This, I believe, is what is behind the success of the scientific enterprise. Our methodological constraints buy us our linguistic precision or, at the very least, permit us to move in that direction.

The success that can be achieved by a well integrated, well defined scientific community was first demonstrated in physics precisely because that was the easiest domain within which to achieve communality of experience, in the context of physical events. Since that time we have pushed the boundary conditions into other areas of interest - through chemistry to biology and, following Wundt, into a scientific community that would like to explain "the facts of consciousness."

What I see, then, as the emerging goal of theoretical psychology, is to define the domain or scope of phenomena to be addressed and then to specify how best to constrain - in a linguistic, experiential, and experimental sense - the various approaches to the investigation of those phenomena so that we will be able, as best as possible, to grasp just what it is that each of us is on about when we try to communicate with each other. I do not, then, see unification as something to be pursued as an end in itself. I do not know if psychology should or could be unified. I would suspect that, if we could all get it right, unification might be a natural consequence of that (if, indeed, it is at all possible), but that seems to be somewhere well beyond the search for the "Holy Grail" at this point.

What we are pursuing - in a very real sense, what has been demonstrated at this conference - is the development of a common language through which our very real differences can be explored, examined, and compared. I doubt very much if anyone at any of these paper sessions has gone through a 'crisis of conversion,' but I am quite convinced, from listening to your multifaceted conversations, that a great number of you, representing remarkably different perspectives on psychology, have come to understand - quite independent of being persuaded - what it is that the 'other side' is really after. That, in my view, is the making of an extremely successful conference, and I believe it bodes well for the development of theoretical psychology as a valuable pursuit.

References

Baker, W. J., Hyland, M. E., van Rappard, H., & Staats, A. W. (Eds.). (1987). *Current issues in theoretical psychology.* Amsterdam: North-Holland.

Deese, J. (1965). *The structure of associations in language and thought.* Baltimore: Johns Hopkins Press.

Deese, J. (1984). *Thought into speech: the psychology of a language.* Englewood Cliffs, NJ: Prentice-Hall.

Durkheim, E. (1953/1911). *Sociology and philosophy.* Glencoe, IL: Free Press.

Feyerabend, P. (1976). On the critique of scientific reason. In R. Cohen & M. Wartofsky (Eds.), *Boston Studies in the Philosophy of Science. Vol. 34.* Boston: Reidel.

Gibson, J. J. (1979). *The ecological approach to visual perception.* Boston: Houghton Mifflan.

Jenkins, J. J. (1974). Remember that old theory of meaning? Well, forget it! *American Psychologist, 29,* 785-795.

Kuhn, T. (1970a). Logic of discovery or psychology of research? In I. Lakotos & A. Musgrove (Eds.), *Criticism and the growth of knowledge.* Cambridge: Cambridge University Press.

Kuhn, T. (1970b). *The structure of scientific revolutions. (2nd ed.)* Chicago: University of Chicago Press.

Lakotos, I. (1978). *The methodology of scientific research programs.* Cambridge: Cambridge University Press.

Madsen, K. B. & Mos, L. P. (Eds.). (1985). *Annals of theoretical psychology, Vol. III.* New York: Plenum.

Mos, L. P. (Ed.). (1986). *Annals of theoretical psychology, Vol. IV.* New York: Plenum.

Royce, J. R. & Mos, L. P. (Eds.). (1984a). *Annals of theoretical psychology, Vol. I.* New York: Plenum.

Royce, J. R. & Mos, L. P. (Eds.). (1984b). *Annals of theoretical psychology, Vol. II.* New York: Plenum.

Staats, A. W. & Mos, L. P. (Eds.). (1987). *Annals of theoretical psychology, Vol. V.* New York: Plenum.

AUTHOR INDEX

Page numbers refer to text citations. Italicized numbers refer to the reference lists at the ends of the papers.

- M -

- S -